D1236717

Migration, Minorities and Citizenship

General Editors: **Zig Layton-Henry**, Professor of Politics, University of Warwick; and **Danièle Joly**, Professor, Director, Centre for Research in Ethnic Relations, University of Warwick

Titles include:

Muhammad Anwar, Patrick Roach and Ranjit Sondhi (*editors*)
FROM LEGISLATION TO INTEGRATION?
Race Relations in Britain

James A. Beckford, Danièle Joly and Farhad Khosrokhavar
MUSLIMS IN PRISON
Challenge and Change in Britain and France

Christophe Bertossi (*editor*)
EUROPEAN ANTI-DISCRIMINATION AND THE POLITICS OF CITIZENSHIP
Britain and France

Sophie Body-Gendrot and Marco Martiniello (*editors*)
MINORITIES IN EUROPEAN CITIES
The Dynamics of Social Integration and Social Exclusion at the Neighbourhood Level

Malcolm Cross and Robert Moore (*editors*)
GLOBALIZATION AND THE NEW CITY
Migrants, Minorities and Urban Transformations in Comparative Perspective

Thomas Faist and Andreas Ette (*editors*)
THE EUROPEANIZATION OF NATIONAL POLICIES AND POLITICS OF IMMIG-RATION
Between Autonomy and the European Union

Thomas Faist and Peter Kivisto (*editors*)
DUAL CITIZENSHIP IN GLOBAL PERSPECTIVE
From Unitary to Multiple Citizenship

Adrian Favell
PHILOSOPHIES OF INTEGRATION
Immigration and the Idea of Citizenship in France and Britain

Agata Górny and Paulo Ruspini (*editors*)
MIGRATION IN THE NEW EUROPE
East-West Revisited

James Hampshire
CITIZENSHIP AND BELONGING
Immigration and the Politics of Democratic Governance in Postwar Britain

John R. Hinnells (*editor*)
RELIGIOUS RECONSTRUCTION IN THE SOUTH ASIAN DIASPORAS
From One Generation to Another

Simon Holdaway and Anne-Marie Barron
RESIGNERS? THE EXPERIENCE OF BLACK AND ASIAN POLICE OFFICERS

Danièle Joly
GLOBAL CHANGES IN ASYLUM REGIMES (*editor*)
Closing Doors

SCAPEGOATS AND SOCIAL ACTORS
The Exclusion and Integration of Minorities in Western and Eastern Europe

Christian Joppke and Ewa Morawska
TOWARD ASSIMILATION AND CITIZENSHIP
Immigrants in Liberal Nation-States

Atsushi Kondo (*editor*)
CITIZENSHIP IN A GLOBAL WORLD
Comparing Citizenship Rights for Aliens

Zig Layton-Henry and Czarina Wilpert (*editors*)
CHALLENGING RACISM IN BRITAIN AND GERMANY

Jørgen S. Nielsen
TOWARDS A EUROPEAN ISLAM

Pontus Odmalm
MIGRATION POLICIES AND POLITICAL PARTICIPATION
Inclusion or Intrusion in Western Europe?

Peter Ratcliffe (*editor*)
THE POLITICS OF SOCIAL SCIENCE RESEARCH
'Race', Ethnicity and Social Change

Jan Rath (*editor*)
IMMIGRANT BUSINESSES
The Economic, Political and Social Environment

Carl-Ulrik Schierup (*editor*)
SCRAMBLE FOR THE BALKANS
Nationalism, Globalism and the Political Economy of Reconstruction

Steven Vertovec and Ceri Peach (*editors*)
ISLAM IN EUROPE
The Politics of Religion and Community

Maarten Vink
LIMITS OF EUROPEAN CITIZENSHIP
European Integration and Domestic Immigration Policies

Östen Wahlbeck
KURDISH DIASPORAS
A Comparative Study of Kurdish Refugee Communities

John Wrench, Andrea Rea and Nouria Ouali (*editors*)
MIGRANTS, ETHNIC MINORITIES AND THE LABOUR MARKET
Integration and Exclusion in Europe

Migration, Minorities and Citizenship
Series Standing Order ISBN 0–333–71047–9 (hardback) and 0–333–80338–8 (paperback)
(*outside North America only*)

You can receive future titles in this series as they are published by placing a standing order. Please contact your bookseller or, in case of difficulty, write to us at the address below with your name and address, the title of the series and the ISBN quoted above.

Customer Services Department, Macmillan Distribution Ltd, Houndmills, Basingstoke, Hampshire RG21 6XS, England

---

Dual Citizenship in Global Perspective

From Unitary to Multiple Citizenship

Edited by

Thomas Faist

Professor of Sociology, Center on Migration, Citizenship and Development, Bielefeld University, Germany

Peter Kivisto

Richard Swanson Professor of Social Thought and Chair of Sociology, Augustana College, USA

First published 2007 by
PALGRAVE MACMILLAN
Houndmills, Basingstoke, Hampshire RG21 6XS and
175 Fifth Avenue, New York, N.Y. 10010
Companies and representatives throughout the world

PALGRAVE MACMILLAN is the global academic imprint of the Palgrave Macmillan division of St. Martin's Press, LLC and of Palgrave Macmillan Ltd. Macmillan® is a registered trademark in the United States, United Kingdom and other countries. Palgrave is a registered trademark in the European Union and other countries.

ISBN-13: 978–0–230–00654–6 hardback
ISBN-10: 0–230–00654–X hardback

This book is printed on paper suitable for recycling and made from fully managed and sustained forest sources. Logging, pulping and manufacturing processes are expected to conform to the environmental regulations of the country of origin.

A catalogue record for this book is available from the British Library.

Library of Congress Cataloging-in-Publication Data
Dual citizenship in global perspective:from unitary to multiple
   citizenship/edited by Thomas Faist, Peter Kivisto.
      p. cm.
Selected papers from a conference entitled "Dual citizenship:
democracy, rights, and identity in a globalizing World," held March 17–19,
2005 at the University of Toronto.
Includes bibliographical references and index.
ISBN 0–230–00654–X (alk. paper)
   1. Dual nationality—Congresses. 2. Citizenship—Congresses.
   3. Globalization—Congresses. I. Faist, Thomas, 1959–.
   II. Kivisto, Peter, 1948–
   JF801.D83 2007
   323.6—dc22   2007023299

10   9   8   7   6   5   4   3   2   1
16   15   14   13   12   11   10   09   08   07

Printed and bound in Great Britain by
Antony Rowe Ltd, Chippenham and Eastbourne

Contents

List of Figures and Tables

Figures

Tables

Contributors

Rainer Bauböck is Professor of Political Theory at the European University Institute (EUI) at Florence in Italy. His research interests are in normative political theory and comparative research on democratic citizenship, European integration, migration, nationalism and minority rights. His book publications in English include *Transnational Citizenship: Membership and Rights in International Migration* (1994); *Blurred Boundaries: Migration, Ethnicity, Citizenship* (1998) (co-editor); *The Challenge of Diversity: Integration and Pluralism in Societies of Immigration* (1996) (co-editor); and *From Aliens to Citizens: Redefining the Legal Status of Immigrants in Europe* (1994) (editor). He is also the author or editor of several books in German.

Seyla Benhabib is Eugene Meyer Professor of Political Science and Philosophy at Yale University, where she also obtained her PhD in 1977. She has previously taught at Harvard University (1993–2000) and the New School for Social Research (1991–1993). Benhabib was a Russell Sage Foundation Fellow during 2000–2001. Among her recent publications is her book *The Claims of Culture: Equality and Diversity in the Global Era* (Princeton University Press, 2002). During the summer of 2000, she held the Baruch de Spinoza Distinguished Professorship at the University of Amsterdam. Her Spinoza lectures are published as *Transformation of Citizenship: Dilemmas of the Nation-State in the Era of Globalization* (Amsterdam, Van Gorcum, 2000). Articles drawing upon her current research on multiculturalism in liberal democracies and transformations of citizenship have appeared in *Die Zeit, Daedalus, Dissent and Political Theory*. She also delivered the John Seeley lectures in Cambridge, UK, on *Aliens, Citizens, and Residents: Political Theory and Membership in a Changing World* (Cambridge University Press, 2004).

Irene Bloemraad is Assistant Professor in the Department of Sociology at the University of California, Berkeley. She studies citizenship, political participation and the impact of migrants on nationalism and state ideologies. She is currently finishing her first book, *Assimilatory Multiculturalism*, an examination of naturalisation, advocacy and electoral success among Vietnamese and Portuguese newcomers in Boston and Toronto. Professor Bloemraad has presented her work in a variety of academic and public policy settings and has published in journals such as *International Migration Review, Journal of Ethnic and Migration Studies, Journal of International Migration and Integration* and *Research in Political Sociology*. Her research has been supported by the US National Science Foundation, the Social Science and Humanities Research Council of Canada, the Russell Sage Foundation and the Social Science Research Council.

Thomas Faist is Professor and Chair of Transnational Relations and Development Studies at the Faculty of Sociology, Bielefeld University. He formerly directed the International Program in Political Management at the University of Applied Sciences Bremen. His research has dealt with transnational migration and social spaces, immigrant integration and social policy. His most recent books are *Dual Citizenship in Europe: From Nationhood to Societal Integration* (2007), *The Europeanization of National Immigration Policies: Between Autonomy and the European Union* (2007, with Andreas Ette) and *Citizenship: Theory, Discourse and Transnational Prospects* (2007, with Peter Kivisto).

Jürgen Gerdes is Research Fellow at Bielefeld University in Germany. He is currently working with the research project 'Democratic Legitimacy of Immigration Control Policy'. He received his MA in politics and sociology at Bremen University, Germany. He previously worked on an international research project on dual citizenship, supported by the Volkswagen Foundation, which compared the politics of dual citizenship in several immigration and emigration countries. His research focuses on the relationship between democracy, human rights and immigration. He is the author of reviews and articles on questions of multiculturalism, minority rights, tolerance, cultural recognition and dual citizenship including 'Dual Citizenship as a Path-Dependent Process', *International Migration Review* 38, no. 3: 913–44, co-authored with Thomas Faist and Beate Rieple (2004).

José Itzigsohn is Associate Professor of Sociology at Brown University. His research focuses on nationalism, immigrant incorporation and the forms and determinants of transnational social links. His most recent articles on these topics are 'Incorporation, Transnationalism and Gender', *International Migration Review* (2005, with Silvia Giorguli Saucedo), and 'Unfinished Imagined Communities: The Theoretical Implications of Nationalism in Latin America', *Theory and Society* (2006, with Mathias vom Hau).

Peter Kivisto is the Richard Swanson Professor of Social Thought and Chair of Sociology at Augustana College. He is the author or editor of more than 20 books, including *Citizenship: Discourse, Theory, and Transnational Prospects* (2007, with Thomas Faist), *Intersecting Inequalities* (2007, with Elizabeth Hartung), *Incorporating Diversity: Rethinking Assimilation in a Multicultural Age* (2005) and *Multiculturalism in a Global Society* (2002). His articles have appeared in a number of journals, including *Acta Sociologica, British Journal of Sociology, Ethnic and Racial Studies, Ethnicities* and *Sociological Quarterly*. He has served as Secretary-Treasurer of the American Sociological Society's Theory Section and International Migration Section. He is a board member of the International Sociological Association's Research Committee on Migration (RC-31). Currently, he is the editor of *Sociological Quarterly*.

Audrey Kobayashi is Professor and Queen's Research Chair in the Department of Geography at Queen's University. She has published extensively in the areas of immigration, racism, gender, multiculturalism and employment equity, and on the development of Japanese-Canadian communities. She is the principal investigator (with David Ley, Valerie Preston, Myer Siemiatycki and Guida Man) of a research project on Hong Kong immigration to Canada. She is the editor of the *Annals of the Association of American Geographers: People Place and Region.* She recently co-edited the *Blackwell Companion to Gender Studies* (2005, with Philomena Essed and David Goldberg).

Mária M. Kovács is Professor of History at the Central European University (CEU) and Director of the Nationalism Studies Program at CEU, Budapest. Before teaching at CEU she was on the faculty of the History Department at the University of Wisconsin-Madison. Her main research interests are in the history of self-determination and international minority protection throughout the twentieth century up to the latest developments in the 1990s. Her latest book entitled *Liberal Professions, Illiberal Politics* focuses on the collapse of liberal institutions in Central Europe and, more specifically, in Hungary, after the First World War, and on the institutional expressions of interwar xenophobia and anti-Semitism. She has also published in the problem area of the conjunction of gender and ethnicity, focusing on the problem of ethnic cleavages within feminism in the interwar era. Professor Kovács is also a member of the Institute of History of the Hungarian Academy of Sciences and the History Compass.

Audrey Macklin is Associate Professor of Law at the University of Toronto. From 1994 to 1996 she adjudicated asylum claims as a Member of the Refugee Division of Canada's Immigration and Refugee Board. Prof. Macklin's areas of research interest include immigration, refugee and citizenship law, multiculturalism, gender and law, corporate social responsibility and human rights. She has published widely on many aspects of migration and citizenship, including gender-related persecution and refugee status, trafficking in persons, migrant workers, and the securitisation of migration post 9/11.

Valerie Preston is Professor of Geography at York University, where she has served as Director of the Graduate Programme in Geography, Associate Director and Chair of the Management Board of the Joint Centre for Research on Immigration and Settlement, Toronto, and Director of the Institute for Social Research. She teaches urban social geography and refugee and migration studies. Her research, which has been published widely in international journals and edited collections, examines how gender shapes geographical access to employment for minority women in North American cities and the ways that immigration is transforming contemporary urban landscapes. Currently, she is completing comparative research about the impact of transnationalism on citizenship identities and practices.

Myer Siemiatycki is Programme Director of the MA Programme in Immigration and Settlement Studies at Ryerson University. He is Professor of Politics and Public Administration, and serves as Community Domain Leader with the Centre of Excellence for Research on Immigration and Settlement in Toronto. His research and publication subjects have examined immigrant civic participation, minority religion in the public realm, transnationalism and dual citizenship.

Waldemar A. Skrobacki was educated at the University of Wroclaw and the University of Toronto, where he received his doctorate. He is Lecturer in Politics in the Department of Political Science at the University of Toronto. The main focus of his research is European politics, and the emergence of a common European identity. Among his most recent publications is 'The European Union and Globalization', in R. B. Day and J. Masciulli, eds, *Globalization and Political Ethics*, Brill Academic Publishers (2005).

Peter J. Spiro is Rusk Professor of International Law at the University of Georgia Law School. He is a former law clerk to Justice David H. Souter of the US Supreme Court and has also served as an Attorney-Adviser in the Office of the Legal Adviser in the US Department of State and on the staff of the National Security Council. Professor Spiro's research interests include citizenship law and theory, the intersection of constitutional and international law and the role of non-state actors in international decision-making. In addition to academic writing, his work has also appeared in such publications as *Foreign Affairs*, *The Wall Street Journal* and *The New Republic*. Professor Spiro is at work on a book, *Decentering Citizenship*, which is under contract to Oxford University Press.

Triadafilos Triadafilopoulos is Assistant Professor of Political Science at the University of Toronto. His research focuses on how immigration and citizenship policies intersect with and help define boundaries of national belonging in liberal democratic states. He received his PhD from the New School for Social Research and was a Social Sciences and Humanities Research Council of Canada Postdoctoral Fellow at the University of Toronto and a German Academic Exchange Service (DAAD) Visiting Research Fellow at the Institute for Social Sciences at Humboldt University in Berlin. Triadafilopoulos is the co-editor of *European Encounters: Migrants, Migration and European Societies since 1945* (2003, with Rainer Ohliger and Karen Schönwälder).

Acknowledgments

This book is based on selected contributions to a conference entitled 'Dual Citizenship: Democracy, Rights and Identity in a Globalizing World', held from 17 March to 19 March 2005 at the Munk Centre for International Studies at the University of Toronto. Special gratitude goes to Professors Susan Solomon and Jeffrey Kopstein, who were inspiring hosts. They supported the endeavours of Thomas Faist during his tenure as a DAAD Visiting Professor during the academic year 2004–2005. Several foundations and institutions generously supported the conference: the VolkswagenStiftung, the Institute of European Studies at the Munk Centre through funds from the European Union (EU), the Fritz-Thyssen-Stiftung, the New York Office of the Deutscher Akademischer Austauschdienst (DAAD), the Social Science Research Council (SSRC) in New York, and the Consulat Général de France à Toronto. Finally, the Stiftung für Bevölkerung, Migration und Umwelt (BMU) supported the editorial work for this book.

This book has a strong focus on the North American context, but also includes comparisons with Europe. Those interested in systematic studies of European developments on dual citizenship may want to consult a companion volume. It is a set of case studies on Germany, the Netherlands, Sweden, Turkey and Poland: *Dual Citizenship in Europe: From Nationhood to Societal Integration*, funded by the VolkswagenStiftung and edited by Thomas Faist (2007). These country studies are set within a common conceptual framework and focus on explaining legislative changes on dual citizenship. And those studying the overall aspects of the expansion or erosion of contemporary citizenship in advanced industrial democracies may want to refer to our co-authored book *Citizenship: Discourse, Theory, Transnational Prospects* (2007).

We are grateful to Edith Klein at the University of Toronto, who improved the readability of the contributions to this book, to Heiderose Römisch and to Judith Ehlert, who took care of the proofreading. We would like to thank them sincerely—even if, of course, the contents of the book commit no one except the authors and editors.

Thomas Faist and Peter Kivisto

1
Introduction: The Shifting Boundaries of the Political

Thomas Faist

Over the last few decades, sovereign states have shown an increasing tolerance of dual citizenship, sometimes also called multiple or plural citizenship.[1] This is astonishing when one considers that a few decades ago citizenship and political loyalty to a state were still considered to form an inseparable unity. Citizenship—here referring to full membership in a national state—is a crucial case for the pluralisation of citizens' ties across the borders of sovereign states. This pluralisation is a case of overlapping citizenship. Certainly, dual citizenship is not a completely new phenomenon but it is only recently that we have witnessed its rapid spread. First, there is the truly global scale of the acceptance of dual citizenship. More than half of all the states in the world, countries of immigration as well as emigration, now tolerate some form or element of dual citizenship. Second, quite a few immigration countries nowadays tolerate and in a few cases, such as Sweden, even accept dual citizenship. Toleration of dual citizenship is rationalised mainly as a tool to promote the naturalisation of immigrants and to close the gap between the resident population and the demos. Third, emigration countries have strengthened the rights of expatriates and introduced various forms of dual citizenship. Previously, emigrants were mostly excluded from political participation in their countries of origin. And fourth, source country governments actively promote dual citizenship and dual nationalism. Dual nationalism is broader than dual citizenship in that the former connotes practices of emigration countries to appeal to their citizens abroad as part of a national collective beyond borders

The author would like to thank Peter Kivisto, Edith Klein and Triadafilos Triadafilopoulos for helpful and critical comments on an earlier draft of this chapter.

for purposes of national unity and nationalist goals. Dual or transnational nationalism goes beyond tolerating dual citizenship in a *de facto* manner, such as Italy since 1912 and the United Kingdom for decades, while publicly condemning it.

The contributions to this book probe the proposition that the increasing tolerance of dual citizenship is a test case for an ambivalent relationship: the growing liberalisation of citizenship law on the one hand, and the increasing securitisation of citizenship, the erosion of popular sovereignty and the changing role of nationalism and nationhood for full membership on the other hand. Indeed, the liberalisation of dual citizenship and resistance to it constitutes a case of changing boundaries of the political, and changes in the very core of the political sphere, namely state-citizen-relations. It is the change of the political sphere itself which is at stake (see Kivisto and Faist 2007). Dual citizenship occurs in two relevant situations and thus applies to two categories of persons. It may be a result of moving persons as in the case of transnational migrants, or as a result of moving borders, as in the case of national minorities.

Often, the increase in global governance, or more modestly, cross-border ties, transactions, social structures and political formations is associated with the decline in the capacity of nation-states to shape political life. Some observers even correlate global and transnational processes, such as the internationalisation of human rights, to a decline in state sovereignty and capacity, or even the significance of national citizenship (Ohmae 1996). In the field of citizenship studies, similar claims can be found. For example, postnationalists such as Yasemin Soysal have maintained that norms guiding membership in advanced democracies are based on global human rights discourses which diffuse from the international to the national level (Soysal 1994). Moreover, the claim is made that for certain categories of persons, immigrants in advanced liberal democracies in particular, membership based upon residence has assumed a more prominent role than citizenship. Yet, the precise mechanisms of diffusion have never been empirically substantiated. Also, and this is important for our purposes, the postnational thesis assumes that the causes of the two processes—the extension of cross-border transactions, such as the spread and importance of human rights discourses and norms on the one hand and the declining sovereignty of states, exemplified by the disjunction of rights (residence membership) and collective identity (a prime dimension of national citizenship), on the other hand—are the same.

The case of the liberalisation of dual citizenship and the associated conflicts, however, point in another direction. First, dual citizenship puts in sharp relief a dimension neglected by the postnational approach. The first and defining notion of citizenship is equality of political freedom. This means very simply that those who are affected by political decisions should have a say in how they are made (Habermas 1992; see also Rousseau 1966). As a matter of fact, one of the most frequent arguments in favour of tolerating dual citizenship made in debates on dual citizenship legislation has been the congruence of the resident population and the demos (Faist, Gerdes and Rieple 2004). To postulate a disjuncture of the second dimension of citizenship (rights and obligations) from the third (collective identity) without considering the essential political dimension of citizenship is to miss the most crucial change in the liberalisation vs restriction of (dual) citizenship, namely the shifting boundaries of the political sphere.

In democracies, the growing tolerance towards civil rights has indeed been part of the 'rights revolution', as the postnational argument would suggest. However, this change can only be understood as a result of long and protracted struggles contesting the state–citizen boundaries (Tilly 2004), that is conflicts around claims for rights. Second, while dual citizenship is a case of overlapping citizenship, and also a consequence of international norms on gender equity and statelessness, the consequence is not a sharp decline of nation-state sovereignty. Interestingly, while attachments and even loyalties of citizens to two or more states arise, this has not entailed the disjunction of rights and collective identity. And emigration states have even tried to use dual citizenship in order to foster ties among emigrant citizens. Rather, the discursive, institutional and territorial boundaries of membership in and across states are being renegotiated. The conflicts around dual citizenship give credence to the hunch that state sovereignty and the internationalisation of human rights and membership norms are not trade-offs. Instead, more intricate and complex processes are emerging. The boundaries between states and citizens are shifting.

More concretely, the core intellectual tension explored in this book is that between the liberalisation of citizenship and the implications for state–citizen relations in central fields such as security, sovereignty and nationhood. Sovereignty, security and nationhood are core issues animating the political sphere. A useful starting point for exploring the shifting boundaries of the political is the obvious trend towards the expansion of individual rights on the one hand, and the continued prerogatives of states over full membership in the political community on the other hand. One of the main tendencies over the past decades has been the growing emphasis on individual rights vis-à-vis state prerogatives in liberal democracies, many of which are immigration countries. The increasing tolerance of dual citizenship which has resulted must be interpreted in the context of the so-called 'rights revolution'. Among the major causes contributing to liberalisation have been, first, the increased prominence of human rights norms, expressed in court decisions and public policies relating to statelessness, and growing gender equity in international and national laws. Exemplary fields, in which these processes have advanced, concern the independent citizenship of women since the 1950s and the European Council's latest convention on citizenship in 1993, which provides that both fathers and mothers are allowed to pass on their citizenship to their children. For an even longer time international law has included provisions that allow for dual citizenship in cases where individuals would otherwise be stateless. Second, in many immigration countries dual citizenship has been justified by referring to the so-called 'congruence principle'. In these cases it implies fulfilling one of the main principles of democracy towards denizens, namely achieving congruence between the resident population and the demos. Other factors driving the increasing tolerance of dual citizenship include the gradual dissolution of the nexus between the warfare state and citizenship after the Second World War, exemplified by the decline of conscription and the spread of armies consisting of professional soldiers. On the emigration side, instrumental considerations have been numerous. These expressions of dual nationalism include, for example, the interest of emigration states, which act as patronage or kin states, in maintaining ties for political and economic reasons.

However, the tendency towards liberalisation stands in stark contrast to the potentially negative implications for security, sovereignty, nationhood and nationalism raised by opponents to the increasing toleration of dual citizenship. As to state sovereignty, the question is whether the pluralisation of citizens' cross-border ties dilutes loyalty and allegiance and thus the very monopoly of states to exercise control over their territory. Issues of popular sovereignty surface when there is a disjuncture between the demos and the resident population. Also, there are conflicts over the fact that some dual citizens *exit* but still exert *voice* without being necessarily affected by the decisions they help to bring about. Finally, national collective identities refer to both nationalism and nationhood. As mentioned before, some states appeal to expatriates abroad, including dual citizens, as a diaspora or even a lobby group. And some 'stateless diasporas' (see Shain and Barth 2003) vie to establish states, carved out of the territory of their states of origin. Both are forms of dual or transnational nationalism. Nationhood proper is a particularly contentious issue in academic analysis. While the distinction between ethnic and republican concepts of nationhood and their implications for core cases such as Germany is highly dubious, references to nationhood abound in citizenship discourse. The shift from ethnic to republican nationhood observed in some cases is not the end of the history of shifts. Boundaries may be currently shifting again, this time towards a more market-oriented understanding of citizenship (see, for example, Ong 1999). There is no claim that liberalisation of citizenship via increasing toleration of dual citizenship necessarily dilutes collective (national) identity, weakens state sovereignty or undermines security. Instead, the studies assembled here probe into the shifting boundaries of rights, membership and thus also democracy in both immigration and emigration situations.

Throughout this book, citizenship is used as a normative-empirical concept in two ways: as a legal construct and as a political idea. Both the legal and the political sides are intricately related but constitute distinct dimensions. Citizenship as a legal concept means full membership in a state, the corresponding tie to state law and the subjection of citizens to state power. Legal scholars sometimes call this 'nationality'. The interstate function of citizenship is to define a people within a clearly delineated territory and to protect the citizens of a state against the outside, at times hostile, world. The intrastate function of citizenship is to define the rights and duties of members. According to the principle of *domaine réservé*—exclusive competence—each state decides within the limits of sovereign self-determination on the criteria required for access to its citizenship. One general condition for membership is that citizens as nationals have some kind of close ties to the respective state, the so-called 'genuine link'. If we extend the perspective and view citizenship as a contested political concept, the problem becomes one of the relationships between citizens, the state and democracy. In essence, citizenship builds on collective self-determination, that is democracy, and essentially comprises three mutually qualifying dimensions: first, the legally guaranteed status of equality of political freedom and democratic self-determination; second, equal rights and obligations; and third, membership in a political community.

To generate a broad range of cases and evidence, the contributions draw on examples from immigration countries in Europe and North America and from emigration countries. Moreover, the book brings together contributions from various sub-disciplines in political science, such as political theory and comparative politics. It also features leading researchers on dual citizenship in legal studies and related social science disciplines, such as sociology and political science.

One caveat on the notion of tolerance towards dual citizenship should be added. Often, authors simply speak of a growing tolerance. Yet, at the very least, distinctions need to be made between *de facto* and *de jure* tolerance, and between different forms of *de jure* tolerance or even acceptance. *De jure* tolerance of dual citizenship arises when children are born in countries where the *jus soli* (and applicable to *all* countries: the *jus sanguinis*) principle holds, and the countries of their parents' origin apply the *jus sanguinis* principle. *De facto* tolerance may also be present when states are indifferent to dual citizenship for various reasons. For example, the 'oath of allegiance' notwithstanding, the United States of America does not require evidence that immigrants have actually renounced a previous citizenship. Other countries, such as the United Kingdom, do not bother to regulate dual citizenship. The most restrictive cases are characterised by the following criteria: (1) assignment by birth: only one citizenship possible; (2) obligation to choose one citizenship on reaching maturity; (3) renunciation requirement (in some cases also proof required) upon naturalisation in another country; and (4) forced expatriation upon naturalisation in another country. The more strictly the acquisition of a citizenship is governed by principles (1)–(4), the more restrictive is the state in question—and conversely, the more lenient the procedure, or the more exemptions there are from these requirements, the more open the state is to dual citizenship. The most important form of *de jure* tolerance in this respect is the abolishment of the renunciation requirement in the naturalisation process, and the option principle in birthright citizenship. However, it is important to note that even countries which fall on the restrictive end of an imagined scale, such as Germany, have rules governing exceptions, which have resulted in almost half of all new naturalised citizens keeping their original citizenship (Faist 2007a: chap. 1). Therefore, a simplistic operationalisation which uses a dichotomous variable—for example, the (non-)existence of legal provisions allowing for dual citizenship as part of a composite measure of the openness of a national citizenship regime—is incorrect, and may point in the wrong direction.

State and popular sovereignty: Exit, voice and loyalty

States still decide unilaterally who they admit to full membership based on constitutional rules they have set for themselves. This principle of *domaine réservé* is a clear expression of state sovereignty connoting legal belonging of citizens to a state. This dimension of citizenship is sometimes called 'nationality' by legal scholars and is to be distinguished from national consciousness. By contrast, popular sovereignty refers to a dimension of citizenship as a political idea. It is basically a reflection of equal political freedom which enables citizens to exercise their rights and duties and, in so doing, to determine the fate of their political communities. Both state and popular sovereignty are encased in the nation-state model, which is characterised by a trinity of stateness, that is the congruence of (1) state territory, (2) the demos and (3) state authority (see Jellinek 1964)—notwithstanding the emergence of more functional forms of governance, such as the European Union (EU).

There is no evidence that state sovereignty is challenged by dual citizenship, other than in a very general way which would be hard to define. The 'rights revolution' is touted as having tilted the balance of rights more in favour of citizens (Jacobson 1997). The rights revolution may not be so much a result of international or global discourses but a consequence of norms embedded in state constitutions of liberal democracies which came to fruition internationally because 'security communities' in selected parts of the world after the Second World War provided a propitious opportunity structure. Among the changing boundaries was also the discrediting of racial discrimination for liberal-democratic states. Yet there is no right to dual citizenship. Only a few exceptional groups, such as stateless persons and refugees—namely officially recognised asylum seekers—could be said to enjoy something of a quasi-right to citizenship. National states in general have been very careful in protecting their *domaine réservé*. Thus, with rare exceptions, we see only states *tolerating* dual citizenship; indeed, only one immigration country *accepts* dual citizenship—Sweden, since 2001 (Gustafson 2005). Mostly, states attach certain stipulations to those holding dual citizenship. For example, many source countries do not allow their expatriates holding another citizenship to vote in the elections of the country of origin or to hold significant official posts. Moreover, various states attach limit eligibility for citizenship. Often, the descendants of dual citizens have to prove a genuine link to the country of origin. In point of fact, the rise of plural citizenship may actually augment state power, insofar as its acceptance is used instrumentally by state actors for purposes of cementing ties with diaspora communities or of projecting influence through immigrant dual citizen populations in countries of origin (Chapter 6).

The dimension of popular sovereignty has been an important subject in political debates on dual citizenship. After all, higher naturalisation rates can be interpreted as a sign of successful integration by those favouring an equal rights approach. This view is contested because a communitarian interpretation would insist that individual integration is a prerequisite for naturalisation. Nonetheless, from the point of view of emigration countries, dual citizenship, seen as transnational citizenship, seems to reflect the continuing engagement of migrants. From a strictly normative point of view, one may advance a critique arguing that many governments may be primarily interested in financial remittances or social remittances such as knowledge and ideas. Thus, it may be more a reflection of 'market citizenship' (Goldring 2002) than an interest in continuing political participation.

The age of dual citizenship has substantially altered emigrants' opportunities to partake in liberal democratic rights. Emigrant political rights were practically non-existent in the early twentieth century. As a matter of fact, states of origin sometimes even denaturalised emigrants (Zolberg 2007). A frequent objection to emigrant political rights is what could be called the exit-voice dilemma. Those who exit and still participate in the country of origin are most often not affected directly by the decisions taken and thus by the rules they helped to bring about. This state of affairs could signal a changing balance of rights and obligations. However, the exit-voice dilemma usually does not constitute a major challenge to the basis of popular sovereignty on the national level. Most often the number of emigrants who are officially registered to vote is actually quite low. For example, when the dual nationality legislation was passed in Mexico in 1998, the state authorities believed that several million people were eligible. After all, close to 10 million persons born in Mexico lived in the United States in the late 1990s. Yet in the first 5 years following the law's implementation, only 67,000 people re-acquired their Mexican nationality (Fitzgerald 2006: 99). This datum suggests that perhaps dual citizenship in and of itself does not enhance orientation towards the home country.

Yet the exit-voice dilemma could be more relevant on levels of political participation in which the ratio of those who exited and those who have stayed is more balanced, for example on the local or communal level. We do know, for instance, that emigration from the same administrative unit such as a state is very uneven across regions and municipalities (Faist 2000: chap. 1). One would expect, therefore, that this dilemma would be of greater relevance on the communal than on the national level. Indeed, recent research on the workings of hometown associations in the Mexican–United States context suggests that decision-making procedures are fundamentally altered in communities with a high proportion of emigrants. In such situations the terms 'trans-local' or 'trans-national citizenship' may not adequately capture the asymmetries of power developing in the course of transnational migration (Fox 2005).

In sum, there is no evidence that dual citizenship has significantly challenged state and popular sovereignty. As to state sovereignty, there seems to be modest evidence that emigration states have successfully used the debates over dual citizenship discursively and institutionally to strengthen ties to their diasporas abroad. Instead, the weakening of both state and popular sovereignty has to be understood with reference to very different causal chains. Much more relevant factors than the liberalisation of citizenship which may have contributed to the erosion of both state and popular sovereignty can be found in the dynamics of global capitalism, such as 'law without states' (Chapter 12), the spread of the politics of fear in the wake of 11 September and the justifications for military interventions to combat terrorism operating transationally.

State and human security: Concomitant desecuritisation and resecuritisation

While state security is about avoiding threats to the institutional integrity of states, human security is primarily concerned with threats to the physical integrity of persons. The two are intricately related as security can be construed as a duty of the state to protect its citizens, both abroad, through diplomatic services, and 'at home'. Security can thus be conceived very broadly as bodily integrity, and also in more far-reaching terms as protecting civil and other rights. Dual citizenship, like few other institutional developments, exemplifies tendencies towards both the desecuritisation and resecuritisation of state–citizen ties (Faist 2005).

The increasing toleration of dual citizenship as a sign of liberalisation is a clear sign of the overall desecuritisation of citizenship, a shift from the nationalist warfare state to security communities (Chapter 2). Securitisation reigned supreme when total war and changes in militarism in the nineteenth and twentieth centuries coincided with and helped reinforce the 'nation under arms'. Such processes placed obvious limits on multiple affiliations and led to the normalisation of unitary citizenship. State–citizen ties in Europe and North America were forged in the classical age of nation-state formation. Direct rule and mass national politics evolved together and reinforced each other. Quite importantly, the subordinated classes had to be motivated for sacrifices, and no method yielded better results than state-sponsored nationalism. Yet, as Triadafilopoulos indicates, shifts in military doctrine and the conduct of war after the Second World War led to the erosion of the classical warfare state and loosening of membership boundaries. The latter half of the twentieth century witnessed the emergence of 'security communities' such as the EU (Deutsch 1966). One of the results of this development was the gradual decoupling of citizenship and military service, illustrated by the steady erosion of conscription and the turn to professional armies. The improbability of war between advanced industrialised democracies made the issues of loyalty and allegiance less important. Even further down the chronological road, the 1990s saw the definitive end of the Cold War which had pitted ideologically defined blocs consisting of nation-states against each other. New forms of warfare, above all asymmetrical wars—such as civil wars and military interventions—became even more dominant, and overtook warfare between states as the main form of combat (Münkler 2004).

The events of 11 September 2001 served as a catalyst for the intensification of processes of resecuritisation. Resecuritisation means that states attempt to increase their hold over citizens and aliens alike. Moreover, state authorities claim that state security automatically increases human security. This leads to a priority of state over human security, and involves a conflation of state with human security without due regard to human security. On the one hand, one may not see a direct threat to the toleration of dual citizenship as a consequence of resecuritisation. Triadafilos Triadafilopoulos concludes that the trend towards greater tolerance for multiple citizenships is likely to persist because countermeasures would pit the state against groups that enjoy political rights and have—in some cases—demonstrated a capacity to use them to guard their interests. Audrey Macklin (Chapter 3) shifts the perspective to state practices and suggests that dual citizenship is more attractive nowadays for states that can take away one's citizenship, that is denaturalise a citizen, without making a person stateless as a result. In other words, dual citizenship enables citizenship revocation without rendering the person stateless because the person can be deported to the other country of citizenship. Conversely, citizens for whom multiple citizenships would otherwise be an asset now have reason to relinquish their other citizenship, especially in relation to states that engage in persecution, torture or execution. Ironically, some states, especially in the Arab world, make the voluntary renunciation of citizenship extremely difficult and thus contribute to the potential revocation of citizenship in other states. In the end, what has been praised as a sign of the liberalisation of citizenship has potentially turned into an instrument allegedly protecting state security and threatening the human security of dual citizens. We may argue that threats have not emerged through the institutional authority of states; but through a combination of discursive and institutional changes—such as the diminishing of civil rights—to the human security of dual citizens and less protected categories of mobile persons, such as asylum seekers and undocumented migrants.

As Macklin poignantly argues, shifting discursive boundaries conflate state and human security in portraying the 'other'—immigrants, minority citizens and aliens alike—as a menace through manifold labelling processes. The construction of discursive boundaries can even be seen as a necessary precursor of the conflation of state with human security to the detriment of the latter. The resecuritisation of immigration prioritises the surveillance, control, physical exclusion and expulsion of non-citizens in the name of protecting the body politic from infection by menacing strangers. Whether resecuritisation will spread as a trend across states remains to be seen.

Nationalism and nationhood: Multiculturalism, transnational nationalism and integration

An important dimension of citizenship beyond legal belonging, equal political freedom and rights is collective identity or, more precisely, affiliation to a politically constituted collective. This dimension refers to a sense of belonging to the political community making up a state. Most often, this collective is the so-called 'nation', underpinned by nationalism as a discursive formation (Calhoun 1998: 3), and nationhood as one of the, albeit often misrepresented, elements of understanding national citizenship models (Faist 2007a). The understandings and uses of nationalism and nationhood for forging state–citizen ties have experienced especially profound boundary changes over recent decades.

The end of the Cold War and the remapping of states in Central and Eastern Europe, which involved the movement of state borders, have offered new ways of nationalist expressions across borders, of 'home' states relating to 'host' states and national minorities abroad. And new constellations in global and regional politics have offered incentives to emigrant states and diasporas alike to engage in transnational nationalism. For example, dual citizenship has been used as an instrument by home states to forge ties to national minorities abroad, thus raising the spectre of irredentist politics.

The case of national minorities shows in exemplary ways that dual citizenship is not a deterritorialised form of membership but a cross-border modality of national citizenship. Often analysts have claimed that dual citizenship should be tolerated in the case of migrants because immigrant loyalties which overlap several states do not pose insurmountable security risks for the states concerned. In the case of national minorities, at least hypothetically, dual citizenship could be connected to claims of minorities in the 'host' state towards self-government, or even irredentism and secession (Chapter 4).

In particular, in Central and Eastern Europe policies on dual citizenship are pervasively shaped by a history of moving borders rather than of people moving across borders (Shevchuck 1996). In these contexts promoting multiple nationalities can serve as an instrument for an aggressive and revisionist nationalist agenda. Rainer Bauböck argues that we need to evaluate dual citizenships within a broader theory of political boundaries and self-government rights. This may help to overcome the apparent inconsistency of advocating, on the one hand, permissive policies on dual citizenship with respect to international migrants and, on the other hand, restrictive policies in the context of relations between national minorities and their kin states. Dual citizenship for migrants does not raise concerns about the demarcation of political boundaries between sending and receiving countries. This is quite different in the Central and Eastern European context, where actors outside the host state perceive dual citizenship as a menace by an external kin state to the jurisdiction of a neighbouring state over a part of its citizen population and over the territory in which these minority citizens live. According to Rainer Bauböck, perceived threats are not a sufficient justification for restricting minority rights. He explores criteria to assess the aspirations of minorities and their kin states.

The case of Hungarians in Romania is a case in point (Chapter 5). In December 2004, Hungary held a referendum on whether the country should extend an offer of Hungarian citizenship to trans-border Hungarians living in the neighbouring states of Romania, Slovakia, Serbia-Montenegro and Ukraine. A majority 'yes' vote would have obliged lawmakers to remove residency requirements from among the preconditions for granting citizenship and thus make Hungarian citizenship easily available to members of Hungarian minorities living outside the borders of the Hungarian state. Conservative estimates put the number of potential claimants between 3 and 3.5 million people. Assuming that the majority of those made eligible by the reform would actually claim citizenship, the proportions of the resulting demographic change would exceed that in the size of Germany's citizenry after unification, but, of course, without a corresponding territorial enlargement. Mária M. Kovács reviews the story of the Hungarian referendum in a domestic and international perspective. The analysis proposes that the arguments for the Hungarian dual citizenship initiative are, in fundamental respects, different from those advanced in favour of dual citizenship in the major immigration states of Western Europe. But this does not mean that the Hungarian initiative would be an isolated or idiosyncratic episode in contemporary Europe. Parallel initiatives have emerged in quite a number of East-Central and South-East European countries as well as in Italy, and continue to serve as a model for mutual adoption in a growing number of states in the region.

The increased discursive, economic and political relevance of migrant expatriates and their new definition as diasporas abroad after the end of the Cold War is also related to political openings in sending countries, which in turn provided for increased leverage for emigrants in their countries of origin (Chapter 6). In addition, as José Itzigsohn points out in referring to the cases of Mexico and the Dominican Republic, rising levels of migration and globalising economies contributed to the increasing importance of remittances in the economies of the two countries. Remittances have increased manifold since the 1970s when they amounted to about \$2 billion globally to over \$230 billion in 2005 (Faist 2006). Generally, during the 1990s these two countries went from a policy of ignoring their migrant communities to the recognition of dual citizenship and an attempt to woo 'their' migrant communities in the United States. Thus, both the political openings and the increased role of emigrants as an economic factor gave incentives for migrants to organise and exert political pressure in cases such as Mexico and the Dominican Republic.

Turning from states to migrants, we note that, somewhat surprisingly, participation in trans-border politics is positively correlated with length of residence in the United States. José Itzigsohn thus disconfirms the conventional wisdom that ties to country of origin weaken over time. Long-term residents are more likely to enjoy a secure legal status and levels of economic well-being that facilitate cross-border travel and political activities. Yet dual citizenship and concomitant political rights are important not only for the highly active and vocal part of the emigrant population. True, the participants in trans-border politics are most often restricted to a narrow slice of the immigrant population; in the case of Latin American immigrants in the United States only about 10–20 per cent of the overall immigrant population (Guarnizo, Portes and Haller 2003). And the majority of immigrants are mainly interested in achieving legal status and improving their position within the United States. Yet for both categories dual citizenship constitutes a potentially important asset, albeit for different reasons.

While political participation focuses on citizens and their involvement in a (national) political community, nationhood refers to symbolic ties between states and citizens and among citizens, such as social relations of generalised reciprocity and diffuse solidarity. There is a close relationship between discursive and institutional boundaries when it comes to collective identity and citizenship laws. Often, the interrelationship comes to light in debates on legislative changes governing rules of access to citizenship, such as the combination of principles attributing citizenship—such as *jus sanguinis, jus soli* and *jus domicili*—and the toleration of or resistance to overlapping citizenship. The variations of tolerance of and resistance to dual citizenship can be seen in comparisons among immigration states, among emigration states and, largely neglected in a literature shaped by legal scholars and normative political theorists, empirical analyses that explore the layers of the migrants' points of view.

Rather than explaining the variance in the adoption of dual citizenship policies by the dominant nationhood approach (Brubaker 1992), a comparative analysis of Germany, the Netherlands and Sweden reveals that dual citizenship policies can be best understood with reference to the belief systems held by the influential national political parties which in turn are shaped and stabilised by the particular institutional structure of the respective political system of nation-states. The whole spectrum of arguments used in public debates on dual citizenship has resonated with different elements and interpretations of the concept of citizenship itself and the related basic principles of legitimacy in liberal and democratic states (Chapter 7). Moreover, irrespective of country-specific features and national traditions, the objections against dual citizenship voiced by politicians and experts were cast in the language of duties, obligations and commitments. However, these objections usually do not relate to understandings of nationhood in civic-republican or ethno-cultural terms. In general, citizens are expected to possess and develop certain capacities of self-reliance, individual autonomy, personal responsibility and primary identification with the respective national state. Dual citizenship is regarded as a serious obstacle to such orientations, because it is held to impede national unity based on shared values. What counts in such a perspective are not ascriptive features such as ethnicity, nationality or religion but rather the abilities and the contributions immigrants are expected to make to economic development and to social welfare systems. The trend of making citizenship acquisition dependent on individual performance corresponds, interestingly, with far-reaching reinterpretations of social rights in the context of so-called 'activation' and 'workfare' programmes in the areas of labour market and social policy.

Though it may not appear so at first sight, dual citizenship debates in European countries have not simply been about immigrants and national minorities or, less obviously, about one's own citizens as emigrants. Despite the association with these debates and conflicts of certain populist features, such as the petition against dual citizenship in Germany in 1999, one should not conclude that resistance to the pluralisation of citizens' cross-border ties is primarily or mainly about immigration, and a platform for anti-immigrant campaigns. Such a conclusion leads to concerns about the illiberal tendencies of citizenship legislation when large-scale popular mobilisation occurs (see, for example, Howard 2006). This interpretation, however, conflicts with empirically observable facts. After all, several years earlier the proponents of citizenship reform, in this case the Green Party, had engaged in similar political tactics to liberalise citizenship laws. This also means that citizenship politics is not simply a carbon copy of immigration politics in general. In immigration politics, some analysts have argued that political and economic elites usually push for liberalisation while the voting masses are much more resistant, once the follow-up economic costs and sociocultural consequences become visible (Freeman 1995). While this observation may capture important interest dynamics revolving around the easing and restriction of immigration, it would be myopic to reduce citizenship politics to the dynamics of immigration politics. Citizenship politics is—although the immediate driving force may be the presence of many newcomers—first and foremost about integration of societies which conceive of themselves as polities. While the criteria are applied to those clamouring to be full members, the discursive boundaries are, at least in the case of liberal democracies, centrally related to the self-understanding and self-perception of the respective political collective.

Even countries with allegedly similar concepts of nationhood show significant differences regarding the tolerance and encouragement of dual citizenship. Canada and the United States are cases in point (Chapter 8). Paradoxically, greater tolerance for dual citizenship in Canada appears to generate greater political loyalty among immigrant newcomers, at least as judged by naturalisation statistics. Relatively few immigrants actively pursue dual citizenship, but—according to Bloemraad—they do like knowing that the option exists, and that their new home is open to dual nationality. Dual citizenship consequently functions less as a legal status and more as a symbol of openness to immigration and diversity. In the United States, immigrants who become US citizens must 'absolutely and entirely renounce and abjure' all former allegiances. Defenders of exclusive American citizenship claim that multiple attachments weaken American civic culture and nationhood. Dual nationals could bring foreign interference into domestic politics and, more generally, dual citizenship undermines the sovereignty and integrity of the United States. In contrast, Canada's Ministry of Citizenship and Immigration takes pains to explain to immigrants that they can hold multiple nationalities. Both countries have long histories of immigration and yet they take strikingly different positions on dual citizenship. Bloemraad suggests that Canada's distinctly different history of nation-building gave rise to its greater tolerance of dual citizenship.

While the foregoing analyses have conceptualised dual citizenship mainly as a variation of national citizenship, it can also be conceived as a postnational construct (Chapter 9; see also Bosniak 2002). Peter Spiro identifies 'identity dilution' among citizens as one of the main consequences of the multiplication of citizenship. He argues that expanded state acceptance of dual citizenship is defensive, and needs to be seen as part of a retreat in which states must lower membership thresholds by way of maintaining membership levels. Moreover, Spiro goes on to argue, insofar as plural citizenship migrates into the realm of international human rights, states will lose autonomy in their choice of how to regulate dual citizenship through citizenship rules. Ultimately, this means that citizens' ties to the state are multiplying and states' hold on citizens is weakening. Clearly, Spiro's reflections refer to liberal democracies. As we have already seen, an increasing number of emigration country governments have used dual citizenship as a means of strengthening ties with their citizens abroad. Yet it is also to be remembered that governments often engage in this as a reactive and not as a proactive move, in response to the urgings of well-organised migrant groups.

The pluralisation of national identities from the point of view of migrants and their perspective on dual citizenship are addressed in the empirical analysis carried out by Preston, Siemiatycki and Kobayashi (Chapter 10). The authors are interested in understanding how individuals are able to maintain ties to more than one country. In what is a welcome departure from premature assumptions about migrants favouring one end or the other of either–or dichotomies such as commitment versus convenience, Preston, Siemiatycki and Kobayashi explore through surveys and focus group transcripts the citizenship decisions made by Hong Kong immigrants to Toronto and Vancouver. The findings reveal that immigrants make a wide range of choices about citizenship in the context of a highly commodified regime of citizenship in Canada and the complex and uncertain regime of Hong Kong citizenship. Government policies in Canada and Hong Kong have created ideal conditions for the emergence of 'flexible citizenship' (Ong 1999), which some have derided as a 'citizenship of convenience'. Contrary to prevailing images and entrenched assumptions about citizenship, identity and belonging, there is no monolithic experience of Hong Kong–Canadian citizenship. For many Hong Kong migrants, dual citizenship also entails deep attachment to Canada. In a way, these findings confirm central tenets of the old pluralism literature, which posits that the multiple attachments of citizens help to deflect ideological polarisation (Dahl 1971). In the case at hand, this insight would not apply to loyalties within states but across states. Indeed, the findings of Preston, Siemiatycki and Kobayashi lead us to question the validity of framing discussions of dual citizenship around competing, binary norms. Instrumental and symbolic meanings of citizenship are thus intertwined. It also seems that political theorists need to overcome binary thinking in theorising citizens' allegiance—a route already taken by transnationally oriented and postmodern thinkers. In other words, conceptual boundaries in the study of citizenship need to be rethought in order to accommodate substantive empirical findings.

Citizenship and democracy beyond borders

Again, it is worthwhile to remember that the very core of citizenship as a political idea in contrast to a purely legal construct is the norm of equality of political freedom, formerly conceptualised as popular sovereignty. Rights, duties and collective identity, often touted as the core of citizenship, are in fact dimensions to be derived from democratic norms. Otherwise, it would simply not be possible to distinguish authoritarian subjecthood from democratic citizenship. Therefore, any effort to place the growing overall tolerance of dual citizenship in the perspective of other forms of cross-border politics and policies has to place the meta-norm democracy at the very centre. This would apply to cross-border (territorial) boundaries of democracy and to non-territorial functionalist forms. Two aspects of democracy across and beyond the territorial borders of states are addressed. First, there is an effort to contextualise dual citizenship within the broader processes of the changes in governance (Chapter 12). Second, one needs to distinguish cross-border forms of citizenship, such as dual citizenship—overlapping citizenship—from other forms of citizenship beyond borders, such as the EU citizenship—nested citizenship (Chapter 11).

Can the trend towards the erosion of the capacity of nation-states to protect and provide for their citizens be compensated by regional citizenship and regional efforts to counter these effects, as in, for example, the EU? Not really; yet it is a form of citizenship beyond nationhood, which is nonetheless based on national citizenship: only citizens of member states hold EU citizenship. EU citizenship is thus derivative of member state citizenship. Therefore, *extracommunitari*—third-country citizens— still face considerable limitations on their rights to travel across the borders of member states, taking up employment across Europe, and other rights. In the literal sense of the word, 'European Union citizenship' is really transnational and thus transcends national citizenship. This is not the case with dual citizenship. Nevertheless, one may speculate that dual citizenship may be an ideal intermediate step in between national and EU citizenship. Actually, as Skrobacki holds, the causality has been in the reverse direction. EU citizenship has facilitated dual citizenship in member states because they do not require citizens from other member states to renounce their original citizenship upon naturalisation.

Although it originates from national citizenship, EU citizenship is different in nature and function. Most studies on EU citizenship compare it to national citizenships, presuming that this is the way to examine its characteristics. Also, EU citizenship is to be considered as a citizenship *sui generis*, rather than a form of aggregated national citizenship. The European Economic Community (EEC) and later the EU was designed from the beginning to become a polity, and one of the essential aspects of political community tends to be a commonality of legal norms collected in the *acquis communautaire*. Most studies on EU citizenship compare it to national citizenships, presuming that this is the way to examine its characteristics. Such studies can only lead to analysing what EU citizenship is not about.

Certainly, EU citizenship looks extremely feeble and incomplete when compared to national state citizenship. For example, first, the EU's legitimacy and acceptance have been hampered by the pervasive democratic deficit, which has not (yet) been successfully tackled by recent reforms such as increasing the powers of the European Parliament somewhat incrementally. Second, EU citizenship by itself does not (yet) include core elements of what T. H. Marshall defined as the third stage of citizenship, namely social citizenship. Social citizenship is restricted to important but limited elements, which include mainly the transfer of social security entitlements of migrants, who are EU citizens, across borders, and some aspects of gender equity. Social citizenship thus does not show any of the hallmarks of national social citizenship of the latter part of the twentieth century; it does not contain redistributive elements, only rudimentary regulatory ones. Those elements very much resemble market citizenship, accompanying economic integration but not dealing with its social consequences, which are left to the national member states (Faist 2001). This being said, the debates around the democratic deficit of the EU are a prominent example of the difficulties of postnational politics described by Seyla Benhabib (Chapter 12). Benhabib observes that we are experiencing a reconfiguration of citizenship, with tolerance of dual citizenship being one example. The very foundations of citizenship are also being reshaped. For example, in her view, popular sovereignty is threatened by macromechanisms such as global capitalism which has resulted in 'global law without a state' (Günter Teubner). Also, fast-tracked legislation in the aftermath of 9/11, legitimised in order to enhance human security with respect to terrorist threats, has strengthened state security and has actually resulted in decreasing civil rights for citizens and aliens alike (see also Chapter 3). Benhabib holds that the disaggregation of citizenship cannot be conceptualised simply as the disaggregation of sovereignty. The two processes do not run parallel to each other. The fact that the internationalisation of human rights norms and the weakening of state sovereignty are developing in tandem with each other does not mean that the one can be reduced to the other. The reconstitutions of citizenship means that we are moving away from citizenship as national membership increasingly towards a citizenship of residency, which strengthens the multiple ties to the locality, to the region, and to transnational and international institutions. Accordingly, the tolerance of dual citizenship fits well with this trend, as it encourages the congruence of demos and the resident population, on the one hand, and recognises cross-border ties of citizens, on the other. It is an expression of cosmopolitan norms. Yet the reduction of state and popular sovereignty means that the efforts of legislators to conduct open and public deliberations on legislation impacting the movements of capital and other resources are sabotaged. Furthermore, many states in the OECD-world are privatising their own activities by disbursing authority over prisons and schools to private enterprises. Benhabib argues that whereas cosmopolitan norms lead to the emergence of generalisable human interests and the articulation of public standards of norm justification, global capitalism tends to verge towards the privatisation and segment-ation of interest communities and the weakening of standards of public justification through the rise of private logics of norm generation. This results in the deterioration of the capacity of states to protect and provide for their citizens—finally, a decline in substantive citizenship (cf. Faist 2007b).

Outlook

Is there something new created by the addition of two or more national citizenships? If dual citizenship is neither a self-evident absurdity nor the harbinger of postnational citizenship beyond the state, what is it then? The manifold forms of tolerating dual citizenship signal changing insti-tutional and discursive boundaries of membership across the territorial borders of states. It may signal trends usually held to be contradictory. On the one hand, dual citizenship may be a sign of increasing tolera-tion and even acceptance of ties of citizens to more than one national state. It could thus be interpreted as a hallmark of the acceptance by liberal democracies of overlapping loyalties and new configurations of exit and voice. It is postnational insofar as it envisions citizenship at the international level beyond the *domaine réservé* of states and considers transnational ties of citizens. Clearly, when viewed from this angle, the institutional and discursive boundaries around national citizenship have become more permeable, and individual rights of citizens seem to have been strengthened vis-à-vis state prerogatives. On the other hand, dual citizenship has been a useful tool for both emigration states and stateless diasporas to advance nationalist goals and identities. Of course, this observation applies not only to emigration states in the 'South' but also to immigration states in the 'North' insofar as the latter focus on their emigrants abroad. Moreover, as several contributors to this book point out, immigration states have come to use dual citizenship as a convenient tool in their 'war against terrorism' in that the forced renun-ciation of citizenship is an option because the respective citizen has yet another citizenship left. Less dramatic but equally relevant is the use of dual citizenship in the case of national minorities in contexts of unsettled nation-state borders. All these considerations on nationalism, sovereignty and security run counter to the liberalisation of citizenship. In sum, the empirical evidence is mixed at best.

Dual citizenship will continue to be a crucial and strategic research site: we are dealing neither with exclusive citizenship in tightly bounded political communities nor with denationalised citizenship, but rather with a sort of multinationalised citizenship. In short, dual citizenship is an instance of internal globalisation: it is an example of how nation-state regulations implicitly or explicitly respond to ties of citizens across states. Mobile citizens may be interested in dual citizenship for a variety of reasons, among them symbolic ties such as attachment to significant others in the country of origin, or instrumental reasons such as increased opportunities for entry across borders and access to assets in the emigration country. Dual citizenship is distinct from citizenship in a single national state on the one hand and from emerging forms of citizenship beyond the nation-state in supranational governance structures such as the EU on the other hand. Dual citizenship is a simultaneous rather than successive form of citizenship by which one may retain only one citizenship at a time. Recognition of dual citizenship may contribute to the further blurring of the boundaries between immigrants and citizens across borders. Examples include the liberalisation of naturalisation rules (Aleinikoff and Klusmeyer 2001), the complementation of *jus sanguinis* by *jus soli*, and the expansion of *denizenship* between some categories of immigrants—permanent residents—and natives within one country. In the end, the pluralisation of citizens' ties across borders and the growing tolerance of states towards dual citizenship do not necessarily signal the foreboding of a world civil society in a Kantian way (Kant 1907). Yet the move from unitary to more plural forms of citizenship certainly reflects growing transnational interdependence. The trends mark a new morphology of social and political structures in the ongoing contestation between state sovereignty and individual rights, based on collective action.

Note

1. Throughout the book the terms 'multiple citizenship', 'dual citizenship' and 'plural citizenship' are used interchangeably.

References

Aleinikoff, T. A. and D. Klusmeyer (2001) 'Plural Nationality: Facing the Future in a Migratory World'. In T. A. Aleinikoff and D. Klusmeyer, eds, *Citizenship Today: Global Perspectives and Practices*. Washington, DC: Carnegie Endowment for International Peace, pp. 63–88.

Bosniak, L. (2002) 'Multiple Nationality and the Postnational Transformation of Citizenship'. *Virginia Journal of International Law* 42, 4: 979–1004.

Brubaker, R. (1992) 'Citizenship and Nationhood in France and Germany'. Cambridge, MA [u.a.]: Harvard University Press.

Calhoun, C. (1998) *Nationalism*. Minneapolis: University of Minnesota Press.

Dahl, R. (1971) *Polyarchy: Participation and Opposition*. New Haven, CN: Yale University Press.

Deutsch, K. W. (1966) *Nationalism and Social Communication: An Inquiry into the Foundations of Nationality*. 2nd rev. edn. Cambridge, MA: MIT Press.

Faist, T. (2000) *The Volume and Dynamics of International Migration and Transnational Social Spaces*. Oxford: Oxford University Press.

Faist, T. (2001) 'Social Citizenship in the European Union: Nested Membership'. *Journal of Common Market Studies* 39, 1: 39–60.

Faist, T. (2005) 'The Migration-Security Nexus'. In Michal Bodemann and Gökce Yurdakul, eds, *Migration, Citizenship and Ethnos: Incorporation Regimes in Germany, Western Europe and North America*. Houndmills, UK: Palgrave Macmillan, pp. 103–120.

Faist, T. (2006) 'Espacio Social Transnacional y Desarrollo: Una Exploración de la Relación entre Communidado, Estado y Mercado'. *Migración y Desarrollo* 5: 2–34.

Faist, T. ed. (2007a) *Dual Citizenship in Europe: From Nationhood to Societal Integration*. Aldershot, UK: Ashgate.

Faist, T. (2007b) 'Die Transnationale Soziale Frage. Soziale Rechte und Bürgerschaften im Globalen Kontext'. In Jürgen Mackert and Hans-Peter Müller, eds, *Moderne (Staats)Bürgerschaft: Nationale Staatsbürgerschaft und die Debatten der Citizenship Studies*. Wiesbaden: VS.

Faist, T., J. Gerdes and B. Rieple (2004) 'Dual Citizenship as a Path-Dependent Process'. *International Migration Review* 38, 3: 913–44.

Fitzgerald, D. (2006) 'Rethinking Emigrant Citizenship'. *New York Law Review* 81: 90–116.

Fox, J. (2005) 'Unpacking "Transnational Citizenship"'. *Annual Review of Political Science* 8: 171–201.

Freeman, G. (1995) 'Modes of Immigration Politics in Liberal Democratic States'. *International Migration Review* 29, 4: 881–903.

Goldring, L. (2002) 'The Mexican State and Transmigrant Organizations: Negotiating the Boundaries of Membership and Participation'. *Latin American Research Review* 37, 3: 55–99.

Guarnizo, L., A. Portes and W. Haller (2003) 'Assimilation and Transnationalism: Determinants of Transnational Political Action among Contemporary Migrants'. *American Journal of Sociology* 108, 6: 1211–48.

Gustafson, P. (2005) 'International Migration and National Belonging in the Swedish Debate on Dual Citizenship'. *Acta Sociologica* 48, 1: 5–19.

Habermas, J. (1992) *Faktizität und Geltung*. Frankfurt a.M.: Suhrkamp.

Howard, M. M. (2006) 'Comparative Citizenship: An Agenda for Cross-National Research'. *Perspectives on Politics* 4, 3: 443–56.

Jacobson, D. (1997) *Rights Across Borders: Immigration and the Decline of Citizenship*. Baltimore, MD: Johns Hopkins University Press.

Jellinek, G. (1964 [1905]) *System der subjektiven öffentlichen Rechte*. Aalen: Scientia Verlag.

Kant, I. (1907) 'Die Rechtsordnung als denknotwendige Bedingung allgemeiner Freiheit und Gleichheit'. *Die Metaphysik der Sitten*, Werke (Akademie-Ausgabe 7), Vol. 6, Berlin: Reimer, pp. 229–38.

Kivisto, P. and T. Faist (2007) *Citizenship: Theory, Discourse and Transnational Prospects*. Oxford: Blackwell.

Münkler, H. (2004) *Die neuen Kriege*. Reinbek: Rowohlt.

Ohmae, K. (1996) *The End of the Nation-State*. New York: The Free Press.

Ong, A. (1999) *Flexible Citizenship: The Cultural Logics of Transnationality*. Durham, NC: Duke University Press.

Rousseau, J. -J. (1966 [1762]) *Du contrat social: Ou Principes du droit politique*. Paris: Garnier.

Shain, Y. and A. Barth (2003) 'Diasporas and International Relations Theory'. *International Organization* 57, 3: 449–79.

Shevchuck, Y. I. (1996) 'Dual Citizenship in Old and New States'. *European Journal of Sociology* 37, 1: 47–73.

Soysal, Y. N. (1994) *The Limits of Citizenship: Migrants and Post-National Membership in Europe*. Chicago: University of Chicago Press.

Tilly, C. (2004) *Contestation and Democracy in Europe, 1650–2000*. Cambridge: Cambridge University Press.

Zolberg, A. R. (2007) 'The Exit Revolution'. In Nancy L. Green and Francois Weil, eds, *Citizenship and Those Who Leave: The Politics of Emigration and Expatriation*. Champaign, IL: University of Illinois Press.

Part I
States and Human Security

2
Dual Citizenship and Security Norms in Historical Perspective

Triadafilos Triadafilopoulos

During the 1990s, a great deal of scholarly interest was shown in the ways that the dawning of 'post-military societies' and the demise of the 'warfare state' were transforming conceptions of nationhood and citizenship (Linklater 1996; Shaw 1991). Theorists posited that the transformation of the global-strategic field was one of the key factors driving the loosening of relations between citizens and states, thus contributing to the proliferation of multiple allegiances, transnationalism and hybridity. As the threat of war receded, they claimed, so did the need for conscription and mandatory military service—two factors that had long made multiple nationalities anathema and assisted nation-states in defining membership in narrow, unitary terms. The demise of the classical warfare state, steady unraveling of the post–Second World War welfare state and globalisation of international human rights norms beckoned a new 'postnational' age.

This chapter revisits these claims in three steps. I begin by briefly reviewing the literature on war and state formation, focusing on how scholars have theorised the connection between the rise and consolidation of the warfare state in the nineteenth and twentieth centuries and developments in citizenship policies and practices. This literature suggests that the rise of the modern state and mass-industrialised war made nationality an increasingly unitary affiliation, jealousy guarded by states keen on enhancing their extractive capacities and ensuring their subjects' loyalty. This general trend in military affairs influenced international norms concerning dual nationality, leading to formal prohibitions on multiple nationalities by the middle of the twentieth century.

I then turn to the post–Second World War period and discuss factors that have arguably led to the loosening of the citizen–state relationship and the introduction of more expansive international norms concerning multiple nationality in the 1990s. Key in this regard was the rise of the concept of 'mutually assured destruction' via nuclear weapons and the shift to smaller and better-trained professional military forces (Art and Waltz 1983: 79). As the likelihood of war between industrialised states decreased, societies shifted to a post-military posture, marked by a decline in the importance of conscription and mandatory military service. The emergence of a more 'permissive international environment', underlain by pacific 'security communities', intersected with other trends, including gender equality, human rights and the policies of emigration countries to spur the proliferation of dual citizenship throughout the industrialised world (Koslowski 2003).

The chapter's third and concluding section asks whether the emergence of what are typically referred to as 'new' security threats, such as non-state actors and 'asymmetrical warfare', portends a new phase in citizen–state relations and a possible shift back to more rigid forms of membership. I offer a speculative response to this question, arguing that the trend towards greater tolerance for multiple nationalities is likely to persist. Any serious effort to check the rise of dual citizenship would require rolling back well-entrenched rights and thus be politically costly. What we are more likely to see are tighter restrictions on international migration, especially against the very weakest groups, namely asylum seekers and undocumented migrants.

Citizenship, security and the rise of the modern state

The rise of the modern state involved a 'revolution in loyalties', in which an 'inner circle of loyalty expanded' and 'an outer circle of loyalty shrank'. New allegiances to the state replaced the inner web of customary loyalties to immediate feudal superiors and the outer web of 'customary religious obedience to the Church and Pope' (Wight 1978: 77). This shift in loyalties was driven in large part by changes in military affairs. In Michael Howard's words, 'the entire apparatus of the state primarily came into being to enable princes to wage war' (Howard 2001: 15). Similarly, Charles Tilly has famously declared that '[w]ar made the state, and the state made war' (Tilly 1975: 42; see also Tilly 1990: 114–17).

From their beginnings, modern states sought to secure control over their territories to mobilise the necessary financial and human resources required for military action. This led to the deepening of the reach, or 'embrace', of the state through the imposition of uniform, rational administration across its entire territory—a process Tilly describes as the move from 'indirect' to 'direct' rule (Tilly 1990; Torpey 2000: 10–13). Administration moved from being based on the personal authority of the officeholder to the mandate conferred on him by the (centralising) government. This was pursued through the framework of a uniform, rational code of law, first developed (not coincidentally) by Napoleon Bonaparte. Under Napoleon, France developed a highly centralised system that could quickly mobilise and deploy vast numbers of citizens to fight. This system was also used as a model for guiding the reconstruction of conquered states (Tilly 1990: 110).

Intense competition for power prompted states to adopt policies conducive to the creation of a sustainable tax and manpower basis for their military endeavours. This ultimately included creating an administrative infrastructure for the direct application of uniform and rational laws that governed most aspects of citizens' lives. The same factor also prompted states to draft segments of the population that had hitherto eluded their grasp: '[S]ubordinate classes [that] had been largely indifferent to or had sought to evade states ... were now caged into national organization, into politics, by two principal zookeepers: tax gatherers and recruiting officers' (Mann 1986: 250).

While pressure for strategic innovation necessitated political and administrative changes, these reforms also fed back into the military field. Constitutional reform was therefore as much a *precondition* of effective military mobilisation and strategic innovation as a *result* of it; in a reflexive process of institutional back-and-forth, the two fields developed concurrently:

> European states began to monitor industrial conflict and working conditions, install and regulate national systems of education, organize aid to the poor and disabled, build and maintain communication lines, impose tariffs for the benefit of home industries, and the thousand other activities Europeans now take for granted as attributes of state power. The state's sphere expanded far beyond its military core, and its citizens began to make claims on it for a very wide range of protections, adjudication, production, and distribution. As national legislatures extended their own ranges well beyond the approval of taxation, they became the targets of claims from well-organized groups whose interests the state did or could affect. Direct rule and mass national politics grew up together, and reinforced each other mightily. (Tilly 1990: 110)

Similarly, nationalism and the sorts of unitary citizenship it engendered were simultaneously products of these forces and preconditions for their success. They provided legitimacy for an evermore intrusive national administration posing ever-greater demands on the population.[1] Once drafted into armies and confronted with developments on the battle-field, the 'subordinate classes' who bore the bloody costs of total war had to be motivated for that sacrifice, and no motivational practice yielded better results than state-sponsored nationalism (Posen 1993). Where the ruling classes failed to adopt this highly successful model—as was the case initially with Prussia and the other German states during the Napoleonic wars—nationalism from within and without drove them from power or forced them into the belated acceptance of the new system out of sheer necessity. By the end of the nineteenth century, '[w]ar was no longer...a matter for a feudal or ruling class or a small group of professionals, but one for the people as a whole. The armed forces were not regarded as part of the royal household, but as the embodiment of the Nation' (Howard 1976: 110). Thus, while changes in military technology determined the conduct of warfare and prompted new forms of preparation for war, these new forms also influenced the way political leaders justified war, formulated war aims and envisioned societies. '[W]ar again became the business of the people...all of whom considered themselves to be citizens.... The full weight of the nation was thrown into the balance.... There seemed to be no end to the resources mobilized; all limits disappeared in the vigor and enthusiasm shown by governments and their subjects' (Clausewitz 1976: 591–93).

For the first time in modern history, a good share of the adult male population became potential belligerents, as the mass army became the primary tool of state survival. A previously unarticulated population was transformed into soldiers and citizens. The mass army brought its own developmental pressure with it, as the mobilisation of large numbers of conscripts proved to be a formidable administrative task. The veterans of wars and their families made demands on states, catalysing the devel-opment of early welfare schemes and other social services. Thus war helped to cement connections between the state and its populace through affective ties and an increasingly complex network of institutions. In Aristide Zolberg's apt formulation, 'national citizenship emerged as a pivotal element in the awesome social contract fostered by the West-phalian system of states.... [T]he transformation of subjects into citizens was universally coupled with the imposition of some form of military obligation upon them' (Giddens 1985: 233; see also Tilly 1990: 116; Zolberg 2000: 515).

As modernisation became a prerequisite for state survival all aspects of social and political life were affected by the rationalisation and centralisation of government and public administration. Free, public mass education was introduced and had wide-ranging implications for cultural minorities, especially linguistic minorities, as linguistic diversity was seen to have an especially strong potential to undermine the effectiveness of social and military mobilisation (Weber 1976). In a highly stratified sub-culture such as the military, what were seen as 'unassimilable' differences became suspect, and even milder forms of difference were a source of distrust. National minorities—especially those with a 'kin' state across the border—were seen as potential fifth columns and exposed to particularly harsh treatment (Karakasidou 1997; Rae 2002). The same was true of immigrants, particularly those from 'enemy states' and 'backward civilizations' (Gosewinkel 2001; Jacobson 2000). The modern warfare state demanded a thoroughgoing loyalty and viewed heterogeneity as a weakness to be avoided (Gellner 1983: 138). Thus, nationality laws became evermore restrictive, and efforts to thoroughly assimilate and 'naturalise' outsiders became the norm. By the early twentieth century, the idea that nations constituted quasi-biological entities competing with one another in a zero-sum game was entrenched in both scientific and popular discourses and practices (Zolberg 1997: 279–80).

Restrictive domestic immigration and citizenship policies played an important part in furthering the consolidation of the nation-state form (Triadafilopoulos 2004). These, in turn, informed emerging international norms aimed at limiting the incidence of multiple nationalities, which had risen as a consequence of vastly increased levels of international migration and states' insistence on defining membership idiosyncratically.[2] The arrival of immigrants from countries which conferred citizenship through *jus sanguinis* (ancestral lineage) in countries where citizenship was based on the *jus soli* principle (birthplace) led to an increase in the number of dual nationals, as both naturalised individuals and children born in immigration countries took on multiple nationalities (Kerber 1997; Koslowski 2003).

Migrants and their children were often caught between two sets of duties, beset by demands from both adopted states and countries of origin. In cases where rival states found themselves in competition for military personnel, tensions increased. Britain's insistence that naturalised American sailors born in Britain remain subjects of the British

Crown drew a sharp rebuke from the United States, ultimately, triggering the War of 1812 (Koslowski 2003). Later in the nineteenth century, conflicts over multiple military obligations for American citizens of German descent complicated relations between the United States and Prussia (Gosewinkel 2001).

Efforts to address such problems led to the formulation of bilateral agreements, such as the Bancroft Treaties, and later to international accords negotiated under the auspices of the League of Nations. Efforts pursued through the League's International Codification Conference produced the 1930 Hague Convention on Certain Questions Relating to the Conflict of Nationality Laws, whose preamble stated that '[a]ll persons are entitled to possess one nationality, but one nationality only'. In essence, international law reinforced 'the congruence of an almost holy trinity of territory, people and political regime' (Faist 2004b: 923). The 1930 Hague Convention's rejection of multiple nationality was strengthened by the 1963 Convention on the Reduction of Cases of Multiple Nationality and Military Obligations in Cases of Multiple Nationality. As its title suggests, the Convention aimed at reducing the incidence of multiple nationality by providing for the 'automatic loss of one's original nationality upon foreign naturalization (subject to exceptions) [and the elimination] of various constraints on a dual national's voluntary renunciation of one nationality' (Legomsky 2002: 17).

Thus, both domestic and international law and practice reinforced the norm of 'one citizen, one state', even in the face of massive international migration (Spiro 2007). Dual citizenship was seen as a 'self-evident absurdity' and a sign of potential disloyalty (Martin 2005). As such, it was to be vigorously avoided. In practical terms this meant that the acquisition of a new nationality entailed giving up one's former affiliation. In cases where dual nationality was unavoidable because of the intersection of *jus sanguinis* and *jus soli*, domestic legislation and international agreements defined rules whereby individuals either chose one of their affiliations, risked expatriation or were deemed nationals of the state in which they had established permanent residence (Flournoy 1921). Whatever the precise nature of the remedy happened to be, the normative impulse driving it was the ideal of unitary citizenship. Multiple affiliations and heterodox identities were problems to be confronted, minimised and, to the greatest extent possible, eliminated. Moreover, it was the interests of states which dominated these discussions; at best, individuals' rights and interests were of secondary concern.

War, the state and the expansion of citizenship after the Second World War

Changes in war fighting, militarism and strategic environments after the Second World War had a tremendous impact on attitudes towards nationality and dual citizenship. In Western Europe the gradual unification and integration of individual states' economic, political and military systems and the democratisation of members' political regimes led to a marked reduction in intra-European hostilities and the gradual emergence of 'security communities' linked by shared interests and norms (Deutsch et al. 1957). The European project was driven in large part by the desire to avoid the internecine strife that had marked so much of the previous decades (Monnet 1978: 221–22). This required the conscious downgrading of traditional militarist virtues and mind-sets and a rejection of the integral nationalisms of the past. Economic rebuilding and the emergence of a pacific consumer society characterised the European project in its early years, as did the strong commitment to building democratic political institutions (Pollard 1981: 81–85).

While military concerns and strategic affairs certainly did not disappear from the agendas of politicians and policy-makers—an impossibility given the exigencies of the Cold War—they were seen in new light and were no longer defined by traditional conceptions of sovereignty and nationalism that had so marked the rise of the warfare state. In contrast to the past, war was no longer 'the normal condition' of the intra-European system of states, nor the 'normal means of defending or enhancing a position within the system' (Tilly 1985: 104). Other methods of conducting international relations were developed so that by the latter part of the twentieth century, the idea of West European states going to war to settle their disputes was ridiculous.

The 'dwarfing of Europe' (Barraclough 1964) in the postwar period facilitated this shift. With the coming of the Cold War and the retreat of European colonial powers throughout the 'Third World', Europe ceased to play its central role in international strategic affairs and was incorporated into the broader global struggle between the superpowers. The 'delicate balance of terror' which characterised the Cold War's bipolar system also played a crucial role in making conventional wars in Europe far less likely, given the huge consequences for both sides. The devastating potential of nuclear weapons acted 'as an inhibiting factor on military operations. As time went on, fear of escalation no longer allowed...countries to fight each other directly, seriously, or on any scale' (Creveld 1999: 344).

As the likelihood of armed conflict between great powers receded, the size of standing armies also shrank. Whereas France, Germany, Italy, Japan and the Soviet Union all possessed armies numbering in the millions on the eve of the Second World War, 'since 1945 there has probably not been even one case when any state used over twenty full-size divisions on any single campaign' (Creveld 1999: 345). Advances in weapons, transportation and communications technologies helped drive this 'revolution in military affairs', leading to important changes in how states interacted with their respective peoples:

> Civilian populations, which at the beginning of the century had been regarded as reservoirs of military manpower... were now no more than hostages. Wars between states might continue, but – at least in the developed world – *they could no longer in any sense be regarded as wars between peoples*. (Howard 2001: 78, emphasis added)

These changes in how wars were being fought contributed to the gradual decoupling of citizenship and military service, illustrated most vividly in the steady erosion of conscription and the turn to professional armies throughout the industrialised world in the years since 1945. Today, the nation is no longer 'under arms' but is increasingly a 'spectator' of televised wars waged in distant lands by professional troops (Shaw 1991). Demands for sacrifice and participation have receded as war has become essentially reprivatised. While this trend has its roots in the 1960s and 1970s, its pace has accelerated in the post–Cold War period, as states in Continental Europe that had maintained conscription either repealed it (for example, Belgium, the Netherlands and France) or entered into renewed debates over its fate (Germany). Even mention of 'the draft' in the United States is studiously avoided by politicians from both major political parties, as it is simply too risky to suggest that fighting wars may require significant sacrifices on the part of the general population. Rather, the burden of fighting is left to professional soldiers, whose ranks are disproportionately made up of young men and women from relatively disadvantaged backgrounds. As David M. Kennedy has noted,

> no American is now obligated to military service, few will ever serve in uniform, even fewer will actually taste battle—and fewer still of those who do serve will have ever sat in the classrooms of an elite university.... Americans with no risk whatsoever of exposure to

military service have, in effect, hired some of the least advantaged of their fellow countrymen to do some of their most dangerous business while the majority goes on with their own affairs unbloodied and undistracted. (Kennedy, cited in Didion 2006)

The decline of conscription has removed one of the most important arguments against dual citizenship, freeing citizens from their long-standing relation to the state's military function. Other factors, including the widening and deepening of economic and political integration in Europe and elsewhere and the improbability of war between advanced industrialised democracies, have also made issues of loyalty and allegiance less pressing (Rusett 1993). Consequently, the trend in many advanced industrialised states has been towards the toleration of dual citizenship (Faist 2007). Canada's 1977 Citizenship Act led the way in this regard, allowing for the toleration of multiple nationalities and facilitating the acquisition of nationality through liberal naturalisation requirements (Galloway 2000: 99). Even in countries where dual citizenship is formally rejected, such as Germany and the United States, *de facto* toleration of dual citizenship is common (Green 2004: 104). Important immigrant-sending states, such as Mexico, have contributed to this trend by allowing their nationals to naturalise in their adopted countries without losing their citizenship status. The granting of voting and other rights to members of 'overseas diasporas' has also worked to extend links between immigrants and sending states (Brubaker 2005; Davies 2000; Faist 2004a; Østergaard-Nielsen 2001).

The growing acceptance of dual citizenship at the state level has its counterpart in international law. Both the 1993 Second Protocol Amending the Convention on the Reduction of Cases of Nationality and Military Obligations in Cases of Multiple Nationality and the 1997 European Convention on Nationality mark an important move away from prior practice in that they formally reject the long-standing principle of avoiding dual nationality. Instead, the principal norm driving both the Second Protocol and the Convention is inclusion: dual citizenship is now touted as a means of promoting and facilitating the naturalisation of legally resident foreigners and deepening the integration of second and third generations (Checkel 1999). Whereas immigration drove the development of exclusionary citizenship laws at the turn of the twentieth century, it is helping drive the formation of more expansive membership regimes today (Joppke 2006; Triadafilopoulos and Schönwälder 2006).

Dual citizenship still creates problems regarding military obligations, but the stakes raised by such conflicts are less pressing than in the nineteenth and early twentieth centuries. Certainly, a replay of the War of 1812 is unlikely—indeed, it is difficult even to imagine. Rather, liberal-democratic states are responding to the challenge of multiple nationality and military service by developing practical solutions that increasingly take the interests of dual nationals into consideration.

While dual citizenship remains a contentious issue, catalysing pitched debates in Canada, Germany, the Netherlands and elsewhere, here, too, one gets the sense that the stakes are simply not as high as in the past. The fact that dual citizenship is increasingly tolerated in Germany and other states which still officially oppose it speaks to this point. Even in countries where dual citizenship has not been 'embraced', it is increasingly accepted as a largely unalterable fact of life. And while fears of disloyalty have not disappeared, they have been displaced away from questions of which side one would side with in a fight to whether or not one has demonstrated a sufficient commitment to integrating into his or her host society.

Conclusion

I have argued that the rejection of dual citizenship in the nineteenth and early twentieth centuries was driven in part by the rise and consolidation of the classical warfare state. Waging war successfully required massive, highly motivated armies united in their commitment to defending their respective homelands and advancing the interests of their 'peoples'. In an age of conscription and mandatory military service, dual citizenship was a nuisance and a threat. It was therefore rejected in favour of an idealised notion of unitary citizenship, which assisted in universalising the nation-state form as the standard mode of political organisation throughout the world.

The transformation of war through the development of nuclear weapons and the turn to smaller professional armies has helped lift the stigma attached to dual citizenship. Perhaps most importantly, the abolition of mandatory military service across a growing number of advanced industrialised states constituting contemporary security communities has removed a long-standing barrier to the toleration of multiple allegiances. This is not to suggest that the decline of the warfare state has been the sole or even most important factor behind the normalisation of dual citizenship and the proliferation of individuals with multiple nationalities. As several of the contributions to this book make clear, other factors, including the rise of gender equality and the policies of sending states, have played a more direct, and arguably more important, role in generating momentum for this trend. My point is simply that changes in broadly encompassing strategic environments have influenced war fighting and, consequently, relations between states and citizens.

This is an admittedly simple point, but one that merits recognition. It helps us to see that the emergence of an incipient 'postnational' order has been driven not solely by the rise and diffusion of human rights, but also by changes in how states themselves interact with individuals within their territorial boundaries. The decline of the classical warfare state and pacification of relations among advanced industrialised countries in the postwar period prompted the emergence of a new 'postnational' order in which multiple nationality and other forms of plural membership are increasingly common. In contrast to those who see postnationalism as a solvent of traditional citizenship, I suggest that changes in the nature of citizenship *preceded* and spurred the development of postnationalism.

Yet even this may be too limited a view. International Relations scholars have rightly noted that considerations of national security among industrialised states are no longer driven solely, or even mainly, by interstate competition; rather, threats from non-state actors operating within and across states are becoming increasingly important (Adamson 2002). This view has taken on added significance in the years since the terror attacks in New York, Washington, DC, Madrid and London. The threat of similar terrorist strikes has catalysed noteworthy responses on the part of states, including the development of new approaches to the use of military force abroad and greater surveillance of citizens and non-citizens at home (Adamson and Grossman 2004; Andreas 2003; Ceyhan and Tsoukala 2002). Arguably, the 'war on terrorism' is creating opportunities for the expansion of state power and the tightening of the state's embrace of those within its boundaries. Given all this, it is reasonable to ask whether and how this most recent change in the nature of threat might lead to changes in citizenship policy. Might we be on the cusp of a reversal of the liberal trends of the recent past and a return to more rigorous notions of unitary membership?

There is evidence to suggest that such a reversal is not beyond the realm of possibilities. The growing popularity of 'integration contracts' and other means of compelling the assimilation of immigrants into dominant national 'cultures' suggest that fears of disloyal foreigners have increased in the years since the attacks of 11 September 2001 (Kofman 2005). Interest in stripping naturalised citizens of their nationality in cases where they are dubbed 'security threats' has also become more common (Nyers 2006). And, as Audrey Macklin points out in her contribution to this book, liberal-democratic states are considering—and, in the case of Great Britain, actually pursuing—means of facilitating the denaturalisation of individuals born in their jurisdictions and granted nationality through *jus soli*. Furthermore, liberal and illiberal states alike are taking an increasingly harder line towards the most powerless individuals in their grasp, namely asylum seekers and undocumented migrants (Kerwin 2005; Nyers 2003). Lacking political rights and influential advocates, these groups are being subjected to increasingly draconian measures that fly in the face of domestic liberal principles and international human rights norms. Fear of 'dangerous foreigners' has tended to dampen popular sympathy for asylum seekers and illegal migrants, leaving them evermore vulnerable to the whims of states intent on demonstrating their ability to maintain control of their borders (Benhabib 2007).

Yet, there have been relatively few efforts to limit access to dual citizenship in liberal-democratic states. One could speculate as to why this is the case. To begin with, in liberal-democratic countries where dual citizenship has been entrenched, attempts to restrict it would be politically contentious and potentially costly in electoral terms. Thus, it is not surprising that politicians in Canada and elsewhere have opted to maintain the status quo. Moreover, respect for dual citizenship has become a way of measuring liberal-democratic states' commitment to core principles, such as gender equality. One would assume that levels of insecurity would have to increase to extreme levels for policy-makers in liberal-democratic states to consider meddling with these principles. Finally, restricting dual citizenship would prompt disagreements among states interested in maintaining ties with their co-nationals abroad, complicating international relations. Again, such a move would only make political sense in an extremely fraught environment where suspicion and insecurity had reached a fevered pitch. In the absence of such a frightening condition, the trend towards tolerating dual citizenship is likely to persist.

Notes

1. For a discussion of consensual and coercive models of governance, see Hall 1994.
2. Rey Koslowski has pointed out that 'in the 1850s 67 per cent of the members of the US Army were born abroad and 50 per cent of enlistees between 1865 and 1875 were foreign-born, primarily from Germany and Ireland' (Koslowski 1997: 5).

References

Adamson, F. B. (2002) 'Mobilizing at the Margins of the System: The Dynamics and Security Impacts of Transnational Mobilization by Non-State Actors'. (PhD dissertation, Columbia University).

Adamson, F. B. and A. D. Grossman (2004) *Reframing 'Security' in a Post-9/11 Context*. New York: Social Science Research Council.

Andreas, P. (2003) 'Redrawing the Line: Borders and Security in the Twenty-First Century'. *International Security* 28, 2 (Fall): 78–111.

Art, R. J. and K. Waltz (1983) 'Technology, Strategy, and the Use of Force'. In Robert J. Art and Kenneth Waltz, eds, *The Use of Force*. Lanham, MD: University Press of America.

Barraclough, G. (1964) *An Introduction to Contemporary History*. New York: Basic Books.

Benhabib, S. (2007) 'Twilight of Sovereignty or the Emergence of Cosmopolitan Norms? Rethinking Citizenship in Volatile Times'. In Thomas Faist and Peter Kivisto, eds, *From Unitary to Multiple Citizenship*. UK: Palgrave Macmillan. Ch. 12.

Brubaker, R. (2005) 'The "Diaspora" Diaspora'. *Ethnic and Racial Studies* 28, 1: 1–19.

Ceyhan, A. and A. Tsoukala (2002) 'The Securitization of Migration in Western Societies: Ambivalent Discourses and Policies'. *Alternatives* 27: 21–39.

Checkel, J. (1999) 'Norms, Institutions, and National Identity in Contemporary Europe'. *International Studies Quarterly* 43: 83–114.

Clausewitz, C. von (1976) *On War*. Eds and trans. Michael Howard and Peter Paret. Princeton, NJ: Princeton University Press.

Creveld, M. van (1999) *The Rise and Decline of the State*. Cambridge: Cambridge University Press.

Davies, R. (2000) ' "Neither Here Nor There?" The Implications of Global Diasporas for (Inter)national Security'. In David T. Graham and Nana Poku, eds, *Migration, Globalisation and Human Security*. London: Routledge, pp. 23–46.

Deutsch, K., Sidney A. Burrell and Robert A. Kann (1957) *Political Community and the North Atlantic Area*. Princeton, NJ: Princeton University Press.

Didion, J. (2006) 'Cheney: The Fatal Touch'. *New York Review of Books* 53, 15: http://www.nybooks.com/articles/19376 [accessed on 19 January 2007].

Faist, T. (2004a) 'Towards a Political Sociology of Transnationalization. The State of the Art in Migration Research'. *Archives Européennes de Sociologie* 45, 3: 331–66.

Faist, T. (2004b) 'Dual Citizenship as a Path Dependent Process'. *International Migration Review* 38, 3 (Fall): 913–44.

Faist, T. (2007) 'The Shifting Boundaries of the Political'. In Thomas Faist and Peter Kivisto, eds, *From Unitary to Multiple Citizenship*. UK: Palgrave Macmillan. Ch. 1.

Flournoy, R. W., Jr (1921) 'Dual Nationality and Election'. *Yale Law Journal* 30, 6 (April): 545–64.

Galloway, D. (2000) 'The Dilemmas of Canadian Citizenship Law'. In T. Alexander Aleinikoff and Douglas Klusmeyer, eds, *From Migrants to Citizens: Membership in a Changing World*. Washington, DC: Carnegie Endowment for International Peace, pp. 82–118.

Gellner, E. (1983) *Nations and Nationalism*. Ithaca, NY: Cornell University Press.

Giddens, A. (1985) *The Nation-State and Violence. Volume Two of A Contemporary Critique of Historical Materialism*. Berkeley and Los Angeles: University of California Press.

Gosewinkel, D. (2001) *Einbürgern und Ausschließen: Die Nationalisierung der Staatsangehörigkeit vom Deutschen Bund bis zur Bundesrepublik Deutschland*. Göttingen: Vandenhoeck & Rurecht.

Green, S. (2004) *The Politics of Exclusion: Institutions and Immigration Policy in Contemporary Germany*. Manchester: Manchester University Press.

Hall, J. (1994) *Coercion and Consent*. Cambridge: Polity.

Howard, M. (1976) *War in European History*. Oxford: Oxford University Press.

Howard, M. (2001) *The Invention of Peace: Reflections on War and International Order*. London: Profile Books.

Jacobson, M. F. (2000) *Barbarian Virtues: The United States Encounters Peoples at Home and Abroad, 1876–1917*. New York: Hill and Wang.

Joppke, C. (2006) 'Citizenship between De- and Re-Ethnicization'. In Y. Michal Bodemann and Gökçe Yurdakul, eds, *Migration, Citizenship, Ethnos*. New York: Palgrave Macmillan.

Karakasidou, A. N. (1997) *Fields of Wheat, Hills of Blood: Passages to Nationhood in Greek Macedonia, 1870–1990*. Chicago: Chicago University Press.

Kerber, L. K. (1997) 'The Meanings of Citizenship'. *The Journal of American History* 84, 3 (December): 833–54.

Kerwin, D. (2005) 'The Use and Misuse of "National Security" Rationale in Crafting U.S. Refugee and Immigration Policies'. *International Journal of Refugee Law* 17, 4 (December): 749–63.

Kofman, E. (2005) 'Citizenship, Migration and the Reassertion of National Identity'. *Citizenship Studies* 9, 5: 453–67.

Koslowski, R. (1997) 'Changing Norms on Dual Nationality and Military Service'. Unpublished paper presented at the German American Summer Institute on Immigration, Incorporation, and Citizenship in Advanced Industrialized Countries, Berlin, July.

Koslowski, R. (2003) 'Challenges of International Cooperation in a World of Increasing dual Nationality'. In Kay Hailbronner and David Martin, eds, *Rights and Duties of Dual Nationals: Evolution and Prospects*. The Hague: Kluwer, pp. 157–82.

Legomsky, S. (2002) 'Dual Nationality and Military Service: Strategy Number Two'. Washington University in St. Louis School of Law Faculty Working Paper Number 02-9-07 (September).

Linklater, A. (1996) 'Citizenship and Sovereignty in the Post-Westphalian State'. *European Journal of International Relations* 2, 1: 77–103.

Mann, M. (1986) *Sources of Social Power*. Cambridge: Cambridge University Press.

Martin, D. A. (2005) 'Dual Nationality: TR's "Self-Evident Absurdity"'. *UVA Lawyer* (Spring): http://www.law.virginia.edu/html/alumni/uvalawyer/sp05/martin_lecture.htm [accessed on 19 January 2007].

Monnet, J. (1978) *Memoirs*. Garden City, NY: Doubleday.

Nyers, P. (2003) 'Abject Cosmopolitanism: The Politics of Protection in the Anti-Deportation Movement'. *Third World Quarterly* 24, 6: 1069–93.

Nyers, P. (2006) 'The Accidental Citizen: Acts of Sovereignty and (Un)making Citizenship'. *Economy and Society* 35, 1 (February): 22–41.

Østergaard-Nielsen, E. (2001) 'Diasporas in World Politics'. In Daphné Josselin and William Wallace, eds, *Non-State Actors in World Politics*. New York: Palgrave, pp. 218–34.

Pollard, S. (1981) *The Integration of the European Economy Since 1815*. London: George Allen and Unwin.

Posen, B. R (1993) 'Nationalism, the Mass Army, and Military Power'. *International Security* 18, 2 (Fall): 80–124.

Rae, H. (2002) *State Identities and the Homogenisation of Peoples*. Cambridge: Cambridge University Press.

Rusett, B. (1993) *Grasping the Democratic Peace: Principles for a Post-Cold War World*. Princeton, NJ: Princeton University Press.

Shaw, M. (1991) *Post-Military Society*. Philadelphia: Temple University Press.

Spiro, P. (2007) 'Dual citizenship – A postnational view'. In Thomas Faist and Peter Kivisto, eds, *From Unitary to Multiple Citizenship*. UK: Palgrave Macmillan. Ch. 9.

Tilly, C., ed. (1975) *The Formation of National States in Western Europe*. Princeton, NJ: Princeton University Press.

Tilly, C. (1985) 'War Making and State Making as Organized Crime'. In Peter B. Evans, Dietrich Rueschemeyer and Theda Skocpol, eds, *Bringing the State Back In*. Cambridge: Cambridge University Press, pp. 169–91.

Tilly, C. (1990) *Coercion, Capital, and European States AD 990–1990*. Cambridge: Basil Blackwell.

Torpey, J. (2000) *The Invention of the Passport: Surveillance, Citizenship, and the State*. Cambridge: Cambridge University Press.

Triadafilopoulos, T. (2004) 'Building Walls, Bounding Nations: Migration and Exclusion in Canada and Germany, 1870–1939'. *Journal of Historical Sociology* 17, 4: 385–427.

Triadafilopoulos, T. and K. Schönwälder (2006) 'How the Federal Republic Became an Immigration Country: Norms, Politics and the Failure of West Germany's Guest Worker System'. *German Politics and Society* 24, 3: 1–19.

Weber, E. (1976) *Peasants into Frenchmen, 1870–1914*. Stanford, CA: Stanford University Press.

Wight, M. (1978) *Power Politics*; cited in Linklater 1996: 77.

Zolberg, A. R. (1997) 'Global Movements, Global Walls: Responses to Migration: 1885–1925'. In Wang Gungwu, ed., *Global History and Migrations*. Boulder, CO: Westview Press, pp. 279–307.

Zolberg, A. R. (2000) 'The Dawn of Cosmopolitan Denizenship'. *Indiana Journal of Global Legal Studies* 7, 2 (Spring): 511–18.

3
The Securitisation of Dual Citizenship

Audrey Macklin

Introduction

The securitisation of immigration operates by directing the first question asked about migration towards potential harm to the receiving state. It prioritises surveillance, control, physical exclusion and expulsion of non-citizens in the name of protecting the body politic from infection by the menacing foreigner. The securitisation of citizenship complements this process by facilitating the discursive and sometimes literal mutation of the citizen into the foreigner. Investing in mechanisms that enable the conversion or reversion of risky people to the status of foreigner simplifies the equation of state security with citizen security. Ordinarily, an elision of national security with citizen security founders on the realisation that a state's pursuit of the former almost invariably involves individual rights violations that jeopardise the latter. However, if a population can be persuaded that alleged security risks are, or ought to be regarded as, essentially 'foreign', then it becomes easier to promote what is done in the name of state security as coeval and consonant with advancing citizen security.

This trend carries with it certain implications for discourses and practices of dual citizenship in Western industrialised states. I contend that the securitisation of citizenship operates by making acquisition of a second citizenship less attainable for refugees and other forced migrants and, paradoxically, by making birthright citizenship itself less secure for certain members of diasporic communities who already possess dual nationality.

Refugees and asylum seekers

Hannah Arendt famously identified the refugee's fundamental loss (and need) as membership in a human community (Arendt 1951). To the extent that Arendt elided the refugee and the stateless person, her characterisation does not accurately reflect the corresponding categories in post-war international law. The vast majority of refugees are not stateless, and not all stateless persons fit within the refugee definition. Nevertheless, one might contend that the legal citizenship possessed by the refugee is substantively hollow insofar as membership in a state from which one reasonably apprehends persecution is the cause and not the solution for insecurity. In such cases, it is unsurprising that refugees in industrialised states might seek durable security in the form of citizenship in the global North.

The nexus between refugees and security is contradictory: the most insecure of migrants are simultaneously construed as security threats. September 11 did not produce this tension, though it surely exacerbated it. Two systemic factors account for the tenacity of the negative association of asylum seekers and national security. First, self-selected asylum seekers bodily and insistently refute the sovereigntist fantasy of invincible borders. In an era marked by globalisation and the attendant loss of state sovereignty in other domains, politicians can ill afford to concede their impotence by disabusing their citizenry of the illusion of control.

If asylum seekers reach the border and meet the refugee definition, the receiving state's international obligations under Article 33 of the 1951 UN *Convention Relating to the Status of Refugees*[1] prohibit *refoulement* (return). States experience their voluntarily assumed obligations under the Refugee Convention as an acute loss of sovereignty. One consequence is that states have made it virtually impossible for an asylum seeker to reach the European Union (EU), North America or Australia/New Zealand through lawful means. As a result, asylum seekers, along with other migrants from the global South, often resort to smugglers who furnish false documents or otherwise circumvent border control. Persons who enter through duplicitous means are depicted as illegal immigrants, and illegal immigrants represent a breach of security. *Ergo*, asylum seekers are a danger to national security, and the aspersion cast by their unauthorised entry often persists despite recognition as refugees.

If one portrays the refugee regime as foisting the uninvited upon the unwilling, how better to demonstrate the catastrophic consequences of this loss of sovereignty than by linking terrorism to the asylum regime?

This visceral anxiety about sovereignty offers an important insight into the dynamics behind the demonisation of refugees as the figurative culprits for September 11 and its progeny. From the perspective of receiving states, the arrival of asylum seekers signifies the failure of border control and, thus, of sovereignty itself, quite apart from the ultimate outcome of the determination process. As such, asylum seekers always already embody a breach of the state's imperfect gate-keeping apparatus.

A second factor that accounts for the singling out of refugees and asylum seekers as inherently risky relates to a certain trepidation about the dissident citizen that is shared by state authorities across the ideological spectrum. As Reg Whitaker explains,

> The very nature of a Convention Refugee claim: a 'well-founded fear of persecution for reasons of face, religion, nationality, membership in a particular social group or political opinion' arises out of political conflicts that are unlikely to be contained within the country of origin. Spread of such conflicts is always a fear, and in the age of international terrorism and the global telepolitics of violence, this fear is not always imaginary. There is always some suspicion that attaches to anyone who has had to flee one state on political grounds, a kind of irreducible aura of political instability that could potentially threaten the order of the host country. (Whitaker 1992: 416)

One would thus expect the securitisation of migration and citizenship to affect forced migrants disproportionately. In this regard, the controversy surrounding the citizenship of Ayaan Hirsi Ali, erstwhile Dutch politician and Somali refugee, is instructive in both its typical and idiosyncratic aspects.

Ayaan Hirsi Ali migrated to the Netherlands in 1992 at the age of 25. She made an asylum claim and within weeks was recognised as a Convention refugee on the basis of a well-founded fear of persecution in Somalia. Five years later, she acquired Dutch citizenship. International law encourages but does not require states to facilitate naturalisation by Convention refugees (UN *Convention Relating to the Status of Refugees*, Article 34; *European Convention on Nationality*, Article 6(4)(g)). The Netherlands is one of many industrialised states that permits Convention refugees to eventually acquire citizenship.

During her years of study at university and subsequent employment with immigrant communities in the Netherlands, she became a

self-described 'Muslim atheist' and an outspoken critic of Islam, especially in its treatment of women. In 2002, she entered Dutch politics
as a candidate for the Dutch Liberal Party (VVD) and was elected in
2003. Members of the Dutch Liberal Party are known to take tough
stances on migration and multiculturalism, especially Rita Verdonk,
Dutch Minister of Immigration and Integration. In 2004, Hirsi Ali rose
to international prominence with the gruesome murder of Dutch film-
maker Theo van Gogh, with whom she collaborated on a film depicting
Islam as misogynist.[2]

Hirsi Ali described her goals as a politician in the following terms:

> First of all I wanted to put the oppression of immigrant women—
> especially Muslim women—squarely on the Dutch political agenda.
> Second, I wanted Holland to pay attention to the specific cultural
> and religious issues that were holding back many ethnic minor-
> ities, instead of always taking a one-sided approach that focused
> only on their socio-economic circumstances. Lastly, I wanted politi-
> cians to grasp the fact that major aspects of Islamic doctrine
> and tradition, as practiced today, are incompatible with the open
> society. (Hirsi Ali 2006)

When she entered public life in 2002, Hirsi Ali revealed that she had lied
on her asylum application in 1992 by using a false name and date of
birth, and by fabricating her story. She claimed to have travelled to the
Netherlands directly from Somalia. In fact, she and her family fled when
she was 6 years old, and she had spent the previous 10 years in Kenya
as a refugee under the aegis of the United Nations High Commissioner
for Refugees (UNHCR). She had also passed through Germany before
reaching the Netherlands. Hirsi Ali explained her deception by claiming
that she had been forced by her father into a marriage in Kenya with
a distant cousin who lived in Canada. En route to Canada, she had a
stopover in Germany, where she slipped away to the Netherlands. She
made her asylum claim under a false identity in order to evade angry
clan members and relatives, and did not reveal her years in Kenya or
her forced marriage in order to expedite her claim and strengthen her
chances of success (*Expatica News*, 12 May 2006).

In 2006, a television documentary revived the story of Hirsi Ali's
misrepresentation, and supplemented it with accounts that cast doubt
on the credibility of her alleged forced marriage. Immigration and
Integration Minister and party colleague Rita Verdonk surprised and

dismayed almost everyone by announcing that in the light of Hirsi Ali's deception, 'the preliminary assumption must be that she is considered not to have obtained Dutch citizenship' (BBC News, 16 May 2006).

The public, the Dutch Parliament (including other members of the Dutch Liberal Party) and many international observers denounced Verdonk and rallied to Hirsi Ali's defence. The validity of Hirsi Ali's legal citizenship was fortified by her compliance with the normative requirements of Dutch citizenship. How had she performed as the ideal Dutch citizen? Not only by exercising the highest form of citizenship in the classical sense, by achieving elected office; she also demonstrated her integration and allegiance to the Netherlands by vehemently criticising Islam and publicly endorsing her party's restrictionist immigration and asylum policies.

By the time the dust had settled, Hirsi Ali had resigned from Dutch politics and accepted a position at a conservative US think tank. Verdonk had retreated from her declaration that Hirsi Ali's citizenship was void, and disavowed any intention to exercise her discretion to revoke it. (Verdonk did, however, guard her reputation by insisting that had she been Minister when Hirsi Ali made her original asylum claim, Hirsi Ali would have been deported. 'I don't like lies', the Minister proclaimed.) Verdonk's bungling of the matter cost the Dutch Liberal Party coalition the support of one of its partners, and the government fell.

Obviously, Hirsi Ali's remarkable trajectory is an unusual one among migrants from the South to the North, but it is worth contemplating hypothetical scenarios arising from this episode for purposes of illuminating the particular significance of dual citizenship for refugees and other forced migrants. First, what might have happened had Hirsi Ali been stripped of her Dutch citizenship? Many states permit revocation of citizenship in cases where it was obtained by fraud or misrepresentation. Revocation is rarely automatic, and usually involves the exercise of discretion by a government official. The fraud or misrepresentation may relate to the acquisition of the status that ultimately led to citizenship, in this case refugee status.

Had the Minister stripped Hirsi Ali of Dutch citizenship on account of her fabricated asylum claim, logic would dictate that her refugee status would also be vacated.[3] After all, if the misrepresentation was not material to the decision to confer refugee status, penalising Hirsi Ali would serve no rational purpose. Deprived of refugee status, Hirsi Ali would then revert to a Somali citizen with no legal entitlement to reside in the Netherlands, and would then face expulsion. The only state with a legal duty to admit her is her state of nationality, namely Somalia. Of course, given Hirsi Ali's notoriety, it seems reasonable to suppose that return to Somalia would expose her to a well-founded fear of persecution on account of her political opinion and her religion (or, more precisely, her atheism). In effect, Hirsi Ali's exercise of her rights as citizen of the Netherlands would probably make her a refugee *sur place* today. Moreover, physically returning people to Somalia is difficult, and sometimes impossible, owing to the absence of any functioning government in Somalia. The 'failed state' label often attached to Somalia only underscores the emptiness of Somali citizenship and the impetus driving many Somalis to obtain citizenship elsewhere.

A second inquiry of relevance concerns some of the reasons why Hirsi Ali lied in her asylum application. According to her statements to the media, she concealed her residence in Kenya, her passage through Germany and her real motive for flight, namely escape from a forced marriage, because she believed that disclosure of these facts would lead to rejection of her asylum claim.

She was probably right. In 1992, the Netherlands regarded Kenya as a viable alternative for Somalis, even though conferral of refugee status by the UNHCR did not actually ensure security of residence for Somalis in Kenya. The fact that she did not make an asylum claim in Germany might also have prejudiced her asylum application in the Netherlands, even though her application pre-dates the entry into force of the Dublin Convention (now Dublin Regulation).[4] Finally, forced marriage would not have been viewed as persecution in 1992. As with many practices oppressive to women, forced marriage would have been regarded as a private matter that did not sufficiently engage the state to amount to persecution. Similarly, most countries at the time resisted recognising sex/gender as a ground of persecution.

At present, many Western states (including the Netherlands) recognise gender-related persecution in some form, and forced marriage has been successfully invoked as the basis of a refugee claim (*Gao v. Gonzales* 2006; RPD TA2-00417, 2002; RRT N98/25465, 2001). It is also a practice associated with Islam that attracts considerable condemnation from EU states, and UK parliamentarians recently adopted criminal legislation to prohibit it. It does not follow inexorably that Hirsi Ali would succeed even today in a claim based on forced marriage, but it is almost certain that she would have failed in 1992 (*Guardian* 2006).

Like many asylum seekers, Hirsi Ali lied because the asylum regime in countries of the North was so restrictive that the truth would probably have led to her rejection. Hirsi Ali would not have received refugee status, which means she would not have acquired permanent residence, which in turn means that she would not have been in a position to apply for and obtain Dutch citizenship within 5 years of her arrival. Since only citizens can run for public office, she would never have become a member of the Dutch parliament. Suffice to say that if governments actually undertook to revoke the citizenship of all refugees who made misrepresentations comparable to Hirsi Ali's, the fate of untold numbers of refugees would be cast into doubt.

The year of Hirsi Ali's arrival in the Netherlands marked the high point of asylum applications in Europe. More than 670,000 asylum seekers entered the EU in 1992 (Guild 2003: 341). The UNHCR reported that in 2006, 180,160 asylum seekers lodged applications in 15 EU states (UNHCR 2006). What changed in the intervening years? One answer is that the asylum regime in Europe, North America and Australia became drastically stricter. One indicator of this trend is an ever-widening distance between the forced migrant and citizenship in the industrialised states. The prospects of bridging this gap are increasingly remote.

A sketch of the technologies of physical and legal exclusion developed and deployed over the last 15 years by refugee-receiving states of the global North (EU, Canada, the United States and Australia/New Zealand) helps explain the mounting difficulty in locating points of convergence between forced migrants and dual citizenship. Not all states employ each of these tactics, but all states use some of them and tacitly or explicitly justify their policies by exploiting and encouraging the belief that the overwhelming majority of asylum seekers are making fraudulent claims. Domestic politics and the sovereign conceit are best served by fostering the view that all the 'real' refugees are passively languishing in refugee camps, patiently awaiting Western aid or selection for resettlement, whereas those who take the initiative and seek asylum are both bogus and risky. The result of this discursive sleight of hand is that, by definition, real refugees are always already 'over there'. The very fact of their arrival 'here' as asylum seekers means they are not genuine refugees.

The catalogue of deflection and deterrence strategies continues to expand in number and in geographic range, with attendant national and regional variations. The following list identifies general mechanisms, rather than detailed description of the particular features of any one state or region (Crépeau and Nakache 2006; Gilbert 2004; Junker 2006; Mandal 2002; McAdam 2002; Taylor 2002).

1. Visa requirements for citizens of poor and/or 'refugee-producing' countries.
2. Physical deflection via interception of ships, or posting of immigration officers at airport boarding gates abroad to scrutinise documents and screen passengers.
3. Capacity-building in weaker surrounding states to prevent migrants from transiting through them *en route* to destination country.
4. Carrier sanctions for airlines and shipping companies who transport undocumented or improperly documented passengers or 'stowaways'; increased surveillance and enforcement of anti-smuggling/trafficking laws.
5. Legal excision of airport transit lounges, islands, coastline perimeters from state territory for purposes of denying that asylum seekers are at the frontier or inside or outside state territory.
6. Deterrence of present and future asylum seekers via the use of detention, fingerprinting, denial of access to work, shelter, social assistance; general immiseration.
7. Offshore processing of asylum claims on remote state territory or the territory of weak states.
8. Deflection of asylum seekers to 'first country of arrival' from among states party to a 'safe third country' agreement.
9. Ineligibility or presumptive denial of asylum seekers as 'manifestly unfounded' if claiming against designated 'safe countries of origin'.
10. Narrow interpretation of the Convention refugee definition, compounded by a 'culture of disbelief' among decision-makers that leads to rejection on the basis of non-credibility.
11. Diversion of asylum seekers from refugee status into complementary or subsidiary forms of protection that are temporary and do not segue into permanent residence or citizenship;[5] denial of access to permanent residence or citizenship by onshore asylum seekers recognised as Convention refugees.

Many of these measures derive additional legitimation from, and simultaneously reinforce, the securitisation of immigration. For example, Elspeth Guild observes that the concept of the safe country of origin reinforces the equation of asylum seeker and security threat:

> Nationals of those [safe] countries are thus defined as probable tellers of lies and untruths, disloyal to their state and unworthy of protection. They are then, by this form of definition, presented as a security threat.... Their act of seeking protection is then categorized by the

host state as showing a disregard for the obligations and duties of citizenship. From here, the connection between treason and terrorism becomes a close one. (Guild 2003: 333)

A similar rationale also applies to safe third-country agreements such as the EU's Dublin Regulation and the Canada–US Safe Third Country Agreement. The failure of an asylum seeker to lodge his or her refugee claim in the first country of arrival is interpreted as indicative of a lack of desperation signifying the 'genuine refugee', thereby justifying the refusal of other states to consider his or her claim (Macklin 2005). Having said this, presenting safe third-country agreements as security-enhancing is problematic on its own terms. For example, the Canada–US Safe Third Country Agreement requires asylum seekers to lodge their applications in the first country of arrival (usually the United States), but it is not obvious how allocating asylum seekers according to first country of arrival promotes state security. Even if one provisionally accepts that the mere presence of asylum seekers on one's territory somehow diminishes national security, then the 'gain' to Canada's security by diverting asylum seekers to the United States presumably redounds as a 'loss' to United States' security (Macklin 2005).

One anomalous case warrants mention, however. The recent European Council *Directive on Minimum Standards for the Qualification and Status of Third Country Nationals or Stateless Persons as Refugees* renders EU citizens ineligible for refugee protection within the EU. Membership in the EU does, sooner or later, ensure free mobility and labour market access throughout the Union. Apart from Sweden, the United Kingdom and Ireland, these rights were not immediately extended by all EU members to the ten new accession states of Central Europe. Nevertheless, on 1 May 2004, all asylum seekers from the accession states who were residing in other European states ceased to be refugees and became citizens of the EU. It remains to be seen if and how EU citizenship will affect the asylum claims of Central Europeans in non-EU states.[6]

In addition to policies designed to deflect or legally exclude a potential refugee from naturalised citizenship, a small but significant number of states have contracted *jus soli* citizenship to eject from the ambit of birthright citizenship those children whose parents lack a requisite legal status. The United Kingdom, Australia and Ireland once guaranteed *jus soli* (birth territory) without restriction, but now limit it to children born of parents possessing a designated lawful resident status (British Nationality Act, s. 1; Australian Citizenship Act, s. 10(2), Irish Nationality and Citizenship Act, s. 6). Although this rule is often represented as a modified *jus soli* test when introduced by traditional *jus sanguinis* states such as Germany, it acquires a different cast when situated in the context of extant *jus soli* states. Rather than depicting it as 'modified *jus soli'*, it is more accurate to understand it as an expanded form of *jus sanguinis*, in which the state extends attribution of parental membership to include legal residents for purposes of citizenship transmission to children.

The citizenship amendments in Australia and Ireland were cata-lysed by public and governmental reaction to judicial pronouncements affecting the removal of non-citizen parents with citizen children *Chen and Zhu v. Secretary of State for the Home Department* [2004]; (*Kioa v. West* [1985]; *L and O v. Minister for Justice*, Equality and Law Reform [2003]). The limitation on *jus soli* denies access to citizenship by children of temporary residents, non-status migrants, asylum seekers and refugees in order that the future expulsion of the family not be impeded by the inconvenient fact that the children are citizens of the deporting state. In the Irish case, the momentum for the referendum was stoked by a moral panic evoking the spectre of pregnant foreign women from outside the EU (and therefore more likely to be racialised as non-white) travelling to Ireland for the express purpose of giving birth. Not only would the child acquire *jus soli* citizenship, but the mother might thereby resist her own removal by claiming that the best interests of the citizen child and respect for family life required that both remain in Ireland. The ostensible benefit to non-citizen mothers of bearing citizen children was characterised as an inducement to illegal migrants and asylum seekers to choose Ireland as a destination. Some 80 per cent of Irish voters supported the referendum (Mullally 2005).

Whereas the stereotypical asylum seeker/security threat is male, public discourse around the Irish referendum unmistakably cast female asylum seekers as the threat to the security of the Irish nation. Through repro-ducing 'inauthentic' Irish citizens, they disrupted the integrity of Irish identity. Under the revised Irish citizenship law, a child's legitimacy *qua* Irish citizen is disavowed unless her mother's legitimacy *qua* refugee has already been recognised by the state. Opinions may differ about the normative basis for *jus soli* citizenship; my objective in raising the Irish example is simply to illustrate the deployment of citizenship law to deter asylum seekers.

It is extraordinarily difficult for most refugees to reach an industrial-ised country in order to claim asylum. If they manage to run the gauntlet of states' interdiction strategies (often by resorting to smugglers and traffickers), they are unlikely to succeed in their claim for Convention refugee status. At best, they may receive some form of subsidiary protection. At worst, they will be deported if their claim for protection fails, or repatriated (with greater or lesser degrees of coercion) once the refugee-receiving country determines that conditions in the country of origin have improved sufficiently. Given the low prospects of success for those who declare themselves as asylum seekers, forced migrants may bypass the regime entirely and join the ranks of the 'illegals' who enter, work and reside in the country without status and in constant fear of detection.

The physical exclusion of forced migrants from industrialised states operates in tandem with a web of legal exclusions initiated outside the border with the imposition of visa requirements, and resumed inside the border with the classification and sorting of migrants from the South into categories of temporariness, insecurity, confinement and illegality. With the exception of Australia, industrialised states retain the *de jure* entitlement of Convention refugees to eventually acquire citizenship on the same terms as other lawful permanent residents. This generosity is revealed as chimerical once one realises how few people gain legal recognition as Convention refugees. The physical disappearance of the refugee operates synergistically with the discursive disappearance of the refugee, who is assimilated through operation of law into the despised category of illegal migrant. Even if forced migrants manage to surmount the physical borders of the state, an elaborate system of legal barriers defines and confines them outside the domain of citizenship. By design, those most in need of a second citizenship are those least likely to obtain it.

The birthright foreigner

The physical and legal exclusion of forced migrants and their children from access to citizenship operates on the external frontier of the securitisation of citizenship by keeping the alien out. Like many states, the Dutch law enabling the state to revoke citizenship applies only where the original grant of citizenship was invalid, owing to fraud or misrepresentation that materially affected the acquisition of citizenship.

The internal dimension consists of the transformation of citizens into aliens from within the geopolitical space of the state. This move is accomplished through popular, political and ultimately legal deprivation of birthright citizenship. The first is represented by the saga of the Khadr family, dubbed 'Canada's first family of terror' by the tabloid press. The second is exemplified by the case of Yaser Hamdi, a dual US-Saudi citizen whose detention as an 'unlawful combatant' in the war on terror was ultimately resolved through his renunciation of US citizenship. Finally, recent amendments to the UK nationality law raise the prospect of revocation of birthright citizenship.

There are numerous definitions and typologies of citizenship circulating in the academic literature. For present purposes, I contrast the legal dimension, which refers to the juridical status of membership held by an individual in relation to a territorial nation-state, and the normative dimension, whereby members of the polity are adjudged as 'good' or 'bad' citizens in a substantive sense. Legal citizenship (nationality in international law) is sometimes disparaged as merely formal, meaning that it does not necessarily denote a thick relationship between individual and state. Instead, it merely signifies a legal status entitling the holder to certain rights denied to non-citizens. The short catalogue of enforceable rights held exclusively by citizens typically comprises the unqualified right to enter and remain in the country of citizenship, the national franchise, access to consular protection and certain public service positions. The criteria for the acquisition of legal citizenship through naturalisation may be more or less demanding in terms of the requisite indicia of integration into the host society, and oaths of citizenship sometimes require a declaration of loyalty to the national community. But subject to the exceptions described below, these signifiers of the threshold-crossing moment are transitory and ultimately unenforceable. Different historical and theoretical accounts of birthright citizenship are available, but from an institutional perspective one can reasonably suggest that birthright citizenship is premised on the notion that birth to existing citizens and birth on the territory of the state are reasonable predictors of an impending 'thick' relationship to the state. Nevertheless, retention of birthright citizenship does not depend on validation of that hypothesis, at least not in the first generation.[7]

In popular discourse, the normative dimension of citizenship deploys various criteria to classify people as better and worse, good and bad, deserving and undeserving, genuine or not. Among academics the criteria themselves are subject to contestation and critique, and the critical/normative vector of citizenship is usually oriented towards defining and achieving equality among formal citizens. The existence of 'second-class citizens' or 'partial citizens' signals a moral defect in the body politic. My suggestion is that securitisation of citizenship manifests through the seepage of the normative into the formal or, put another way, the imposition of the performative onto the status of legal citizen.

I begin with the saga of the Khadr family, whose exploits have been featured in Canadian headlines periodically since 11 September 2001.

Ahmed Said Khadr emigrated from Egypt to Canada in 1977 and married Maha Elsamnah, a Palestinian Canadian already living in Canada. Ahmed obtained Canadian citizenship and then, with the Soviet invasion of Afghanistan in full force, went to Afghanistan in 1980. Ahmed Said's family joined him a few years later. It appears that the Khadrs met Osama bin Laden during this period. In 1996, Ahmed Said Khadr was arrested and detained in Pakistan on suspicion of funding the bombing of the Egyptian embassy in Islamabad. Proclaiming his innocence and his Canadian citizenship, he successfully petitioned Prime Minister Jean Chretien to intercede on his behalf, and was released from Pakistani custody. Ahmed Said subsequently encouraged his sons to attend al-Qaeda training camps in Afghanistan. The second son, Abdurahman, a self-described black sheep of the family, lacked enthusiasm for pursuing holy war, much less a career as a suicide bomber. During the years the family spent in Pakistan and Afghanistan, the Khadr and bin Laden families socialised and even attended the weddings of one another's children.

Following the course of the US invasion of Afghanistan after September 11, Abdurahman (then aged 19) and his younger brother Omar (15) were arrested separately and detained at Guantánamo Bay. In October 2003, Ahmed Said was killed in a shoot-out with US soldiers in Afghanistan. The youngest son Karim, then 13, was shot and paralysed by a bullet lodged near his spine. The whereabouts of Abdullah, the eldest son, remained unknown until 2005.

Omar remains at Guantánamo, charged with murder for throwing a grenade that killed a US soldier, as well as other offences. Abdurahman was released, taken to Afghanistan by the US, and eventually made his way back to Canada in late 2003.

In early 2004, a Canadian television crew managed to interview Maha Elsamnah and her daughter Zaynab in Pakistan. In the course of the interview, mother and daughter defended bin Laden and al-Qaeda, enthused about the prospect of Khadr sons becoming 'martyrs' like their father and expressed admiration for suicide bombers. About the events of September 11, Maha stated that 'You don't want to feel happy, but you just sort of think [the US] deserve it, they've been doing it for such a long time, why shouldn't they feel it once in a while?' (CBC 2004a). She also condemned what she saw as Canadian decadence:

You would like me to raise my child in Canada and by the time he's 12 or 13 he'll be on drugs or having some homosexual relation or this and that. Is it better?... For me, no. I would rather have my son as a strong man who knows right and wrong and stands for it even if it's against his parents. It's much better for me than to have my child walking on the streets in Canada taking drugs or doing all this nonsense. (CBC 2004b)

Soon after the interview, Maha publicly expressed her intention to return to Canada with Karim. Karim was paralysed and in need of proper medical care. Both lacked valid passports. Maha complained that the Canadian government was refusing to reissue their passports, but eventually they did receive emergency single-entry passports. Maha returned to Canada with wheelchair-bound Karim in March 2004.

When Canadian officials first explained that, as citizens, the Khadr family had the legal right to enter and remain in Canada, opposition Members of Parliament and others demanded that Maha and Karim be stripped of their citizenship and refused admission. Once mother and son had entered, the demand shifted from exclusion to expulsion. The court of public opinion put the Khadrs on trial for crimes against citizenship. The following excerpt from an online petition (Campbell 2004) distills the latter sentiment:

1) To: Canadian Government

The Canadian government has granted emergency passports to Maha Elsamnah Khadr and her 14-year-old son Karim. Members of this family have made statements in support of al-Qaeda. They should not have been allowed back into Canada, and I, as a Canadian citizen, do not feel safe knowing that we have fundamentalists living in our own backyard. My fear is that our government will set this woman up on welfare, as well as dole out free health care for her injured child. I don't want Canadian tax dollars going toward looking after this family. They should be stripped of their citizenship and sent on their way.

...

Sincerely,

The Undersigned

The petition depicts Khadrs' legal citizenship as a cheap and thin veneer which, when stripped away, exposes their indelible foreignness.

The Khadrs personify an anomalous category one might call 'foreign citizen'. From the perspective of legal citizenship, this 'foreign citizen' disturbs the sharp citizen/non-citizen binary and undermines the assumption of equal citizenship. Even the distinction between foreign-born and native-born citizen does not fully account for the alienation of the Khadrs. Four of the six Khadr children were born in Canada, and all are birthright citizens via *jus soli* or *jus sanguinis*. All Khadr children attended Canadian schools for at least part of their education, and all spent significant periods of their childhood in Canada (*National Post* 2002). Despite this pedigree, their foreignness seemed to exceed their citizenship.

The assimilation of Maha and Karim (and ultimately the entire family) to the category of foreigner was certainly facilitated by the intermittence of the family members' residence in Canada and their long sojourns in Afghanistan and Pakistan. The Khadrs' support for the ideology and actions of al-Qaeda—a transnational assemblage whose membership criteria are wildly inimical to any plausible conception of citizenship within Canada—supplements their territorial absence with profound social distance. They represent the antithesis of Hirsi Ali: The Khadrs' legal citizenship was discredited by their failure to fulfill the normative requirements of Canadian citizenship.

No one suggested that Maha Elsamneh obtained Canadian citizenship by fraud or misrepresentation, and so the legal basis for revocation was completely spurious. Nevertheless, the fact that it is legally conceivable to expatriate a naturalised citizen opens up a space of imaginative possibility: some citizens *can* be stripped of citizenship, and non-citizens *can* be refused entry or removed, so why not the Khadrs? It is almost trite to observe that Canadians classified as non-white or non-Christian (especially Muslim) or allophone are perennially perched on the precipice between member and stranger, regardless of legal status. Even if the thin but resilient guard rail of legal citizenship saves them from toppling over into alienage, it does not prevent others from pushing hard on that rail. The formal equality of all legal citizens, whether by birthright or by naturalisation, is what protects the Khadrs. The fragility of that equality in public consciousness is what enables the petition. Exploiting this vulnerability is crucial to translating societal denunciation of the Khadrs as bad Canadians into a demand upon the state to de-Canadianise them.

Given the legal impossibility in Canada of revoking birthright citizenship, the speed and ease of the slide from 'bad citizen' to 'not citizen' seems surprising, at least in the case of the children. But perhaps I overestimate public awareness of the fact that the link between naturalised citizens and the state is severable, whereas the link between birth-right citizens and the state is not. Another possibility is that the Khadr children were virtually assigned to the category of naturalised citizens because everything else about their ascribed identity—their immigrant parents, their religion, skin colour, ethnicity, divided residence—signifies that they do not really 'come from' Canada.

The petition author's assertion that she feels insecure 'knowing we have fundamentalists living in our backyard' draws on familiar metaphors of home and nation. By 'backyard' she presumably means the geographical territory of Canada. Similarly, when she demands that the Khadrs be 'sent on their way', the unuttered collocation is 'back where they came from'. And wherever that place is, it is not Canada.

But where is it? Pursuing this question may ascribe more rationality to a polemical document than it merits, but also provides a useful mechanism for surfacing the dormant issue of dual citizenship. The Khadr matriarch, Maha Elsamnah, was a stateless Palestinian before immigrating to Canada, and would be rendered stateless again if deprived of her Canadian citizenship. She has no citizenship other than Canadian to pass on to her children. The Khadrs are not citizens of Pakistan or Afghanistan, the two countries where they resided for extended periods in order to advance the parents' particular vision of religious militancy.

Ahmed Said was an Egyptian citizen by birth. His children would thus possess birthright Egyptian citizenship by virtue of descent from an Egyptian citizen (*jus sanguinis*). If expelled from Canada, Egypt would have a legal duty under international law to admit the children *qua* Egyptian nationals. There is, however, no evidence that any of the Khadr children ever visited, much less resided in Egypt. In what sense could the Khadr children be considered more Egyptian than Canadian? Only if the basis for assigning citizenship is religion (Islam) and ethnicity (Arab) could the Khadr children be construed as more authentically Egyptian than Canadian. But of course, this ethno-religious conception of citizenship is antithetical to Canada's self-understanding as a multicultural, secular state; it is downright un-Canadian.

The campaign to strip the Khadrs of their citizenship attracted some 15,000 signatures in less than two weeks, although it had no prospect of success. In response to media queries, then Prime Minister Paul Martin swatted the issue away by pointing to the absurdity of punishing the exercise of civil citizenship by revoking legal citizenship:

> I believe that once you are a Canadian citizen, you have the right to your own views and to disagree....If in the process you break

the law or you threaten the nation, there are means of dealing with that and obviously the government would exercise those means, but fundamentally there are rights of citizenship and they are the rights of dissent. (*National Post* 2004)

Though the petition's supporters did not prevail, it would be a mistake to dismiss their project as a failure. It is true that the signatories could not attach legal consequences to their judgment that the Khadrs were bad citizens. The Khadrs' right to enter and remain in Canada, and their freedom of expression, emerged more or less intact. On the other hand, the popular verdict that the Khadrs 'are not Canadians, no matter what their passports say' (Canadian Press 2004) was delivered to the Khadrs via mail, phone, e-mail and Internet, television, radio and newspapers. They got the message.

The case of US citizen Yaser Hamdi demonstrates the next step in the process of securitising birthright citizenship. Hamdi was born in Louisiana to Saudi parents and was therefore a *jus soli* citizen of the United States and a *jus sanguinis* citizen of Saudi Arabia. He left the United States at age three and spent most of his life in Saudi Arabia. Northern Alliance forces captured and transferred him to the US military in late 2001, and he was eventually detained in South Carolina as an enemy combatant. He challenged his designation and detention via a *habeas* petition. The United States Supreme Court acknowledged that Louisiana-born Hamdi was indeed a US citizen. Dissenting Justice Scalia disdainfully refers to Hamdi as 'a presumed American citizen' as if there were some doubt regarding his *jus soli* citizenship. The plurality concluded that 'a citizen-detainee seeking to challenge his classification as an enemy combatant must receive notice of the factual basis for his classification, and a fair opportunity to rebut the Government's factual assertions before a neutral decisionmaker' (*Hamdi* 2004: 2647).

In order to circumvent the consequences of the Supreme Court decision, the US government negotiated an agreement with Hamdi that would enable him to leave prison and fly to Saudi Arabia in exchange for renouncing his US citizenship and abiding by various other restrictions on his future conduct. The government did not revoke his citizenship, nor did it claim that Hamdi expatriated himself through his alleged affiliation with the Taliban. Instead, after 3 years in solitary confinement, Hamdi relinquished his US citizenship and, therefore, his legal right to enter and remain in the United States in exchange for release from incarceration.

On one reading of this narrative, Hamdi's legal citizenship effectively withstood the challenge to its authenticity and formal power. After all, a majority of the US Supreme Court accepted that he was a lawful citizen of the United States and that his citizenship mattered in terms of his legal rights. At the same time, the resolution of his case implies that his legal citizenship was eclipsed politically by a popular rejection of the normative legitimacy of Hamdi's US citizenship. To borrow Peter Nyers' expression, Hamdi was rendered an 'accidental citizen', a status that is 'securitized and made into a status that is dangerous to the body politic' (Nyers 2006: 26). The agreement that Hamdi reached with the United States could not have been compelled by law.[8] The political resolution achieved can only be understood in the context of public denunciations that Hamdi acquired his citizenship by an accident of birth and was not genuinely (read: deservedly) an American.

Yet birth on the soil of a particular state is no more or less accidental than birth to a citizen of a particular state. Was it Hamdi's parentage or his residence in Saudi Arabia that made him 'more' Saudi than American? If it was the former, would Americans have claimed him as one of their own had he been born to a US citizen mother? It seems doubtful. If it was the fact that he spent most of his life in Saudi Arabia, then the measure of Hamdi's membership (to borrow the language of the famous *Nottebohm* decision of the International Court of Justice) derives more from the 'social fact of attachment, a genuine connection of existence, interests and sentiments'. The pejorative labelling of Hamdi as an 'accidental citizen' of the United States was enabled by the fact that he had lived with his family in Saudi Arabia since the age of three, thereby making Saudi Arabia a plausible candidate for designation as his 'real' home (cf. Nyers 2006: 35). The same rationale would not apply to the Khadrs.

The resolution of Hamdi's case was achieved politically through a surrender of citizenship in circumstances where Hamdi had already been detained in solitary confinement for several years, and could not confidently anticipate when or whether he would be released. At a minimum, the line between voluntary renunciation of citizenship and citizenship revocation by the state begins to blur under conditions of state-induced duress.

Meanwhile, various European states have contemplated instituting or strengthening citizenship tests as a means of thickening legal citizenship. In Germany, the citizenship test adopted by the *Land* Baden-Württemberg intersperses questions about German geography, history, politics, culture and arcana with such pointed inquiries as 'Some people consider the Jews responsible for all the evil in the world and even claim they are behind the September 11 attack in New York. What do you think about such suggestions?' (*Los Angeles Times* 2006). Other questions concerned the wearing of head scarves, homosexuality, arranged marriages, and Israel's right to exist.

The questions are not merely crude attempts to ferret out Muslims holding extremist views. The exam also contains a contractual term (surely of dubious legal validity) that provides for citizenship revocation if an applicant has concealed his or her authentic beliefs in answering the exam questions. Naturalised legal status thus acquires an ongoing disciplinary element through a requirement of compliance with a particularised normative conception of German citizenship.

Only Britain, however, has extended the performativity of citizenship to birthright as well as naturalised citizens. Until 2002, only naturalised citizens were at risk of citizenship revocation, albeit for reasons that included serious criminal conduct within 5 years post naturalisation (British Nationality Act 1981, s. 40(3)). In 2002, the government amended the *British Nationality Act* to permit the Secretary of State to revoke citizenship of naturalised *and* birthright citizens 'if the Secretary of State is satisfied that the person has done anything seriously prejudicial to the vital interests of the United Kingdom, or a British overseas territory' (Nationality, Immigration and Asylum Act, s. 4). Expansion of citizenship revocation to birthright citizens is unprecedented among industrialised states post the Second World War. One would expect that this startling derogation from the security of legal citizenship would rarely be invoked, but that is not the sole measure of its impact or significance.

The revelation that the men accused of the 7 July 2005 London subway attacks were birthright citizens of the United Kingdom reveals the targets of the citizenship law amendment in stark relief: the so-called 'home-grown terrorists' who are birthright citizens of the United Kingdom. The message it sends is clearly directed at second-generation children of immigrants (especially Muslims) who likely possess UK citizenship as well as the citizenship of their immigrant parents. The law signals that for these dual nationals, UK citizenship remains tentative and subordinate to their 'real' nationality, which aligns with the ethno-religious identity transmitted by their parents. Their entitlement to equal citizenship with other British citizens is provisional, precarious and continually under surveillance. Indeed, in March 2006, the UK government diluted the standard for citizenship revocation to permit the Secretary of State to act where 'satisfied that deprivation is conducive to the public good' (Immigration and Nationality Act 2006, s. 56). This is the same standard applied to the exclusion of non-citizens for immigration purposes, thereby recruiting law in the explicit elision of the second-class citizen and the non-citizen.[9]

The United Kingdom is going further than simply thickening the criteria for obtaining legal citizenship. It is engaging in a project of infusing legal citizenship with an ongoing performative aspect. The normative implications of this project are dire and disturbing. They exceed the compass of the term 'accidental citizen', and illustrate how securitisation accomplishes the 'unmaking' of citizenship in law as well as politics (Nyers 2006).

These citizenship-stripping strategies also reveal a paradox, however. The capacity to revoke citizenship and deport depends on the subject holding at least dual nationality, because the current s. 40(4) of the *British Nationality Act* as well as Britain's legal obligations under the 1961 *Convention on the Reduction of Statelessness* (Article 8(2)(b)) and/or the 1997 *European Convention on Nationality* (Article 7(3)) preclude thrusting a person into statelessness unless citizenship was obtained by fraud or misrepresentation of material facts.[10] Because Britain tolerates dual citizenship across the range of possible modes of acquisition (*jus soli, jus sanguinis*, naturalisation), the prospect of revoking birthright British citizenship becomes feasible if the subject possesses at least one other nationality.

The revocation strategy thus creates anomalous incentives. Dual citizenship now appears attractive to the state because it enables citizenship revocation without rendering the person stateless. The state can thus deport to the other country of nationality. Conversely, citizens— for whom multiple citizenship would otherwise be an asset—now have reason to relinquish other nationalities, especially in relation to states that engage in persecution, torture or execution. To complicate matters further, certain of the latter states, including Iran, Syria and Egypt, make it extremely difficult to renounce citizenship voluntarily. Syrian-born Canadian Maher Arar experienced the horrific consequences of his dual citizenship when, *en route* back to Canada from a family vacation in Tunisia in 2003, he was detained by US immigration authorities. On the basis of information obtained from Canadian officials, US authorities suspected him of terrorist associations. Arar was then rendered against his will to Syria, his original country of nationality, where he spent 10 months being confined and tortured in a Syrian jail.

To the extent that the securitisation of citizenship makes legal citizenship more vulnerable in industrialised states, the ironic outcome is that among those citizens likely to arouse the state's suspicion, two citizenships provide less security than one.

Conclusion

Evaluating dual citizenship in the context of securitisation invites critical enquiry into who or what constitutes the subject of security. Security in relation to the state, the nation, the citizen and the human being are not synonymous. Most obviously, policies propounded in the name of state or national security can have a direct and negative impact on citizen and human security. Thinking about citizenship in general, and dual citizenship in particular, contributes to the critical literature on securitisation by exposing the discursive and legal regulation of citizenship acquisition and loss as part of what Didier Bigo describes as the 'management of unease' (Bigo 2002). In earlier periods of human history, before the consolidation of the state system, exile was a preferred method of ridding the community of the traitorous citizen, who was then both free and condemned to wander the world. According to some commentators, the figure of the transnational terrorist stands accused of treason to the global order of sovereign states, loyal to no country, an enemy of all and, in normative terms, deserving of citizenship nowhere. Between this global outlaw and the idealised citizen stand the foreigners, the immigrants, the 'illegals', the refugees and the asylum seekers, whose legal identities, substantive entitlements and normative recognition as actual or potential citizens are being reconfigured and recalibrated in accordance with this new normative geography.

Didier Bigo remarks that 'Immigration is problematized in Western countries in a way that is very different from the distinction between citizen and foreigner. It is not a legal status that is under discussion, but a social image concerning… "the social distribution of bad" ' (Bigo 2002). I would diverge from Bigo's analysis only to observe that revisions to the legal distinction between citizen and foreigner are precisely about the social distribution of 'bad'. Not only do they aspire to keep the alien out, they actively produce the 'alien within' in order to cast him or her out, figuratively and literally. Within this security field, the possibilities and limitations of border control and the constraints imposed by international law regarding statelessness shape the form and meaning of dual citizenship for diasporic communities and forced migrants living in industrialised states today.

Notes

1. Convention Relating to the Status of Refugees, 28 July 1951, 189 U.N.T.S. 2545 (entered into force 22 April 1954), supplemented by the Protocol relating to the Status of Refugees, 606 U.N.T.S. 8791 (entered into force 4 October 1967) [hereinafter Refugee Convention].

2. The film outraged certain Muslims because it depicted naked female bodies painted with Qur'anic verses sanctioning women's subordination. Van Gogh's assassin pinned a note to his victim's chest declaring 'You, oh America, will go down. You, oh Europe, will go down... You, oh Netherlands, will go down... You, oh Hirsi Ali, will go down.' (*The Guardian*, 17 May 2005).

3. Under Dutch law, however, it is not actually clear that Convention refugee status is revocable.

4. See text at p. 50, infra [re: Dublin Regulation].

5. The 2004 European Council *Minimum Standards for the Qualification and Status of Third Country Nationals or Stateless Persons as Refugees or as Persons who Otherwise Need International Protection and the Content of the Protection Granted* remains conspicuously silent on the naturalisation of recipients of subsidiary protection.

6. For example, might the EU as a whole be seen as constituting an 'internal relocation alternative' for Central European asylum seekers?

7. The picture is slightly more complicated than I portray; some states limit the transmission of *jus sanguinis* citizenship by requiring second- or third-generation citizens by descent to reside on the territory of the state in order to retain legal citizenship.

8. Although American law recognises expatriation, whereby citizens can be imputed with the intention to renounce US citizenship through their conduct, the doctrine seems to have fallen into desuetude and was not invoked against Hamdi or against John Walker Lindh, another birthright citizen of the United States accused of fighting for the Taliban against the United States.

9. The new law has been applied once: David Hicks, an Australian citizen detained by the United States at Guantánamo Bay, applied for registration as a UK citizen based on his mother's British citizenship, in the hopes that the United Kingdom would advocate more effectively for his release than had the Australian government. The British government refused to confer British citizenship, and in December 2005 an English Court ordered the government to do so (*Hicks v. Secretary of State for Home Department*). On 6 July 2006, Hicks received his British citizenship; on 7 July, the Secretary of State revoked Hicks' citizenship on the ground that 'deprivation is conducive to the public good'.

10. Since Germany does not generally permit naturalised citizens to retain their original citizenship, a naturalised German citizen would perforce become stateless if denaturalised. It is theoretically possible (though impracticable) to enquire into the sincerity of the responses given to the citizenship test questions on subjective matters of attitude, and this would be the tenuous hook upon which evidence of 'fraud' or 'misrepresentation' would hang in the Baden-Württemberg case. On 24 May 2006, the Federal Constitutional Court

of Germany ruled that revocation of naturalised citizenship on grounds of fraud or misrepresentation was constitutionally permissible under the German Basic Law (Magen 2006).

References

Statutory instruments and government documents

National

Australian Citizenship Act 1948, Act No. 83 of 1948 (as amended).
British Nationality Act 1981, UK St. 1981, c. 61 (as amended).
Immigration, Asylum and Nationality Act 2006, C. 13 (U.K).
Irish Nationality and Citizenship Act 1956 (No. 26 of 1956, as amended).
Nationality, Immigration and Asylum Act 2002, UK St. 2002, c. 41.
http://www.multiplecitizenship.com/wscl/ws_EGYPT.html.
http://www.multiplecitizenship.com/wscl/ws_IRAN.html.
http://www.multiplecitizenship.com/wscl/ws_SYRIA.html.

Europe

European Convention on Nationality, 6 November 1997, ETS no. 166 Council Regulation (EC) No 343/2003 of 18 February 2003 establishing the criteria and mechanisms for determining the Member State responsible for examining an asylum application lodged in one of the Member States by a third-country national (Dublin Regulation), OJ L 50, 25.2.2003 (http://www.uvi.fi/download.asp?id = Dublin + II + asetus+eng;979;%7B8C0EC6FC-E189 - 4ED9-88C1-FC4132E6E978%7D).

Council Directive 2004/83/EC of 29 April 2004 on minimum standards for the qualification and status of third-country nationals or stateless persons as refugees or as persons who otherwise need international protection and the content of the protection granted, OJ L 304, 30.9.2004 (Asylum Qualification Directive) (http://europa.eu.int/eur-lex/pri/en/oj/dat/2004/l_304/l_30420040930en00120023.pdf).

UNHCR, Asylum Levels and Trends in Industrialized Countries 2006. Overview of Asylum Applications Lodged in Europe and Non-European Industrialized Countries in 2006. Table 1: Asylum applications submitted in Europe and non-European industrialized countries, 2002–2006. http://www.unhcr.org/statistics/STATISTICS/460150272.pdf.

International

Convention relating to the Status of Refugees, 28 July 1951, 189 U.N.T.S. 2545 (entered into force 22 April 1954), supplemented by the *Protocol relating to the Status of Refugees*, 606 U.N.T.S. 8791 (entered into force 4 October 1967).
Convention on the Reduction of Statelessness, 30 August 1961, UNTS vol. 989: 175.

Popular media

A. H. Ali, 'Persverklaring Ayaan Hirsi Ali', 16 May 2006 (http://www.vvd.nl/index.aspx?FilterId=974&ChapterId=1147&ContentId=4977).

'The asylum process is failing too many women'. *The Guardian*, 23 May 2006 (The Guardian http://www.guardian.co.uk/comment/story/0,1780804,00.html).

CBC (2004a) 'Al Qaeda Family – Al Qaeda Attacks,' http://www.cbc.ca/news/background/khadr/alqaedafamily5.html (last accessed 20 May 2007).

CBC (2004b), 'Al Qaeda Family – The Black Sheep', http://www.cbc.ca/news/background/khadr/alqaedafamily4.html (last accessed 20 May 2007).

"Danger Woman", The Guardian, 17 May 2005, http://film.guardian.co.uk/interview/interviewpages/0,,1485810,00.html.

David Gordon Smith. 'Failing the Tolerance Test'. *Expatica Comment*, 11 January 2006 (http://www.expatica.com/source/site_article.asp?channel_id=2&story_id=26707), accessed 9 August 2006.

Donna Campbell, www.PetitionOnline.com/Khadr/petition.html (accessed 10 April 2004; no longer available).

'German naturalisation officials given list of questions to ask Muslim citizenship applicants in Baden-Württemberg', 7 January 2006 (http://www. militantislam-monitor. org/article/id/1524), accessed 9 August 2006.

'In Germany, Citizenship Tests Stir Up Muslims and Cultural Debate', *Los Angeles Times*, 9 April 2006 (http://www.latimes.com/news/printedition/asection/la-fg-test9apr09,1,7945159.story?coll_la-news-a?section&ctract=1&cset=true).

'Khadrs Entitled to Equal Treatment, McGuinty Says', Canadian Press, 13 April 2004.

'Liberals Don't Care Hirsi Ali Lied to Get Asylum in 1992'. *Expatica News*, 12 May 2006 (http://www.expatica.com/source/site_article.asp?channel_id=1&story_id=29954).

'Martin Says Khadrs Have Right of Dissent'. *National Post*, 16 April 2004, A5.

'Profile: Ayaan Hirsi Ali'. BBC News, 16 May 2006 (http://news.bbc.co.uk/go/pr/fr/-/2/hi/europe/4985636.stm).

Stewart Bell. 'US Denies Access to Khadr Teen', *National Post*, 10 September 2002, A1.

Scholarly articles, research papers and monographs

Arendt, H. (1951) *The Origins of Totalitarianism*. New York: Harcourt, Brace & Company.

Bigo, D. (2002) 'Security and Immigration: Toward a Critique of the Government-ality of Unease'. 27 *Alternatives: Global, Local, Political* (Supplement): 63–92.

Crépeau, F. and D. Nakache (2006). 'Controlling Irregular Migration in Canada'. Institute for Research on Public Policy Choices, 12 (1), February (http://www.irpp.org/indexe.htm).

Gilbert, G. (2004) 'Is Europe Living Up to Its Obligations to Refugees?' *European Journal of International Law* 15: 963.

Guild, E. (2003) 'International Terrorism and EU Immigration, Asylum and Borders Policy: The Unexpected Victims of 11 September 2001'. *European Foreign Affairs Review*, 8L 331–46.

Junker, B. (2006) 'Burden Sharing or Burden Shifting? Asylum and Expansion in the European Union'. *Georgetown Immigration Law Journal* 20: 293.

Macklin, A. (2005) 'Disappearing Refugees'. *Columbia Human Rights Law Review* 36: 101–61.

Magen, S. (2006) 'Naturalizations Obtained by Fraud – Can They Be Revoked? The German Federal Constitutional Court's Judgment of 24 May 2006'. *German Law Journal*, 7 (*http://www.germanlawjournal.com*), accessed 19 September 2006.

Mandal, R. (2002) 'Protection Mechanisms Outside of the 1951 Convention ("Complementary Protection")'. UNHCR Department of International Protection, Legal and Protection Policy Research Series, PPLA/2005/02, June.

McAdam, J. (2002) 'The European Union Proposal on Subsidiary Protection: An Analysis and Assessment'. UNHCR Evaluation and Policy Analysis Unit New Issues in Refugee Research Working Paper No. 74, December.

Mullally, S. (2005) 'Citizenship and Family Life in Ireland: Asking the Question "Who Belongs"?' *Legal Studies* 25: 578–600.

Nyers, P. (2006) 'The Accidental Citizen: Acts of Sovereignty and (Un)Making Citizenship'. *Economy and Society* 35, 1 (February): 22–41.

Taylor, S. (2002) 'Guarding the Enemy from Oppression: Asylum-Seeker Rights Post-September 11'. *Melbourne University Law Journal* 26: 396.

Whitaker, R. (1998) 'Refugees: The Security Dimension'. *Citizenship Studies* 2(3): 413.

Jurisprudence

Chen and Zhu v. Secretary of State for the Home Department, E.C.J. Case C-200/02, Opinion of Advocate General Tizzano delivered 18 May 2004; Judgment of the Court delivered 19 October 2004.

Gao v. Gonzales, 440 F.3d 62 (2d Cir. 2006).

Hamdi v. Rumsfeld, 124 S. Ct. 2633 (2004).

Kioa v. West (1985), 159 CLR 550.

L and O v. Minister for Justice, Equality and Law Reform [2003] IESC 1 (23 January 2003).

The Nottebohm Case (Liechtenstein v. Guatemala) [1955] I.C.J. 4.

R (Hicks) v. Secretary of State for the Home Department [2005] EWHC 2818 (Admin).

RRT Reference: N98/25465 (12 January 2001) (Australian Refugee Tribunal).

RPD TA2-00417, November 13, 2002 (Canadian Immigration and Refugee Board).

Part II
Nationalism and Nationhood

4
The Trade-off Between Transnational Citizenship and Political Autonomy

Rainer Bauböck

Multiple citizenship in Central and Eastern Europe

On 2 March 2005, *The New York Times* reported that the Hungarian town of Hódmezuővásárhely, which had up until then 50, 000 citizens, could soon become the country's biggest in virtual terms. The municipal authorities had decided to grant honourary citizenship to all ethnic Hungarians living abroad and were then receiving about 100 applications a day. This decision was taken in response to a failed referendum initiative in December 2004 to grant dual citizenship to ethnic Hungarians in neighbouring countries (Chapter 5). The referendum had been initiated after a widely perceived failure of the so-called Hungarian Status Law adopted under the right-wing populist Orban government in 2001. That law called for providing Hungarian identity cards to ethnic Hungarians living in neighbouring states (with the notable exception of Austria) and not only offered card holders various cultural and educational benefits in their countries of citizenship but also facilitated admission to Hungary and access there to certain social and health benefits and short-term employment. The law had been substantially watered down after protests from Romania and Slovakia and from international European organisations, but in the end satisfied neither these nor Hungarian nationalists (Kántor et al. 2004). The Romanian government strongly opposed the law on the grounds that its extraterritorial effects infringed on Romanian sovereignty. It also argued that the law discriminated between Romanian citizens according to their ethnicity, which was unacceptable under Romania's conception of civic rather than ethnic citizenship.

Romania itself, however, has vigorously pursued a policy of extending dual citizenship to the majority population in Moldova, whom Romania considers to be ethnic Romanians. This policy has been supported by some groups in Moldova who campaign for reunification in a Greater Romania, but is strongly resented by those who consider Moldova to be a distinct nation. The offer of dual citizenship for Moldavians looks very attractive, however, since Romanian citizens now enjoy visa-free travel within the European Schengen area and even more so since the European Union (EU) has accepted Romania as an accession candidate.

Moldova is also a deeply divided country that includes within its boundaries an autonomous Gagauz region and Transnistria, the latter controlled by separatist forces and now issuing its own passports. Transnistrian political leaders want to unite their province with Russia; indeed, many inhabitants of the province have successfully claimed Russian citizenship. It was estimated in August 2003 that 40 per cent of Moldavian citizens also hold citizenship of Romania, Russia or Israel (Iordachi 2004: 257).

This story is by no means unique. Similar ones could be told about Bosnia-Herzegovina and its Serbian and Croatian neighbours or about Russian minorities in Russia's 'near abroad'. I have summarised it here not because I want to suggest a particular solution to any of these complex conflicts, but because it raises two fascinating questions for comparative studies and theoretical analyses of citizenship. The first concerns the stark contrast with debates about multiple citizenship in Western Europe or North America. In Hungary, Romania and Moldova, dual nationality is seen as a tool for expanding the national community beyond state borders, whereas in the West it is promoted by liberals as a means for helping to overcome antiquated notions of state sovereignty and national homogeneity. The second question concerns the normative implications of the story. Is there not only a geographic chain of interconnected claims but also some underlying principle that links the innocuous honourary citizenship of Hódmezővásárhely with the rather turbulent conflicts in Moldova? Should this lead us to reject dual citizenship in all these cases? And if so, how can we reconcile such rejection with well-established arguments for tolerating multiple nationality among migrants in the West? (see Aleinikoff and Klusmeyer 2002, Martin and Hailbronner 2002).

The standard response to both questions among Western liberals is probably that citizenship in the West is civic, whereas in Eastern Europe it is ethnic. This distinction seems to explain easily why multiple citizenship is a source of territorial conflict in the latter region but not in the former and why we should accept it in the West, but reject it in the East. This answer is, however, deeply flawed. First, as many scholars have shown, the idea of a purely civic citizenship is straight ideology without any real world cases that live up to the model. Modern state-building has invariably involved the establishment of particular national languages, histories and cultural traditions, and every modern citizenship law includes transmission by descent (*jus sanguinis*) for those who are born to citizen parents outside the state borders. Second, dual citizenship by definition has two components. Immigrants in Western societies generally conceive of their relationship to their country of origin in ethnic terms. If those countries permit or promote multiple nationality among their expatriates, they do so based on ideas about the permanent nature of the ethnic bond and about a wider national community extending beyond the state's borders. This rhetoric is hardly different from what we find in Central and Eastern Europe. So why should our political response be different? Finally, just as citizenship conceptions in the West are never purely civic, it is equally false to claim that citizenship conceptions in Eastern Europe are purely ethnic. The Hungarian–Romanian conflict is a case in point. As mentioned above, Romania claims that it adheres to a civic conception. Its policy of inviting Moldavians to adopt Romanian citizenship is indeed formally neutral with regard to ethnicity because it rests on a claim to restoration of citizenship for previous holders of Romanian citizenship, who had lost it involuntarily, as well as for their descendants (Iordachi 2004). The apparent contrast with the Hungarian Status Law is, however, easily accounted for once we consider that Hungary before the 1920 Treaty of Trianon had a much more ethnically diverse population than Romania between 1918 and 1940, when it included what is now Moldova as well as Northern and Southern parts of Bessarabia that were subsequently incorporated into the Ukrainian Soviet Republic. The impact of Romania's apparently civic conception for the integrity of Moldova is arguably worse than that of Hungary's ethnic conception for Romania.

Other arguments that have been used to defend transnational citizenship[1] in the context of migration appear to apply just as well to minorities in Central and Eastern Europe. And, vice versa, most objections against the Hungarian Status Law could also be raised against transnational citizenship for migrants.

The core argument in the migration context can be described as a stakeholder principle for the allocation of citizenship (Bauböck 2005).

Migrants who are permanent residents in a receiving society but retain strong economic, social, cultural and family ties with a sending country have a plausible claim to citizenship in both polities since they are in a position where their lives will be strongly affected by political decisions in both states and where protection of their rights may depend on formal recognition as citizens of these states. Couldn't a similar case be built for minorities who have been shifted into another state's jurisdiction through the drawing of a new international border?

The critique of the Hungarian Status Law focused on the following points: the definition of the beneficiary group as ethnic Hungarians; the creation of a political and legal status that went beyond cultural support for kin minorities; the extraterritorial effects of the law, namely the provision of benefits for ethnic Hungarians living in neighbouring states rather than only for those who migrate to Hungary; and the unilateral nature of the policy that was adopted without prior negotiations with neighbouring states.[2] In other words, most critics of the Law said that they would not have objected to external cultural support for ethnic Hungarians (which would have made identity cards unnecessary since only ethnic Hungarian would claim such support), to immigration privileges and social benefits for external minority members who migrate to Hungary, and even to more extensive schemes than these as long as these could be agreed upon in bilateral negotiations with the states concerned (Kis 2004). Yet each of the points listed above applies *a fortiori* to giving minorities access to a second nationality, which is a legal status, has extraterritorial effects and is nearly always granted unilaterally without consulting other states. And all these points apply not merely to the Romanian policy towards Moldova, but also to migrant-sending states that allow their expatriates to retain their nationality when they naturalise.

Two further considerations might justify a differential evaluation of multiple citizenship in the two contexts. First, in the standard migration case the external citizenship is *retained*, whereas it is *restored* for transborder minorities who held kin state citizenship prior to the border change, or *newly created* for their descendants. One could argue that sending states are under no duty to withdraw an existing citizenship from those who acquire a new one abroad, while they may have a duty to refrain from restoring or bestowing a new citizenship on those who are already citizens of another country where they reside permanently. Yet some sending states, among them Turkey and Spain, have also permitted their expatriates to restore a citizenship that they had previously lost because the nationality laws of the country of residence did not allow for dual nationality. Moreover, several European states, among them Italy and Germany, have restored citizenship based on ancestry in cases where the populations concerned had not held this citizenship for more than a generation. This policy may be criticised in many respects, for example, because access to citizenship is so much more difficult for long-term resident immigrants in Germany and Italy hailing from outside the EU. However, there have been few complaints that the granting of Italian citizenship to Argentinian citizens of Italian ancestry or to Polish citizens of German ancestry violates the interests and sovereignty of Argentina or Poland.[3] Thus, Western states seem to get away with the same policies that are protested when pursued by Central and Eastern European kin states of transborder minorities.

Second, in the migration context multiple citizenship increases gradually over time through a process of individual decisions about naturalisation. In Central and Eastern Europe, new legislation offering dual nationality may generate a sudden and substantial increase in the numbers of multiple citizens. This may not only be harder to digest for the country of minority residence, but it may also have a strong impact on domestic politics in the external kin state, especially if these dual citizens are granted absentee voting rights. In the Hungarian case, a positive result in the referendum could eventually have led to a stable right-wing majority in national elections brought about by citizens who do not even live under the government whose political colour they determine through their vote (Chapter 5). The argument about the disproportionate impact of naturalisations on election outcomes also applies, however, in immigration contexts whenever legislation is changed to become more inclusive. And similar objections have indeed been raised by conservative parties in Western Europe and North America against naturalisation campaigns or reforms under liberal and left-wing governments who are more likely to embrace the migrant vote. Finally, population transfers and border changes in several Western European countries, from Greece in 1922 to Germany in 1990, have also brought about dramatic changes in the size and composition of the electorate without being challenged in the same way as the Hungarian Status Law. In both the migrant and the transborder minority cases the prior question is whether ties to an external kin state or country of origin are strong enough to support a claim for citizenship status and voting rights. If they are, then it is the exclusion from the demos rather than the inclusion of these individuals in an extended transnational polity that needs to be justified.

None of the general arguments for or against multiple and transnational citizenship seems to supply us with a clear normative criterion that justifies treating migrants and transborder minorities differently. We need to explore more closely, then, the particular contexts that distinguish the two cases. One could argue that multiple citizenship is always a problem when relations between the states involved are not friendly. Yet in the case of Hungary, Slovakia, Romania and Moldova, it is not bad relations that make transnational citizenship a problem but the other way round. Relations between these countries are not generally bad—indeed, if they are occasionally unfriendly this is *because* of national identities that extend beyond borders and corresponding fears in neighbouring countries about external interference on behalf of minority populations. To claim that this is the reason not to accept transnational citizenship in this region simply begs the question and does nothing to explain why similar escalations do not occur in the case of immigrants in Western democracies.[4]

I want to suggest instead a somewhat different hypothesis. In a migration context, the main impact of transnational citizenship is to make the political boundaries of the states involved more porous and open for flows of persons, money and cultural practices. In a context of heightened security concerns these flows may indeed be perceived as a threat, and governments in countries of immigration are likely to constrain transnational citizenship for this reason. The securitisation of migration policies after 11 September 2001 and concerns about undocumented immigration, human trafficking and abuse in the asylum system have already produced a deterioration of legal protection for resident aliens and of their opportunities for transnational movement and activities. Yet transnational citizenship for migrants does not raise concerns about the demarcation of political boundaries between sending and receiving countries. This is fundamentally different in the Central and Eastern European context where transnational citizenship is not perceived as a facilitator for migratory movements but as a challenge by an external kin state to the jurisdiction of a neighbouring state over a part of its citizen population and over the territory in which these minority citizens live. From a liberal perspective we must not accept perceived threats as sufficient justification for restricting minority rights. Whether these fears are reasonable and whether they justify constraints on transnational citizenship depend on how we assess the aspirations of minorities and their kin state.

Identity options and political goals among transborder minorities

Liberal immigration countries provide international migrants with several options for their life plans, group identities and political aspirations (Table 4.1). They may choose between the alternatives of returning to their country of origin or full assimilation into the receiving society. Yet some move back and forth between countries and develop corresponding transnational identities. Others cannot go back to where they have come from because violent conflicts or oppressive regimes keep them from returning. But they may still develop a strong diasporic identity that entails a commitment to eventual return in order to rebuild the country they had to leave. Finally, many migrants who do not maintain strong relations to their countries of origin will still develop a sense of distinct ethnic identity fostered by experiences of discrimination as well as by pride in their own traditions and origins. There are numerous examples in the history of human migration for each of these different orientations. What is historically new is the willingness of liberal democracies to recognise transnational modes of citizenship and to develop a more pluralistic public culture through policies that recognise diversity. All of these identity options open to migrants are also relevant to transborder minorities that have been historically cut off from neighbouring kin. Yet the range of possibilities is considerably broader in their case. The four basic options for them are to emigrate to their kin state, to assimilate into the dominant national community, to claim the status of an autonomous nation within their state of residence or to wage an irredentist struggle for secession and reunification with their kin state.[5]

Table 4.1 Identity options and political goals among transborder minorities

Main alternatives	Mixed alternatives	Kin-state support options
Emigration		Promoting return
	Diasporic identity	Providing exit option
Assimilation		None
	Ethnic identity	Cultural support
Autonomy		Political support
	Condominium	External citizenship
Secession		Territorial incorporation

The options of emigration and assimilation are normatively ambiguous since both may be either an expression of voluntary individual choice or imposed by coercive policies of the state of residence. The mass exodus of large and territorially concentrated minorities from their traditional homeland, whether it is a spontaneous movement or an organised population transfer, is always the result of oppression. Minorities may also, however, through cumulative individual decisions to emigrate in search for better opportunities in the kin state, gradually shrink to a size where they can no longer maintain their distinct identities.[6]

Assimilation has been the preferred option for many individual minority members for whom abandoning their language and culture of origin is a price worth paying for upward mobility. The attractiveness of this option is diminished, however, by the experience of discrimination and the persistence of social exclusion based on origin that cannot be overcome through assimilation. Moreover, individual choices about assimilation are also influenced by public policies that range from soft incentives to naked coercion.

The third alternative for transborder minorities is to demand recognition and self-government as a national minority within the state of residence. This claim will nearly always be more strongly resisted by that state than the former two options. Yet a contemporary understanding of liberal norms does not permit active pursuit of either the assimilation or the emigration of native minorities while still allowing for states to resist secession. Devolving political power in such a way that a minority can realise its aspiration for self-government is thus the only choice for such states that are neither normatively constrained nor in violation of their own legitimate interests. Minority self-government transforms the nation-state into a multinational democracy with vertically nested dual citizenship. If the minority is granted special autonomy status (as in Scotland, South Tyrol or the Åland islands), then only minority members will be dual citizens in this sense; if a federal constitution is adopted (as in Canada, Belgium or Switzerland), then this applies to every citizen of the state.

The alternative of secession denies the possibility of reconciling minority self-government with citizenship in the encompassing polity. A secession claim may be a legitimate response to illegitimate annexation of territory and to oppression or violent conflict that dim the prospect for future cohabitation within a multiethnic state. Alternatively, it may be the result of aggressive minority nationalism that does not respect the territorial integrity of the parent state. Many cases will be more ambiguous than these two clear-cut ones, but if territorial integrity is an important value for self-governing polities, then secession rights for minorities should be normatively constrained in a similar way as assimilation and expulsion policies are for liberal states. Secession should therefore be accepted as a remedial right only (Buchanan 1997, 2004).[7]

There are three further possibilities that represent half-way solutions between the four basic alternatives. First, torn between the options of emigration and assimilation, minorities may develop diasporic identities by retaining a strong orientation towards the external kin state while postponing the actual decision of emigration to a more distant future.

Second, instead of either fully assimilating or claiming political autonomy, groups that were once part of an external kin state may become ethnic minorities that retain elements of their original language and distinct identity and claim cultural recognition and resources from the state of residence. Such developments are often caused by geographic dispersal, demographic decline and the resulting need for minority members to operate primarily within the language and culture of the wider society. This has been the historic development path for several transborder minorities in Western Europe, such as the Danish and German minorities on both sides of the German–Danish border or the Slovene, Croatian and Hungarian minorities in Austria.

The third possible half-way solution is between autonomy and secession: a condominium status for a territory inhabited by the minority. Such an arrangement combines institutions of autonomous self-government with direct involvement in the government of the territory of two external kin states (or one such state alongside the state into which the territory is incorporated). The 1998 Good Friday Agreement in Northern Ireland exemplifies to a certain extent this very rare arrangement. I will discuss in the following section the particular circumstances and possible justifications for condominium solutions to nationality conflicts.

Even after including these mixed cases, the typology remains to a large extent ideal-typical in the sense that these options will nearly always be internally contested or pursued simultaneously by different minority members. Only three of these possibilities—political autonomy, secession and condominium—are purely collective political goals, and various political factions will favour different outcomes. The other types (those also relevant for migrant groups), namely emigration, assimilation, diasporic and ethnic identity, are at least partly determined by individual choices. A liberal democratic environment will make minorities less homogeneous simply by creating more opportunities for different identity choices by individuals. The result is that minorities will be less homogeneous than in a regime where individual liberty is strongly constrained. On the other hand, autonomy and condominium solutions provide minority elites with institutional resources and incentives for maintaining distinct collective identities and will therefore lead to rather stable, even if internally heterogeneous, minority identities.

Among the seven types, transnational citizenship is a defining feature only of condominium. Minorities who choose the option of emigration or who are pushed out of the country will indeed require the citizenship of the state where they settle. They may also seek to obtain its passport already for the purpose of moving there, but they will not need to combine over an indefinite time the citizenship of their current country of residence with that of an external kin state. Demands for a more durable affiliation are, however, likely to arise among diasporic minorities who want to connect on a permanent basis with the kin state while still maintaining their cultural community in the state of residence. For them, the primary purpose of obtaining citizenship in an external homeland is as a reassurance that they will be able to 'return' to this country if and when they so decide.

Transnational citizenship is obviously incompatible with a desire or need to assimilate into mainstream society. Ethnic minorities may rely on an external kin state for cultural support but since they no longer form a distinct political community in their state of residence they are unlikely to establish external citizenship relations, as are fully assimilated groups. Similarly, transnational citizenship cannot be a stable feature in the case of secession. An external kin state that supports an irredentist movement among a minority may hand out its passports to this group as a proclamation of its claim to jurisdiction, but this is a highly unstable form of multiple citizenship that must be resolved either way by reestablishing a singular membership.

The most interesting cases are political autonomy arrangements. If the state of residence denies the minority self-government rights, the minority may turn to the kin state for support. The latter can then seek to conclude a bilateral agreement in which it acts as an external protector of its kin minority's domestic autonomy.[8] It can also provide this minority with cultural support and open its borders for those who want to emigrate. However, it cannot consistently maintain support for domestic autonomy arrangements in the group's state of residence and at the same time include this minority in its own political community by granting it external citizenship status.

I suggest therefore that there is a general trade-off between political autonomy and transnational citizenship, in other words, between vertical multiple citizenship within a state and horizontal multiple citizenship across international borders. Neither migrants and their countries of origin nor transborder minorities and their kin states can have it both ways by combining citizenship in the external polity with political autonomy in the state of residence. What distinguishes the two types of minorities is the range of their options for choosing different points on the trade-off curve. Unless they come as colonial settlers, migrants who are offered full citizenship in the receiving country will hardly ever develop a sense of being a distinct political community with a claim to territorial autonomy or even to secession. And if some migrant group ever raised such claims, the receiving state would be justified in rejecting them. By contrast, transborder minorities incorporated into a newly formed state territory have a *prima facie* claim to be treated as a constituent group within a multinational polity.[9] And if their political elites can successfully mobilise them for this goal, then states should be willing to accommodate them through autonomy and power-sharing arrangements. Once national minorities realise in this way their aspirations to self-government through dual citizenship in their autonomous polity and in the larger state, then adding to this a further claim to external citizenship in another independent state subverts the integrity of a multinational polity to which each of its constituent groups must be committed.

Complex cases

The various alternatives described above are still fairly schematic and do not exhaust the full range of struggles over transnational citizenship and minority self-government. Let me therefore briefly discuss four types of conflicts that do not fit neatly into either of the two categories. In these cases, several assumptions that have been built into the simplified models of migrant and national minority citizenship presented here no longer apply. The four constellations emerge from successively dropping, one by one, the following assumptions: (1) that the conflict is between a majority within a nationalising state and a minority with an external kin state; (2) that the conflict occurs within a state with internationally recognised borders and a *prima facie* claim to territorial integrity and independence; (3) that for each group with strong external ties there is a kin state with which it identifies; and (4) that each group has at least some territorial homeland where it can or could realise aspirations of national self-government. My contention is that we will still find evidence for the normative trade-off in each of these cases, but that the political responses that I have suggested may have to be somewhat modified.

Divided countries with several external kin states

In discussing standard cases of transborder minorities, such as the Hungarian minorities in Romania or the German-speaking population in northern Italy, I have assumed that there is a dominant majority that regards the entire state territory as the site for its nation-building project and a non-dominant minority with historic links to an external kin state in which it was once incorporated. Yet the Moldavian case does not fit this description perfectly since there is within the majority a movement that considers Moldavians as part of a greater Romanian nation and strives for eventual (re)unification. Moldova may thus be described as a deeply divided state in which none of the three large ethnic groups has an unequivocal commitment to the integrity of the state, and in which two of them maintain strong links to external kin states that undermine this commitment.

Cyprus provides another example for this constellation. Since the failed 1974 coup, the Greek majority has given up on *enosis*, the attempt to incorporate Cyprus into the Greek state, and has confined its nation-building aspirations to the island. Nevertheless, its representatives have not been willing to return to the earlier power-sharing arrangements with the Turkish minority. Turkey intervened militarily in the conflict in 1974 and established a separate Turkish-Cypriot republic in the north whose dependency on the external kin state was reinforced through a policy of resettling Anatolian peasants there. The 2002 UN plan for this island suggests reunification in a multinational federation. The essential *quid pro quo* is that the Greek majority would have to agree to federal devolution and power-sharing with the Turkish minority while the latter would have to substantially reduce its transnational links with the Turkish state. Given the history of violence and distrust, it is indeed plausible that the role of the two kin states as external protectors of their respective co-ethnic populations on the island is a major part of the problem and should be replaced as far as possible by international guarantees for a domestic arrangement that combines autonomy for each community with power-sharing between them and with a common overarching Cypriot citizenship.

Disputed territories and condominium solutions

For Moldova and Cyprus, it seems in each case at least possible and worth trying to maintain an independent multinational state in its currently recognised international borders. The alternative scenario of partition is likely to escalate the conflict partly because majorities identify with the larger state rather than just the part with which they would be left after dividing the territory. This makes such cases harder than, say, the peaceful separation of Norway and Sweden in 1905 or the Czech and Slovak 'velvet' divorce in 1992. Yet there are still other constellations where borders are essentially contested and where independence for the disputed territory is an unlikely solution.

Kashmir and Northern Ireland illustrate this state of affairs. In both provinces the population is deeply divided over the question into which of the neighbouring states it should rightfully be incorporated. In Kashmir there is no internationally recognised border, and neither India nor Pakistan have renounced their claims to the province. Northern Ireland is different because it is recognised as part of the United Kingdom, but the British government has itself stated that it would respect a plebiscite in the province in favour of (re)unification with Ireland. The Irish–British relationship includes several elements of transnational citizenship. Until 2004, every child born in Northern Ireland automatically acquired the citizenship of the Irish Republic.[10] At the same time, Irish citizens enjoy immigration and voting rights in Britain. The Good Friday Agreement of 1998, which has yet to be fully implemented, extended these transnational dimensions significantly by adding a North–South Ministerial Council and a British–Irish Council to autonomy and power-sharing arrangements within the province itself.

This seems, therefore, to constitute an example where political autonomy would be combined with ongoing involvement of external kin states. A similar solution might be envisaged for Jerusalem in the context of establishing an independent Palestinian state. Instead of fully dividing the city, Israel and Palestine could agree to preserve common institutions of municipal self-government. What makes these arrangements different from the Central and Eastern European ones is that leaving undecided the territorial affiliation of the disputed territory and involving the external kin states in its government appears to be a fair solution.

This condominium dimension is, however, an irregularity within an international state system that requires clearly demarcated territorial jurisdictions. In past nationality conflicts, condominiums were avoided either through the prevailing military power of one state over the other or through border settlements enforced in the wake of the two World Wars by the victorious Allied Powers. Although these imposed borders appear in retrospect often unwise and unjust, revising them would cause more harm and injustices than accommodating aggrieved minorities within the present boundaries. Condominiums may, however, be envisaged today as solutions for violent conflicts where no stable border has yet been established, where small size, lack of economic viability and the orientation of divided populations towards their kin states excludes the option of independence, and where these groups live so intermixed and economically interdependent that partition would require extensive population transfers.

This is a rare combination of circumstances.[11] And even where they are present, condominium arrangements ought to be combined with autonomous self-government and citizenship for the entire disputed territory and power-sharing between its ethnic groups, or else each of them will constantly perceive that it is ruled by a foreign power. Stefan Wolff suggests that, as an accommodation of ethno-territorial conflicts, '[t]he concept of a condominium needs to be taken out of the traditional context of territorial settlements, i.e., conceiving of it as rule of two states over the same area' and should instead be 'redefined as the group-specific integration of parts of the population of an area into the polities of either of the two states' (Wolff 2004: 208). For the external kin states the latter model involves divided sovereignty and non-territorial jurisdiction rather than joint territorial sovereignty. My trade-off hypothesis still suggests that the combination of nested self-government within the territory with external jurisdiction of kin states will rarely be stable over a long time. The two stable solutions that could emerge from a temporary condominium are full independence for the territory or a confederation between the external kin states that would transform it into an autonomous province within a larger federal polity. In both cases transnational citizenship would have to give way to nested multiple citizenship—within the independent territory or the larger regional confederation.

Transborder minorities without kin states

Many minorities with a strong desire for autonomous self-government do not have kin states that include them in their imagined national community. Most of these 'stateless nations' (Keating 2001) live in a traditional homeland that is confined within the borders of a state. In these cases, the appropriate solutions will be some combination of domestic autonomy and power-sharing. The transnational dimension does not come into play.

Some diaspora groups, however, hail from ethnic and national minorities in their countries of origin and emigrated because they felt oppressed by the state's institutions. Instead of expecting external support from their state of origin, they mobilise their political support among co-ethnics remaining in the homeland. In this constellation both the transnational relation and the minority autonomy in the country of origin involve an *aspiration* for citizenship rather than an effective institutional form. If the struggle succeeds, the diaspora will have to make a choice between returning in order to join the nation-building project, and gradually transforming themselves into regular immigrants with the usual combination of external and internal identity components.

Dropping the assumption that there is an independent external kin state generates yet another type of transborder minorities that I had set aside in the previous discussion. These are minorities whose culture has not been established in any state and who live in a traditional homeland that stretches across an international border. In Europe, the Catalans and Basques might be characterised in this way. There is, however, little credibility to nationalist claims that the population on the French side of the Pyrenees aspires to be included in minority nation-building projects. The international border subdivides the linguistic groups into ethnic minorities on the French side and national ones on the Spanish side. So the transnational dimension appears once again rather weak and largely irrelevant for the robust self-government claims of the Catalan and Basque provinces in the Spanish state.

The Kurdish case illustrates more fully the problems of transborder nations without kin states. Two alternative outcomes could be said to satisfy Kurdish aspirations for self-government: an independent Kurdish state or comprehensive regional autonomy in Turkey, Iraq, Iran and Syria, combined with some joint institutions for transborder cooperation between these regional Kurdish governments. The former outcome would involve a major redrawing of international borders and could severely destabilise the whole region. It would also create large dissatisfied non-Kurdish minorities in an independent Kurdistan. The second outcome is therefore preferable but it requires a delicate balancing between self-government and transnational institutions of joint government. This would resemble the Good Friday Agreement and may work if the larger states themselves can agree on such cross-border cooperation. The further complication compared with Northern Ireland is that autonomy arrangements would have to be implemented within several states, none of whom has a record of respecting minority claims.

Dispersed transnational minorities

What if the group has neither a kin state that provides external support nor a territory where it could realise aspirations to self-government? The simple answer is that these groups are unlikely to develop such aspirations in the first place. If we reject a primordialist view of national identities and see them instead as the contingent outcome of political and economic processes and constellations (Brubaker 2004), then a lack of territorial and institutional bases will generally prevent the transformation of ethnic into national identities. This answer is, however, not entirely sufficient because extreme forms of segregation and oppression might generate in such dispersed ethnic groups a sense that independent nation-building is their only hope for protection or even for sheer survival. This explains the attraction of the Zionist response to European anti-Semitism in the first half of the twentieth century. For other groups that have suffered from racist segregation no such option was available or plausible. In the 1920s Marcus Garvey failed to convince African Americans that they should return and build their own African nations. Answers to what Gunnar Myrdal identified as the 'American dilemma' must be found within American society itself.

The group that today fits the description most closely as a dispersed transnational minority is the European Roma populations. One particular faction among the small Roma elites has proclaimed them as a non-territorial European nation.[12] This is a largely symbolic and internally disputed claim to a status under international law and a transnational citizenship that would operate on a European scale and would not be tied to a particular state or homeland. I think that this agenda deserves to be taken seriously in a specific sense. Protection of Roma against discrimination should not be regarded as an internal matter within the several European states. The EU has implicitly recognised this by including minority protection among the Copenhagen criteria for accession to membership and by monitoring candidate states for the 2004 enlargement primarily with regard to their policies towards Roma minorities (Sasse 2004). Any substantive improvement for the Roma must involve social development and anti-discrimination policies as well as affirmative action in the realms of education and access to public administration. Roma should also be recognised as ethnic and cultural minorities and receive public funds for language protection and cultural activities. Yet given their geographic dispersal and deep internal divisions there is little prospect for comprehensive political autonomy in any of the countries where they live. A transnational Roma citizenship could then fulfil two important tasks: providing a thin common identity for all Roma that makes them aware of their shared concerns and attributing a strong and ongoing responsibility for monitoring and enforcing Roma minority rights to European institutions rather than relying only on voluntary compliance by national governments.

Conclusions

In the Westphalian state system, sovereign states are considered as the only relevant political communities and their sovereignty excludes overlapping affiliations of their citizens to other states. What we see emerging instead is a proliferation of multiple citizenships that are either vertically nested within each other in federal arrangements or overlap horizontally in transnational relations. This transformation is not merely an empirical development, but also a normative one (Bauböck 2007). The norms of homogenous and singular citizenship that have underpinned the Westphalian system have been gradually eroded and especially so in liberal states whose commitment to human rights, minority protection and democracy made them aware that the old conception of indivisible sovereignty clashes with their most fundamental political values.

I hesitate, however, to describe both phenomena as a 'denationalisation' or 'deterritorialisation' of political community. Such concepts certainly do not apply to autonomy and self-determination struggles of national minorities that challenge existing state borders because these impede their own projects for building distinct self-governing polities. They are also generally misplaced for transnational migrants, whose external citizenship is firmly anchored in the institutions of a sending state, or for diasporic groups, who define their identity through their relation to an unredeemed homeland.[13]

What I have tried to show in this chapter is that it is also important not to confound the distinct claims of such minorities with each other. Migrants' transnational citizenship is sometimes misinterpreted as generating a potential claim to autonomy or even to irredentism in the receiving society.[14] Yet in other contexts demands for transnational citizenship are indeed linked to projects of nation-building beyond international borders. It is misguided to welcome such border transgressions as part of a cosmopolitan agenda of overcoming state sovereignty and territoriality. De-escalating and accommodating these conflicts between interlocking nation-building projects generally requires reframing them as internal ones within state borders and promoting multilevel citizenship as a substitute for transnational citizenship.

Liberal states and international organisations are more willing to tolerate multiple citizenship for migrants because its main effect is to enhance the permeability of political boundaries between states without affecting the demarcation of their separate territorial jurisdictions. In an age of global terrorism, such greater openness may be experienced as an exposure to security risks. But open borders do not challenge the jurisdiction of the state over all those who enter and live in its territory. And providing the citizens of one state with unfettered admission to another state does not interfere with the former state's rights, either. Even rights to participate in elections in several countries do not undermine democratic equality in any of these electoral arenas as long as their territorial jurisdictions are clearly demarcated and separated since each vote cast by a multiple national will be counted as one and one only in each election.

Extending the citizenship of a kin state to transborder minorities is a different matter because it tends to challenge this demarcation. In contexts where borders are still to a certain extent contested and where states engage in nation-building projects beyond their territory transnational citizenship becomes a natural concern not merely for the state in which these minorities reside, but also for the international community that has a vital interest in the stability of territorial jurisdictions.

From a liberal perspective, state concerns about security and territorial integrity are not necessarily sufficient reasons for rejecting minority claims to cultural as well as legal and political ties with sending or kin states in either the migrant or the transborder minority case. Instead we have to look for arrangements that reconcile conflicting conceptions of political communities and their boundaries in mutually acceptable ways.

Immigration countries must not only give immigrants access to citizenship but ought to accept also that these new citizens have relevant stakes in their countries of origin that they cannot be asked to abandon as a precondition for citizenship in the receiving society (Bauböck 2003). Immigrants who are offered such opportunities for transnational citizenship will have to accept in turn that as citizens of the new country they do not form a separate polity with a claim to self-government. They are admitted as individuals with liberties and opportunities to form ethnic, religious and cultural groups, but not as national minorities.

Members of transborder minorities may often make similar choices as immigrants. But if they demand recognition as a distinct political community, then their claim is much stronger. In the process of state formation no nation has a right to take possession of the state and establish itself at the expense of all other groups with a distinct identity and historic presence in the territory. Minorities generated through the very process of boundary-drawing that created a new state therefore have rights to autonomy and power-sharing, and majorities must be willing to accept that the larger polity will then become a multinational state rather than a nation-state. Yet these arrangements will be stable and acceptable to the majority only if they are fully internalised within the state. A self-governing minority in a multinational state cannot at the same time define itself as part of an external nation-state.

Does this mean that a stakeholder principle for allocating citizenship will be overridden by stability concerns in the case of transborder minorities?[15] The question for transborder minorities, which does not arise at all for international migrants, is, what are the boundaries of the polities in which they have a claim to be citizens? In the first instance, they must be recognised as full and equal citizens of the state in which they live. Beyond this, they can claim a second membership that realises their national aspirations either through diasporic citizenship in an independent kin state or through autonomous citizenship in a substate entity within the state where they live. Both solutions should satisfy their claims as stakeholders and minorities should enjoy some freedom to choose between them.

Combining the two would, however, undermine the integrity of multinational democracy that accepts the minority as a constitutive community even if it does so in less obvious ways than a unilateral right to self-determination and secession. Adding transnational citizenship to domestic autonomy may instead be interpreted as a claim to condominium status in which the citizens of a self-governing territory are at the same time included in the jurisdictions of two independent states. As I have argued above, condominium may work as a temporary solution for externally disputed and internally deeply divided territories. However, condominium cannot be achieved through unilateral extension of a state's personal jurisdiction to the citizens of an autonomous territory in another state. Promoting condominium as a general model for transborder minorities would undermine the conditions of trust and cooperation between states that are required for this solution to work.

We might imagine a different world in which there were neither Westphalian constraints on all kinds of transnational citizenship nor post-Westphalian trade-offs between nested and overlapping modes of citizenship. This could be a world in which political communities were nothing more than voluntary associations.[16] They would have boundaries of membership that could broadly overlap with other associations but they would no longer claim comprehensive territorial jurisdiction. I can see why this libertarian utopia is attractive as a thought experiment about human freedom. I am not sure that it would also provide a response to the human need for protection. But I am sure that our most basic ideas about citizenship and democracy would no longer apply in this world and that imagining it does not help us improve the conflict-ridden one in which we live.

Notes

1. I have introduced the concept of 'transnational citizenship' to describe an overlapping structure of membership in two or more polities, with significant elements of citizenship status and rights in each (Bauböck 1994). This includes residential citizenship for immigrants disconnected from their nationality (for example, local voting rights for foreign nationals), external citizenship in relation to a country of origin or nationality (such as absentee voting rights for expatriates) and multiple nationality. The Hungarian Status Law grants external citizenship rights to co-ethnics abroad who are not formally Hungarian nationals.
2. See the Report of the Venice Commission of the Council of Europe on the Hungarian Status Law, reprinted in Kántor et al. (2004).
3. The distribution of German passports among ethnic Germans in the Polish Silesia region in the early 1990s resembles in some ways Romanian policy towards Moldova. There are, however, two main differences that explain the acquiescence of the Polish government: first, the prior recognition of Polish borders and territorial integrity by Germany; and second, the lack of political aspirations among the German minority in Poland. German government promises for economic assistance and advocacy of Polish accession to the EU certainly helped, too.
4. The traditional rejection of multiple nationality in international law is grounded on the premise that relations between sovereign states are always dominated by security concerns. If we view the international state system as resembling a Hobbesian state of nature then transnational citizenship must be regarded as an evil in the two contexts that I consider here.
5. Will Kymlicka (2001: 347) suggests a somewhat different typology of minority responses to dominant nation-building projects: mass emigration, renegotiating the terms of integration, autonomous self-government or accepting marginalisation through self-insulation. My typology has a narrower purpose since I discuss here only minorities with external kin states, but it still suggests that there are more possibilities than the four listed by Kymlicka.
6. The formerly quite strong German-speaking minorities in Romania were often forced out of the country by Ceausescu's dictatorship but have shrunk further after the democratic transition due to the pull-factor of the German *Aussiedler* policy.

7. The case of the German-speaking minority in Italian South Tyrol illustrates the interplay and implications of all four alternatives. Under Mussolini's regime this group was exposed to a policy of coercive assimilation. In 1939 Hitler and Mussolini concluded a pact that left its members with the option of either fully assimilating or emigrating into distant parts of the German Reich. This resettlement plan was, however, largely blocked by the unfolding war. In 1946 Italy and Austria agreed on a strong form of provincial autonomy, which was, however, initially not fully honoured by the Italian side. In response to this, a group of activists engaged in the 1960s in a violent campaign for self-determination and reunification with Austria. The gradual implementation of the autonomy agreement from 1969 onwards has marginalised the secessionist option and has thus reconciled the rival claims to an extent that none of three other solutions could achieve.

8. As Austria did with regard to South Tyrol when Italy violated the autonomy agreement.

9. This claim is weaker if the minority in question is primarily composed of recent immigrants resettled in the territory under an authoritarian regime. In Estonia and Latvia this has been used as a justification for excluding Russian minorities from citizenship after the restoration of independence. Such exclusion is, however, a heavy burden for building a liberal democracy and cannot be reasonably maintained for more than a short time. Had the Russian minorities raised demands for extensive political autonomy rather than for inclusion into a common citizenship, then the Baltic governments would have had much stronger reasons for rejecting such claims.

10. On 11 June 2004 a majority voted for amending the Irish Constitution in such a way that birth in the territory alone is no longer sufficient for acquiring citizenship. The referendum was triggered by the case of Man Levette Chen, a Chinese citizen who went to Belfast to give birth to her second child in order to avoid deportation to China where having this second child would have violated the one-child policy. Her child automatically acquired the citizenship of the Irish Republic and therefore also citizenship of the EU, which would allow Mrs Chen to stay in Britain. The European Court of Justice upheld this claim against a British Court (European Court of Justice (2004) *Chen v. Secretary of State for the Home Department*, C-200/02, ECR 2004, I-3887).

11. Stefan Wolff points out that condominiums such as Andorra before 1993 and the New Hebrides (1906–1980) 'have historically not been set up to accommodate ethnic conflicts; rather they were meant to settle territorial disputes between states' (Wolff 2004: 196). Yet condominium arrangements may in some cases help to settle 'cross-border conflicts that involve an ethnically mixed disputed territory with actually or potentially high levels of inter-ethnic conflicts' (ibid.: 196).

12. See the 'Declaration of Nation', adopted by the 2000 Prague Congress of the International Romani Union, which describes the Roma as a non-territorial 'nation, which does not want to become a state' (http://www.tolerance.cz/, accessed 1 April 2005).

13. The notion of deterritorialised community is more plausible for religious transnationalism, such as the idea of a global Islamic *umma* (Mandaville 2001).

14. A prominent example for this misinterpretation is Huntington (2004).
15. Thanks to Audrey Macklin for raising this question.
16. Or, in Chandran Kukathas' version, associations of voluntary associations (Kukathas 2003).

References

Aleinikoff, T. A. and D. Klusmeyer, eds (2002) *Citizenship Policies for an Age of Migration*. Washington, DC: Carnegie Endowment for International Peace and Migration Policy Institute.
Bauböck, R. (1994) *Transnational Citizenship. Membership and Rights in International Migration*. Aldershot: Edward Elgar.
Bauböck, R. (2003) 'Towards a Political Theory of Migrant Transnationalism'. *International Migration Review* 37, 3: 700–23.
Bauböck, R. (2005) 'Expansive Citizenship: Voting Beyond Territory and Membership'. *Political Science and Politics* 38, 4: 683–87.
Bauböck, R. (2007) 'Political Boundaries in a Multilevel Democracy'. In Seyla Benhabib and Ian Shapiro, eds, *Identities, Affiliations and Allegiances*. Cambridge: Cambridge University Press, pp. 85–109.
Brubaker, R. (2004) *Ethnicity Without Groups*. Cambridge, MA: Harvard University Press.
Buchanan, A. (1997) 'Theories of Secession'. *Philosophy and Public Affairs* 26, 1: 31–61.
Buchanan, A. (2004) *Justice, Legitimacy and Self-Determination. Moral Foundations for International Law*. Oxford: Oxford University Press.
Huntington, S. (2004) *Who are We? The Challenges to America's National Identity*. New York: Simon and Schuster.
Iordachi, C. (2004) 'Dual Citizenship and Policies Toward Kin Minorities in East-Central Europe: A Comparison between Hungary, Romania and the Republic of Moldova'. In Zoltán Kántor, Balázs, Majtényi, Osamu Ieda, Balázs Vizi and Iván Halász, eds (2004) *The Hungarian Status Law: Nation Building and/or Minority Protection*. 21st Century COE Program Slavic Eurasian Studies, 4, at http://src-h.slav.hokudai.ac.jp/coe21/publish/no4_ses/contents.html., pp. 239–69.
Kántor, Z. and B. Majtényi, O. Ieda, B. Vizi and I. Halász, eds (2004) *The Hungarian Status Law: Nation Building and/or Minority Protection*. 21st Century COE Program Slavic Eurasian Studies, 4, at: http://src-h.slav.hokudai.ac.jp/coe21/publish/no4_ses/contents.html.
Keating, M. (2001) *Plurinational Democracies*. Oxford : Oxford University Press.
Kis, J. (2004) 'The Status Law: Hungary at the Crossroads'. In Zoltán Kántor, Balázs Majtényi, Osamu Ieda, Balázs Vizi and Iván Halász, eds (2004) *The Hungarian Status Law: Nation Building and/or Minority Protection*. 21st Century COE Program Slavic Eurasian Studies, 4, at: http://srch.slav.hokudai.ac.jp/coe21/publish/no4_ses/contents.html., pp. 152–76.
Kukathas, C. (2003) *The Liberal Archipelago. A Theory of Diversity and Freedom*, Oxford: Oxford University Press.
Kymlicka, W. (2001) *Contemporary Political Philosophy*. 2nd edn. Oxford: Oxford University Press.
Mandaville, P. G. (2001) *Transnational Muslim Politics – Reimagining the Umma*. London: Routledge.

Martin, D. A. and K. Hailbronner, eds (2002) *Rights and Duties of Dual Nationals. Evolution and Prospects.* The Hague: Kluwer Law International.

Sasse, G. (2004) 'Minority Rights and EU Enlargement: Normative Overstretch or Effective Conditionality'. In Gabriel von Toggenburg, ed., *Minority Protection and the EU: The Way Forward.* New York: Open Society Institute.

Wolff, S. (2004) *Disputed Territories. The Transnational Dynamics of Ethnic Conflict Settlement.* Oxford: Berghahn Books.

5

The Politics of Dual Citizenship in Hungary

Mária M. Kovács

In Hungary the issue of dual citizenship has recently emerged as a controversial issue and, for a few months in 2004 it even captured centre stage in politics. On 5 December 2004, 6 months after Hungary's accession to the European Union (EU), voters were asked in a referendum to decide whether Hungary should offer extraterritorial, non-resident citizenship to ethnic Hungarians living outside Hungary by lifting all residency requirements from among the preconditions for obtaining a second, Hungarian citizenship. The novel aspect of the proposal was not the introduction of dual citizenship itself, since the option of obtaining a Hungarian second citizenship had long been available for permanent residents within the country.[1] The innovation would have been to remove all residency requirements from among the preconditions of obtaining a Hungarian second citizenship. The question posed at the referendum was as follows:

> Do you wish that Parliament pass a law which would enable an applicant who declares himself/herself to be of Hungarian nationality, but is not a Hungarian citizen and does not live in Hungary, to enjoy the right of preferential naturalisation at his/her request, provided he/she can provide proof of his/her Hungarian nationality with the possession of a 'Hungarian identity card' issued on grounds of Law LXII.19, 2001, or in any other way to be determined by the law.[2]

Accordingly, Hungarians living outside Hungary were to be granted Hungarian citizenship merely upon declaring themselves to be of Hungarian linguistic affiliation at a Hungarian consular office, or upon possessing an identity card issued by the Hungarian state since 2002 for non-citizen Hungarians confirming their Hungarian nationality.[3]

Although the referendum question left the precise criteria of eligibility open to future law-making, an approximation of potentially eligible claimants can be made on the basis of the size of transborder Hungarian ethnic minorities whose numbers are estimated at around 3 million. If Hungarians from all over the world were included, the number of potentially eligible claimants would rise to 5 million.[4] Thus the number of those eligible for Hungarian citizenship would be augmented by at least a third of Hungary's current citizenry of 10 million.[5] Assuming that the majority of those deemed eligible would actually claim citizenship, the proportions of the resulting change would exceed the growth of Germany's citizenry after unification but, of course, without the corresponding territorial enlargement. Or to give another analogy, the resulting change would be proportionate to the entire population of Mexico being made eligible for US citizenship. This points to the first specificity of the Hungarian story, namely that the dimension of Hungary's kin-minority problem is unusually large: nearly a quarter of all Hungarians live outside Hungary's borders in neighbouring states located in more or less compact settlements.

The proposed reform failed to win popular mandate in the referendum of 2004.[6] But the movement towards citizenship reform is not exhausted. Powerful endorsers of the reform within the Hungarian political establishment, among them the Chairman of the main right-wing party (FIDESZ), Viktor Orbán, pledged to pursue the reform and to create non-resident dual citizenship should the right achieve electoral victory in the 2006 elections ('Modernizációs' 2005). The President of the republic, László Sólyom, also expressed sympathy for the initiative ('MTI' 2005). Meanwhile, the Federation of World Hungarians, the organisation that had initiated to 2004 referendum, announced plans for a new referendum to be held in 2006 ('Patrubány' 2005).

Debates over the Hungarian citizenship reform raised a number of contentious issues characteristic of citizenship debates worldwide, but also brought forth problems that are specific to the East Central European region. The Hungarian initiative was directed at external co-ethnic minorities living in neighbouring states as well as the Hungarian diaspora living elsewhere in the world. As such, the reform would amount to what Christian Joppke identified as the 're-ethnicisation' of citizenship, a process in which states provide preferential access to citizenship to people who are considered ethnic or linguistic relatives (see also Bauböck 2004b; Joppke 2003: 13). Within Europe, such policies are pursued by a number of countries including Germany, Portugal, Spain, Italy and Greece. In the East Central European region, Croatia and

Romania introduced similar legislation. But while such reforms in the West and East may look similar in terms of the legal techniques involved, they address different concerns and carry different implications.

In Western Europe, citizenship reforms aimed at the preferential treatment of ethnic relatives abroad mostly emerged in the context of migration and were adopted without drawing much international attention. As Christian Joppke put it, such reforms constituted a 'little-noticed side plot' alongside more important reforms aiming at easing access to citizenship, by receiving states, for ethno-culturally foreign immigrants. Even in a country like Spain, which introduced an elaborate regime for the preferential treatment of ethnic relatives abroad, these reforms were counterbalanced by measures easing access to citizenship for ethnically foreign labour migrants.

As compared to Western immigration countries, the context in which the issue was raised in East Central Europe is fundamentally different. Here, the defining events of the first decade following the fall of communist regimes had less to do with labour migration and all the more to do with the dissolution of multinational federations and the formation of 12 new states in the region (Brubaker 2000: 1). Therefore in East Central Europe, questions of membership, of who does or does not belong to the nation, touch upon sensitive issues of state sovereignty and evoke problems of historically disputed borders and transborder ethnic kin minorities. For example, when in 1991 Romania created non-resident second citizenship for ethnic Romanians in neighbouring Moldova, the reform had been based on the expectation that Moldova, a successor state of the Soviet Union, would, in time, cease to exist as a sovereign entity, and the country that used to be a part of Romania before its incorporation into the Soviet Union would again be unified with Romania.[7] At the same time, the ethnic Russian population of the separatist Transdnistrian region of Moldova was allowed by Russia to retain Soviet passports. Eventually, in 2000, the authorities of the split Moldavian republic, 40 per cent of whose population hold a dual citizenship status of some sort, retaliated in despair and passed a citizenship reform that mandated the denaturalisation of holders of dual citizenship unless they had acquired that status through mixed marriages (Iordachi 2004: 255). Although the application of the law had been minimal until its eventual revocation in 2003, the story is a telling indication of the interstate tensions created by the use of dual citizenship towards nationalist-revisionist purposes.[8] In this light it is hardly surprising that Romania would be extremely sensitive about the Hungarian offer of external citizenship to Hungarians in Romania, suspecting Hungary of intentions similar to those informing Romanian policies towards Moldova.

Paradoxically, the expansion of the EU into the East Central European region also raised the political stakes involved in non-resident dual citizenship. When, in 1992, Germany offered citizenship to Silesian Germans living in Poland, a part of the population of Poland had received the benefits of European citizenship ahead of their ethnically Polish counterparts who had to wait over a decade to acquire the same status. Were Hungary to offer non-resident dual citizenship to Hungarians in neighbouring states, Hungarians in those states would become EU citizens ahead of their counterparts belonging to the majority nation. The Hungarian case is not altogether unique in Europe: Albanian misgivings about creating a privileged 'European' minority within a majority nation that is not part of the EU have led to pressures on Greece to surrender its plans to offer non-resident dual citizenship to the Greek minority in Albania.

Political debates

Political debates on the referendum initiative were tremendously polarised. In 2003, the initiative to call a referendum had not come from Hungarian parliamentary parties, but from a diaspora organisation not well integrated into Hungarian politics, the World Federation of Hungarians. Prior to 2003, the Federation had contested the policies of the Hungarian governments on citizenship matters, claiming that Hungary was not doing enough for minority Hungarians. In the year 2000, the presidency of the Federation was assumed by the Transylvanian politician Miklós Patrubány, who made a series of moves, including a call for the revision of Hungary's so-called Trianon borders established after the First World War, that gravely overstepped the limits of what was generally seen as acceptable by the Hungarian political establishment, creating an image of himself as a political gambler (Debreczeni 2004: 7). Understandably, with Hungary scheduled to join the EU in 2004, no part of the Hungarian political establishment was ready to risk being associated with Patrubány's straightforward revisionism.

In the following year the Orbán government (1998–2002) introduced the status law that was designed to provide some form of state-membership for transborder Hungarians without the creation of dual citizenship. The law was, in fact, explicitly formulated for transborder Hungarians who are not dual citizens: it provided benefits and grants for

Hungarians, their spouses and children in neighbouring states as long as they retained their residence abroad. The entitlement to benefits was to cease in case the claimant was granted residence permit or citizenship in Hungary. The law established a Hungarian Identity Card and provided its holders with the most favourable conditions of entry into Hungary, free work permits within Hungary for a fixed period, awards and grants within Hungary, support for teaching in Hungarian in neighbouring countries and benefits in health care, education and cultural services within Hungary itself (Law 2001, LXII. 'On the Hungarians in Neighbouring States').

Minority politicians in the neighbouring countries were split in their response to the status law. Most of them supported the law on grounds best expressed by Mikós Duray, a leader of minority Hungarians in Slovakia, namely that the law avoided the obstacles inherent in the claim for dual citizenship (Györgyi 2004: 57). Already at this time, however, some influential minority leaders rejected Duray's argument that posited the status law as a permanent alternative to dual citizenship. Rather, they based their support for the law on the explicit expectation that the law would, in the course of time, prepare the ground for full citizenship rights for transborder Hungarians. At the same time, the Chairman of the World Federation of Hungarians, Patrubány, insisted that the benefits provided by the law were simply no substitute for what minority Hungarians really needed, which was full Hungarian citizenship.[9] Responding to objections that an extension of Hungarian citizenship to non-resident minorities would be incompatible with the terms of Hungary's accession to the EU, in the spring of 2003, the Federation called on Hungarian voters to say 'no' to Hungary's accession to the Union (Duray 2000).[10] This radicalism alienated not only the political public within Hungary proper, but also mainstream Hungarian minority politicians in neighbouring states.

The status law provoked an angry response in neighbouring states. Hungary was accused of irredentist nationalism, of creating a 'veiled form of dual citizenship' the ultimate effect of which was to call the sovereignty of the neighbouring states into question. Hungary was also criticised by the EU for the unilateral adoption of the legislation without appropriate consultations with the states in question and for the fact that the law provided for a set of extraterritorial rights for ethnic Hungarians. Eventually, the Hungarian Parliament amended the legislation. In the years since, approximately one out of every four transborder Hungarians has applied for the Hungarian ID.

But hardly had the implementation of the status law begun when the World Federation of Hungarians launched a new campaign in favour of dual citizenship. What gave the issue special urgency, the Federation claimed, was that Hungary's upcoming accession to the EU was going to make millions of non-Hungarian EU citizens legally 'less alien' within Hungary, while transborder Hungarians would continue to qualify as 'legal aliens' falling under restrictions in their labour opportunities, and in their movement across borders (Duray 2004: 1).[11] The only way to remedy this absurd situation, the Federation contended, was by extending full Hungarian citizenship to ethnic Hungarians (Csergő and Goldgeier 2004). In October 2003, the Federation began collecting signatures for a referendum on establishing non-resident citizenship for transborder Hungarians.[12] This, then, points to the second specificity of the Hungarian story, namely that the initiative to create non-resident transborder dual citizenship did not come from within the Hungarian political establishment, but from the outside, or as some analysts put it, 'from below', from a radical organisation that was not well integrated into Hungarian politics and pursued aims that were not in line with the policies of Hungary's major political parties, or the government. Only this can explain the puzzle of why any organisation would take the risk of launching a referendum initiative that had only limited support within Hungary itself and therefore carried the prospect of its own defeat.

Initially, mainstream Hungarian parties on all sides reacted very cautiously to the initiative as did transborder Hungarian minority leaders who were especially worried about the possibility of a negative outcome of a referendum which, in their view, could do serious harm to minority Hungarians ('Hírösszefoglalónk' 2004). Miklós Kovács, Chairman of the Cultural Association of Ukrainian Hungarians, for instance, branded the referendum initiative the action of a 'marginalized swindler', and other minority leaders, such as József Kasza of Serbia, were also sceptical. Within Hungary itself, even those parties of the right that, a few months later, came out in support of the referendum, remained conspicuously passive in the beginning. Besides the anticipation of failure, the other reason for the initial passivity of rightist parties may be the explicit commitment, made only 2 years earlier in 2001, by the Orbán government to the European Council on the occasion of the EC's investigation of the status law that Hungary had no intention of extrapolating citizenship rights from the status law which, as they said, was in fact based on the 'rejection of dual citizenship' for kin minorities. As the position paper of the Orbán government submitted to the Venice Commission in 2001 stated,

> In fact, the Act [status law] recognises that Hungarians abroad are citizens of the relevant states and clearly rejects the idea that the self-identification as Hungarians can be based on dual citizenship. Hungarian assistance to Hungarians abroad has always been and will continue to be carried out according to the practice of other European states, taking European norms into consideration in good faith and giving due attention to the spirit of co-operation between neighboring states. In the expression of its kin-state role, Hungary has always acknowledged that it has no citizen-like relationship whatsoever with Hungarians living in the neighboring countries when dealing with them. ('Paper' 2001)

After a few months, however, the mainstream right-wing parties along with the President of the Republic declared their support for the referendum, while the socialists and liberals turned against it ('Kettős állampolgárság kronológia' 2005). What followed was an agitated, hysterical campaign leading up to the referendum that fulfilled the prophecy of its own failure by turning out as invalid on account of the low number of participants.[13] This, then, points to a third feature of the Hungarian story, namely that an 81 per cent majority of the Hungarian electorate either stayed away from the voting, or voted against the creation of non-resident dual citizenship for transborder Hungarians. Among those who cast their ballots, amounting to 37.67 of the electorate, 51.57 per cent voted in favour of the reform, 48.43 per cent against ('A kettős állampolgárságról' 2005).

Little research is available on what precisely motivated Hungarian voters in their choices. Welfare protectionism could well have played a role, given the fact that, apart from Slovakia, the average living standards of transborder Hungarians are way below those of Hungarians in Hungary, and that the arguments of the Socialist Party against dual citizenship relied primarily on the costs of the reform. According to one poll, 31 per cent of 'no' voters mentioned the problem of social costs and pensions as their main concern. Another motive may have been the fear of instability on the borders resulting from tensions with Hungary's neighbours. Moreover, voters may also have been influenced by the perception that the mass appearance of transborder voters in Hungarian elections might overturn the balance of Hungary's parliamentary system. What is sufficiently clear is that the plan to introduce non-resident transborder citizenship failed to win a popular mandate within Hungary itself and that in the future it can only be created against the back story of a failed referendum. To quote an outspoken liberal opponent of the initiative, János Kis, 'the offer was made to a nation of ten million to enlarge its homeland above the state-borders to the entire Carpathian basin. The nation refused to take the risk and accept the costs' (Kis 2004a: 5). But the issues raised by the referendum are likely to remain on the agenda of Hungarian politics for some time to come. Despite the fact that a few months after the failed referendum, in June 2005, the socialist–liberal coalition passed new legislation that provides a simpler process and a shorter waiting period for citizenship for those ethnic Hungarians who are permanent residents in Hungary, introduced a new form of 'national visa' for trans-border Hungarians and shortened the process of preferential natural-isation, demands for dual citizenship have not subsided ('Tájékoztató' 2005).

Ethnicity and citizenship

Before summarising the arguments of endorsers in favour of the reform and the arguments of opponents against the reform, a brief outline is in place on the general implications raised by the initiative.

The Hungarian suggestion associates eligibility for non-resident dual citizenship with membership in an ethnic community. Thus, dual citizenship would purposefully reaffirm the connection between ethno-cultural nationality and citizenship. Citizenship for transborder ethnic kin would create a legal tie between the Hungarian state and the members of an ethnically defined community (Fowler 2002).

Advocates of the reform wished to overcome this difficulty by presenting the plan as based on a traditional *jus sanguinis* concept rather than the concept of ethnicity. In this view, transborder Hungarians would be 'regaining' the citizenship of their ancestors who had possessed the citizenship of the Hungarian state before the First World War.[14] However, there are several difficulties with this approach.

The first difficulty is political. After the First World War those Hungarians who ended up as minorities in neighbouring states were obliged, by the Peace Treaties, to opt for the citizenship of their new home state or, if they declined to do so, they were obliged to move to Hungary. Therefore, in the eyes of Hungary's neighbours, any unilateral change in the citizenship status of minority Hungarians would amount to a unilateral breach of treaty obligations, to a revision of the terms of the peace treaty that still serves as the basis of international legitimacy for the borders of these states.

Second, transborder populations whose ancestors bore the citizenship of a larger Hungarian state in the Dual Austro-Hungarian Monarchy include millions of non-Hungarians. So even if the *jus sanguinis* view was applied, the only way to narrow down eligibility for Hungarian dual citizenship to those with a Hungarian ethno-cultural affiliation would be to apply an ethnic definition that restricts eligibility to Hungarians.

A third difficulty has to do with the dimensions of the population potentially affected by the *jus sanguinis* view. Given the fact that in 1920 Hungary's population had been reduced to half of what it had been before the war (with a corresponding reduction of two-thirds of its territory), the idea that *jus sanguinis* transmission could automatically create dual citizens after any number of generations would amount to the obligation to reactivate the 'dormant' citizenship of people whose numbers may well surpass the current number of Hungarian citizens.[15] Moreover this approach would also go against current international standard practice that citizenship should express a genuine connection between the citizen and the state resulting in an unwritten consensus of contemporary states on an 'informal second generation cap' on ties of states with members abroad (Joppke 2003: 13).

Dual citizenship and voting rights

The next issue that emerged in the debate was the problem of voting rights. Although the referendum question did not clarify the substantive content of non-resident citizenship, the general perception that emerged within Hungary was that even if, initially, transborder citizenship were to be created without voting rights, in the long run it would still lead to the enfranchisement of would-be transborder citizens. Were this to happen, opponents of the reform argued, the appearance of masses of transborder voters in Hungarian elections would run counter to the principle of popular sovereignty and democratic self-determination within Hungary itself, putting Hungarian democracy under pressures it might not be able to withstand.

The reform initiative projected a potentially weak distinction between active and inactive citizenship for dual citizens. Hungarian transborder citizenship, if ever instituted, is likely to be in line with that of Croatia, where transborder dual citizens retain some of their rights associated with Croatian citizenship, including voting rights, even at times when their alternate citizenship is active.[16] This is partly because Hungarian regulations on the declaration of residence are rather lax, requiring only 3 months of residence for the citizen to activate his/her right to vote. Moreover, in order to avoid the disenfranchisement of the homeless, voters can be admitted to the voters' registry without actually possessing an address or residence permit, but simply based on a declaration of residence at a given locality at the communal office. Thus, in the present legal framework, transborder citizens would find it technically easy to assume permanent residency in Hungary without surrendering permanent residency in their country of first citizenship, thus, in effect, becoming not only dual citizens, but also dual residents with dual voting rights (see Ostrow 2002). And even if, as experts for the Council of Europe argued in a recent study (Council of Europe 1999), 'a hypothetical mass invasion of electors from abroad' is unrealistic, given the experience of most European countries that allow expatriate voting, in Hungary, where elections are usually won by a narrow margin, the appearance of transborder voters would most likely mean that 'the outcome of Hungarian elections would regularly be decided by voters who do not pay taxes in Hungary and who are, in general, not subject to its laws' (Kis 2004b). In the absence of clear criteria of eligibility, even a rough assessment of the number of potentially eligible new voters in the Hungarian elections remains in the realm of speculation. What we may safely presume is that those transborder Hungarians who, after 2001, decided to apply for a Hungarian Identity Card would most likely apply for extraterritorial Hungarian citizenship, if instituted. Their numbers by 2004 added up to 774,288 people of whom approximately 514,000 were of voting age (Kántor and Császár 2005). In the 2002 elections, a quarter of this number would have sufficed to produce the swing votes necessary to change the outcome of the parliamentary elections. Whatever the estimates, voting rights for transborder Hungarians could easily mean that external voters may acquire a crucial influence on the result of an election. In its opinion of March 2002, the Venice Commission of the European Council considered this kind of decisive influence by external voters as highly problematic ('Venice Commission, Croatia' 2002: 7).

A further element of organised irresponsibility inherent in such a solution would be that those casting the swing votes may be people who are not only not subject to Hungarian law, but had never even lived in Hungary proper so that their political choices would be made on a highly selective image of issues and candidates. A call for electoral mobilisation on such grounds was already given by the Chairman of FIDESZ, who, in the summer of 2005, urged transborder Hungarian communities 'to regard themselves as mirrors and assess parties within Hungary in the light of how these parties respond to their claims'. They should, then, 'do their share in mobilising public opinion and convince people of trans-border origin to participate in the elections in large numbers' ('Modernizációs' 2005). No wonder then that another concern with transborder expatriate votes has been the potentially radicalising effect of such a system. Based on a survey of countries that allow non-resident voting, David Martin argued that votes by non-resident citizens may easily lead to more extremist election outcomes, as people do not have to live with the consequences of their vote ('Citizenship in Countries of Immigration' 1988). In view of the possible consequences of non-resident external citizenship on the Hungarian political system, as well as on the welfare state and the country's international relations, it is hardly surprising that the proposal created passionate debates within Hungary. At stake in the debate for some participants was the question of whether or not Hungary is in fact experimenting with ideas that are pulling her away from, rather than bringing her closer to, 'mainstream' Europe. As János Kis summarised it, all in all, he concluded, 'the victory of "yes votes" would pull us back to the murky nationalism of past ages, it would lock up Hungarian politics in the prison of revisionist nostalgias, it would poison public life within Hungary as well as our relationship with neighbouring states and with transborder Hungarians, and it would damage the level of our acceptance within the European Union' (Kis 2004b: 7).

Compatibility with European norms

In stark contrast, advocates of the initiative argued that their proposal is modelled on concepts that are part and parcel of an integrated Europe, putting into effect a small-scale version of the European process, some kind of small-scale Hungarian integration across state borders.

Responding to objections that non-resident transborder citizenship would be incompatible with European norms and practices regarding the connection of citizenship to ethnicity, advocates pointed to the fact that all European states accept ethnicity as part of the basis of citizenship. Most of them even 'make provisions for the acquisition of benefits, including citizenship, for ethnic kins who are citizens of another state' (Schöpflin 2004: 22). To substantiate this claim they pointed to examples of non-resident citizenship for ethnic kin populations within the EU.

Indeed, examples of ethnic preferentialism abound in EU member states. Italy created non-resident citizenship for people of Italian descent and has recently expanded eligibility for non-resident citizenship;[17] Germany offered non-resident citizenship to Silesian Germans in the early 1990s, thus providing dual citizens of Poland and Germany with access to EU citizenship; in 2002, Greece announced plans to offer non-resident transborder citizenship to the Greek minority in Albania; and Spain waived the residence requirement for children of emigrants to recover Spanish citizenship, and reduced residency requirements for naturalisation for descendants of Spanish ancestors. In 1997, Britain granted the right to opt for British citizenship to part of Hong Kong's population and in 2002 most British Overseas Territories Citizens became European citizens through their having been granted British citizenship. In none of these instances did the European Commission or other member states voice protest, nor did the amendments of the treaties on dual nationality—concluded between Spain and Latin American countries, which entitled persons of dual Spanish–Latin American nationality to apply for a Spanish passport—lead to protests. These precedents, one could argue, point to the legitimacy, even within the core nations of the EU, of using dual citizenship and external citizenship for the inclusion of ethnic relatives from abroad in the citizenry of the homeland.

Arguments against

Opponents of the reform challenged this interpretation of larger European processes. First, even though the EU left the regulation of citizenship in the competence of member states, opponents claimed, it would still regard the ethnicist turn in Hungarian legislation as a breach of common principles laid down in European agreements. Second, they argued that the 1997 European Convention on Nationality, ratified by Hungary in 2001, restricted the recovery of former nationality of a given state to those having an 'effective link' to the state in question which involves habitual residence in the territory of the state (see Tóth 2004 and Kis 2004b). According to this view, the apparent inconsistency between this restriction and the failure of the EU to challenge the permissive policies of its member states in granting non-resident citizenship is explained by the fact that the Convention did not require the elimination of preferential provisions that had already been in force before the adoption of the Convention. It is perhaps no coincidence that most member states that have permissive preferential policies of granting citizenship have not yet ratified the convention (for example, Italy, Greece, Spain and the United Kingdom). Germany introduced an explicit sunset clause according to which persons of German origin cannot apply for German citizenship if they were born after 1984. Hungary, however, ratified the convention in 2001, becoming one of the 14 EC member countries to have ratified the convention.

Second, opponents criticised the suggestion of unilateral legislation for its implied confrontational posture. The problem with unilateral action is not so much that it violates international law, but that it is self-defeating. To quote János Kis again, the unilateral creation of Hungarian citizens on the territory of other states is nothing but a 'mirage' that provokes 'phony wars over phony questions and phony answers' (Kis 2004b: 4). Endorsers of the reform do not share in Kis's critique: as long as Hungarian minorities are mistreated or disadvantaged, they argue, Hungary must use the instrument of 'unilateral steps' to respond to mistreatment ('Válságban' 2005).

Nor can the creation of dual citizenship be justified, opponents argued, by reference to the fact that transborder minorities would approve of such a move. First, transborder minorities are themselves divided over the issue. For example, before 2003, the largest Hungarian party of the robust Hungarian minority of Romania, with substantial representation in the Romanian parliament and government, had been lukewarm about dual citizenship. But at the same time, the most vocal advocates of transborder Hungarian citizenship also came from Romania and they also relied on a substantial constituency. Minorities themselves do not speak with a single voice because the attitudes of the different groups of which they are composed are derivative of the long-term view each of these groups takes on the possibilities of negotiating a better status for themselves in their host states. The fact that less than half of the transborder Hungarian population has applied for a Hungarian Identity Card since its creation in 2001 points to the absence of a clear majority for a single solution among those involved. But even if the idea of dual citizenship enjoys the support of the majority of transborder Hungarians, so the argument goes, this support is based on a populist misrepresentation of the possibilities connected to dual citizenship (Bauer 2004). At the end, any unilateral move by Hungary to create dual citizenship would remain 'a game of illusions played between Hungarian nationalists and a minority within the Hungarian minority' in a useless, but 'ritual display of imagined political togetherness' (Kis 2004c: 22).

Third, critics argued that dual citizenship is incompatible with the claims of autonomy by transborder minorities. Concurring with Rainer

Bauböck, critics maintained that 'claims for multiple citizenship and territorial autonomy should be seen as mutually incompatible. They would create fears in the host society about irredentist threats to its territorial integrity that cannot be easily dismissed as unreasonable' (Bauböck 2004a: 23).

Therefore, according to the opponents of dual transborder citizenship, in the final analysis, Hungary must take a new look at the ultimate aims of its homeland policies. One—bad—option would be to remain with the discourse advocated by the two mainstream right-wing parties of recreating a 'unitary Hungarian nation' over and above existing state borders (Stewart 2004: 23). The need for self-reflection by Hungary is all the more pressing, as the discourse of 'national unification' has already become standard in Hungarian legislative language. The concept of a 'unitary Hungarian nation' was used in the original formulation of the Status Law of 2001, though it was later deleted from the version of the law amended after criticism from the European Commission.

According to the critics, Hungary should revise this confrontational approach and instead it should clearly articulate, or rearticulate, its policies in the conceptual framework of minority protection. Hungary must accept that transborder Hungarians are the citizens of the states where they reside and that their long-term well-being depends on the solutions they are able to work out with majority societies. As the Transylvanian sociologist Béla Bíró put it, 'what can help us is not national unification above existing borders, but collective integration into the political community of the states in which we live' (Bíró 2004: 6). One of these states, Slovakia, is already a member of the EU. Another, Romania, is a candidate for accession in a year or two. Yet others, such as Serbia–Montenegro and Ukraine, are likely to remain outside the Union for some time to come. The way Hungary should promote the protection of Hungarian minorities differs from case to case, but they should all be able to count on Hungarian support in their efforts to secure equal individual and collective rights, including the right to autonomy, in their home states. They should all have access to completely free travel to and from Hungary as well as support for maintaining cultural and educational links with Hungary.

Fourth, as indicated above, critics objected to the impact the reform could have on democratic institutions within Hungary with the appearance of masses of transborder voters in Hungarian elections. Their enfranchisement would put Hungarian democracy under pressures it may not be able to withhold.

Final remarks

In conclusion, a few words on the ambiguities with regard to the arguments of both sides in the debate. The idea of dual citizenship emerged in Hungary with reference to a larger international process of the increasing tolerance of dual citizenship. However, while in the major immigration states of Europe dual citizenship has been espoused above all by the political left as an instrument of integrating labour migrants, in Hungary, as in many other states of the region, the demand for dual citizenship has mostly, if not exclusively, emanated from the nationalist right and is predominantly directed at transborder ethnic relatives. Thus, in the Hungarian referendum debate, the battle over dual citizenship has been cast as a debate between the nationalist right, as supporters, on the one hand, and the Europe-oriented liberals, as opponents, on the other.

This representation of the debate is, however, to some extent self-made and arbitrary, especially as it relies on rather strong assertions, both by the left and by the right, of what 'Europe' 'really' stands for. In fact, the nationalist right has partly been drawing on the arguments of European liberals for transnational dual citizenship, amounting, in Christian Joppke's terms, to a 'piracy' of the arguments of the left, by the right (Joppke 2003: 19). Meanwhile liberals relied on counter-arguments they claimed to have extrapolated from relevant European norms and practices. But these practices are much too diverse to form the basis of a coherent interpretation (Joppke 2003: 13). Recent debates on dual citizenship in other European countries, for instance in the Netherlands, show that, just as in the case of Hungary, 'European' arguments can be brought into the discussion on all sides of the debate on extending access to citizenship based on the principle of dual nationality (Vink 2001: 880). In fact, a number of EU states, such as Italy, Portugal, Germany or Spain, have had generous ethnic preference regimes written into their citizenship law, some quite recently, without having had to confront a negative response by the EU (De Groot 2004: 9–11). To the extent that such reforms are challenged, these challenges usually arise from domestic pressures, as was the case in Germany. At the same time, references to 'European pressures' to eliminate ethnic preferences rely on arguments about what Europe 'would' prefer, rather than actual precedents of European pressure (Joppke 2005: 155). Admittedly, when, in the summer of 2005, the socialist-liberal coalition called together experts from the EU to discuss the international legal aspects of a possible citizenship reform, the conclusions of the conference supported the Hungarian opponents of the reform on grounds that any offer of Hungarian citizenship to descendants of Hungarian citizens must be based on the test of effective link, including lawful and habitual residence of the applicant in Hungary ('Működik-e a külhoni állampolgárság?' 2005). However, endorsers of non-resident citizenship rightly claim that the Union has not, so far, interfered with countries that introduced non-resident citizenship with or without testing the existence of effective link to the 'home' state.

Not surprisingly, in the end neither side in the Hungarian debate was able to present a fully convincing, coherent interpretation of those principles and international norms and practices to support their respective positions. In the final analysis it is quite possible that the conflicting stances of the left and the right may stem from concerns that are only partially connected to the problems of transborder Hungarians. After all, even those forces of the political right who have, in the recent referendum debate of 2004, emerged as the staunchest supporters of non-resident citizenship had, only a few years before that, opposed the idea themselves and would have rather wished to address the problem of transborder Hungarians through the status law and special visa arrangements. It is perhaps not too far-fetched to suggest that these conflicting stances may, at least in part, be a result of conflicting opinions and concerns about the long-term stability of Hungary's transitional democracy. After all, in Hungary post-communist parliamentary practices are little more than a decade old. The creation of transborder non-resident citizenship would most likely amount to a mass enfranchisement of a new electorate that, as in all episodes of mass enfranchisement in the past, would introduce new uncertainties in the system and could lead to an internal destabilisation of Hungarian democracy itself. In this respect, both sides share the same intuition, namely that, if instituted, transborder citizenship would most likely have the effect of freezing the regular rotation of parliamentary forces for some time to come in favour of the nationalist right—a prospect that is as welcome on one side as it is feared on the other.

Notes

1. According to Law LV.4§ of 1993 the residency requirement for the 'preferential naturalization' of ethnic Hungarians is a minimum of 1 year of legal residence in Hungary. For other applicants the residency requirement is 8 years of continuous residence. For non-citizen spouses of Hungarian citizens the residency requirement is 3 years and the same applies to parents of children who are Hungarian citizens, children adopted by Hungarian citizens and refugees.

2. 'A kettős állampolgárságról' (2005). For the law establishing the Hungarian ID, see: Kantor et al. (2004: 501–509). This law applied only to Hungarians living in Serbia–Montenegro, Croatia, Slovenia, Ukraine and Slovakia, but not to those Austria.

3. The question posed in the referendum did not restrict non-resident citizenship to Hungarians in neighbouring states.

4. 'Határon túli' (2004). According to the numbers published in 2004 by the Hungarian Government Office for transborder Hungarians, the number of Hungarians amounted to 2,429,000; in Romania, 1,435,000; in Ukraine, 156,000; in Serbia and Montenegro, 293,000; in Slovakia, 516,000; in Croatia, 16,000; and in Slovenia, 8,500. The number of potential claimants globally was estimated at around 5 million by the Undersecretary for Foreign Affairs, András Bársony, in 'Határok nélkül' (2003).

5. 'Népességnyilvántartási' (2004). The Hungarian Ministry of Interior put Hungary's population at 10,207,006 and the number of Hungarian Identity Cards issued to transborder Hungarians was 774,288.

6. In Hungary a referendum is valid if at least 25 per cent of the electorate returns identical votes, or if participation reaches above 50 per cent of the total number of eligible voters. In this case neither criterion was fulfilled.

7. Article 37 of the Law on Romanian Citizenship of 1991 established non-resident Romanian second citizenship for those who had been Romanian citizens in the past and for their descendants (Iordachi 2004: 246–47). Ethnic Romanians constitute two-thirds of the population of Moldova (4.3 million). Of these, 300,000 were granted Romanian citizenship between 1991 and 2000.

8. A smaller number of Moldova's dual citizens have Israeli second citizenship, while most of them carry a Russian or Romanian second passport (Iordachi 2004: 257).

9. As a result of the federation's conflict with Prime Minister Viktor Orbán on the issue of the Status Law, in the fall of 2000 the Orbán government withdrew public funding from the Federation.

10. On the Federation's negative position on EU accession, see 'Az MVSZ' (2003).

11. Before its accession to the EU in 2004, Hungary concluded an agreement with Serbia and Ukraine (2003) on providing citizens of those states with visas free of charge and eliminating the visa requirement for those from Hungary to travel to these states.

12. Even after FIDESZ declared its full support of the referendum, the future content of citizenship remained unclear. The President of the party, Viktor Orbán, spoke of nothing else but a passport while a few days later, his deputy, László Kövér, said in Parliament that 'a passport without citizenship' is a 'kind of animal that does not exist in international law' (Kövér 2004).

13. Of the eligible voters, 63.33 per cent stayed away from the referendum. Among those who cast their ballots, 51.57 per cent voted in favour of the reform, 48.43 per cent against ('A kettős állampolgárságról' 2005).

14. According to paragraph 69. § 2 of the Hungarian constitution, Hungarian citizens who had emigrated from Hungary retain their Hungarian citizenship. This does not, however, apply to former citizens of Hungary in neighbouring states who had lost their Hungarian citizenship as a result of the

peace treaties that redrew the borders of the Hungarian state. The possibility of inheriting Hungarian citizenship applies only to people whose right to Hungarian citizenship is derived from their connection to the territory of the state of Hungary as delineated in the Paris Peace Treaty of 1947.

15. The peace treaty of 1920 reduced Hungary's population from 18.2 million to 7.9 million and its territory from 282 thousand sq. kilometers to 93 thousand sq. kilometers.

16. Transborder Croat dual citizens retain their right to vote in Croatian elections. Italian non-resident citizens may also vote in referenda and national elections for 12 fixed seats. However, Italian non-resident citizens make up approximately 3 per cent of the resident-citizenry of Italy as opposed to the transborder Hungarian population which makes up 30–35 per cent of the current citizenry of Hungary (Vizi 2003).

17. Law 2000/379 offered Italian citizenship to descendants of the territories that were ceded to Italy by the post-First World-War treaties in case their ancestors emigrated from these territories before 1920, but did not extend this offer to the descendants of Italians in Dalmatia, Istria and Fiume, which were ceded from Italy to Yugoslavia by the postwar treaties.

References

Bauböck, R. (2004a) 'Citizenship and Political Integration' (Second Workshop on Global Migration Regimes, Stockholm, 11–12 June 2004.) (http://www.framtidsstudier.se/eng/globalMobReg/CitizenshipandPoliticalIntegration.pdf, [06.03.2005]).

Bauböck, R. (2004b) 'Western European Countries Tend to Follow a Liberalizing Trend towards Citizenship Policies'. Interview with Rainer Bauböck (http://www.migrationonline.cz/news_f.shtml?x=230291).

Bauer, T. (2004) 'Kettős Kapituláció' [Dual Capitulation]. *Népszabadság*, 1 August 2004.

Bíró, B. (2004) 'Nem jó, de haszos' [Not Good, but Useful]. *Népszabadság*, 12 August 2004.

Brubaker, R. (2000) 'Accidental Diasporas and External Homelands'. *Political Science Series*, 71, Institute for Advanced Studies, Vienna, October, 2000.

Csergő, Zs. and J. Goldgeier (2004) 'Nationalist Strategies and European Integration'. In Z. Kántor et al., eds, *The Hungarian Status Law: Nation Building and/or Minority Protection*. Hokaido University, *Slavic Eurasian Studies*, 4, October (http://src-h.slav.hokudai.ac.jp/coe21/publish/no4_ses/contents.html).

Debreczeni, J. (2004) 'Hazárdjáték' [Gambling]. *Népszabadság*, 27 November 2004 [05. 05. 2005].

De Groot, G. (2004) 'Towards a European Nationality Law'. *Electronic Journal of Comparative Law* 8 (http://www.ejcl.org/83/art83-4.html#N_54 [08.08.2005]).

Duray, M. (2000) 'Státustörvény, kettős állampolgárság vagy külhoni állampolgárság' [Status Law, Dual Citizenship or Trans-border Citizenship]. *Magyar Nemzet*, 18 November 2000.

Duray, M. (2004) 'Állampolgárság és nemzetpolgárság: a kettős vagy a többes állampolgárságról' [Citizenship and National Citizenship: On Dual or Multiple Citizenship] (http://www.aprilisiifjak.hu/index.php/?csz=31778,1May 2004 [25.11.2004]).

Fowler, B. (2002) 'Fuzzing Citizenship, Nationalising Political Space: A Framework for Interpreting the Hungarian "Status Law" as a New Form of Kin-state Policy in East-Central Europe'. Centre for Russian and East European Studies, European Research Institute, University of Birmingham, Working Paper 40/02. (www.one-europe.ac.uk/pdf/w40fowler.pdf, [22.02.2005]).

Györgyi, A. (2004) 'A mumusok és a kék madár, Mi történt? Miről beszél(t)ünk?' [Monsters and the Blue Bird, What Happened, What Did We Talk About?] *Regio*, 2004/4: 57.

'Határok nélkül' (Without Borders) (2003) *Kossuth Rádió*, 16 January 2003 (http://www.hhrf.org/hatnelk/4_030216kallampg.htm, [05. 05. 2005]).

Iordachi, C. (2004) 'Dual Citizenship and Policies Toward Kin Minorities in East-Central Europe: A Comparison Between Hungary, Romania and the Republic of Moldova'. In Z. Kántor et al., eds, *The Hungarian Status Law: Nation Building and/or Minority Protection* Hokaido University, *Slavic Eurasian Studies*, 4, October (http://src-.slav.hokudai.ac.jp/coe21/publish/no4_ses/contents.html [06.03.2005]).

Joppke, C. (2003) 'Citizenship Between De- and Re-Ethnicization'. (http://www.russellsage.org/publications/workingpapers/Citizenship%20between[18.07. 2005]).

Joppke, C. (2005) *Selecting by Origin, Ethnic Migration in the Liberal State.* Cambridge, MA and London, UK: Harvard University Press.

Kántor, Z. and M. Császár (2005) 'A státusztörvény hatása a határon túli magyarokra' [The Effect of the Status Law on Trans-border Hungarian]. Manuscript from author's files.

Kis, J. (2004a) 'Nemzetegyesítés vagy kisebbségvédelem' [Nation Unification or Minority Protection]. *Élet és Irodalom*, 48/51.

Kis, J. (2004b) 'Miért megyek el szavazni?' [Why am I Taking Part in the Voting?]. *Népszabadság*, 20 November 2004.

Kis, J. (2004c) 'The Status Law: Hungary at the Crossroads'. In Z. Kántor et al., eds, *The Hungarian Status Law: Nation Building and/or Minority Protection*. Hokaido University, *Slavic Eurasian Studies*, 4, October (http://src-h.slav.hokudai.ac.jp/coe21/publish/no4_ses/contents.html).

Kövér, L. (2004) 'Speech in Parliament'. 17 November 2004. (http://www.mkogy.hu/naplo37/187/187.htmnov.17).

Ostrow, A. P. (2002) 'Dual Resident Voting: Traditional Disenfranchisement and Prospects for Change'. *Columbia Law Review*, 102/7.

Schöpflin, G. (2004) 'Citizenship and Ethnicity: The Hungarian Status Law' In Z. Kántor et al., eds, *The Hungarian Status Law: Nation Building and/or Minority Protection*. Hokaido University, *Slavic Eurasian Studies*, 4, October (http://src-h.slav.hokudai.ac.jp/coe21/publish/no4_ses/contents.html).

Stewart, M. (2004) 'The Hungarian Status Law: A New European Form of Transnational Politics?' In Z. Kántor et al., eds, *The Hungarian Status Law: Nation Building and/or Minority Protection*. Hokaido University, *Slavic Eurasian Studies*, 4, October (http://src-h.slav.hokudai.ac.jp/coe21/publish/no4_ses/contents.html).

Tóth, J. (2004) 'Kettős állampolgárságot Népszavazással?' [Dual Citizenship by Referendum?]. *Fundamentum*, 2004/2.

Vink, M. (2001) 'The Limited Europeanization of Domestic Citizenship Policy: Evidence from the Netherlands'. *Journal of Common Market Studies*, December, 2001: 880.

Vizi, B. (2003) 'A határon túli olaszoktól a külföldön élő olasz állampolgárokig – az olasz állampolgárság kiterjesztése az ezredfordulón' (From Italians Living Abroad to Italian Citizens – the Extension of Italian Citizenship During the Milleneum). *Kisebbségkutatás*, 2003/4.

Documents and collections

'A kettős állampolgárságról – Adatok, állásfoglalások, elemzések' (2005) [On Dual Citizenship – Data, Opinions, Research] (http://www.martonaron.hu/ kettosallampolgarsag/nepszavazas_eredmenyek.html, [17.02.2005]).
'Az MVSZ nemet mond az EU-ra' (2003) Index, 03. 22. 2003. (http://index.hu/ politika/belhirek/?main:2003.03.22&123591 [09.09.2005]).
'Citizenship in Countries of Immigration: Australia, Canada, and the United States'. (1988) Conference on Comparative Citizenship, Carnegie Endowment for International Peace, 4 June 1988 (http://www.ciaonet.org/conf/cei06/ceip [11.07.2005]).
Council of Europe (1999) Recommendation 1410 (1999) 'Links Between Europeans Living Abroad and Their Countries of Origin' (Extract from the Official Gazette of the Council of Europe – May 1999) (http://assembly. coe.int/Documents/AdoptedText/TA99/EREC1410.HTM [07.05.2005]).
'Határon Túli Magyarok Hivatala' (2004) (http://www.htmh.hu/korszak.pdf [05.05.2005]).
'Hírösszefoglalónk' (2004) (News summary) *Népszabadság*, 7 December 2004: 7.
'Kettős állampolgárság kronológia' (2005) [Chronology of Dual Citizenship] (http:// www.martonaron.hu/kettosallampolgarsag/kronologia.html[17/02/2005]).
Law (2001) LXII. 'On the Hungarians in Neighbouring States' (http://www. kettosallampolgarsag.mtaki.hu/statusz/stv_04.html).
'Modernizációs és kortesduma' (2005) [Modernization and Electioneering], Report on the Speech by Viktor Orbán on Tusnád, 23. 07. 2005. (http://politika.transindex.ro/?cikk=3424 [23.07.2005]).
'Működik-e a külhoni állampolgárság?' (2005) [Does Trans-border Citizenship Work?] Transindex 29. 07. 2005. (http://belpol.transindex.ro/?hir=9000 [02.08.2005]).
'MTI' (2005) ugyelet@mail.index.hu, 04.08.2005. [09.09.2005].
Népességnyilvántartási füzetek (2004) (http://www.okmanyirodak.hu/fixhtml/ nepessegfuzet/2004/2004ertekeles.doc. [09.09.2005]).
'Paper Containing the Position of the Hungarian Government in Relation to the Act on Hungarians Living in Neighbouring Countries' (2001) (http://www.venice.coe.int/docs/2001/CDL(2001)080-e-asp [09.09.2005]).
'Patrubány újra szavaztatna' (2005) [Patrubány Suggests to Repeat the Referendum] *Népszabadság*, 14 February 2005.
'Tájékoztató a magyar állampolgárságról szóló 1993. évi LV., valamint a külföldiek beutazásáról és tartózkodásáról szóló 2001. évi XXXIX. törvényekben foglalt rendelkezések fontosabb változásairól' (2005) [Information on the Modification of Rules Relating to Law LV. of 1993 on Hungarian Citizenship and to Law XXXIX of 2001 Relating to the Entry and Residence of Foreigners in Hungary), Government Office for Hungarians Abroad (HTMH), (http://www.htmh.hu/?menuid=0605&news034_id=1857 [09.09.2005]).
'Válságban a hivatalos magyar nemzetpolitika' (2005) [Official Policies for Hungarian Nationhood are in a Crisis]. *Magyar Nemzet*, 16 September 2005.

'Venice Commission, Croatia' (2002) European Commission for Democracy Through Law_(Venice Commission), Consolidated Opinion, on the law on the election of members of the representative bodies of local and regional self-government units of Croatia, 12 March 2002. (http://www.venice.coe.int/docs/2002/CDL-AD(2002)003-e.asp. [18.07.2005]).

6
Migration and Transnational Citizenship in Latin America: The Cases of Mexico and the Dominican Republic

José Itzigsohn

States, citizenship and migration

In the modern world, nationality and citizenship, understood as membership in a political community, have been organised within nation-states. Non-members in the political community, or those who have left it, have normally been excluded from the full package of rights that define nationality and citizenship. The geographic and political boundaries of the states have been the defining units of peoplehood and full membership in the nation. Today, however, we are witnessing the blurring and the overlapping of nationality, citizenship rights and states. Large-scale migration is reshaping the boundaries of national belonging. States that until not so long ago treated their populations abroad with disdain are suddenly rethinking this relationship and reaching out to migrant populations. Dual nationality and dual citizenship are increasingly becoming global norms.

The cases of Mexico and the Dominican Republic illustrate this process of redrawing of the boundaries of national membership. During the 1990s, Mexico and the Dominican Republic went through drastic changes in their attitudes and policies towards their populations abroad. Until then, both countries had basically ignored their emigrants. Furthermore, those who naturalised in their new places of residence were stripped of their nationality of origin. All this changed radically during the 1990s. During that decade, both countries recognised the rights of migrants to hold dual nationality and to vote abroad. These changes marked a fundamental shift in the terms of inclusion in the nation and its political community. This chapter describes and analyses these changes.

In the last few decades, many countries in the Americas and Europe expanded their definitions of citizenship and granted dual nationality and voting rights to their populations abroad (Calderón Chelius 2003). In fact, it is necessary to differentiate between two related yet different elements in the process of redrawing of the boundaries of the nation. The first one is the granting of dual nationality, that is the right of migrants to keep their nationality of origin while they adopt the nationality of their place of residence. This is an issue where migrant demands and the interests of the country of origin often coincide. The second element is the granting of the citizenship rights attached to nationality—mainly, the right to vote—to people who do not reside within the territorial boundaries of the country. Migrants and states of origin do not necessarily see eye to eye regarding this issue.

Analysing how these processes unfolded in Latin America, Jones-Correa (2001) distinguishes between early and late adopters of dual nationality and between top-down and bottom-up processes of extension of citizenship rights. Correa argues that Mexico and the Dominican Republic, together with Colombia and Ecuador, are late adopters of dual nationality. According to Jones-Correa, in both cases the extension of citizenship rights was a bottom-up process.[1] I focus on Mexico and the Dominican Republic because the proportionally large size of their migrant communities makes them critical cases through which to investigate the processes of change in national belonging. My argument is that in these two cases the extension of the boundaries of nationality and citizenship has been a process shaped by both the interests of the state of origin and the activism of immigrant groups. Through the analysis of these two cases I intend to delineate the causes that led to the changes in the relationship between sending states and migrant populations and also to address tensions generated in the process of establishing this new form of national membership.

Global economic integration and international migration

Mexico and the Dominican Republic are among the largest senders of migrants to the United States. Mexican migration is, of course, larger, but relative to their domestic populations the size of the migrant populations of both countries is rather similar. Mexican migration goes back to the nineteenth century while Dominican migration is newer, having begun only in the 1960s. However, both countries experienced the rise of large-scale migration in the last two decades—about half of the Mexican-origin population in the United States arrived since the mid-1980s. In addition, there are interesting similarities in the ways in which the process of granting dual nationality and voting rights to migrants abroad took place in both these countries. In both cases, the redrawing of the boundaries of the nation and citizenship has resulted from a process of social, political and economic integration of the sending and receiving societies (Itzigsohn 2000a). In particular, this process is linked to the following three factors: first, the increasing importance of remittances both for the subsistence of increasingly larger numbers of households and for the national economy as a whole; second, a process of democratic opening that created a window of opportunity for migrant communities to intervene in debates concerning issues of citizenship; and third, the emergence of organised immigrant groups engaged in the politics of the country of origin.

The sharp change in the policies of the Mexican and Dominican states towards their migrant communities is rooted in the pattern of integration into the global economy that emerged in the last decades of the twentieth century. Until the early 1980s, the prevalent economic model followed by both countries was based on industrialisation directed towards the internal market, also known as import substitution industrialisation (ISI). The normative aspiration of that economic model was the universalisation of formal wage employment. During the middle decades of the twentieth century, Mexico and the Dominican Republic witnessed large-scale rural–urban migration to their main cities where manufacturing and public employment were concentrated. The inward-looking industrialisation model expanded formal employment but not fast enough to absorb the rural migrant population. The result was that large cities saw the emergence of large informal economies. At the same time, however, informal economies provided subsistence and mobility opportunities.

The 1980s brought a profound economic crisis that led the political and economic elites to search for a new model of insertion into the global economy. Mexico and the Dominican Republic—and Latin American countries in general—searched for a solution to the crisis of the import substitution model by promoting export activities and the opening of their economies to trade and foreign investment. In this way, the countries switched the focus of economic growth from expanding the internal market to a tighter integration with global markets. In the case of Mexico and the Dominican Republic this meant a closer integration of their economies with that of the United States, as their exports were oriented mainly towards this market. The process of economic integration with the North American economic region reached its peak when Mexico signed the North American Free Trade Agreement (NAFTA) and the Dominican Republic joined the Central American Trade Agreement (CAFTA).

The move towards an export-oriented model of growth yielded some of its expected results. The two countries saw periods of rapid economic growth and exports indeed multiplied. At the same time, and as the result of the same policies, the two countries witnessed the overall informalisation of domestic labour relations. Precarious forms of employment became predominant, even in the new leading economic sectors (Itzigsohn 2000b). The new model of economic growth does not provide enough opportunities for subsistence for all of the population. The presence of established Dominican and Mexican communities in the United States provided the networks that transformed economic and social exclusion into a process of mass migration. As a result, the new economic model created a new kind of export, namely workers, and a new kind of import, namely migrant remittances.

Tables 6.1a and 6.1b illustrate this situation. Both tables show the large growth of exports in the economies of the two countries. Since the 1980s, exports grew in absolute numbers and as a percentage of GDP. Yet, the tables also show the exponential growth of remittances during the same period.[2] The weight of remittances in the national economy is larger in the Dominican Republic than in Mexico, but even in the latter the money sent by migrants constitutes one of the largest sources of foreign income for the country.

Table 6.2 shows the steep rise in migration in the last two decades and particularly during the 1990s. This table, however, shows only the tip of the iceberg, because the numbers represent only legal migrants. Passel (2005) convincingly shows that during the 1990s the number of Mexican undocumented migrants to the United States was much larger than the number of documented migrants. He estimates that undocumented migration constituted 28 per cent of migration from Mexico during the 1985–1990 period. Since then, the proportion has risen exponentially. Undocumented migration constituted 70 per cent of total migration from Mexico in the 1990–1994 period, 80 per cent in the 1995–1999 period, and 85 per cent in the 2000–2004 period (Passel 2005). While there are no similar calculations of undocumented Dominican migrants, Passel (2005) shows that the source of undocumented migration was first Mexico and then Latin America in general. Hence we can be confident that the data in the table significantly

Table 6.1a Economic indicators for Mexico, 1980–2004

	1980	1985	1990	1995	2000	2004
GDP per capita (constant 2000 US$)	5,086	5,014	4,971	5,309	5,935	5,968
Exports of goods and services (current US$, millions)	20,859	28,487	48,866	87,053	180,219	203,414
Exports of goods and services as % of GDP	11	15	19	30	31	30
Workers' remittances (current US$, millions)	698	1,157	2,492	3,673	6,572	16,612
Workers' remittances as % of exports of goods and services	3.3	4.0	5.1	4.2	3.6	8.1

Source: World Bank, World Development Indicators (http://devdata.worldbank.org/dataonline/).

Table 6.1b Economic indicators for the Dominican Republic, 1980–2004

	1980	1985	1990	1995	2000	2004
GDP per capita (constant US$)	1,508	1,492	1,565	1,765	2,359	2,450
Exports of goods and services (current US$, millions)	1,271	1,420	2,392	3,893	8,870	9,269
Exports of goods and services as % of GDP	19	28	34	31	45	52[1]
Workers' remittances (current US$, millions)	183	242	315	794	1,689	2,266
Workers' remittances as % of exports of goods and services	14.4	17.0	13.2	20.4	19.0	24.4

[1] Data for 2003.
Source: World Bank, World Development Indicators (http://devdata.worldbank.org/dataonline/).

Table 6.2 Immigration by country of last residence, 1980–2004 (the numbers in parentheses represent the percentages of Mexican and Dominican migration out of total migration to the United States)

	Mexico	Dominican Republic	All countries
1961–1970	453,937 (13.6)	93,292 (2.8)	3,321,677
1971–1980	640,294 (14.2)	148,135 (3.2)	4,493,314
1981–1990	1,655,843 (22.5)	252,035 (3.4)	7,338,062
1991–2000	2,249,421 (24.7)	335,251 (3.6)	9,095,417
2001–2004	710,810 (18.8)	99,936 (2.6)	3,780,019

Source: Yearbook of Immigration Statistics, 2004, Table 2 (http://uscis.gov/graphics/shared/statistics/yearbook/YrBk04Im.htm).

underestimate the actual number of Dominicans who came to the United States during this period. Integration in the global economy results therefore in movements of capital, merchandise as well as people. Large-scale migration is an inherent part of globalisation. The two countries increasingly depend on remittances for access to hard currency, and low-income households within Mexico and the Dominican Republic depend on remittances for daily subsistence.

Remittances and dual nationality

The new social and economic links between the countries of origin and reception have forced the sending countries to rethink their relationship to their migrant populations. The continuation of the flow of remittances is now an explicit goal of economic policy. As a result, the two countries started to have a proactive policy towards their migrant communities. The paradoxical outcome of this situation is that the Mexican and Dominican Republic political leaders have become interested in the dual—and potentially contradictory—task of reinforcing the ties of migrants to the society and economy of the country of origin while at the same time encouraging them to incorporate in the society and politics of the United States. While there are differences in the policies of these two countries towards their migrant populations, there are also important commonalities: both states have started to reach out to migrant organisations abroad, and their consulates have worked to build ties with the migrant communities.

In the late 1980s the Mexican state began to reach out to the migrant communities in the United States. The Salinas administration (1988–1994) had the strategic goal of linking Mexico's economy with that of the United States through the signing of NAFTA. Salinas hoped to gain the support of migrant communities for this new trade agreement, which would entail a radical shift in the way Mexico related to the United States: a shift from a nationalist discourse to the embrace of globalisation (Calderón Chelius and Martinez Saldaña 2002). As part of this strategy, the Salinas administration created the Programa para las Comunidades Mexicanas en el Exterior (PCME—Program for the Mexican Communities Abroad), which was in charge of the promotion of Mexican cultural programmes abroad and developing coordination with home-town associations. The Salinas administration also created Solidaridad Internacional and the Programa Paisano. The former aimed to match the resources sent by migrants for local development projects, while the latter was meant to protect migrants travelling to Mexico from abuse by customs and police officers. The Zedillo administration (1994–2000) continued the PCME and Paisano programmes. Boggled by internal problems, however, it paid less attention to the migrant communities abroad than the Salinas administration. Nevertheless, it was during this administration that the crucial legal changes that are the concern of this chapter were enacted. The end of the long dominance of the *Partido Revolucionario Institucional* (Institutional Revolutionary Party, PRI) over Mexican politics brought more cooperation between the Mexican state and the Mexican migrants. In 2002, the Fox administration (2000–2006) created the Instituto para los Mexicanos en el Exterior (Institute for Mexicans Abroad, IME). This Institute coordinates the relationships between the Mexican government and the Mexican communities abroad. It is unique in having a consultative council composed of Mexican migrants. In this way, the Mexican government has incorporated representatives from migrant organisations abroad into an official government organisation.

The Dominican government did not go as far as Mexico in institutionalising its links with migrant communities but it did reach out to migrants and migrant organisations. During his first administration (1996–2000), Leonel Fernandez aimed to facilitate the investment of migrants in the Dominican Republic. The Fernandez government also played an active role in supporting the creation and activities of the Dominican American Round Table (DANR), an umbrella organisation of

Dominican-American groups in the United States. DANR works towards developing a Dominican-American political agenda with the goal of improving the social and economic position of Dominican-Americans in the United States. Dominican diplomatic and elected officials have been invited to and participated in the organisation's annual meetings, and the DANR elected officers have travelled to the Dominican Republic to meet with Dominican authorities. The DANR and the Dominican government share a common agenda in that both want to help immigrants achieve a more stable position in the United States: both aim to secure the legal status of migrants, to promote migrant citizenship and to reduce the number of people who are deported from the United States. These common interests have provided a basis for collaboration between the state and the Dominican migrant organisations abroad.

It is in this context, a political moment in which both the Dominican Republic and Mexico were reaching out to migrant communities, that the two countries enacted legal changes which granted their citizens the right to hold dual nationality and to vote abroad. Until the mid-1990s, in both countries, taking on a second nationality implied losing the nationality of the country of origin. However, in 1994 the Dominican Republic legislated that people could maintain Dominican nationality even if they became citizens of another country. Mexico did something similar in 1996, and went even further by allowing thousands of Mexicans who had naturalised in the United States to reclaim their Mexican citizenship. Dual nationality legislation has the purpose of allowing migrants to naturalise in the country of reception without losing their attachment to the country of origin. It is predicated on the notion that immigrants want to keep their nationality of origin and that allowing them to do so will facilitate their incorporation into the country of reception.

There are two reasons for the sudden interest of Mexico and the Dominican Republic in their migrants becoming American citizens. First, naturalisation creates stability in the lives of migrants (meaning that they will not be deported or will be less likely to return to their countries of origin). Sending states hope that stability will secure the flow of remittances. Second, naturalisation allows for political participation and, in an old tradition of migrant advocacy for issues concerning their countries, both Mexico and the Dominican Republic hope to affect US policy through the political participation of the Mexican and Dominican populations. For these reasons, Mexico and the Dominican Republic have broadened the bounds of their political community and provided a degree of flexibility to citizenship.

Table 6.3 Mexican and Dominican naturalisation 1991–2004

	1991–1995	1996–2000	2001–2004
Mexico	187,190	907,454	299,698
Dominican Republic	48,582	110,732	58,692
Total	1,785,167	3,834,706	2,182,268
Mexico and Dominican Republic as percentage of total naturalisations	13.2	26.5	16.4

Source: Yearbook of Immigration Statistics, 2004, Table 32 (http://uscis.gov/graphics/shared/statistics/yearbook/YrBk04Im.htm).

The 1990s indeed saw a high surge in naturalisation rates by Dominican and Mexican immigrants in the United States (see Table 6.3). In part, the surge was the result of timing: in the early 1990s, after completing the required 5 years of legal permanent resident status, people who had obtained legal residence through the 1986 Immigration Reform and Control Act of 1986 were able to naturalise. In part the surge was also a response to the anti-immigration climate of the 1990s, a hostility towards immigrants that was expressed in the passage of Proposition 187 in California, the legislation of the Personal Responsibility and Work Opportunity Reorganization Act (PRWORA), better known as welfare reform, and the Immigrant Responsibility and Reform Act (IRIRA) in 1996. Yet, there is evidence that the new laws of Mexico and the Dominican Republic, which granted the right of dual nationality, also contributed to the surge in naturalisations; in this sense, the strategy followed by the sending states was validated (Jones-Correa 2001; Mazzolari 2005).

Both Mexico and the Dominican Republic have found that migrant organisations have their own agendas. While these migrant agendas and those of political leaders in the home country sometimes coincide, they sometimes diverge in important ways. Migrant organisations have been lobbying their states of origin with their own demands. While states have an interest in keeping migrant's loyalty, they are less interested in hearing the voices and divergent demands of immigrants. At the same time, immigrants do not want only symbolic membership, they want to be heard.

Democratisation and dual citizenship

The granting of dual nationality was driven in part by state interests in the context of globalisation. Yet, this is only a partial picture.

The process was also driven by grassroots demands for inclusion and participation in the political life of the country of origin. A political opening in both countries, particularly the rise of competitive elections, facilitated this 'bottom-up' pressure, which ultimately led to the reconfiguration of national political boundaries. The consolidation of democracy created an opening for the contestation of existing limits on the political participation of immigrants in countries of reception. These debates created an incentive for political parties to search for a constituency among the large number of migrants abroad. At the same time, these new national debates created an opening for the voice of immigrant groups to be heard. The grassroots character of the process propelled it forward: migrants had a more comprehensive understanding of dual nationality than political actors in sending states. For migrant organisations, nationality included also the right to have a voice in the politics of the country of origin.

In both countries, the changes in citizenship laws took place amidst political crises that ended the hegemony of long-established political elites. During most of the twentieth century, Mexican politics was dominated by the PRI. In 2000, a non-PRI government was voted in for the first time in seven decades. Yet, the downfall of the PRI was a protracted process during which new political actors emerged. A key event in undermining PRI's hegemony was the 1988 elections. That year Carlos Salinas de Gortari beat Cahuautemoc Cardenas, the candidate of the *Partido de la Revolucion Democratica* (PRD—Democratic Revolution Party) and the son of the famous Lazaro Cardenas, the Mexican President from 1934 to 1940 and an iconic figure in Mexican—and PRI—history. The legitimacy of this election, however, was seriously challenged; as a result, the PRI was forced to begin opening up the political system.

Until 1988, Mexican national elections were a ritualistic exercise with predetermined results. That year, however, for the first time in several decades the election results were strongly contested and a serious challenge to the PRI rule emerged. From then on, the idea of beating the PRI in elections seemed achievable. The potential for a credible challenge to the ruling party led to the emergence of grassroots activism among migrant communities in the United States: the rise of electoral competition created a new constituency with its own demands. As a result, political parties began to campaign among migrant communities. Migrant activists in turn organised in order to place demands on the Mexican state, foremost among these the right to vote abroad. The PRI held office for two more periods after 1988, but the legitimacy of its rule rapidly disappeared.

The decay of PRI's hegemonic rule forced the Zedillo administration (1994–2000) to the negotiation table to establish the bases of an electoral reform and a new and legitimate political order. The new laws, which allowed migrants dual nationality and the right to vote while abroad, were the result of these political negotiations. In 1996 the Mexican congress passed a constitutional amendment establishing that Mexicans born in Mexico do not lose Mexican nationality if they take a second citizenship. The decision took effect in 1998, after it was ratified by the Mexican states. The Mexican congress also ruled to allow those Mexicans who had previously relinquished their nationality by naturalising abroad to recuperate their Mexican nationality by applying for it before 2003. Because so few people chose to exercise this right, the Mexican congress extended this provision even further by removing the time limits on the recuperation of Mexican nationality (Calderón Chelius 2003; Jones-Correa 2001).

In 1996, the Mexican congress also reformed the electoral law in ways that made it possible for migrants to vote abroad. The new law, however, only established the right of migrants living abroad to vote indirectly: the PRI had opposed the explicit recognition of migrants' voting rights. For this reason, the new law only stipulated that people were not required to vote in their place of residence. The specific ways in which voting was to take place was left for future study and regulation. This fact opened the door to a series of negotiations, manoeuvrings and political pressure by migrant organisations, which, after 10 years, ultimately led to the 2005 decision by the Mexican congress to allow migrants to vote in domestic presidential elections.

Calderón Chelius (2003) points to two important differences between the reform which allowed dual nationality and the decision allowing migrants to vote abroad. First, dual nationality legislation only matters to those Mexican immigrants for whom naturalisation in the United States is a legal option. Most notably, this option does not apply to undocumented migrants, who constitute the majority of recent migrants from Mexico to the United States. On the other hand, undocumented migrants can take advantage of the extension of the right to vote abroad. Second, the dual nationality legislation was initiated by the political parties and enjoyed the support of the state apparatus for the reasons described above. The right to vote abroad, on the other hand, was a grassroots demand that was opposed by important segments of the political system. In fact, the implementation of the right to vote abroad took 10 years of lobbying and activism by immigrant organisations in the United States. In the 2000 elections, migrants did not participate. These elections, however, marked the end of the PRI regime. The winning candidate, Vicente Fox, had before and after the election expressed his support for the right of migrants to vote abroad. Yet, only in the twilight of his administration and only due to the political pressure of migrant groups—a leverage given by the weight of remittances—was this right finally implemented.

The organisation of migrants in favour of the vote abroad started through the mobilisation of groups in support of the Cardenas candidacy in 1988. Initially, it was the organisation of the PRD in the United States that carried the demand for immigrant political rights. And it was the PRD that brought the topic of migrant political rights into the political negotiations in 1996. Yet, the PRD did not have the power to transform those legal changes into actual policies. It was the grass-roots organisation of migrant groups that swayed the Mexican congress and government (Calderón Chelius and Martinez Cossío 2003; Martinez Saldaña 2002).

Once it became clear to migrant organisations that the Zedillo government did not intend to implement the right to vote abroad, migrants mobilised to press the Mexican congress. Martinez Saldaña (2002) describes how in 1998 a coalition of migrant organisations was formed with the goal of achieving the right to vote in the 2000 elections. Starting that year, migrant organisations began sending delegations to talk with members of congress and government officers to demand the implementation of the vote abroad. The 2000 elections passed without participation of immigrant voters, but immigrants found in Vicente Fox a President friendly to their demands. Immigrant organisations stepped up their pressures, sending delegations and receiving ample press coverage as well as the support of academics and intellectuals. As the deadline for registration to vote in the 2006 elections approached, some migrant organisations started to talk of a remittances strike. In 2005, the Mexican congress finally approved the regulations that allow the Instituto Federal Electoral (IFE—Federal Electoral Institute) to implement the vote abroad.

The changes in the relationship between the Dominican state and the Dominican migrant community follow a pattern that parallels the Mexican case. Change in legislation came as a result of a political opening coupled with the pressure of migrant groups abroad. Since 1966, Dominican politics was dominated by Joaquin Balaguer. Balaguer became President in 1966, in elections that ended the long and contested political transition out of the Trujillo regime. Rafael Leonidas Trujillo had headed an authoritarian patrimonial regime since 1930—a regime in which Balaguer occupied numerous political offices, including a figurehead presidency. The killing of Trujillo in 1961 ended his dictatorship and initiated a 5-year period of political turmoil that included the American intervention of 1965. The election of Balaguer to the presidency launched a three-decade-long transition towards democracy (Hartlyn 1998).

The first 12 years of Balaguer rule—from 1966 to 1978, a period in which he was elected twice in fixed elections—were characterised by heavy repression of political oppositional forces. This period also marked the beginning of large-scale Dominican migration to the United States. Many members of the opposition found their way to exile in New York City, a move facilitated by the US administration's interest in alleviating political pressure in the island. In 1978, in the first truly contested elections since the start of Balaguer's regime, the *Partido Revolucionario Dominicano* (PRD—Dominican Revolutionary Party) gained the presidency. Yet, its 8 years of rule were marked by corruption and a deep economic crisis, and in 1986 Balaguer was reelected as a result of the fragmentation within the PRD. Balaguer was reelected again in 1990, despite allegations of fraud: Juan Bosch, the candidate of the oppositional Partido de la Liberación Dominicana (PLD—Dominican Liberation Party), challenged the legitimacy of the election results but did not mobilise the party base to demand transparency. In 1994, another dubious Balaguer victory led to a political crisis. This time the opposing candidate—the alleged losing candidate, PRD leader Jose Francisco Peña Gomez—called for mass mobilisations in order to stop Balaguer from stealing another election. The result was a crisis of legitimacy of Balaguer's political regime.

A political compromise quelled the crisis: Balaguer agreed to constitutionally forbid consecutive presidential reelections[3] and to hold new elections in 1996. In exchange, he served half of his term. As part of this compromise, the constitution was also changed to allow Dominicans to hold dual nationality. Migrants had made demands for such a right, and Dominican political parties had also been debating the issue. However, it was not until the political crisis of 1994 created a window of opportunity that the demand for dual nationality was taken seriously by the Dominican congress.

With the consolidation of competitive elections, the migrant communities in the United States have become a new constituency that politicians court for funding and political support. Dominican political parties, particularly those who opposed Balaguer, have had a lively presence in New York since the late 1960s and have long demanded recognition from their sister organisations in the Dominican Republic. After 1994, however, the US-based organisations of the Dominican political parties gained unprecendented strength. Dominican politicians operate under the assumption that the opinions of family members abroad—the family members who send remittances—can sway the opinion of voters on the island. Hence campaigning abroad and the party apparatuses abroad acquired sudden relevance. Moreover, party organisations abroad demanded with new vigour that their members be given candidacies for office and administrative appointments.[4]

In the 1996 elections Leonel Fernandez, the PLD candidate, was elected to the presidency for the first time.[5] Fernandez grew up in New York as a legal permanent resident. As such, he well understood the demands and aspirations of the migrant community in the United States. With the election of Fernandez, Dominican migrant organisations and political parties abroad were able to push through additional electoral reforms. In 1997, the Dominican congress legislated the right to vote abroad. Yet this legislation, as in the Mexican case, would have to wait a number of years before being implemented. Unlike the law which had assured migrants access to dual citizenship, the right to vote abroad met with opposition within the Dominican political system (Itzigsohn 2003).

The Dominican state had readily passed the dual nationality law, a law that served a major interest of the state—securing continuous flows of remittances—by renewing the attachment of migrants to their country of origin while allowing them to consolidate their position abroad. Providing migrants the right to vote abroad, on the other hand, posed a threat to the state's political elites. This right would create a new and large constituency that would not only reside beyond the borders of the country, but as such would also not be subjected to the clientelistic mechanisms that assured political control. For this reason, the Dominican state, like the Mexican state, stalled the implementation of the right to vote abroad as long as it could. Sending states may be able to facilitate migrants' return to or investment in the country of origin by providing consular services. However, living beyond the reach of state power and clientelistic cooptation, the migrant population is well positioned to contest the status quo and refuse to comply with state interests. For the state political elites, the unpredictability and autonomy of the migrant population was a reason to worry. Nevertheless, pressure from migrant organisations and party organisations abroad proved strong enough to force the political elites finally to put into practice the law which had legally enfranchised Dominican migrants.

The mobilisation of Dominican migrants for citizenship rights started earlier and was broader than that of Mexican migrants. A key difference was that Dominican migrants were instrumental in achieving both dual nationality and political rights. Guarnizo (1998) shows that already in the 1970s, successful Dominican transnational entrepreneurs in New York started demanding the recognition of dual nationality. They demanded dual nationality in order to be able to conduct their businesses easily both in New York and in the country of origin. At the same time, during the 1980s, organisations of migrants and migrant returnees held several conferences in New York and the Dominican Republic to demand both dual nationality and dual citizenship.

The Dominican political parties abroad also played a central role in these demands. They were an integral part of the initiatives mentioned above. Also, after 1996, once competitive elections were institutionalised and the right to vote legislated, the US organisations of the Dominican parties began to press the Dominican party organisations to come through with putting into practice the migrants' right to vote. As Dominican politicians toured the United States in search of financial and political support, party members greeted them with questions concerning the implementation of the right to vote abroad. Finally, 7 years of constant pressure by migrant organisations and political parties yielded results: Dominicans voted abroad for the first time in the 2004 elections.

In both Mexico and the Dominican Republic, migrant organisations successfully pressured the state into extending citizenship rights together with dual nationality. The sending states' interest in remittances provided the 'top-down' impetus for the expansion of the national political community. The economic importance of remittances, however, and the need of the sending states to ensure their continuous flow also provided the political leverage that ultimately allowed migrant organisations to make their 'bottom-up' demands for citizenship rights heard. Dominican and Mexican migrants who straddle multiple political communities embody a kind of transnational citizenship that characterises the lives of many under contemporary globalisation. The processes that enable transnational political membership, however, are not without contradictions and tensions.

Paradoxes of transnational citizenship

Granting dual nationality and citizenship rights to migrants in effect redraws the boundaries of the nation. During a historical moment of large-scale migration this reconfiguration of national communities creates paradoxes concerning the construction of identities and forms of national belonging. The first paradox is related to the potentially contradictory results—for the sending state—of granting dual nationality. Through this measure sending states aim on the one hand to increase the loyalty of immigrants towards the home country, and on the other hand to facilitate and promote migrants' incorporation into the country of reception. The state elites of the sending countries believe that once dual nationality is granted and immigrants are not afraid of losing their nationality of origin, they will naturalise and participate in the political process of the receiving country, while at the same time they will maintain their attachment—and their financial contribution—to their home country.

Indeed, there is some evidence that dual nationality does promote naturalisation in the United States: since the mid-1990s the rates of naturalisation for both Mexicans and Dominicans have gone up (Jones-Correa 2001; Mazzolari 2005). There is also evidence that migrant incorporation into US society, achieved by acquiring legal status and gaining access to economic resources, facilitates all forms of transnational engagement (Itzigsohn and Giorguli Saucedo 2002). Yet, at the same time there is evidence that migrants' incorporation into receiving countries, the achievement of economic and legal stability, and in particular family reunification lead to a decline in the sending of remittances, the opposite of what the governments of the sending countries aim to achieve (Suro 2003). Furthermore, the governments of the countries of origin hope that migrants will lobby for issues of interest to sending states. These states learn, however, that migrant groups often organise to make demands on the sending states themselves.

Key amongst the demands that migrant organisations place upon sending countries is the demand for the right to vote. Nevertheless, the response of the migrant populations once they have received this vigorously sought right presents a second paradox. Mexican and Dominican organisations in the United States engaged in many years of active campaigning and organising in order to obtain the right to vote. Yet, when it came time finally to exercise this right, very few people actually registered and voted.

Table 6.4 shows the levels of registration and voting in the last Dominican presidential elections for various locations abroad. The table clearly shows the low rates of participation in these elections. The reasons for the low participation rates are not clear. It may be that migrants did not trust that the counting of the overseas ballots will be

Table 6.4 Migrant Dominican vote in the 2004 presidential elections (the numbers in parentheses represent percentages)

	Registered	Voted	PRD	PLD
Boston	4,202	3,536	683	2,702
		(84.1)	(19.5)	(77.4)
Barcelona	2,989	1,336	231	970
		(44.7)	(17.3)	(72.9)
Madrid	5,944	2,913	485	2,264
		(49.0)	(16.6)	(77.7)
Miami	2,399	1,776	376	1,299
		(74.0)	(21.5)	(74.4)
Montreal	404	306	84	217
		(75.7)	(27.7)	(71.6)
New Jersey	6,418	4,502	993	3,283
		(70.1)	(22.3)	(73.9)
New York	24,343	16,608	3,511	12,061
		(68.2)	(21.4)	(73.6)
Orlando	282	191	45	140
		(67.7)	(23.6)	(73.6)
Puerto Rico	4,622	3,300	563	2,576
		(71.4)	(17.4)	(79.8)
Tampa	261	205	53	139
		(78.5)	(26.1)	(68.4)
Venezuela	576	369	111	247
		(64.1)	(31.7)	(66.9)
Total Migrant Vote[1]	52,440	35,042	7,135	25.898
		(66.8)	(20.3)	(73.9)
Total National Vote	5,020,703	3,656,850	1,215,928	2,063,871
		(72.8)	(33.6)	(57.1)

[1] In the case of the Total Migrant Vote the PRD and PLD percentages were calculated by the author using the number of the total people who voted. In the rest of the table, the percentages of PRD and PLD vote are given by the Junta Central Electoral and were calculated using the valid votes. So the actual percentages of the vote for the PRD and PLD should be slightly higher but not much as the percentage of valid votes abroad was consistently higher than 95 per cent of the total vote.
Source: Junta Central Electoral. *Boletín Nacional Electoral* 10 (www.jce.do/Boletines 2004/Boletines/B10.html).

clean and transparent. Such concerns had been voiced prior to the last Dominican elections and may have discouraged people from voting: many migrants feared that the widely distrusted government of Hipolito Mejia would manipulate the votes cast from abroad to shore up its numbers regardless of the actual vote. Such fears were rooted in their experience of Mejia's ruthless political machinations, which had forced a change in the constitution with the sole purpose of allowing Mejia to run for consecutive reelection. It should be remembered that after the long years of Balaguer's political domination, Dominicans were weary of allowing the consecutive reelection of the President, and they were therefore distrustful of Mejia's intentions. In fact, the 2004 elections were clean, perhaps only because the victory of Leonel Fernandez was so decisive that only massive fraud would have changed the actual results. Fernandez won in the first of a two-round election, and despite any fears of vote fraud, the counting of votes cast abroad proved to be transparent. In fact, as the table shows, the migrant community vote went predominantly to the opposition candidate, following the pattern of the national vote, but with even larger proportions supporting Fernandez.

In the Mexican case, the number of people who have registered to vote abroad is also very low: only around 50,000 out of an eligible population of several million people. There are a number of possible explanations for this low rate of participation. First, the right to vote abroad as it is currently implemented still excludes many Mexicans residing in the United States. This is so because only those who have an electoral credential—a document that can be acquired only in Mexico, not in the consulates abroad—are allowed to vote in the elections. This is without a doubt a limitation, but still registration could be higher and, indeed, existing surveys indicate that most Mexicans in the United States want to vote in the Mexican elections (Suro 2005). Nevertheless, while the desire to vote may be widespread, it may be mitigated by the hassles that come with the actual registration and voting process. For example, another survey of potential voters found that people were indeed interested in voting abroad, but only if the registration process and the actual voting did not take much time or effort (Espinoza Valle 2004). It is not clear whether the method chosen for registration and voting abroad meets this criterion. Whereas Dominican elections were conducted in Dominican consulates, the Mexican authorities chose a method similar to the United States's mail-in ballot that allows absentee voting in US elections: people send their registration application to the Instituto Federal Electoral (IFE—Federal Electoral Institute), the institution that organises and supervises Mexican elections. If their registration is accepted, migrants receive a ballot by mail that they have to post before the election day.

In the case of both Mexico and the Dominican Republic, migrant organisations engaged in a long struggle ultimately to achieve a major change in terms of the political rights of migrants vis-à-vis the country of origin, only to see that most migrants did not take advantage of these victories when the time came to vote. Whether migrants did not vote in large numbers simply because it was the first time elections had been conducted abroad remains to be seen. It may also be the case that the right to vote abroad is a demand felt much stronger by activists than the community in general, which focuses its energy on carving a place in the country of reception. Only time will tell if the exercise of transnational political rights captures the imagination of large numbers of people in the migrant communities.

A third paradox is that the emergence of transnational citizenship is taking place in the context of increasingly strong nativist sentiments in the United States. Since 11 September 2001, immigrants have been marked as criminal suspects or potential terrorists. Recently, Samuel Huntington (2004) identified Mexican migration as a threat to American national identity in general. While Huntington's argument lacks any solid empirical base and its logic is deeply flawed, his work reflects the thinking of important sectors of the US policy-making establishment. During the writing of this chapter (May 2006), we are witnessing mass mobilisation of immigrant groups being met by intense lobbying against the legalisation of undocumented migrants. At the same time, different immigration reform proposals are being discussed in the US Congress. The outcome of these political confrontations is by no means clear. We can be sure, however, that regardless of which type of immigration legislation Congress approves, the debate over immigration will not end. The outcome of the current debates about immigration policies will certainly affect the future of transnational politics. Dual nationality and the right to vote have not yet become hot issues in the US public arena. For the time being, it is the large presence of undocumented migrants that has captured the attention of the American public. Nevertheless, public opposition to transnational citizenship may in fact be looming: there is no telling when such a debate might also erupt.

A final paradox concerns the imagining of the nation. In a period of increasing recognition of the multiethnic and multicultural character of nations, the granting of dual nationality and citizenship rights to migrants implies that the sending states are moving from a territorial basis of state membership to a diasporic understanding of the nation—from *jus solis* to *jus sanguinis*—as the basis for granting membership. This is a process that is taking place worldwide, but its causes and mechanisms differ from location to location. In Mexico and the Dominican Republic dual nationality and citizenship resulted from the combination of a certain pattern of insertion in the global economy, coupled with mass migration and the consolidation of competitive elections. In Italy and Spain, on the other hand, the expansion of the boundaries of the nation took place in countries with economies that are not dependent on remittances and with an apparent absence of political mobilisation by immigrants. In the case of Italy, the move to include the Italian diaspora in the political community was a response to the challenges of immigration and multiculturalism (Joppke 2003). Furthermore, despite the fact that the expansion of citizenship rights in Spain and Italy proceeded in a 'top-down' manner, the process has gone further than in Mexico and the Dominican Republic in that it allows people to vote in more than just the presidential elections. In the 2005 regional elections in Galicia, Spain, the composition of the autonomous regional government was decided by votes from abroad. Italy has recently legislated representation in the senate for Italians abroad, and migrant representatives gave the majority in the senate to the centre–left coalition in the 2006 national elections. In the case of Mexico and the Dominican Republic, the process has been much more contested and the results more limited. There is no official congressional representation for the migrant communities—although migrants have been elected to parliament through their inclusion in electoral lists as representatives of localities in the country of origin. It is precisely the grassroots-based impetus for broadening nationality and citizenship in Mexico and the Dominican Republic that has led the political elites of these sending states to try to limit the scope of citizenship rights for migrants.

The redrawing of the boundaries of the nation is predicated on the transnationalisation of social and economic life. In order to subsist, households have to send family members abroad. Jobs in the sending countries are not available or do not provide access to the standards of living that people expect. The result is that the horizons of meaning for people in sending countries include international migration as a life choice. Migration has been part of the lived experience of Mexicans and Dominicans since both countries started the drive towards modernisation and industrialisation. During the early industrialisation period, however, both countries went through large-scale processes of internal migration, from the countryside to the city. In contemporary circumstances of globalisation, migration continues but it goes from the rural and urban areas of the two countries to the cities of the United States.[6] International migration has become an integral part of people's lives in an economic and social system that binds sending and receiving societies together.

This does not mean that states do not matter anymore, that frontiers are no longer relevant or that a person's place of residence is not important. The fact that many thousands of people from poorer countries risk their lives to gain entry into richer countries, and that people in richer countries mobilise to stop them from doing so, points to the continuing relevance of borders. State boundaries are indeed relevant, but important aspects of the lives of people in sending and receiving societies are not contained within the boundaries of the state of origin or the state of residence. The redrawing of the boundaries of nation and citizenship results from the reshaping of the boundaries of the economic and social practices of subsistence and mobility. Yet, the actual working of transnational citizenship is a paradoxical and contradictory process, and its shape and future are by no means set.

Notes

1. Bottom–up processes are those that are initiated by the action of organised migrant groups, top–down processes are initiated by the state. According to Jones-Correa (2001), the early adopters of dual nationality were Uruguay, Panama, Peru and El Salvador. The late adopters, in addition to Mexico and the Dominican Republic, were Costa Rica, Brazil, Colombia and Ecuador.
2. The exact amount of remittances and their correct measurement is a subject of intense debate (Lozano Ascencio 2004; Suro 2003). The numbers presented here are taken from the World Bank's World Tables. The numbers may suffer from measurement error but the important fact is the growing importance of remittances as a source of foreign currency. The assumption is that whatever measurement error is there, it is the same for all the years for which data is presented.
3. This was changed again during the Hipolito Mejia administration (2000–2004) to allow Mejia to run for a second consecutive term.
4. Since there is no official mechanism of representation of communities abroad—a mechanism that exists in other cases such as Colombia, Cape Verde and now Italy—migrant party members were included in lists of candidates for office in Dominican electoral districts.
5. At the time of the writing of this chapter, the spring of 2006, Leonel Fernandez was again President of the Dominican Republic, after being elected for a second non-consecutive term in 2004.
6. There is also an important migration flow from the Dominican Republic to Europe, particularly to Spain, but it does not reach the scale of US-bounded migration.

References

Calderón Chelius, L., ed. (2003) *Votar en la Distancia*. Mexico, DF: Instituto Mora.
Calderón Chelius, L. and J. Martinez Saldaña (2002) *La Dimensión Política de la Migración Mexicana*. Mexico, DF: Instituto Mora.
Calderón Chelius, L. and N. Martinez Cossío (2003) ' "La democracia incompleta": La lucha de los mexicanos por el voto en el exterior'. In L. Calderón Chelius, ed., *Votar en la Distancia* Mexico, DF: Instituto Mora, pp. 217–67.

Espinoza Valle, V. A. (2004) *El Voto Lejano: Cultura Política y Migración México-Estados Unidos*. México: El Colegio de la Frontera Norte.

Guarnizo, L. (1998) 'The Rise of Transnational Social Formations: Mexican and Dominican State Responses to Transnational Migration'. *Political Power and Social Theory* 12: 45–94.

Hartlyn, J. (1998) *The Struggle for Democratic Politics in the Dominican Republic*. Chapel Hill, NC: The University of North Carolina Press.

Huntington Samuel, P. (2004) *Who are We? The Challenges to America's National Identity*. New York: Simon and Schuster.

Itzigsohn, J. (2000a) 'Immigration and the Boundaries of Citizenship: The Institutions of Immigrant Transnationalism'. *International Migration Review* 34, 4: 1126–54.

Itzigsohn, J. (2000b) *Developing Poverty*. University Park, PA: Penn State Press.

Itzigsohn, J. (2003) 'La migración y los límites de la ciudadanía: el voto de los Dominicanos en el exterior'. In L. Calderón Chelius, ed., *Votar en la Distancia*, Mexico, DF: Instituto Mora, pp. 268–88.

Itzigsohn, J. and S. Giorguli Saucedo (2002) 'Immigrant Incorporation and Sociocultural Transnationalism'. *International Migration Review* 36, 3: 766–98.

Jones-Correa, M. (2001) 'Under Two Flags: Dual Nationality in Latin America and Its Consequences for Naturalization in the United States'. *International Migration Review* 35, 4: 997–1029.

Joppke, C. (2003) 'Citizenship between De- and Re- Ethnicization'. *European Journal of Sociology* 44, 3: 429–58.

Lozano Ascencio, F. (2004) 'Tendencias recientes de las remesas de los migrantes mexicanos en Estados Unidos'. Working Paper 99. San Diego, CA: Center for Comparative Immigration Studies, University of California.

Martinez Saldaña, J. (2002) 'Participación Política Migrante: Praxis Cotidiana de Ciudadanos Excluidos'. In Leticia Calderón Chelius and Jesús Martinez Saldaña, eds, *La Dimensión Política de la Migración Mexicana*. Mexico, DF: Instituto Mora, pp. 159–330.

Mazzolari, F. (2005) 'Determinants of Naturalization: The Role of Dual Citizenship Laws'. Working Paper 117. San Diego, CA: Center for Comparative Immigration Studies, University of California.

Passel, J. S. (2005) 'Estimates of the Size and Characteristics of the Undocumented Population'. Washington, DC: Pew Hispanic Center Report.

Suro, R. (2003) 'Remittance Senders and Receivers: Tracking the Transnational Channels'. Washington, DC: Multilateral Investment Fund and Pew Hispanic Center.

Suro, R. (2005) 'Attitudes about Voting in Mexican Elections and Ties to Mexico'. Washington, DC: Pew Hispanic Center Report.

7
Varying Views on Democracy, Rights and Duties, and Membership: The Politics of Dual Citizenship in European Immigration States

Jürgen Gerdes and Thomas Faist

Introduction

In spite of a general trend towards increasing tolerance of dual citizenship, we can still observe considerable differences between immigration states in the stance they take on the issue as reflected in the spective rules of citizenship law subject to recent reforms. This chapter seeks to answer the question as to which factors account for these differences in citizenship law reforms. To do so, we investigated the policy processes in comparative perspective. We selected three European immigration states where in recent years comprehensive citizenship law reforms took place but which at the same time provided for very different policy outcomes with regard to the regulation of dual citizenship. The three countries selected for comparative analysis—Germany, the Netherlands and Sweden—have at present varying policies on dual citizenship and can be classified accordingly on a continuous scale ranging from restrictive to open. The relevant criteria are, first, whether or not dual citizens by birth are obliged to choose one citizenship on reaching maturity; second, whether renunciation of previous citizenship upon naturalisation is required; and, third, whether or not there is automatic loss of citizenship upon naturalisation in another country. On these criteria, Germany is the most restrictive case while the Netherlands is more tolerant, and Sweden is the most liberal regime since 2001. Although a comparatively generous *jus soli* clause was introduced in Germany, the principle of avoiding dual citizenship is *de jure* adhered to strictly.

The individuals in question must, by the end of their twenty-third year, opt for one or the other citizenship, or else be deprived of their German citizenship. With some exceptions, German citizenship is usually lost when another citizenship is acquired. The Netherlands has been, overall, somewhat more tolerant. Briefly during the early 1990s, dual citizenship there was tolerated upon naturalisation without exception, but relinquishment of the prior citizenship is now once again generally mandatory since 1997. By comparison with Germany, however, there are much more extensive exemption clauses. In Sweden, the recent legislative reform tolerates dual citizenship in general, that is for immigrants and emigrants simultaneously.

On the basis of a comprehensive analysis of the political debates and processes, we argue, in essence, that different belief systems and the related arguments of the relevant political actors should be taken into account in explaining variations in citizenship politics and policies and, consequently, the rules justified and adopted with regard to dual citizenship. However, as we will contend in the next section, we consider the most prominent approach with regard to political belief systems, which emphasises the different understandings of nationhood in civil-republican vs ethno-cultural terms, to be outdated, mainly because it contradicts the basic legitimising principles of liberal democracies. Instead, the arguments on dual citizenship which were raised in the countries under investigation, as outlined in the following section, account for different beliefs of the relevant political actors who interpret and weigh the constitutive elements of citizenship—democracy, rights and duties, and membership—in distinct ways. In the subsequent section we describe briefly how the prevailing discourses in the three countries of research were framed and supported within country-specific institutional opportunity structures. Finally, we conclude that arguments against dual citizenship should be seen in relation to broader tendencies to make citizenship conditional on the assumption of certain duties by immigrants, whereas arguments in favour of dual citizenship emphasise individual rights.[1]

Discursive opportunity structures

Citizenship legislation is of symbolic significance because it opens up fundamental questions about the collective identity of a political community. It is therefore necessary to analyse the politics of citizenship law with regard to the underlying belief systems[2] dominant in different nation-states and held by different political actors. Especially with regard to citizenship politics and policies, it is insufficient to enquire simply who benefits and who loses from a particular policy.[3] The most influential approach in migration research in which belief systems about collective identity are analysed is that which refers to the different understandings of nationhood as a decisive explaining factor of the respective legal rules and conditions for acquisition of citizenship:

> Citizenship in a nation-state is inevitably bound up with nationhood and national identity, membership of the state with membership of the nation. Proposals to redefine the legal criteria of citizenship raise large and ideologically charged questions of nationhood and national belonging.... The politics of citizenship today is first and foremost a politics of nationhood. (Brubaker 1992: 182)

Specifically, a civic-republican understanding of nation-state would lead to more inclusive measures of immigrant integration, while a more ethnically and culturally defined concept of nation-state would tend to be much more exclusive regarding immigrants. On the level of the individual, republican membership is a question of subjective will and of individual readiness for affiliation and loyalty to state and nation. On the level of the political community, inclusion of all permanent residents who are subjected to valid laws into the nation and thus into citizenship is seen as a crucial precondition for public mindedness. By contrast, an ethnic understanding of nation-state emphasises the objective belonging to the cultural and linguistic community, and political membership is acquired predominantly by descent. Accordingly, access to citizenship in ethnic nation-states is often differentiated according to ethnic origin and assumed cultural proximity, whereas it is open under the same conditions and equally for all kinds of immigrants in republican nation-states (see Brubaker 1992; Castles and Miller 1993).

This approach, however, depends upon a long-term historical perspective, and cannot account for relative short-term and far-reaching changes of citizenship politics and policies. From opposite directions, both Germany and the Netherlands are cases in point. In Germany, at least the introduction of *jus soli* for the second generation is a radical departure from an allegedly ethnic understanding of nationhood. Meanwhile in the Netherlands, which until only a few years ago was presented as an example entirely contrary to the model of ethno-cultural Germany (Koopmans 1999), arguments were raised similar to those heard in Germany justifying restrictive rules of citizenship acquisition.[4]

In our view, two kinds of conceptual vagueness lie at the root of applying the concept of nationhood, leading to considerable confusion. First, there is an implicit and general equation, on the one hand, between the civic-republican concept and liberal rules of citizenship acquisition and, on the other hand, correspondingly, between the ethno-cultural understanding and restrictive rules of citizenship acquisition. In Germany, a recent interpretation with respect to dual citizenship applying this logic derives the alleged ethno-cultural understanding of nation-state quite simply from the outcome of citizenship law and its consequences. Because of the relatively stagnant and comparatively low naturalisation rates after the recent reform in the year 2000, it should be concluded that the ethno-cultural nation-state still prevailed: 'For Germany to have truly departed from the ethno-cultural path, its citizenship policy would have needed to achieve a demonstrable increase in naturalisations' (Green 2005: 945). Then, in a kind of *petitio principii*-consideration, it is suggested that at least the intentions of those opposing dual citizenship are governed by an ethno-cultural understanding. The tolerance of dual citizenship, because it would make naturalisation more attractive to non-nationals, 'is unlikely to be supported by those political interests who feel that German national and cultural identities need to be defended' (Green 2005: 943). Such a perspective precludes from the outset, however, that restrictive rules of citizenship law in Germany might be caused by anything other than a still prevailing ethno-cultural understanding of nation-state.

Second, the concept of nation approach not only equates restrictive citizenship policies with an alleged ethno-cultural nation-state, but further assumes, at least implicitly, that the restrictive rules contain criteria of illegitimate discrimination based on ascriptive group distinctions such as race, ethnicity and national origin. This further equation between exclusion and discrimination, however, is in contradiction to the increasing importance of individual human rights and related anti-discrimination norms, essentially defined as excluding consideration of ascriptive features such as gender, descent, religion, ethnicity or national origin. The subsequent implementation of human rights norms in the admission policies of liberal democratic states in the post-Second World War period also led to a replacement of ascriptive and collective modes of exclusion by formal and individualist rules of exclusion (Joppke 2005). While historically during the nation-building process immigration and citizenship rules served partly to (re)produce ethnically and culturally homogenous populations by selecting newcomers according to ethnic and national origin, today's inclusion and exclusion rules of nation-states are based either on immigrants' claims which are considered legitimate, such as asylum or family unification, or on acquired capacities and skills of immigrants which are viewed to be beneficial to the immigration state. These rules, whether restrictive or liberal, are applied for the most part irrespective of group affiliation of immigrants, at least in explicit terms.

Thus, when looking for the crucial belief systems that make sense of the different arguments relating to dual citizenship, instead of departing from the dominant understandings of nation-state it seems more useful to turn to the normative implications which the concept of citizenship itself comprises and how these are interpreted in different countries and by various actors, corresponding with the shared self-understandings and legitimising principles of modern liberal democracies themselves. Apart from deep-rooted historical and particular national traditions of interpretation, the basic legitimising principles of democratic liberal states are a matter of collective self-determination of sovereign states and individual human rights (Habermas 1992). Although the right of the nation-state to control the boundaries of its territory and to determine the rules of access is widely accepted (Weiner 1996), human rights interpretations by various actors constitute the limits of control of these state actions, based on both national constitutions (Joppke 1999) and international treaties (Soysal 1994). This basic tension between two, in certain respects opposing, legitimising principles has been termed a 'liberal paradox' (Hollifield 1992) or a 'paradox of demo-cratic legitimacy' (Benhabib 2004). On the one hand, the principle of collective self-determination of existing nation-states includes the control of the territorial borders and the regulation of access condi-tions for newcomers. The principle of individual human rights, on the other hand, signifies legitimate demands and individual rights of potential or actual immigrants to claim for reception, inclusion and membership. A number of developments in international law illus-trate an increasing trend towards recognition of citizenship as a human right (see, for example, Chan 1991; Orentlicher 1998), most notably the European Convention on Nationality of 1997, which provides that each state 'shall provide in its internal law for the possibility of natur-alization of persons lawfully and habitually resident on its territory'.[5] Thus, the conviction that citizenship, as Hannah Arendt once put it, is the most basic human right because it is 'the right to have rights' by being a member of a political community which is able to guar-antee these rights at all (Arendt 1981) is the one that now seems to be widely shared.

We should therefore also expect that the relevant national political actors in democratic states, when debating issues of citizenship law reform, recognise the normative implications of the very concept itself. Instead of assuming that national political elites represent the traditional ideas and interests of a particular and ethno-cultural homogenous nation-state *as opposed to* the institutional embedded universal principles of democracy and individual rights (cf. Kurthen 1995), the following analysis of dual citizenship politics demonstrates that the different views on citizenship stem from varying interpretations of these universal principles and their inherent tensions in an imperfect world of separated nation-states.[6]

Democracy, rights and duties and membership

In essence, citizenship comprises three important dimensions: the democratic self-determination of the people, equal individual rights and obligations, and membership in a political community. Most of the arguments in favour of or against dual citizenship refer to one or more of these dimensions of citizenship. Nevertheless, the interpretations about the relative weight, the concrete content and the interrelationship of each element differ considerably between the opposing views on dual citizenship.

In the first dimension citizenship means the principle of unity of those governing and those being governed, whatever forms the democratic procedures of each state may take in detail. Ideally, citizens endowed with equal political liberty obey the laws in the creation of which they have participated and to whose validity they thus consent (Walzer 1989). Without democratic procedures guiding citizens' political self-determination, citizenship would mean little more than members of political communities being subjects of a sovereign. The second dimension of citizenship refers to the constitutions of modern states which enshrine human and fundamental rights of liberty as a legal status. In general, citizens' rights fall into various realms; for example, civil or negative rights to liberty, political rights to participation such as the right to vote and to associate, and social rights including the right to social benefits in case of sickness, unemployment or old age, as well as the right to education (Marshall 1964). The duties of citizenship include, in the external sphere, the duty to serve in the armed forces to protect state sovereignty against exterior threats and, in the internal sphere, the duty to pay taxes, to acknowledge the rights and liberties of other citizens and to accept democratically legitimated decisions of majorities.

In a third dimension, citizenship rests on an affinity of citizens with certain political communities, the partial identification with and thus loyalty to a self-governing collective, often a nation or a multi-nation (see Weber 1972: 242–44). In modern national states, citizens, otherwise anonymous to each other, identify with a self-governing collective which claims to establish a balance between individual and common interests on the one hand and rights and responsibilities within the political community on the other. Solidarity and reciprocity are deemed a requirement for peaceful coexistence and welfare state redistribution.

Still, liberal democracies have to cope with a principled tension between the will of the majority and a commitment to the individual rights of persons, or more concretely with the potential contradiction between the pursuit of collective goals, requested by the majority of citizens, and the individual freedom of the citizen. This basic tension between democracy and individual rights is nowhere more present than in migration issues, because the constitutions of liberal democratic states are committed to universal human rights including immigrants' rights, yet democratic participation in the life of the state is usually confined to citizens who are members of the nation-state. It comes as no surprise, then, that political actors take different views about which and to what extent claims of access to territory and membership ought to be considered either a matter of state discretion or an issue of human rights. Dual citizenship is a contested issue in this respect as well. Furthermore, with regard to the third dimension of citizenship, there are important differences between the respective beliefs of different political actors regarding the origin, the kind and the degree of homogeneity and internal cohesiveness of political communities and how they ought to be reproduced, especially in terms of societal or political factors.

Democracy

In all three immigration countries considered here, dual citizenship figured in debates on the validity and extension of democratic principles. Those political actors advocating tolerance of dual citizenship viewed facilitated naturalisation as an alternative to expanding the franchise to non-citizens. In Sweden, the Social Democrats proposed in the early 1980s extending the franchise to denizens at the regional and national level, thus going one step beyond local voting rights for permanent residents, which had been introduced in 1975. Because of strong opposition from the Centre-Right parties, the Social Democrats then moved to dual citizenship as an alternative, and struck the first Commission on the subject in 1985, leading, in a process that took 15 years, to the

eventual acceptance of dual citizenship. The origin of increased tolerance in the Netherlands bears great similarity to the Swedish case in
the early stages. Equal rights proponents also pushed for permanent
residents' voting rights, and here also dual citizenship was developed as
an alternative. The Social Democratic (PdvA) and Christian Democratic
(CDA) coalition then reached a compromise in 1991 to scrap renunciation as a prerequisite for naturalisation. While the PdvA withdrew its
plans for voting rights for non-citizen residents on the national level
and dropped its plans for specific anti-discrimination laws, the CDA,
in return, gave up its opposition to dual citizenship. But the political
consensus backing increased tolerance broke up in 1997 when dual
citizenship within the context of general issues of immigrant integration became an increasingly contentious subject in public debate.
In Germany, local voting rights likewise served as a stepping stone
in the debates on dual citizenship. Regional governments headed by
SPD proposed extending local voting rights to non-citizen permanent
residents in 1989, following the Swedish and Dutch examples. Yet,
when the states of Hamburg and Schleswig-Holstein tried to implement the measure, the Federal Constitutional Court rejected the move,
arguing that only citizens can be granted the franchise. Nonetheless,
the proponents of dual citizenship felt the Court had given them
strong support because it explicitly accepted the underlying claim of
the need to reduce the gap between those who are subject to the law
and those who are entitled to full democratic participation, arguing that
this principle corresponds exactly to the ideas of freedom and democracy. While under valid constitutional law the Court considered alien
voting rights unconstitutional, it affirmed at the same time that political
integration of immigrants could be enhanced by changing the citizenship law and easing naturalisation requirements for permanent resident
immigrants.

Throughout the debates, proponents of dual citizenship tied the issue
to democracy and argued that for reasons of democratic legitimation
immigrants after a reasonable period of stay should enjoy full rights
of political participation. In Germany, some dual citizenship advocates
even referred to the famous 'no taxation without representation' claim
of the American Revolution by arguing that those who for years have
been fulfilling their duties as workers and as tax payers have a legitimate
claim to the full range of participation rights connected to citizenship
status.

But the opponents of general tolerance of dual citizenship tied many
of their arguments to democracy, too. When in Sweden in the second

half of the 1980s and in the late 1990s citizenship law commissions were appointed to investigate the issue, it was the potential violation of the principle of 'one person, one vote' that was regarded as the most important and principled problem of dual citizenship. A common argument among the conservative and Christian Democratic parties in all three countries was that immigrants must be asked to make a reasonable choice between one or the other citizenship. Only if such a choice was made, in the form of renouncing the previous citizenship, could sufficient commitment and loyalty to the political community be expected. In Sweden, the opposing parties argued that such a choice shows that the applicant is prepared to take citizenship seriously and understands and accepts its consequences. In Germany, one of the most important arguments raised consistently by the Christian Democrats (CDU/CSU) was that renunciation of previous citizenship is the central proof of authentic willingness to identify with the new state and society on the immigrants' part and hence can serve as a sort of loyalty oath. In the Netherlands, the growing opposition to dual nationality from the mid-1990s onwards was justified by contending that the temporary abolishment of the renunciation requirement had made naturalisation into a mere 'paper' formality without expressing sufficient connections to the country. The threat of potential 'citizenship shopping' likely to result from allowing dual citizenship was a central image expressed within the opponents' beliefs in Sweden and in Germany. The conviction behind this claim was that dual citizenship finally means devaluing citizenship by undermining the very specific connection between the individual and the state which should not be confused with membership in voluntary associations in civil society, where exit and entry is predominantly a matter of utilitarian calculations. In Germany, the opposing CDU/CSU were also able to connect the claim that dual citizenship contradicts the very 'essence of citizenship' (*Wesen der Staatsangehörigkeit*) with legal arguments. They pointed repeatedly to statements of the Constitutional Court which defined citizenship as a 'comprehensive legal relationship from which certain rights and duties emerge'. Unlike in Sweden, this argument based on the devaluing of citizenship took a particular twist in Germany and in the Netherlands, where the threat to escape from duties and responsibilities tied to citizenship was emphasised if one has another citizenship as an opportunity to return to.

Individual rights and duties

The proponents of dual citizenship in all three immigration countries linked their main arguments to the value of equality. During various debates on the issue, the most important argument put forth was that full legal inclusion of immigrants by means of citizenship acquisition has to be seen as a precondition for equal and basic individual rights of immigrants. Such moral arguments concerned above all the legal equality between immigrants who continuously reside within the state's jurisdiction and citizens. According to this view, equal legal and political status within a nation-state determines in important respects the social position of the individual. The general acceptance of dual citizenship was justified with respect to equality in more specific legal contexts. It is noteworthy, for example, that all three immigration countries allowed for certain exceptions to the granting of dual citizenship in the name of individual rights, thus strengthening the equality argument vis-à-vis internal legal differentiations within the immigrant population. In the Netherlands and in Sweden, the parties favouring dual citizenship frequently pointed to incidents of *de facto* tolerance as a consequence of, for instance, strengthened standards of gender neutrality in regard to citizenship acquisition rules or when the corresponding emigration states refused to release immigrants from citizenship or else made it conditional on unreasonable demands. They considered it as unjustifiable that some immigrants be allowed to retain their original citizenship while other immigrants are required to renounce their original citizenship. In Germany, because of the privileged and unconditional access of East European resettlers to German citizenship for constitutional reasons it was considered as a matter of fairness that dual citizenship be extended to include all immigrant groups.

An argument against dual citizenship related directly to individual rights, which emerged in all three countries, was that giving dual citizens access to rights and citizenship-related opportunities in two states—for instance regarding travel, education, self-employment and employment in the civil service—would constitute something of a privilege. While in Sweden this argument could be refuted in debating and regulating the tolerance of dual citizenship in relation to immigrants and emigrants at the same time, it played a significant role in the German public debate. In the two countries where dual citizenship became increasingly contested, however, the most important claims were related not to rights but rather to the duties and obligations of citizenship. In Germany as well as in the more recent debates in the Netherlands one of the most frequently invoked terms was loyalty. As already mentioned above, those who opposed dual citizenship expressed their fear that dual citizenship constitutes an incentive to make use of the respective rights without fulfilling and possibly even escaping the corresponding duties of citizenship by relocating to another country.

When looking more closely at the relationship between individual rights and democracy prevailing in each country a crucial difference stands out between Sweden on the one hand and the Netherlands and Germany on the other. Whereas in Sweden a continuous consciousness held sway among the political actors that dual citizenship at least could contribute to the preconditions of democracy and help to realise immigrants' individual rights, in Germany and increasingly also in the Netherlands dual citizenship was deemed predominantly a matter for democratic decision and hence state discretion. In Germany especially, the CDU/CSU presented the question of dual citizenship primarily within the framework of the somewhat communitarian claim that the already established political community possesses the basic collective and democratic right to regulate the access of newcomers.[7] The obvious objection that this collective right might be justified with regard to immigration and border control but is seriously constrained when it comes to the naturalisation conditions of long-term residents could be evaded easily by the CDU/CSU in pointing to the already established as-of-right naturalisation under certain conditions in the beginning of the 1990s. Indeed, they stated several times that opposing dual citizenship does not in any way mean denying naturalisation. By agreeing on a necessary citizenship law reform which would ease the conditions of naturalisation, they had already conceded this as a confirmation of the legitimate interests of the persons concerned. But they did not view dual citizenship as an element of such a reform and even less as an aspect of the individual right to citizenship. In persistently mixing questions of immigration with those of integration during the debate, they argued for the priority of state interests with regard to dual citizenship. They repeatedly tried to suggest in public debate that allowing dual citizenship would be an incentive for additional unwanted immigration to Germany. Similarly, when in the Netherlands the issue of dual citizenship became increasingly contested, it was addressed from the perspective of the interests of overall society and the state. Symptomatically, in both countries opponents of dual citizenship tied it in an instrumental way to matters of state security. In Germany, many Christian Democrats claimed that deportation in cases of serious criminal offences would no longer be possible if the persons concerned also hold German citizenship. In reverse order and against the backdrop of previously liberal practice in dual citizenship, the question in the Netherlands was whether dual citizens could be deprived of their Dutch citizenship if they are convicted of crimes or even fail to behave according to desired norms and values.

These observations reveal that political actors on either side of the issue obviously hold different understandings of political legitimacy. In emphasising democratic congruence of the subjects of the law and citizens entitled to political rights of participation, those who advocated dual citizenship espoused a concept of input-related or procedural legitimacy as the basis of political unity. By contrast, the political parties contesting dual citizenship were primarily concerned with an output-related political legitimacy, focusing on upholding the intervention capacities of the sovereign state and its ability to perform political core functions such as guaranteeing public and social security. Thus, they viewed political legitimacy predominantly as the empirical consent of the established citizenry.

Membership

In all three countries the word most often used in the several political and public debates on dual citizenship was 'integration'—a certain indication that the most important element of citizenship distinguishing the arguments of the proponents and opponents of dual citizenship concerned membership. Integration, however, can be understood as pertaining only to the terms of immigrant integration; but it may also refer to the more general conditions of overall integration of society and within the polity. The more that immigrant integration is regarded as a fundamental social and political problem, the greater the likelihood that aspects of immigrant integration and overall societal integration overlap in political debate. Then, the questions at issue are the basics of collective identity and political community and certain continuities and traditions of interpretation with regard to the roles und functions attributed to individual persons, civil society and the state (Favell 1998).

As to how integration and citizenship are connected, the dividing line is clear in the discourse in all three countries. Whereas the proponents thought that citizenship may be seen as a precondition and a tool facilitating the integration of immigrants, the opponents argued that it is necessary for integration to be 'complete' before persons may become citizens. However, in the two countries, where dual citizenship in general was rejected, the question of dual citizenship was deeply embedded in much more general and public debates on immigration, integration and membership. In Germany, for instance, the CDU/CSU accused the government parties of using dual citizenship as a sort of surrogate for patterns of social integration. The debated citizenship draft law in 1999 was in particular viewed as a diversionary manoeuvre in order to avoid mention of the actual social problems of immigrant integration. In the Netherlands, dual citizenship became increasingly contested when all of the established political parties developed a more restrictive attitude towards integration and naturalisation in general. The notion was widely expressed that in the context of a previous multicultural integration approach ethnic minorities had been treated too liberally and without having any demands imposed on them. A prior political consensus that for reasons of political correctness issues of immigration should not be discussed publicly was replaced by the idea that a 'new realism' necessitated open and frank discussion of the problems of immigrant integration.

A closer look at the arguments in these two countries reveals that the proponents and opponents of dual citizenship invoke two fundamentally different understandings of citizenship: 'citizenship-as-legal-status', meaning full legal membership in a particular political community conferring basic individual rights, on the one hand; and 'citizenship-as-desirable-activity', meaning citizenship as a function of one's actual participation in civil society, on the other hand (Kymlicka and Norman 1994). Whereas the proponents understood citizenship primarily as an issue of legal status, the opponents referred to citizenship as an activity contributing to the common good.[8] The opponents rejected dual citizenship precisely on the grounds that they viewed it as conferring rights without imposing sufficient duties. While in the Netherlands a cultural understanding of obligations relating to Western values prevailed, in Germany a focus on economic self-sufficiency of immigrants was dominant. In the Netherlands, the subsequent governments during the 1990s placed a growing emphasis on the duties of active citizenship and loyalty to the Dutch constitutional state. For example, a Government Memorandum of 2001 on integration of immigrants defined citizenship as 'having a part and participating in Dutch society as an autonomous person' and further stated that it can be expected of immigrants 'to contribute actively to this modern, open and dynamic society' (quoted in de Hart 2007). While in former times the principle of equality, to which dual citizenship was related, was perceived as a feature of political institutions, now it was framed increasingly as a sort of faith which Muslim groups especially must adhere to and which must guide their behaviour in civil society. Immigrants should first prove that they are worthy of naturalisation and deserving of the rights of citizens. The more restrictive stance was also reflected in the introduction of a strict test of language skills and knowledge of Dutch society as a requirement for naturalisation. In Germany, the CDU/CSU referred to individual capacities, which are regarded as necessary for participation in civil society but especially in a market society. In a climate of economic crisis and high unemployment rates in the German context, immigrants eligible for naturalisation were deemed to have to meet first and foremost the obligation to support themselves. To avoid the phenomenon of 'immigration into the social security systems', as the CDU/CSU frequently put it, the citizenship law had to contain reliable criteria, suggestive of comprehensive and successful social integration. Full citizens should be expected, on the whole, to undertake sufficient initiatives for vocational training and job search, to earn a living on their own account and to take on responsibilities and commitments for their family members.

These observations point to more general differences between proponents and opponents of dual citizenship with regard to the belief systems of overall societal integration and the various functions and performances attributed to citizens, civil society and the state. In regard to the role of the individual, as already mentioned, there is a fundamental opposition as to whether citizenship is regarded as related to individual rights or to expectations of certain capacities, responsibilities and obligations. Regarding civil society, the emphasis put on citizens' obligations reveals that the opponents of dual citizenship do not regard the overall integration of society as exclusively a function of political institutions. Although the constitutional loyalty of immigrants was increasingly stressed, societal integration goes far beyond political loyalty in a more narrow sense, as in the form of simple obedience to existing laws and the constitution. Rather, in this conceptualisation, social cohesion, moral commitment and internal solidarity are based on social, cultural and occasionally also economic conditions that are prerequisites of political integration. This view resonates perfectly with more general programmatic statements of the CDU/CSU in Germany. In various programmatic assertions they referred to a well-known phrase coined in 1967 by a former judge of the Constitutional Court, according to which the free and secular state builds upon preconditions which it cannot guarantee on its own account (Böckenförde 1991: 112).[9] Such remarks were generally tied to a revival of the principle of subsidiarity, emphasising individual capacities for active citizenship, meaning that a citizen should be able to act on his or her own responsibility and to participate in civil society. In a similar way, in the Netherlands the view became even more widespread that civil capacities such as tolerance and respect for gender equality must be demanded and proved. Moreover, if necessary, failures of integration should be sanctioned rather than presupposed simply by trust in socialisation processes within society and polity. Concerning the role of the state and the function of politics, the dividing line with respect to the various understandings of integration reflects the contradictions among comprehensive beliefs which resemble what have been termed 'the politics of faith' and 'the politics of scepticism' (Oakeshott 1996). The proponents believe that the formative effects of political institutions and the intervention capacities of the state contribute to a betterment of the human condition. For example, the SPD in Germany saw easing naturalisation conditions as a way of contributing to equalise the status of the immigrant and the indigenous populations, as well as an institutional means to change the terms of reciprocal recognition between Germans and immigrants in everyday life. By contrast, the opponents are sceptical about the reach of political interventions and argue for confining the role of the state to core functions such as, most importantly, securing public order. Obviously, these positions also correspond with neo-liberal ideas of redefining different areas of responsibility, the privatisation of former state performances or their delegation to civil society, most visible recently, for example, in the policy area of social security. From that point of view, it is a logical consequence to extend the prerequisites of integration of immigrants in order to enhance the probability that they are able to care for themselves.

Institutional opportunity structures

The different party belief systems on the meaning of citizenship are related to the respective institutional opportunity structures. These structures enable and constrain political attitudes towards consensus or dissent to different degrees. The extent to which the issue at hand also serves as a strategic weapon in the struggle for political power is especially dependent upon structural and institutional features of the political system. The decisive institutional factors influencing dual citizenship legislation in the countries under analysis include the party system, the role of the courts and expert commissions and the degree of public debate.

The search for inter-party consensus, especially in matters relating to constitutional issues and foreign policy, is an important hallmark of Swedish politics, and the enduring treatment of the issue of dual citizenship within parliamentary commissions in the 1980s and late 1990s, involving representatives of all relevant social groups and institutions, led to a careful, level-headed and realistic balancing of the costs and benefits of dual citizenship. For example, whereas initially the problems of dual voting were raised as a serious objection to dual citizenship, these problems were later found to be of minor importance since few persons actually exercised their right to vote in elections in two countries. More importantly, the benefit of having more individuals participating in the politics of the state where they reside was later seen as outweighing the problems of double voting. Interestingly, during the various debates, some major political actors, such as leading members of the Liberal and Centre-Right parties, changed their views in the long run by accepting arguments against the privilege-claim and of inequality caused by *de facto* toleration. The absence of an established right-wing populist party on the national level and the fact that dual citizenship did not become an issue of public discussion contributed further to the pragmatic character of the debate and the ultimate change in the law to allow dual citizenship in Sweden.

Traditionally, Dutch politics have also been oriented towards building consensus and reaching compromises, owing in part to the relatively large number of small political parties represented in parliament. A consequence as well as an expression of this political pragmatism was the compromise achieved between the two major parties PdvA and CDA in 1992 on the general allowance of dual citizenship for immigrants. However, the compromise broke down in the mid-1990s when the earlier political consensus on avoiding public debates on immigration and integration gradually eroded. Moreover, in the course of time both the multicultural 'minority policies' approach adopted in 1983 and the formerly widely shared relationship between naturalisation and integration was increasingly questioned. The far-reaching change in the understanding of integration as linked to individual performance and sanctions was influenced by expert commissions such as the Socio-Cultural Planning Office (SCP), influential statements of intellectuals in public debate and the events of 11 September 2001. The most important factor, however, was the sudden and meteoric rise of the Lijst Pim Fortuyn (LPF), a populist party that has made changing the terms of integration one of its main political issues. The party's indirect but nevertheless considerable influence on Dutch politics can be seen in the adoption by all of the other established parties, to different degrees, of a discourse marked by frankness and openness in immigration matters.

In Germany, the somewhat puzzling content of the German citizenship law enacted in 1999—a very liberal *jus soli* regime and a rather restrictive regulation on dual citizenship—reflects exactly an unintended political compromise between two political camps holding opposing views on integration and the interpretation of citizenship. During several parliamentary debates on citizenship law reform in the 1990s the respective positions of the CDU/CSU on the one hand and the SPD and the Greens on the other remained very constant. In their statements one finds a repetitive exchange of the same arguments in a kind of ritualistic and stereotypical way. This persistent dividing line between the relevant political parties was formed and fuelled by an institutional structure consisting of a competitive party system, the federal system and the influential role of the Constitutional Court, inviting the articulation and mobilisation of dissent in efforts to gain electoral support. The federal system accelerates the competition and conflict structure of the two major political parties with their varying prospective coalition partners, because many decisions need co-ratification by the *Länder*-chamber (*Bundesrat*) and because elections on the regional level are regarded usually as indicators of the actual proportions of political support on the federal level. This constellation leads to intensive election campaigns, especially in cases of slim majorities and possible changes of governments. Consequently, the CDU/CSU, still coping with their severe defeat in the federal elections in 1998 and serious problems regarding irregularities with party financing at that time, quickly used the institutional opportunity to mobilise against the fundamental reform project on citizenship law announced by the newly elected coalition government (SPD and Greens) and organised a petition campaign immediately before the first following regional elections. By mobilising against the plan of the government coalition to tolerate dual citizenship in all cases of naturalisation, they succeeded in winning the elections in Hessen against the previous SPD-led government, contrary to all expectations. As a result, the government coalition was forced to make concessions in the form of retreating from an overall allowance of dual citizenship, because they had in fact lost their majority in the *Bundesrat*. Nevertheless they succeeded in introducing the *jus soli* for the second generation of immigrants. The influential role of the Constitutional Court in Germany and its often-cited 1974 decision in which dual citizenship is described as an 'evil' to be avoided as far as possible in the interests of states and individuals also contributed to the credibility of the Christian Democrats' campaign.

In sum, the institutional opportunity structures play a significant role in shaping the discourses, especially with regard to the principled or pragmatic, contentious or consensus-oriented, and public or non-public character of political debates, which in turn influences the legislation processes regarding acceptance or rejection of dual citizenship.

Conclusion

Citizenship policies can be best understood with reference to the belief systems held by the influential national political parties which in turn are shaped and stabilised by the particular institutional structure of the respective political systems of nation-states. However, as the analysis of the legislation processes regarding dual citizenship in different immigration states reveals, the traditional approach of the prevailing nation concept is outdated when trying to make sense of the several arguments raised in the various contexts of the debates. Rather, the whole spectrum of arguments in favour of or against dual citizenship resonates with different elements and interpretations of the concept of citizenship itself and the related basic principles of legitimacy in liberal and democratic states.

Whereas the beliefs and arguments in favour of dual citizenship tend to be linked to liberalised naturalisation conditions as a way of providing for the individual rights of immigrants, the positions and arguments against dual citizenship should be interpreted in relation to broader tendencies of revisions to liberal policies on naturalisation taking place in a number of states. Several European states have recently introduced stricter language and integration requirements, and in some cases linked certain sanctions regarding conditions of residence permits and transition to citizenship with perceived integration failures measured by the behaviour of immigrants. With regard to the connection between naturalisation and integration, a remarkable feature of—and a noticeable trend in—citizenship policies is the approach traditionally favoured by the German opponents of overly liberal naturalisation rules. The paradigm of 'naturalisation as the crowning of a completed integration process' now seems to prevail, having replaced the previous concept of 'naturalisation as a means of integration' (Bauböck et al. 2006: 7). Requiring the renunciation of previous citizenship upon naturalisation as an indicator of unequivocal choice and loyalty on the part of immigrants can be viewed as one element of such a restrictive and more demanding approach to integration.

Irrespective of country-specific features and national traditions, the objections to dual citizenship voiced by politicians and experts have been cast in the language of duties, obligations and commitments, as recent discussions of dual citizenship among political scientists in the clearly republican context of the United States also show (see, for example, Huntington 2004; Renshon 2001). In this framework, citizens are expected to possess and develop certain capacities of self-reliance, individual autonomy, personal responsibility and primary identification with the respective nation-state. Immigrants should use and invest their resources within the boundaries and to the benefit of the common good of the political community where they want to be citizens. Dual citizenship is regarded as a serious obstacle to such orientations, because it is held to impede national unity based on shared values and/or to undermine national sovereignty.

As the comparison between Germany and the Netherlands reveals, two ideal-typical variants of the citizenship obligations approach can be distinguished. The first reflects a primarily economic perspective. Here, a broader tendency in immigration policies—aiming increasingly to attract highly skilled immigrants but being more restrictive vis-à-vis immigrants who are deemed costly—is partly reflected in naturalisation policies as well. Immigrants were distinguished not so much by their ascriptive features such as ethnicity, nationality or religion, but rather by their actual or expected abilities and supposed contributions to economic development and to the social welfare system.[10] The tendencies to make citizenship acquisition dependent on individual performance correspond, interestingly, with far-reaching reinterpretations of social rights in the context of the so-called 'activation' and 'workfare' programmes in the areas of labour market and social policy. These ideas were initially advocated by neo-conservative theorists (see Kymlicka and Norman 1994) and politicians but meanwhile trickled down deeply into the beliefs of Social Democratic Parties, represented most prominently by the British Labour Party and its theoretical consultant who has coined them 'The Third Way' (Giddens 1998). Here, certain welfare rights, although not citizenship itself, are made 'increasingly conditional upon citizens first agreeing to conform to appropriate patterns of behaviour as defined by the state' (Dwyer 1998: 500).

The second version of the citizenship obligations approach is concerned primarily with political culture. In this variant, the applicant's discernible approval of the state's valid laws and constitutional principles and confirmation of a certain level of language skills are deemed the main preconditions of citizenship acquisition. However, these tendencies should not be viewed simply as a return to assimilation in terms of adaptation to a particular national culture. Although both policies and their accompanying discourses emphasising individual civil obligations are framed as a reaction of some sort to previous multicultural relativism, the criteria used in redefining the boundaries of particularistic inclusion and exclusion obviously pertain to Western values, which are taken as universal principles. A further characteristic feature of this trend is that adaptation of immigrants is no longer considered as a protracted, multistage and automatic process of socialisation within the established social and political institutions of the majority society, but rather a process of integration that has to be proved and tested. In the aftermath of the events of 11 September 2001 and in the context of Islamic fundamentalism, the requirement of language skills and knowledge of basic values was increasingly debated and actually introduced in some countries. Immigrants eligible for naturalisation were to demonstrate not only that they accept the basic political values, such as cultural tolerance, freedom of speech in cases of disparagement of religious beliefs and respect for gender equality, but that they have already internalised these values on faith and in a form resembling civic virtues guiding their behaviour in private relations and civil society.

If renunciation of previous citizenship is interpreted as one element of a naturalisation approach emphasising the activation of citizenship duties, it is nevertheless confronted with contrary and substantive rights-based interpretations. In adhering to principles of individual rights democratic states are compelled to accept dual citizenship in a number of cases. For example, they have had to provide for exemptions from the principle of avoiding dual citizenship in cases when the respective other states, usually authoritarian regimes, make renouncing nationality impossible or conditional on unreasonable demands. If another state were thus to be in a position where it could interfere with the extent of rights and integration of residents within their own jurisdiction, the legitimation principles of liberal democracies would be seriously contradicted. Liberal democracies also tend to accept dual citizenship in the name of gender equity, especially when citizenship is acquired by birth. Furthermore, such states may be inclined to grant dual citizenship based upon reciprocity within regional governance systems such as the EU. Then, as a consequence of instances of *de facto* tolerance, a crucial and dynamic mechanism is set into motion: once certain exceptions have been granted, new interpretations of individual rights and new claims of other categories of persons combined with court cases could easily follow, and lead to yet more exceptions, a process best described as a proliferation of 'exception groups'. The more exceptions granted and thus potential claimant groups, the greater the likelihood that questions of legitimating different treatments for different citizen categories arise because each exemption has to be justified on reasonable grounds.

Problems of justification and rising costs of administrative procedures have had the effect of increasing tolerance of dual citizenship (Faist, Gerdes and Rieple 2004; Faist 2007b), leading to a liberalising trend among EU-countries with regard to dual citizenship policies (Howard 2005), although such a trend cannot be observed in citizenship policies more generally (see Bauböck et al. 2006). In any case, these counter-balancing forces in favour of dual citizenship seem to constrain the opportunities of including the renunciation requirement of previous citizenship in restrictive naturalisation approaches.

Notes

1. The following account is based on the case studies of three immigration countries (de Hart 2007; Gerdes, Faist and Rieple 2007; Spång 2007) and their comparison (Faist 2007a, b) carried out within the research project *Multiple Citizenship in a Globalising World*. We would like to thank the Volkswagen Foundation for funding the project.
2. By belief system we understand existing and familiar ideas such as worldviews (*Weltanschauung*), ideologies, and systems of values and norms, which have intellectually derivable normative implications for how society should be organised (see Converse 1964; North 1981).
3. Max Weber's famous dictum in his *Sociology of Religion* reads, 'Not ideas, but material and ideal interests, directly govern men's conduct. Yet very frequently the "world images" that have been created by "ideas" have, like switchmen, determined the tracks along which action has been pushed by the dynamic of interest' (Weber 1946: 280).
4. Some critical accounts of the ethnic-republican perspective on nationhood instead emphasise the interests of nation-states (see Weil 2001) or the function of citizenship law (see Weinbach 2005) in relation to the actual processes of immigration and emigration. It is assumed that states usually adapt their citizenship laws to changed conditions of immigration and emigration. However, while the first thesis leaves it open which and whose interests are influential and why, the second thesis neglects the possibility of different and alternative paths to such adaptations.
5. ECN, Art. 6, para. 3.
6. A more general version derives ethnicisation processes in citizenship law from the mere fact of coexisting and partly competing nation-states. According to that view, a nation-state is *per se* an ethnic entity because it inevitably provides for criteria to define membership which simultaneously leads to the exclusion of non-members (see Bös 2000). However, such a perspective neglects variations of membership definitions and cannot account for different criteria and whether these are ethnically selective, group-based and particularistic, or of a formal, individualistic and universalistic kind.
7. For a theoretical justification of this communitarian claim, see Walzer (1983, ch. 2).

8. Correspondingly, a theoretical justification of republican citizenship understands it as an 'office' which presupposes certain capacities such as autonomy and independent judgement opposed to 'pure conformity'. Therefore, it would not be illegitimate to make citizenship acquisition conditional on assumed dialogic competence by requesting language skills, supposed willingness and capability of identification with the particular political community by requesting knowledge of its institutions and culture, and presumed autonomy by demanding economic independence (see van Gunsteren 1988).

9. For example, see the CDU-Basic Programme 'Freedom in Responsibility' (1994).

10. Consequently, a justification based on economic theory, which predominantly sees nation-states as clubs providing collective goods for members, names as the decisive criterion of admission of new members whether or not they are willing and able to invest their resources for the common good. This means, in the end, admitting that citizenship can be bought by solvent applicants. Persons who are prepared to pay more taxes than the additional expenditures they cause in terms of, for example, making use of the public health or education systems should be accepted (Straubhaar 2003).

References

Arendt, H. (1981) [1949] 'Es gibt nur ein einziges Menschenrecht'. In O. Höffe, G. Kadelbach and G. Plumpe, eds, *Praktische Philosophie/Ethik*, Vol. 2. Frankfurt: Fischer, pp. 152–67.

Bauböck, R., E. Ersbøll, K. Groenendijk and H. Waldrauch, eds (2006) *Acquisition and Loss of Nationality. Policies and Trends in 15 European States.* Vienna: Institute for European Integration Research.

Benhabib, S. (2004) *The Rights of Others: Aliens, Residents and Citizens.* New York: Cambridge University Press.

Böckenförde, E.-W. (1991) 'Die Entstehung des Staates als Vorgang der Säkularisation'. In *Recht, Staat, Freiheit.* Frankfurt a.M.: Suhrkamp, pp. 92–114.

Bös, M. (2000) 'Die rechtliche Konstruktion von Zugehörigkeit. Staatsangehörigkeit in Deutschland und den USA'. In K. Holz, ed., *Staatsbürgerschaft. Soziale Differenzierung und politische Inklusion.* Wiesbaden: Westdeutscher Verlag, pp. 93–118.

Brubaker, R. (1992): *Citizenship and Nationhood in France and in Germany.* Cambridge, MA, and London: Harvard University Press.

Castles, S. and M. Miller (1993) *The Age of Migration: International Population Movements in the Modern World.* London: Macmillan.

Chan, J. M. M. (1991) 'The Right to a Nationality as a Human Right. The Current Trend towards Recognition'. *Human Rights Law Journal* 12: 1–14.

Converse, P. E. (1964) 'The Nature of Belief Systems in Mass Publics'. In D. Apter, ed., *Ideology and Discontent.* New York: Free Press, pp. 206–61.

de Hart, B. (2007) 'The End of Multiculturalism – The End of Dual Citizenship? Political and Public Debates on Dual Citizenship in the Netherlands (1980–2004)'. In T. Faist, ed., *Dual Citizenship in Europe: From Nationhood to Societal Integration.* Aldershot: Ashgate, pp. 77–102.

Dwyer, P. (1998) 'Conditional Citizens? Welfare Rights and Responsibilities in the Late 1990s'. *Critical Social Policy* 57: 493–517.

Faist, T. (2007a) 'The Fixed and Porous Boundaries of Dual Citizenship'. In T. Faist, ed., *Dual Citizenship in Europe: From Nationhood to Societal Integration*. Aldershot: Ashgate, pp. 1–43.

Faist, T. (2007b) 'Dual Citizenship: Changes, Prospects, and Limits'. In T. Faist, ed., *Dual Citizenship in Europe: From Nationhood to Societal Integration*. Aldershot: Ashgate, pp. 171–200.

Faist, T., J. Gerdes and B. Rieple (2004) 'Dual Citizenship as a Path-Dependent Process'. *International Migration Review* 38: 913–44.

Favell, A. (1998) *Philosophies of Integration: Immigration and the Idea of Citizenship in France and Britain*. London: Macmillan.

Gerdes, J., T. Faist and B. Rieple (2007) 'We are all "Republican" Now – The Politics of Dual Citizenship in Germany'. In T. Faist, ed., *Dual Citizenship in Europe: From Nationhood to Societal Integration*. Aldershot: Ashgate, pp. 45–76.

Giddens, A. (1998) *The Third Way: The Renewal of Social Democracy*. Cambridge: Polity Press.

Green, S. (2005) 'Between Ideology and Pragmatism: The Politics of Dual Nationality in Germany'. *International Migration Review* 39: 921–52.

Gunsteren, H. R. van (1988) 'Admission to Citizenship'. *Ethics* 98: 731–41.

Habermas, J. (1992) *Faktizität und Geltung*. Frankfurt a.M.: Suhrkamp.

Hollifield, J. (1992) *Immigrants, Markets and States: The Political Economy of Postwar Europe*. Cambridge, MA: Harvard University Press.

Howard, M. M. (2005) 'Variation in Dual Citizenship Policies in the Countries of the EU'. *International Migration Review* 39: 697–720.

Huntington, S. P. (2004) *Who are we? The Challenges to America's National Identity*. New York: Simon & Schuster.

Joppke, C. (1999) *Immigration and the Nation-State: The United States, Germany and Great Britain*. New York: Oxford University Press.

Joppke, C. (2005) 'Exclusion in the Liberal State. The Case of Immigration and Citizenship Policy'. *European Journal of Social Theory* 8: 43–61.

Koopmans, R. (1999) 'Germany and its Immigrants: An Ambivalent Relationship'. *Journal of Ethnic and Migration Studies* 25: 627–47.

Kurthen, H. (1995) 'Germany at the Crossroads: National Identity and the Challenges of Immigration'. *International Migration Review* 29: 914–38.

Kymlicka, W. and W. Norman (1994) 'Return of the Citizen: A Survey of Recent Work on Citizenship Theory'. *Ethics* 104: 352–81.

Marshall, T. H. (1964) *Class, Citizenship, and Social Development, Essays by T. H. Marshall*. New York: Doubleday & Company.

North, D. C. (1981) *Structure and Change in Economic History*. New York: W. W. Norton.

Oakeshott, M. (1996) *The Politics of Faith and the Politics of Scepticism*. London: Yale University Press.

Orentlicher, D. (1998) 'Citizenship and National Identity'. In D. Wippmann, ed., *International Law and Ethnic Conflict*. Ithaca, NY: Cornell University Press, pp. 296–325.

Renshon, S. A. (2001) *Dual Citizenship and American National Identity*. Washington, DC: Center for Immigration Studies.

Soysal, Y. N. (1994) *The Limits of Citizenship*. Chicago: University of Chicago Press.

158   *Dual Citizenship in European Immigration States*

Spång, M. (2007): 'Pragmatism All the Way Down? The Politics of Dual Citizenship in Sweden'. In *Dual Citizenship in Europe: From Nationhood to Societal Integration*. Ed. T. Faist. Aldershot: Ashgate, pp. 103–25.

Straubhaar, T. (2003). 'Wird die Staatsangehörigkeit zu einer Klubmitgliedschaft?' In D. Thränhardt and U. Hunger, eds, *Migration im Spannungsfeld von Globalisierung und Nationalstaat*. Leviathan. Special Issue 22. Wiesbaden: Westdeutscher Verlag, pp. 76–89.

Walzer, M. (1983) *Spheres of Justice. A Defence of Pluralism and Equality*. New York: Basic Books.

Walzer, M. (1989) 'Citizenship'. In T. Ball, J. Farr and R. L. Hanson, eds, *Political Innovation and Conceptual Change*. Cambridge: Cambridge University Press, pp. 211–19.

Weber, M. (1946) 'The Social Psychology of World Religions'. In H. Gerth and C. Wright Mills, eds, *From Max Weber*. New York: Basic Books, pp. 267–301.

Weber, M. (1972) [1922] *Wirtschaft und Gesellschaft*. 5th edn. Tübingen: J. C. B. Mohr.

Weil, P. (2001) 'Access to Citizenship: A Comparison of Twenty-Five Nationality Laws'. In T. A. Aleinikoff and D. Klusmeyer, eds, *Citizenship Today: Global Perspectives and Practices*. Washington, DC: Carnegie Endowment for International Peace, pp. 32–81.

Weinbach, C. (2005) 'Staatsbürgerschaft und nationale Zugehörigkeit heute: multikulturell und de-ethnisiert?' In C. Gusy and H.-G. Haupt, eds, *Inklusion und Partizipation. Politische Kommunikation im historischen Wandel*. Frankfurt a. M. and New York: Campus, pp. 187–211.

Weiner, M. (1996) 'Ethics, National Sovereignty and Control of Immigration'. *International Migration Review* 30: 171–96.

8
Much Ado about Nothing? The Contours of Dual Citizenship in the United States and Canada

Irene Bloemraad

Introduction

In August 2003 the United States Bureau of Citizenship and Immigration Services (USCIS) stood poised to introduce a new Oath of Allegiance, required of those applying for US citizenship through naturalisation. The USCIS wanted to modernise the oath's archaic and cumbersome language. Strikingly, although the proposed changes never went into effect—USCIS came under intense criticism for not allowing adequate public debate on the new language—the proposed oath left intact the language emphasising the exclusivity of American citizenship.[1] Unlike many countries around the world, the United States does not explicitly embrace multiple citizenship.[2]

The US attitude stands in contrast to its neighbour to the north. Surfing the website maintained by Citizenship and Immigration Canada (CIC), a prospective Canadian citizen quickly sees an entry on 'Dual Citizenship' under the heading 'Information about Canadian Citizenship.' The would-be citizen learns that, as of 15 February 1977, there are no Canadian restrictions on multiple citizenship.[3] Those desiring further information are encouraged to contact the CIC call centre or a Canadian consulate or embassy.

The seemingly stark difference in American and Canadian stances towards multiple citizenship blurs upon closer examination—the United States actually does tolerate dual passports—but it is clear that the United States is more hostile to dual citizenship than Canada. In the United States, the would-be American citizens must swear, 'I absolutely and entirely renounce and abjure all allegiance and fidelity to any foreign prince, potentate, state, or sovereignty of whom or which I have

159

heretofore been a subject or citizen.'[4] What accounts for the US–Canada difference? What consequences, if any, do these countries' positions carry for immigrant integration? Are fears around dual citizenship— especially its potential to weaken political cohesion—born out of available evidence?

I suggest that distinct security concerns and histories of nation-building gave rise to greater tolerance of multiple citizenship in Canada. Citizenship and its legal predecessor, subjectship, are in large part statuses establishing rights and responsibilities around security: sovereigns or sovereign nations provide security to subjects and citizens, and in return subjects and citizens pledge allegiance to the protector, usually with some understanding that they will contribute to the community's security through military service or other means. In such a context, dual loyalties are suspect. The United States, created from armed revolution and with a long history of participation in hot and cold wars, has held on to a view of citizenship—and immigration more generally—as an issue of national security.

Citizenship is also about national identity. Immigrant-generated diversity raises serious questions for those who fear that excessive pluralism undermines the civic (and cultural) core of the nation (Huntington 2004).[5] Some consequently defend exclusive US citizenship by arguing that in a country lacking the glue of a homogeneous ethnicity, multiple nationalities must be rejected to ensure unity around a common civic bond (Scherner-Kim 2000; Renshon 2001).[6]

From the lens of national identity, Canada's acceptance of dual citizenship is puzzling. While Canada's lesser role in world politics and international security, as well as its incremental break with Great Britain, help explain its greater tolerance of multiple allegiances, Canadian society is also defined by diversity, including a strong and credible challenge to its unity in the form of Quebec separatism. Ironically, this threat and the need to integrate immigrants resulted in greater acceptance of dual nationality. In a sense, embracing multiple citizenship, especially at a symbolic level, is part and parcel of contemporary Canadian nationalism.

Importantly, Canada's tolerance of multiple nationality appears to foster greater political integration among immigrants than in the United States, at least as measured by high levels of immigrant naturalisation and the striking success of foreign-born politicians. Relatively few immigrants actively pursue multiple citizenships, but they like knowing that the option exists and that their new home is open to dual nationality. Dual citizenship consequently functions less as a legal status and more as a symbol of the country's openness to immigration and diversity. Much has been made of sending countries' hope that dual citizenship will secure financial remittances. Dual citizenship might also provide benefits to receiving societies, not the least of which is an increase in immigrants' attachment to their new home. Canada's embrace of dual citizenship, a part of Canada's move to adopt an ideology of multicultural nationalism, appears to have produced greater political incorporation and civic community.

Citizenship law and nation-building

Seymour Martin Lipset (1970, 1986, 1990) argues that American and Canadian political cultures differ markedly because the United States underwent a revolution while Canada was forged in a conservative 'counterrevolution'. This characterisation offers some insight into the American embrace of exclusive citizenship and the concomitant fear of multiple political loyalties. As a country born in revolution, the new nation had to ensure its legitimacy by forcing residents to make a choice—allegiance to the new United States or continued loyalty to the British Crown. Likewise, Canada's greater acceptance of multiple nationality finds its origins in the multiple statuses held by those living in the British Empire and early Canadian Confederation. Lipset's characterisation ignores, however, the way later events and choices reaffirm or alter earlier tendencies. In the United States, subsequent wars and national security fears reinforced—and continue to buttress—suspicion of dual citizenship. In Canada, openness to dual citizenship was bolstered by contemporary efforts to use multiculturalism and citizenship to craft a new, non-British identity.

Dual citizenship: Early foundations

American and Canadian citizenship share British roots, although the common law tradition imported from Great Britain defined individuals' political membership in terms of subjectship rather than citizenship. Anyone born on the King's lands—including the overseas colonies—received the King's protection as a subject in return for allegiance and obedience (Carpenter 1904; Schuck and Smith 1985).[7] Those not born on the King's lands, such as immigrants, could acquire the status of subject—with its attendant property and trading rights—through a process of naturalisation.

The authority to naturalise was subject to fierce competition between the Crown, English Parliament and the colonial assemblies and proprietors. Each wanted control over access to civic and political membership and the rights that came with such status.[8] A two-tiered system developed in which the colonies could grant local citizenship, but England controlled the empire-wide status of British subjecthood.[9] In a certain sense, colonial membership was defined through multiple citizenship.

The trajectories of American and Canadian citizenship parted course soon after London banned colonial naturalisation in 1773. Revolution in the United States ushered in a new sense of membership defined around citizenship rather than subjecthood. Among the grievances outlined in the US Declaration of Independence was the charge that King George III 'has endeavoured to prevent the Population of these States; for that Purpose obstructing the Laws for Naturalization of Foreigners...'. Lawmakers in the new country established a relatively open, easy natur-alisation procedure: applicants could file for citizenship in any court of record after 5 years of residence in the United States and a prior declaration of intention to become a citizen.[10] Would-be citizens had to swear an oath to uphold the Constitution and renounce allegiance to any foreign sovereign. The contours of these criteria continue to define naturalisation today.[11]

Although naturalisation predated the War of Independence, Americans' use of the term 'citizen' rather than 'subject', a new view of member-ship, predicated on Lockean notions of social contract and consent (Kettner 1978). Individuals could become citizens through voluntary adherence to an adopted country. Given the revolutionary period, natur-alisation was not only a question of legal status, but also an affirma-tion of the new state's legitimacy (Schuck and Smith 1985). Multiple allegiances became suspect, an attitude strengthened during the Napo-leonic wars when British sea captains would use press gangs on Amer-icans, arguing that they were born English and thus were British subjects for life (Ueda 1982; Spiro 1997). The American response was that those in the United States could, and should, only hold American citizenship.

In Canada, British influence lasted longer and so, too, did the exist-ence of multiple membership statuses. With Canadian Confederation, residents preserved their status as British subjects, the primary citizen-ship category in the new Dominion.[12] Canadian Parliament gained the right to make most laws for the Dominion, including exclusive legis-lative authority over 'Naturalization and Aliens' under Section 91 of the British North America Act (Constitution Act 1867). However, London retained residual power over British subjecthood since this status gave rights throughout the Empire.

The eighteenth-century tug-of-war between London and the colonies over subjecthood continued through the nineteenth century and into the twentieth. In an 1868 Act of Parliament, the new Canadian government guaranteed that those who had naturalised in the confederating colonies before 1867 would continue to hold equal rights in the new country. The Act also established liberal guidelines for future naturalisation: 3 years of residence, good character and an oath of loyalty to the Crown (Kaplan 1991: 10–11).[13] Two years later the British Parliament approved an imperial statute (Naturalization Act 1870) stipulating that an individual naturalised in one of the colonies enjoyed equal rights with native-born subjects, but that such rights were exclusive to that colony (Hancock 1937). Forty years later, during the Imperial Conference of 1911, Britain and the Dominions agreed to a uniform procedure of naturalisation and recognition of local naturalisation throughout the Empire (Brown 1996). These negotiations were enshrined in the Canadian Naturalization Act, 1914, which largely governed membership in Canada until passage of the Canadian Citizenship Act in 1946.

A patchwork of membership classes thus characterised Canada in the early twentieth century. 'Aliens' designated people born outside the British Empire who were living in Canada. They had no guaranteed right of entry into Canada and could only gain standing as a British subject or Canadian national through naturalisation. Those who naturalised were variously called 'British subjects of Canada', 'Canadian citizens' or 'Canadian nationals'.[14] These individuals enjoyed the right of entry into Canada, but their status elsewhere in the Empire depended on prevailing laws. In contrast, native 'British subjects', born in Canada or elsewhere in the Empire, needed no other status to enter Canada. British subjects born outside Canada could become Canadian nationals, a 'rather hollow distinction', by simply residing in Canada for 5 years (Hancock 1937: 98). At the close of the Second World War, Canada's citizenry thus consisted of native-born Canadians, naturalised Canadians who had affirmatively sought permanent status along the lines of US volitional citizenship, and a third class of individuals who were foreign-born but, because of their status as British subjects, were not required to take any confirmatory action for Canadian membership.

Dual citizenship: Modern evolution

Following the Second World War, Canada established a clear, legal Canadian citizenship, complete with the first Canadian passport, for the first time. As in the United States, the impetus to assert independent citizenship arose from a sense of nationalism and the desire to integrate individuals of diverse backgrounds into one political membership. Absent from the revolutionary context of the United States, however, the process of distancing from Great Britain did not bring a wholesale rejection of multiple membership.

Canadian citizenship came into being on 1 January 1947.[15] By the end of the Second World War, the fragmented state of Canadian nationality law demanded new legislation, as did the growing potency of Canadian nationalism, which had been strengthened in the cauldrons of war.[16] The government took great pains to underscore the symbolic unification accorded by citizenship, a bond that crossed ethnic lines. During the inaugural ceremony organised in January 1947, the first certificate of Canadian citizenship was given to the Prime Minister, but the second went to 'Wasyl Elnyiak, one of the first Ukrainians to farm in western Canada.... We had discovered him after a long search through the immigration department's records' (Martin 1993: 76). Other recipients were of Danish, Italian and Jewish background.

At the same time, British connections remained and thus, too, did multiple memberships. Canadian citizenship was primary, but all Canadians continued to be British subjects. The status of immigrants who were already British subjects elicited vigorous debate in the House of Commons: Did British subjecthood automatically entail Canadian citizenship? Nationalists, especially those from Quebec, wanted to provide few special rights, if any, to British subjects. Conversely, the Conservative party felt that the break with Britain and the rest of the Commonwealth embodied in Canadian citizenship was too radical (Schwartz 1976; Demirjian, Gray and Wright 1996). In the end, the government took a middle road, refusing to make British subjects automatic Canadian citizens, but it extended the vote to them after a year of residence without naturalisation, and it allowed them to gain Canadian citizenship after 5 years of residence without seeing a citizenship judge.

The approach to dual citizenship had a similar compromise character. Under the 1947 Citizenship Act, Canadians could lose their citizenship by naturalising in another country. Affirmatively taking on another nationality would be taken as a renunciation of Canadian citizenship. In contrast, there was no explicit requirement that those acquiring Canadian citizenship need to renounce prior allegiances. An immigrant who became Canadian could retain a prior nationality under the law (Kaplan 1991).

Canada's second major piece of citizenship legislation, the 1977 Citizenship Act, and accompanying Citizenship Regulations ended the long history of special duality with British subjecthood, but it extended full tolerance of dual citizenship with any country in the world. The Act eliminated special provisions for British subjects, requiring all immigrants, regardless of origin, to observe the same naturalisation requirements.[17] At the same time, the new legislation no longer equated naturalisation elsewhere with renunciation of Canadian citizenship. Dual citizenship was permitted through the absence of any language interdicting it. This change ushered in a permissive governmental attitude to dual citizenship.

The reasons behind Canada's acceptance of dual citizenship are not clear. According to Galloway (2000), dual citizenship elicited no debate in Parliament.[18] We can speculate that the government's adoption of official multiculturalism earlier in the decade might have had an influence. Announced in the House of Commons in 1971, Canadian multiculturalism set out a new vision of the country as culturally diverse, but unified under a new Canadian identity. The official languages of Canada would reflect the nation's British and French roots but, as Prime Minister Pierre Trudeau argued to the applause of all the opposition parties in the House of Commons, 'biculturalism does not properly describe our society' (Canada, House of Commons 1971: 8581). Rather, 'National unity if it is to mean anything in the deeply personal sense, must be founded on confidence in one's own individual identity; out of this can grow respect for that of others and a willingness to share ideas, attitudes and assumptions. A vigorous policy of multiculturalism will help create this initial confidence' (Canada, House of Commons 1971: 8545). Thus, immigrants' and ethnic minorities' attachment to other identities became both a precursor and a constituent part of being Canadian. Perhaps this sentiment informed the government's decision to allow multiple citizenship.

It appears paradoxical to build a sense of Canadian unity on acceptance of multiplicity and, indeed, various people have questioned the ideology of multiculturalism and dual citizenship. In the 1990s, as a backlash against multiculturalism was growing in Canada, the Parliamentary Standing Committee on Citizenship and Immigration recommended restricted dual citizenship with an emphasis on unitary, primary loyalty to Canada (Galloway 2000). Yet as discussions over a new Citizenship Act got underway in the late 1990s, there was no talk of ending dual citizenship. A primary reason probably lies in immigrants' appreciation of dual membership, even if they do not actively pursue the option.[19]

In the US case, security concerns generated by the Second World War and fear of Communism reinforced the suspicions of many over the divided loyalties implied by multiple citizenship. Prior to the war, the US Department of Labour oversaw citizenship policy and the administration of naturalisation, but in 1940 the President's Reorganization Plan (Number V) transferred the Immigration and Naturalization Service (INS) to the Department of Justice, refocusing the actions and priorities of the agency around security. The war responsibilities of the INS included recording and fingerprinting every alien in the United States through the Alien Registration Program, organising and operating internment camps and detention facilities for enemy aliens, and guarding national borders with the Border Patrol (Smith 1998).

The 1952 Immigration and Nationality Act, the first major piece of US immigration and citizenship legislation following the Second World War, was crafted at a time of growing concern over Communism. In it, Congress directed the INS to administer a Naturalization Oath of Allegiance to all adult would-be citizens. It is this oath that most dramatically illustrates America's belief in a single citizenship and still guides present-day naturalisation policy.

By the 1990s the imperatives of war and anti-Communism had faded, but border control still dominated the INS. From 1993 to 1999, the border control budget grew by more than $1.5 billion while citizenship and other immigration services saw an increase of only about $270 million (US Immigration and Naturalization Service 2000). In 2000, the INS was the largest law enforcement agency of the federal government. In the words of former INS Commissioner Doris Meissner, 'the dominant culture of the agency ... [is] rooted in a view of immigration as a source of security and law enforcement vulnerability more than of continuing nation building' (2001: 2). President Bush's decision to relocate immigration and naturalisation services to the new Department of Homeland Security, effective 1 March 2003, continues this tradition.

American support for exclusive citizenship appears unequivocal, especially in Congress, but domestic court decisions and foreign countries' acceptance of multiple nationality undermine Congressional desires. Symbolically the United States promotes a single status, but in reality dual citizenship is permissible. Many dual nationals hold their status because numerous countries allow parents to pass on their citizenship to their children, regardless of their children's birthplace. As a result, many children of immigrants born in the United States can access multiple nationalities. US courts have upheld their right to dual citizenship. In

Mandoli v. Acheson (1952), the Supreme Court ruled that Joseph Mandoli, the American-born son of Italian parents, could retain US citizenship even though he had lived most of his childhood and adolescence outside the United States.

Courts have also attacked the US government's ability to take away Americans' citizenship when they violate the principle of national exclusivity. Up to the 1960s, the State Department would denationalise Americans who engaged in activities construed as a renunciation of American citizenship, such as naturalisation in another country or voting in a foreign election (Finifter and Finifter 1995; Schuck 1998). The Supreme Court challenged this practice in its 1967 *Afroyim v. Rusk ruling*. The case revolved around Beys Afroyim, a naturalised citizen who had moved to Israel in 1950. When Afroyim tried to renew his American passport in 1960, the government refused to issue it on the grounds that he had voted in Israeli elections, thereby revoking his American citizenship. The Court, however, ruled that Afroyim was still a US citizen, asserting that the 14th Amendment elevated citizenship to be a constitutionally protected right. The Court found that any action on the part of a US citizen, including swearing allegiance to a foreign country, must be accompanied by intent to renounce American citizenship. Those who acquired another citizenship after becoming American could not automatically lose their US citizenship.[20]

Dual citizenship is thus legal in the United States for those born with multiple nationalities and for Americans—naturalised or native-born— who subsequently acquire another citizenship without an explicit intention of giving up their US status. The case for naturalising immigrants is less clear. Does an immigrant who swears to reject past allegiances but then proceeds to use a former passport commit perjury? The Supreme Court has never ruled on the legality of the Oath of Allegiance and its renunciation clause, but the Court's prior rulings make it extremely unlikely that someone going through the naturalisation process will have their ability to acquire American citizenship challenged simply because they maintain another nationality. Furthermore, many countries today fail to recognise the Oath as a renunciation of their nationals' prior citizenship. Many immigrants consequently find that they retain their former nationality in the eyes of their home countries even after they acquire American citizenship.

Given legal rulings and the actions of foreign governments, officials in the State Department and naturalisation service no longer monitor residents' use of multiple passports. In 1990, then Secretary of State James Baker sent a series of telegrams to diplomatic and consular posts around the world which, while reiterating the US government's dislike of dual citizenship due to 'the problems which it may cause', also specified that officials were to presume US citizens wanted to keep their citizenship even when they obtained the citizenship of another country or made a pro forma declaration of allegiance to another country (Ansgar Kelly 1991–92: 443–44). For the INS, 'Dual citizenship from our point of view is not really a problem. We're in the business of saying who's a U.S. citizen or not. And whether some other country also recognizes that person, we basically think that it's an issue of that country's domestic law. And so, it's really not a big concern for us.'[21] Indeed, some US officials welcome foreign countries' adoption of multiple nationality since it produces dual citizenship without requiring them to enter the American political fray over the issue. As former INS Commissioner Doris Meissner explained, reflecting on her tenure from 1993 to 2000, '[Dual citizenship] was unlikely to change as a matter of U.S. policy, and we really didn't need to raise it because other countries were changing their policies rather rapidly.'[22] In 2001, for example, ten Latin American countries and ten countries in the Caribbean basin allowed their citizens to hold dual nationality (Jones-Correa 2001). The US Oath of Allegiance notwithstanding, American citizens, like citizens of Canada, can hold multiple nationalities even though American acceptance of the practice appears largely grudging and against the wishes of Congress, while the Canadian policy is more openly embraced.

Does dual citizenship matter?

Those worried about multiple citizenship raise at least three sets of concerns. The first set centres on the potential clash of allegiances generated by multiple attachments. Some of these concerns are general, equating dual citizenship with bigamy and lamenting the lack of loyalty alleged to follow from multiple citizenship (Geyer 1996). Other concerns are more specific questions of jurisdiction and dual nationals' conflicting duties. For whom does one fight in the event of military conflict?

A second set of concerns focuses on the political ramifications of dual citizenship. These range from the mistrustful—will dual nationals vote in domestic elections according to the interests of their other nationality?—to the philosophical—is democratic equality undermined when some citizens can vote in two elections? Noah Pinkus (2005: 181–82) wonders about the long-term viability of a political community where some citizens, unhappy with political outcomes, can opt to leave the country for another state rather than be forced to live with the community's political decisions.

A third set of concerns centres on the fear that dual citizenship undermines a country's ability to integrate immigrant newcomers. If citizenship is 'a vital part of patriotic assimilation, in some ways its symbolic heart' (Fonte 2005: 6), won't multiple nationalities undermine foreigners' psychological and political incorporation? Space constraints prevent a detailed examination of all the objections to dual citizenship, but the evidence from Canada suggests that dual citizenship, especially as a symbolic affirmation of immigrants' ties to their land of birth and land of adoption, might enhance political incorporation and the creation of a civic community.[23]

To take up, or not take up, dual citizenship

Many of the fears around dual citizenship assume that individuals actively pursue dual citizenship wherever it is permitted. Surprisingly, despite significant public concern and academic interest in dual citizenship, we know little about the actual number of people who hold multiple nationalities. Some generous estimates suggest that up to 40 million individuals in the United States could access dual citizenship through their ties with one of almost 100 countries that permit some form of multiple allegiance (Renshon 2000, 2001). Such a large figure—suggesting that one in fourteen Americans holds legal, political and affective ties to a country other than the United States—raises red flags for those who worry that multiple attachments challenge the sovereignty and integrity of the United States. We need to distinguish, however, between the number of people who have the legal right to dual citizenship and the number who actually take affirmative steps to adopt another nationality. If few avail themselves of the opportunity, the dangers of dual citizenship are exaggerated.

In fact, relatively few naturalised immigrants, and even fewer US-born dual nationals, appear to avail themselves of citizenship in other countries. Take, for example, Mexico's widely discussed decision to extend dual nationality to Mexicans living abroad through the *No Perdida de la Nacionalidad Mexicana* programme, which ran from 1998 to 2003.[24] Mexicans make up a quarter of all foreign-born individuals in the United States, and the 2000 US Census enumerated just over two million Mexican-born naturalised Americans who could regain Mexican nationality. Newspapers across the United States ran stories about the programme, often with headlines suggesting that large numbers of local residents were applying for the reinstatement of their Mexican nationality. Yet only a tiny fraction of those eligible visited a Mexican consulate to pay the $15 fee and fill out the required paperwork. According to one report, the Mexican Foreign Relations Ministry estimated that only 30,000 former Mexican nationals registered between 2000 and 2003 (Gutierrez 2003). Local news coverage in cities with significant Mexican-American populations reported that between a few dozen to a few hundred individuals—out of immigrant populations numbering in the tens of thousands—sought dual nationality. Full bureaucratic and legal dual citizenship appears to hold little interest for many Mexican Americans.[25]

Mexican Americans are not the only ones who express interest in dual citizenship but fail to take the administrative steps necessary to secure another passport. Indian immigrants around the world have long requested dual citizenship. Prior to January 2004, an Indian citizen who acquired citizenship in another country automatically lost his or her prior nationality. That policy changed in early 2004 when the Indian government extended dual citizenship to Indians living in sixteen countries, including Canada.[26] One poll conducted by a South Asian newspaper in the Toronto area found that 90 per cent of respondents would opt for dual citizenship (Prashad 2005).[27] Yet one year after the policy change, an official with the Indian High Commission in Canada reported that only about 500 Indians out of an estimated population of 350,000 had filed for dual citizenship in metropolitan Toronto (Prashad 2005).

In in-depth interviews with Portuguese immigrants in Toronto and Boston, I found that many were pleased that Portugal changed its laws in 1981 to allow dual citizenship, but relatively few had taken the effort to visit the Portuguese consulate to register as a citizen or reclaim Portuguese nationality.[28] Victor, a naturalised American who had lived in the United States for 30 years, explained,

> I have not yet [applied to reclaim Portuguese citizenship]. I think I will, eventually...I don't have any personal reasons right now. Yeah, I think that it would be nice to have.... having two passports probably will cut five minutes out of my waiting time at the airports in Portugal. But not that much more.

While a number of community leaders had taken the time to seek Portuguese citizenship, and in some cases to be involved in Portuguese politics, the vast majority of ordinary Portuguese evinced little interest in formally reinstating their prior nationality.[29]

Indeed, taking the administrative steps necessary to acquire a second passport can be time-consuming, complicated and expensive. Such hassles help explain the low number of applicants for formal dual citizenship. But even if we consider a less demanding indicator of multiple nationality, immigrants' simple acknowledgment of their status as dual citizens, reports of dual attachments remain modest.

Various scholars have noted the lack of adequate data on dual citizenship (Hammar 1985; Spiro 1997; Aleinikoff 1998). In this context, the Canadian Census stands out as one of the very few sources of broad, nationally representative statistics on reported dual citizenship. Since 1981, residents of Canada have been asked to indicate not only their status as Canadian citizens, but also whether they possess any other citizenship.[30] The question—which does not ask whether an individual holds a valid foreign passport—can be understood as a general query about multiple citizenship.

Examining Canadian residents' response to this question, we find that reports of dual citizenship clearly increased over the past 25 years. As shown in Table 8.1, just under 4 per cent of immigrants in Canada indicated that they held two or more citizenship statuses in 1981.[31] By 1996, the proportion had risen to 12 per cent, a threefold increase.

The significance of this figure is, however, open to debate. If one in eight immigrants reports multiple citizenship, does this indicate widespread multinationalism, or a relatively low level of multiple attachments? The number of dual citizens is far from negligible—more than half a million immigrants reported the status in 2001—but the overall

Table 8.1 Reported dual citizenship among immigrants in Canada, 1981–2001 (in percentages)

Population	1981	1991	1996	2001
Immigrants of all ages	3.9	8.2	12.1	10.3
Naturalised immigrants of all ages	5.5	10.7	16.6	13.7
Naturalised immigrants who moved to Canada as adults	6.1	11.2	17.8	n/a
Naturalised immigrants who moved to Canada as children	4.6	9.9	14.3	n/a

Sources: Author's calculations from 1981, 1991 and 1996 Canadian Census (20% sample); 2001 Canadian Census.

percentage seems low given academics' recent emphasis on transnational and postnational belonging.

Curiously, by 2001 the proportion of immigrants reporting dual citizenship actually *decreased*, to just over 10 per cent, despite an increase in the number of countries around the world allowing dual citizenship. One explanation for the decrease could be a rise in the number of new immigrants in Canada. Although some Canadian residents hold multiple citizenships that do not include Canadian citizenship—5,195 individuals in 2001—the vast majority holds Canadian citizenship and some other nationality. Thus 552,880 individuals reported Canadian citizenship and one other nationality, and 4,030 indicated that they were Canadian and citizens of two other countries in 2001. Since recent immigrants usually have not had a chance to acquire Canadian citizenship, a sudden influx of newcomers decreases the overall proportion of dual citizens.[32]

If we instead consider the prevalence of reported multiple citizenship among naturalised immigrants to Canada, the proportion of multinationals increases. Table 8.1 reveals the same threefold increase in the percentage of dual citizens, but the percentages now rise from 5.5 per cent to almost 17 per cent in 1996. We also see the same fall in 2001, with just under 14 per cent of naturalised Canadians indicating that they have at least one other nationality.

The drop in reported dual citizenship in 2001 might also come from changes in the source of Canadian immigration. Not all sending countries permit multiple citizenship. If the relative proportion of immigrants from permissive and restrictive states changes, the aggregate percentage of dual nationals could decrease. Statistics Canada has not published 2001 citizenship data by country of origin, but analysis of data from 1981 to 1996 shows great variation in reported dual citizenship depending upon country of origin. Both Switzerland and Ireland permit dual citizenship, yet while 57 per cent of Swiss-Canadians report their multiple nationalities—the highest percentage of any immigrant group—only 18 per cent of those born in Ireland do.

Indeed, as we can see in Table 8.2, the majority of naturalised Canadians fail to report dual citizenship when the laws of their birthplace allow them to do so.[33] Take, for example, the case of those born in Uruguay. Since 1919, naturalisation in another country has had no effect on Uruguayans' birth nationality. Legally, almost everyone born in Uruguay and naturalised in Canada should declare dual citizenship. Yet, in 1996 more than 60 per cent did not, reporting only 'Canadian by naturalisation'. The same holds true for other countries

Table 8.2 Percentage of naturalised Canadian adults reporting dual citizenship, by place of birth*

Country of birth	1981	1991	1996	Per cent change from 1981 to 1996 (%)	Adult dual cit. allowed? (Yr allowed, if specified)
Switzerland	28.6	32.1	57.0	99	yes (1952)
New Zealand	26.5	31.7	45.0	70	yes (1949)
Lebanon	10.3	16.8	42.0	308	yes
Israel	10.5	14.5	40.0	281	yes
Uruguay	15.9	24.7	38.7	143	yes (1919)
France	18.7	24.0	37.9	103	yes (1973)
El Salvador	2.3	15.9	35.2	1430	yes (1983)
Argentina	11.0	15.5	32.7	197	yes (limited)
Pakistan	7.4	9.3	30.8	316	yes
Barbados	11.3	17.1	26.2	132	yes (1966)
Poland	1.0	6.8	26.1	2510	de facto
Egypt	7.2	11.4	24.0	233	de facto
United Kingdom	8.3	14.5	21.9	164	yes
U.S.A.	2.8	11.6	20.8	643	de facto
Portugal	2.4	8.4	20.4	750	yes (1981)
Greece	5.9	11.5	20.1	241	de facto
Ireland (Eire)	7.8	13.6	18.1	132	yes (1922)
Guyana	10.0	8.3	16.1	61	yes
Jamaica	7.7	9.0	16.0	108	yes (1962)
Trinidad and Tobago	2.4	5.2	14.7	513	yes (1988)
Hungary	2.5	4.8	11.2	348	yes (1993)
Italy	2.5	4.8	10.3	312	yes (1992)
Philippines	2.6	3.8	8.5	227	no
Haiti	1.8	2.4	7.4	311	no
Vietnam	4.7	5.8	6.7	43	no (de facto)
India	1.2	2.2	3.6	200	yes (2004)
China	1.8	3.4	2.7	50	no
Germany	0.8	1.7	2.5	213	no
Netherlands	0.6	1.5	2.3	283	no

* Here dual citizens include those with, at least, citizenship in Canada and their country of birth.
Sources: Statistics from the 20% sample of the Canadian Census of Population 1981, 1991 and 1996; legal information from government documents, embassy officials, Jones-Correa (2001), Renshon (2000) and Defense Security Service of the US Department of Defense.

that formally accept multiple citizenship. Jamaican law recognised dual citizenship in 1962. Since most Jamaican immigrants naturalised after 1962, all are legally dual citizens. Yet only 16 per cent claimed this status in 1996. Overall, a significant majority of immigrants who are *de jure* dual nationals do not recognise or acknowledge this fact.

Failing to claim dual citizenship might be more telling than its acknowledgment, assuaging some commentators' fears of rampant divided loyalties, or challenging others' belief in widespread transnationalism. Unfortunately, census data do not tell us why respondents mark the particular response they do, so we know little about the content and meaning of dual citizenship for these people. Do those who fail to report their status do so because they do not understand their legal status or because they do not find dual citizenship terribly relevant?

It is likely that some immigrants are not aware of their homeland's stance on dual citizenship. If we consider people born in countries that do *not* allow dual citizenship, we find that there are always a small number who nonetheless claim multiple nationalities. For example, in 1996 Indian law considered naturalisation in another country to be a renunciation of Indian nationality. Yet 4,595 people, or 3.6 per cent of all naturalised adult Indians, reported dual citizenship. Likewise, 4.8 per cent of naturalised Italians reported dual nationality in 1991, a year before Italian law changed to allow dual citizenship. Those who reported dual nationality in 1991 either anticipated that they would get their former citizenship back, or did not understand the legal code, or reported dual nationality as an identity claim rather than as a legal status.[34] At the same time, the number of immigrants who appear to make mistaken claims of dual citizenship is small, implying that most immigrants are aware of dual citizenship laws.[35] In Table 8.2, fewer than 10 per cent of immigrants from countries that do not allow dual citizenship report a double allegiance.

The evidence thus implies that many who are legally dual citizens fail to report their status because dual nationality is not overly salient for them. This is not to say that they have no feeling of attachment to their country of origin. Many probably have multiple identities that include a deep sense of ethnic, national or cultural pride. But it is likely that such feelings do not translate into a strong desire for formal political and legal attachment to the country of origin. The propensity to claim dual citizenship decreases as length of residence in Canada increases, and those who migrate as children are less likely to report multiple attachments than adult migrants. The effects of length of residence and age at migration are stronger predictors of a dual citizenship claim than an immigrant's sex, poverty status, ability to speak basic English or French, marital status or status as a visible minority.[36] Only level of education, language spoken at home and whether the person lived outside Canada 5 years earlier has a larger impact on reported dual citizenship (Bloemraad 2004).

The symbolic significance of dual citizenship and multiculturalism

From the admittedly limited evidence available, it appears that few immigrants embark on the bureaucratic hassle attendant upon claiming formal dual citizenship. Only a fraction of those eligible bother to go to consulates and embassies to get a second passport or register their citizenship status. When we consider a less stringent measure of dual citizenship—just taking the time to mark a box on a census form asking about multiple nationalities—in all cases save one a minority of immigrants report dual citizenship. Most immigrants who are *de jure* dual nationals do not bother to claim it, despite Canada's openness to dual citizenship. One implication is that despite academics' interest in—and, in some cases, concern with—dual citizenship, the vast majority of immigrants care little about their access to multiple political memberships.

We need to make a distinction, however, between actively pursuing dual citizenship in the form of a passport or voting in homeland elections, and the symbolic importance of having the option available. Various studies show that immigrants value the *idea* of dual citizenship. Dual citizenship acknowledges multiple emotional attachments and recognises both where immigrants come from and where they currently make their home (Jones-Correa 1998; Bloemraad 2006). Victoria, a Portuguese-Canadian immigrant from the Azores, spoke somewhat disdainfully of the old Portuguese law that forbade dual citizenship. As she explained, 'I was born in the [Azorean] islands. I think for me I will always—I was Portuguese, and I don't think I've lost it. But they said I did so.' At the same time, Victoria proudly says that she is Canadian and would never return to Portugal, not even when she retires: 'I love Canada, and I consider Canada my home now.' Dual citizenship serves as an acknowledgment of her multiple emotional ties.

In fact, dual citizenship might increase immigrants' attachment to the receiving country. Some immigrants do not want to become citizens of their new country if it means giving up their old nationality. Interestingly, Portuguese immigrants in the United States do not see the US Oath of Allegiance as a barrier to dual citizenship. Rather, they are concerned with the citizenship laws of their birthplace. A number of Portuguese immigrants in Boston and in Toronto said that they did not file naturalisation papers until the Portuguese government allowed dual citizenship, even if they later did not formally file to keep their old nationality. As one organiser of a Portuguese-Canadian citizenship drive in Toronto explained,

> Dual citizenship is very important. . . . a lot of people at the citizenship drive said, 'I don't want to lose my Portuguese citizenship'. We had to tell them hundreds of times, we have told them hundreds of times, that you don't lose your Portuguese citizenship. They want to keep it for patriotic reasons. . . . my generation, people who are older, they are very nationalistic.

Dual citizenship laws in the country of origin consequently promote political integration in the country of adoption.

The dual citizenship laws of the *receiving* society are also critical, though not so much for what the legal code says but for what it symbolises. Combined with policies of multiculturalism or pluralism, dual citizenship in the country of residence communicates acceptance of immigrants and respect for their backgrounds. For some immigrants exclusive American citizenship equates with an attitude of forced assimilation, one that ignores the value of cultures and traditions elsewhere (Jones-Correa 1998). Conversely, some immigrants in Canada view dual citizenship as a natural extension of multicultural acceptance, even if they have little interest in retaining political or legal ties to their birthplace. Dual citizenship thus signals the degree to which the adopted country accepts immigrants' differences.

This symbolic side of dual citizenship probably helps to explain in small part a recent divergence in North American naturalisation patterns. Through most of the twentieth century, the proportion of immigrants who acquired US or Canadian citizenship was remarkably similar: citizenship levels rose and dipped in tandem from 1900 to 1970. Since 1970, a striking divergence has emerged, as shown in Figure 8.1. In Canada, citizenship levels rose from 60 per cent in 1971 to 75 per cent in 2001. In contrast, the percentage of naturalised Americans fell from 64 per cent in 1970 to 40 per cent in 2000. No significant changes in citizenship regulations occurred over this period, and the gap remains even when we consider immigrants' country of origin and various sociodemographic variables such as length of residence, education and ability to speak English (Bloemraad 2004).[37]

The 1970s were, however, marked by a substantial shift in Canadian self-identity towards multicultural nationalism, including the acceptance of dual citizenship in 1977. This ideology, despite its limits

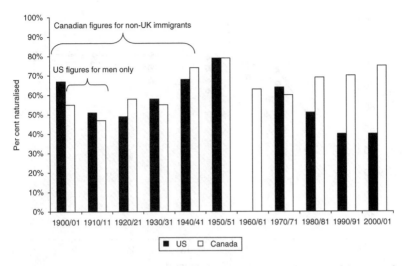

Figure 8.1 Percentage of adult immigrants naturalised in the United States and Canada, 1900–2001

in dealing with problems of discrimination and racism, has proven attractive to many immigrants who have entered Canada in the last three decades. One consequence is increased interest in Canadian citizenship among very recent immigrants, as shown in Figure 8.2. The graph charts the percentage of immigrants who have acquired Canadian citizenship, taking into account the number of years they have spent in Canada. Over the period 1981–1996, successive cohorts of immigrants are more likely to take out Canadian citizenship than immigrants who came earlier, and they do so more quickly than in the past. Thus, in 2001, 80 per cent of immigrants who had lived in Canada for 10 years reported Canadian citizenship, compared to only 60 per cent of immigrants with the same length of residence in 1981. Census data do not allow us to probe the reasons behind citizenship decisions, but in-depth interviews suggest that the Canadian government's openness to multi-culturalism and multiple identities, of which dual citizenship is one manifestation, helps make Canadian society and Canadian citizenship attractive (Bloemraad 2006).

The consequence of higher naturalisation and greater political inclusion is reflected in the number of foreign-born representatives serving in each country's national legislature. In 2001, 45 sitting Members of the Canadian House of Commons, or 15 per cent, were born outside Canada. This percentage stood a bit under the 19 per cent of the total Canadian

178 _Dual Citizenship in the United States and Canada_

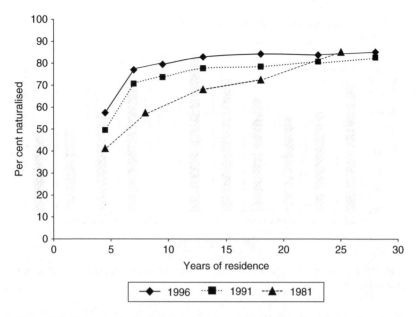

Figure 8.2 Percentage of adult immigrants naturalised in Canada, by length of residence, 1981, 1991 and 1996

population that was foreign-born that year. Though not at parity, the ratio of the proportion of foreign-born in the House of Commons to the proportion in the general population was much more equal than in the United States. In 2000, only 8 foreign-born individuals held office in the 435-seat US House of Representatives. The percentage of foreign-born individuals in the House, 1.8 per cent, stood much lower than the 11 per cent of the population born outside the United States.

Conclusion

According to Scherner-Kim, the role of the US Oath of Allegiance, in particular its renunciation clause, is to further American nationality so that 'newly naturalized U.S. citizens become fully functioning members of the U.S. polity' (2000: 330). A failure to enforce the renunciation clause reduces American citizenship to an instrumental status used to acquire rights and benefits without a true affective tie.

   Given such an analysis, why do immigrants to Canada take up citizenship more quickly and in greater numbers than compatriots in the

United States? The obvious answer is that Canada allows dual nationality, devaluing Canadian citizenship into a passport for material and
legal benefits and undermining the creation of a robust political and
civic community.

This chapter turns such an argument on its head. The available empirical evidence seems to suggest that far fewer people take active steps to
hold multiple passports than some commentators fear. Indeed, when
asked an explicit question about their citizenship status, many people
fail to report dual nationality. Yet at the same time, interviews with
the foreign-born consistently suggest that immigrants want and value
the ability to hold dual citizenship. I would thus suggest that dual
citizenship, at this point in time, is most important for its symbolic
value. It signals a country's willingness to tolerate multiple attachments and recognise the multiple identities many immigrants hold. As
a result, immigrants in countries that explicitly accept dual citizenship
feel a stronger sense of belonging, promoting the creation of a political
community. Facilitating citizenship, rather than policing membership,
can build national unity from diversity.

Notes

1. The bureau tried to bypass the regular review period for administrative
   changes, raising the ire of groups across the political spectrum. Veterans'
   associations and some conservative think tanks also complained that the
   new oath diluted the requirement to defend the United States against foreign
   and domestic enemies.
2. Indeed, since 2003 a number of conservative groups – including the American Legion, Hudson Institute and Center for Immigration Studies in
   Washington, DC – have become increasingly vocal against any weakening in
   the language of exclusive American allegiance. During its summer convention in 2005, the American Legion passed a resolution encouraging Congress
   'to enact measures to enforce the Oath of Renunciation and Allegiance and
   reject dual allegiance in principle and restrict and narrow its application in
   practice' (Fonte 2005: 3).
3. See http://www.cic.gc.ca/english/citizen/dualci_e.html (last accessed 20
   January 2006). CIC also notes the potential dangers of dual citizenship, such
   as compulsory military service or mandatory taxes in other countries of
   citizenship.
4. The entire oath reads as follows:

   > I hereby declare, on oath, that I absolutely and entirely renounce and
   > abjure all allegiance and fidelity to any foreign prince, potentate, state, or
   > sovereignty of whom or which I have heretofore been a subject or citizen;
   > that I will support and defend the Constitution and laws of the United
   > States of America against all enemies, foreign and domestic; that I will

bear true faith and allegiance to the same; that I will bear arms on behalf of the United States when required by law; that I will perform noncombatant service in the Armed Forces of the United States when required by law; that I will perform work of national importance under civilian direction when required by law; and that I take this obligation freely without any mental reservation or purpose of evasion; so help me God.

5. Fear of newcomers probably helps to explain why the dual citizenship of US-born citizens—who hold a second nationality through a foreign citizen parent or because they were born overseas to American parents—generates limited controversy compared to the cries of alarm over the multiple allegiances of naturalising immigrants (Duckett 2000; Scherner-Kim 2000).

6. In certain legal contexts, citizenship and nationality are not the same, providing a different set of rights and benefits. Largely for stylistic reasons, I use the terms 'dual citizenship' and 'dual nationality' interchangeably. In those cases in which an important legal distinction exists, I note the difference.

7. The colonists' membership status was clearly established by William III in 1700 when he decreed that any natural-born subject, whether in the colonies or Great Britain, could inherit even if his father or mother was an alien (Carpenter 1904: 292).

8. The colonies, wishing to lure settlers, generally embraced a liberal policy of naturalisation while Parliament in London favoured restricted access to subjecthood due to religious intolerance and as a limit on trading rights (Ueda 1982; Kaplan 1991). Shifting power dynamics between the Crown and the Parliament, as well as among the parties within Parliament, generated frequent changes in England's policies.

9. The most important step in this evolution was an Act of Parliament passed in 1740 establishing a general naturalisation law. It permitted foreigners in North America to acquire local subjectship (Ueda 1982).

10. At the same time, American citizenship contained important limits to its inclusive vision. The first law on naturalisation restricted its application to 'free white persons'. Black immigrants gained access to naturalisation under legislation passed in 1870, but 12 years later the Chinese Exclusion Act of 1882 prohibited any Chinese immigrant from acquiring US citizenship through naturalisation. Using a narrow interpretation of the fourteenth Amendment, subsequent court decisions made it difficult for any East or South Asian immigrant to naturalise (Ueda 1982; Haney López 1996; Smith 1997). Racial restrictions on naturalisation only ended in the middle of the twentieth century. Chinese immigrants gained access to citizenship in 1943, Filipinos and Asian Indians in 1946. The 1952 McCarran–Walter Act definitively removed race or national origin as a criterion for American citizenship.

11. See Ueda (1982) and Bloemraad and Ueda (2006) for further details on this history.

12. British subjecthood did not necessarily imply adherence to British language or culture. During the Confederation debates the leading French-Canadian advocate of Canadian Confederation, George Etienne Cartier, spoke of political unity and membership rather than ethnic belonging: 'When we are united we shall form a political nationality independent of the national

origin or the religion of any individual...The idea of unity of races is a utopia; it is an impossibility' (Kaplan 1991: 13).

13. The residence period was extended to 5 years in 1914 and brought back to 3 in 1977. Unlike the United States, Canada had no racial restrictions on citizenship; Asians and ex-slaves from the United States could become British subjects and Canadian nationals. However, this status proved hollow since the Canadian system rested on Parliamentary supremacy, not a written Constitution guaranteeing rights to citizens. Thus, the province of British Columbia could and did deny voting rights to Asians on racial grounds, regardless of citizenship status, and the federal government worked to deport Japanese-Canadians during the Second World War (Angus 1937; Kelley and Trebilcock 1998; Galloway 2000).

14. The term 'Canadian citizen' first appeared in the 1910 Canadian Immigration Act, and 'Canadian national' was defined in the 1921 Canadian Nationals Act as a precondition for participation in the League of Nations (Kaplan 1991: 12–13).

15. The Secretary of State had made an earlier attempt to introduce a bill on Canadian citizenship in 1931 but it was withdrawn largely due to protest over the extension of citizenship to Asians in British Columbia (Kaplan 1991: 23; Galloway 2000).

16. According to the Secretary of State responsible for introducing the legislation, Paul Martin, his commitment to establishing Canadian citizenship solidified following a visit to the graves of Canadian soldiers in Dieppe, France (Martin 1993).

17. Canadian citizens still automatically become 'citizens of the Commonwealth' upon naturalisation. This status has little consequence.

18. During the second reading of the bill in December 1975, only two Members of Parliament alluded to dual citizenship, approving the removal of renunciation provisions. My thanks to Chris Anderson for this information.

19. Space considerations prevent an extended discussion of evolving Canadian nationalism, especially the role of Quebec in shaping English-Canadian conceptions of nationhood. Some commentators argue that the goal of multiculturalism was to undermine rising French-Canadian nationalism and Quebec's unique place in Confederation (Labelle, Rocher and Rocher 1995). Similarly, the backlash against multiculturalism in the 1990s stemmed in part from fears over Canadian unity generated by Quebec's election of a separatist provincial government and ensuing referendum on independence in 1995.

20. The Court's distinction between acts that could be construed as renunciation of citizenship and the actual intent behind the act was reaffirmed in *Vance v. Terrazas* (1980). The court shifted the burden of proof in challenges to American citizenship status away from the individual immigrant and onto the government (Duckett 2000). Following this decision, the Immigration and Nationality Act was amended in 1986 to specify that loss of US citizenship only follows from acts committed 'with the intention of relinquishing U.S. nationality' (Ansgar Kelly 1991–92: 439). Ansgar Kelly argues that US law has always provided some room for dual citizenship, but that 'both the government and the judiciary at various levels had a track record of dislike for dual nationals' (1991–92: 440).

21. Interview with a senior INS official, 6 November 2001. Former Commissioner Doris Meissner made similar comments during an interview on 2 May 2002.
22. Interview with the author on 2 May 2002.
23. Other arguments in favour of dual citizenship suggest that allowing the practice might further democracy by facilitating the transfer of American democratic norms back to less democratic countries of origin (Levitt 2001). The Canadian government has also defended the practice as helping build better economic, cultural and political relations with other countries through the activities of dual citizens. More generally, metaphors equating dual citizenship with bigamy ignore alternative models, such as a child's love for two (or more) parents and a parent's love for multiple children, some of whom might be biological, others adopted.
24. This dual nationality programme did not provide full dual citizenship. Mexican nationals in other countries could gain property rights and the right of entry into Mexico, but did not have full political rights unless they resided in Mexico. Expatriate political rights were extended in 2005. The 1998–2003 programme was nonetheless largely seen as an extension of dual citizenship.
25. When it comes to voting in Mexican elections—a political act of particular concern to some opponents of dual citizenship—the numbers are even more modest. Only ten thousand Mexican citizens living in the United States, a number which would include dual citizens and those who hold only Mexican citizenship, registered to vote for the 2006 Mexican presidential election (Enriquez 2006: 3). A survey by Louis DeSipio and colleagues also reports low levels of participation in homeland politics among Mexican, Dominican and Salvadoran immigrants. Depending on the group, between two and six per cent reported contributing money to a candidate or party in their country of origin, and between 9 and 15 per cent reported having voted in a homeland election at least once (DeSipio et al. 2003: 11). In addition, it is quite possible that immigrants in the survey over-reported homeland electoral participation, as native-born Americans and Canadians do in domestic election studies. This would mean that the percentage of active political participation is even lower.
26. In January 2005, dual citizenship was extended to all Indians worldwide living in countries allowing dual citizenship. Indian dual citizenship does not extend political rights to nationals living overseas.
27. The poll, done online, would not meet scientific standards for survey research, but it is an indication of widespread interest in dual citizenship.
28. Portuguese nationals who naturalised in Canada or the United States before the 1981 law automatically lost their Portuguese citizenship. Those who naturalised after the law can keep their Portuguese nationality, but they must register at a Portuguese consulate if they want to vote in Portuguese elections.
29. For more on this study, which includes in-depth interviews with Portuguese and Vietnamese immigrants in Boston and Toronto, see Bloemraad (2006).
30. The 1981 form reads, 'Of what country are you a citizen? *Mark as many boxes as apply.*' The 1991 form asks, 'Of what country is this person a citizen? *Mark more than one circle, if applicable.*' The 1996 form asks, 'Of what country is this person a citizen? *Indicate more than one citizenship, if applicable*' (emphasis

in originals). These questions appeared on the Census 'long form', delivered to every one in five households in Canada. For more details about census methodology and the figures reported below, see Bloemraad (2004).

31. I focus on dual citizenship among immigrants to Canada since these individuals are the most likely to hold multiple nationalities and they have been the focus of debate on the subject. Some native-born Canadians hold dual citizenship by descent from an immigrant parent or grandparent or through marriage to a foreign national. In a very few cases, individuals with large capital assets can buy a foreign nationality. Native-born dual nationals increase the absolute number of dual citizens in Canada, but because they constitute a very small proportion of all Canadian-born individuals, the overall percentage of reported dual citizenship among all Canadian residents is substantially less than among immigrants.

32. Under Canadian law, a foreign-born individual must have 3 years of legal permanent residence before applying for naturalisation; bureaucratic waits might add another year's delay.

33. Because citizenship laws for children sometimes differ from those for adults, and these differences in turn vary by country of origin, the statistics in Table 8.2 count only adults.

34. Dual citizenship for Italians who naturalised before 1992 was not automatic. The government required former nationals to file a formal request to restore their Italian citizenship.

35. It is also possible that special circumstances provide these individuals with legitimate dual citizenship, despite the general interdiction against multiple nationality. Such is the case for the author.

36. 'Visible minority' is the Canadian term for people of colour.

37. Canadian citizenship actually provides fewer rights and gives access to fewer special benefits than American citizenship. US citizens can sponsor relatives more easily to the United States—a valuable benefit to many immigrants—and certain welfare provisions have recently been tied to citizenship. In Canada, citizenship does not facilitate family reunification, nor does it determine access to Canadian social programmes such as universal health insurance. A naturalised Canadian gains guaranteed access to Canadian soil, the opportunity to apply for certain citizen-only jobs, and political rights such as the right to vote and run for office. The same is true for naturalised Americans.

References

Aleinikoff, T. A. (1998) *Between Principles and Politics: The Direction of U.S. Citizenship Policy*. Washington, DC: Carnegie Endowment for International Peace.

Angus, H. F. (1937) 'The Legal Status in British Columbia of Residents of Oriental Race and Their Descendants'. In Norman MacKenzie, ed., *The Legal Status of Aliens in Pacific Countries*. London: Oxford University Press, pp. 58–72.

Ansgar Kelly, H. (1991–92) 'Dual Nationality, the Myth of Election, and a Kinder, Gentler State Department'. *University of Miami Inter-American Law Review* 23, 2: 421–64.

Bloemraad, I. (2004) 'Who Claims Dual Citizenship? The Limits of Postnationalism, the Possibilities of Transnationalism, and the Persistence of Traditionalism'. *International Migration Review* 38, 2: 389–426.

Bloemraad, I. (2006) *Becoming a Citizen: Incorporating Immigrants and Refugees in the United States and Canada.* Berkeley, CA: University of California Press.

Bloemraad, I. and R. Ueda (2006) 'Naturalization and Nationality'. In Reed Ueda, ed., *A Companion to American Immigration.* Oxford, UK: Blackwell, pp. 36–57.

Brown, R. C. (1996) 'Full Partnership in the Fortunes and in the Future of the Nation'. In Jean A. Laponce and William Safran, eds, *Ethnicity and Citizenship: The Canadian Case.* London: Frank Cass, pp. 9–25.

Canada, House of Commons (1971) *Debates.* 28th Parliament. Ottawa: Queen's Printer.

Carpenter, A. H. (1904) 'Naturalization in England and the American Colonies'. *American Historical Review* 9, 2: 288–303.

Demirjian, A., D. Gray, and D. Wright (1996) *The 1947 Canadian Citizenship Act: Issues and Significance.* Report Prepared for Citizenship and Immigration Canada. Ottawa: Consulting and Audit Canada.

DeSipio, L., H. Pachon, R. de la Garza, and J. Lee (2003) *Immigrant Politics at Home and Abroad: How Latino Immigrants Engage the Politics of Their Home Communities and the United States.* Claremont, CA: Tomás Rivera Policy Institute.

Duckett, K. (2000) 'The Meaning of Citizenship: A Critical Analysis of Dual Nationality and the Oath of Renunciation'. *Immigration and Nationality Law Review* 21: 717–34.

Enriquez, S. (2006) 'No Loud Voice for Expats in Mexican Vote'. *Los Angeles Times* (A) 14 January: 3.

Finifter, A. W. and B. M. Finifter (1995) 'Pledging Allegiance to a New Flag: Citizenship Change and Its Psychological Aftermath among American Migrants in Australia'. *Canadian Review of Studies in Nationalism* 22, 1–2: 1–21.

Fonte, J. (2005) *Dual Allegiance: A Challenge to Immigration Reform and Patriotic Assimilation.* Brief in Backgrounder Series. Washington, DC: Center for Immigration Studies.

Galloway, D. (2000) 'The Dilemmas of Canadian Citizenship Law'. In T. Alexander Aleinikoff and Douglas Klusmeyer, eds, *From Migrants to Citizens: Membership in a Changing World.* Washington, DC: Carnegie Endowment for International Peace, pp. 82–118.

Geyer, G. A. (1996) *Americans No More: The Death of American Citizenship.* New York: Atlantic Monthly Press.

Gutierrez, H. (2003) 'U.S. Citizens "Si" Double, Thanks to Mexico's Offer'. *Rocky Mountain News* 16 April: 28A.

Hammar, T. (1985) 'Dual Citizenship and Political Integration'. *International Migration Review* 19, 3: 438–50.

Hancock, M. (1937) 'Naturalization in Canada'. In Norman MacKenzie, ed., *The Legal Status of Aliens in Pacific Countries.* London: Oxford University Press, pp. 88–100.

Haney López, I. F. (1996) *White by Law: The Legal Construction of Race.* New York: New York University Press.

Huntington, S. P. (2004) *Who Are We? The Challenges to America's National Identity.* New York: Simon & Schuster.

Jones-Correa, M. (1998) *Between Two Nations: The Political Predicament of Latinos in New York City.* Ithaca, NY: Cornell University Press.

Jones-Correa, M. (2001) 'Under Two Flags: Dual Nationality in Latin America and Its Consequences for Naturalization in the United States'. *International Migration Review* 35, 4: 997–1029.

Kaplan, W. (1991) *The Evolution of Citizenship Legislation in Canada*. Ottawa: Multiculturalism and Citizenship Canada.

Kelley, N. and H. Trebilcock (1998) *The Making of the Mosaic: A History of Canadian Immigration Policy*. Toronto: University of Toronto Press.

Kettner, J. H. (1978) *The Development of American Citizenship*. Chapel Hill, NC: University of North Carolina Press.

Labelle, M., F. Rocher, and G. Rocher (1995) 'Pluriethnicité, citoyenneté et intégration: De la souveraineté pour lever les obstacles et les ambiguités'. *Cahiers de recherche sociologique* 25: 213–45.

Levitt, P. (2001) *The Transnational Villagers*. Berkeley: University of California Press.

Lipset, S. M. (1970) *Revolution and Counterrevolution*. New York: Anchor Books.

Lipset, S. M. (1986) 'Historical Conditions and National Characteristics: A Comparative Analysis of Canada and the United States'. *Canadian Journal of Sociology* 11, 2: 113–35.

Lipset, S. M. (1990) *Continental Divide: The Values and Institutions of the United States and Canada*. New York: Routledge.

Martin, P. (1993) 'Citizenship and the People's World'. In William Kaplan, ed., *Belonging: The Meaning and Future of Canadian Citizenship*. Montreal: McGill-Queen's University Press, pp. 64–78.

Meissner, D. (2001) *After the Attacks: Protecting Border and Liberties*. Policy Brief. 8. Washington, DC: Carnegie Endowment for International Peace.

Pinkus, N. (2005) *True Faith and Allegiance: Immigration and American Civic Nationalism*. Princeton, NJ: Princeton University Press.

Prashad, S. (2005) 'Few Bites for Dual Citizenship Deal'. *Toronto Star* 19 January: A6.

Renshon, S. A. (2000) *Dual Citizens in America: An Issue of Vast Proportions and Broad Significance*. Brief in Backgrounder Series. Washington, DC: Center for Immigration Studies.

Renshon, S. A. (2001) *Dual Citizenship and American National Identity*. Washington, DC: Center for Immigration Studies.

Scherner-Kim, K. (2000) 'The Role of the Oath of Renunciation in Current U.S. Nationality Policy—to Enforce, to Omit, or Maybe to Change?' *Georgetown Law Journal* 88: 329–79.

Schuck, P. H. (1998) *Citizens, Strangers, and In-Betweens: Essays on Immigration and Citizenship*. Boulder, CO: Westview Press.

Schuck, P. H. and R. M. Smith (1985) *Citizenship Without Consent: Illegal Aliens in the American Polity*. New Haven, CT: Yale University Press.

Schwartz, M. A. (1976) 'Citizenship in Canada and the United States'. *Transactions of the Royal Society of Canada, Series IV* 14: 83–96.

Smith, M. L. (1998) '[Overview of INS History]'. In George T. Kurian, ed., *A Historical Guide to the U.S. Government*. New York: Oxford University Press.

Smith, R. M. (1997) *Civic Ideals: Conflicting Visions of Citizenship in U.S. History*. New Haven, CT: Yale University Press.

Spiro, P. J. (1997) 'Dual Nationality and the Meaning of Citizenship'. *Emory Law Review* 46, 4: 1411–85.

Ueda, R. (1982) 'Naturalization and Citizenship'. In Richard A. Easterlin, David Ward, William S. Bernard and Reed Ueda, eds, *Immigration*. Cambridge, MA: Belknap Press.

United States Immigration and Naturalization Service (2000) 'INS Achieves 2-Year Naturalization Program Goals'. In *News Release from Media Services, Office of Public Affairs*, www.ins.gov/graphics/publicaffairs/newsreels/NatzGoal.htm Washington, DC (Accessed 25 April 2000).

Part III

Postnational and Transnational Citizenship

9
Dual Citizenship: A Postnational View

Peter J. Spiro

Does the dramatic rise of plural citizenship portend a postnational future? Multiple nationality stands among the most understudied incidents of globalisation. It may have profound implications for the state as a form of human association. Where nationality had been long established, normatively and legally, as an exclusive tie, multiple national attachments are increasingly tolerated, accepted, even embraced. As transnational migration increases, the number of individuals holding more than one citizenship will continue to grow. Dual citizenship is well on the way to becoming a commonplace.

But that does not by itself demonstrate its importance. This chapter describes how plural citizenship both reflects and accelerates postnationalism, in the sense that it undermines state-based identities. This proposition may pose an initial paradox, insofar as plural citizenship could be thought to facilitate state-based connections. But acceptance of plural citizenship is likely to lower the intensity of the citizen–state affiliation and, in turn, the intensity of bonds among citizens. A citizenship regime tolerant of dual citizenship will count more members who subordinate the attachment to other national attachments, as an inevitable corollary of the move from an exclusive to a non-exclusive relationship. States, however, now have greater incentives to accept a higher incidence of plural citizenship notwithstanding these identity-diluting effects. Moreover, insofar as international norms begin to require acceptance of plural citizenship, at least in some cases, states will be increasingly constrained from rejecting the status at the same time that acceptance may result in constitutive challenges.

Defining postnationality

The predicted arrival of postnationalism seems to be accompanied by trumpets, a subclass of the celebratory tone that sometimes overwhelms the study of globalisation. It is therefore important to define at the outset what is meant by the term (Bosniak 2002: 983), and whether it is offered along both descriptive and normative valences. I here mean to use postnationality to include the decline of the state as brought about by a dilution in state-based identity and the rise of non-state attachments. The dilution of identity causes a decline in the state insofar as the feelings of solidarity and trust (Faist 2001) are contingent on shared identity. To the extent that identity is diluted, then, members of any particular community (state or non-state) will be less inclined to share among themselves relative to the rest of the world. That goes for resources as well as other forms of protection, including the distribution of rights. As identity weakens, so will the state.

At the same time, I do not believe that postnationalism implies the rise of an undifferentiated global democracy nor of supra-statism (Faist 2001), although in the abstract postnationalism would be consistent with either. In this respect, postnationalism is more about the fall of the old order rather than the content of the new. In my view (although the question is largely beyond the scope of this chapter), the postnational era will be characterised by the rise of non-state communities. State-based communities will be persistent, but in a way that is less privileged; the state will remain a robust form of association, but one situated along a scale with other forms of community rather than standing in a disjunctured category of its own.

Nor do I mean to imply in this discussion that postnationalism promises any sort of utopian future. Insofar as postnationalism allows for the more complete autonomy in the composition of individual identity and associational attachment, it is normatively preferable to the Westphalian regime in which such autonomy was constrained. However, postnationalism does not imply that such autonomy will be complete. (In this respect, I part ways with Franck's [1996] premise of a more completely realised liberal autonomy in the choice of individual affiliations.) Communities are definitionally exclusionary, more or less. Individuals in the postnational order will not be able to determine their own associational composites. Nor does the postnational order promise an end to conflict. Although it may spell a diminution in the occurrence of interstate violence (the major source of violence over the last three hundred years), it does not equate to the end of conflict among communities. In the absence of universal, comprehensive community (which would seem inconsistent with human nature), conflict will always be an element of global interaction. Finally, transitions to a postnational order will destabilise the protection of rights. The liberal nation-state of late modernity has advanced a rights-protection regime, at least within the parameters of the state-based community. Immature postnational structures are unlikely to emulate the state in this respect for many years to come. In the meantime, I cannot agree with those (Soysal 1994: 165; Jacobson 1996) who believe that the ascendancy of international human rights regimes will buttress the nation-state as the location for their enforcement. The enforcement of exogenously determined rights will not suffice to maintain community solidarities.

So 'postnationalism', as I use the term here, is mostly what it sounds like: getting past the state. The rise of dual citizenship will likely play a role in that trajectory. To be sure, dual citizenship may reap short-term gains for both immigrant-sending and immigrant-receiving states. It is clearly being used as an instrument of state policy in the former context, as homeland government's attempt to cement ties to prosperous diasporas. Tolerating dual citizenship also serves receiving states by way of facilitating naturalisation and political assimilation. But in both contexts state policies are defensive, aimed at shoring up the increasingly porous boundaries of national community. Whether they will in fact further state interests, even in the short term, remains to be seen. In the long term, they will almost surely contribute to the dilution of state-based identity.

Dual citizenship in the interest of the state

One cannot, it is true, establish the end of the nation-state by deploying the growth of plural citizenship. Citizenship is about membership in states, plural citizenship as much as singular citizenship; in that respect, plural citizenship evidences the continuing salience of states in the world order. Plural citizenship facilitates the identification of individuals with state-based communities by allowing those individuals to formalise the multiple national attachments they may have as a matter of social fact. In the world that frowned upon dual nationality, in such cases national attachments were obstructed, at least at the secondary level. An individual who would have liked to be associated with each of two states was forced to choose between them, diminishing the attachment to the state not chosen. Today, both attachments can be sustained and cultivated through the channels of full membership.

That plural nationality can serve state interests in immigrant-sending countries is well understood. Through much of the twentieth century, most states terminated nationality upon naturalisation in another state. This expatriation practice reflected an official suspicion of émigré populations, especially pronounced with respect to political ties to the state of naturalisation. The act of naturalisation was conceived of as an act of abandonment, even treachery (Shain 1999: 181–82; Huntington 2004: 279). Such sentiment often masked the political interests of ruling homeland regimes, for whom expatriates (in some cases, 'exiles') represented a threat resistant to domestic forms of discipline (hence also rules under which even those who maintained citizenship as mono-nationals were barred from voting as non-residents). Dual nationals also represented a threat under rules of international law affording their state of naturalisation standing before international law to assert diplomatic protection against mistreatment by a homeland government. An emigrant returning to his country of origin from the United States would have the heft of the US government behind him, complicating internal as well as external governmental control in an era in which states could otherwise treat their own citizens as they pleased.

Late-twentieth-century liberalisation resulted in a diminishment of those control priorities in many states as authoritarian and one-party regimes gave way to some measure of democratic governance. Sending states have come to recognise the economic resource represented by external populations resident in developed economies. In the popular culture, émigrés are taking on something of a heroic stature, sustaining substantial economic and political power in countries of origin. Dual citizenship has emerged as a reflection of that power as well as a potential tool for states to cement relations with external communities. External populations have lobbied successfully for legal acceptance of dual citizenship in such countries as Mexico, India, the Philippines and the Dominican Republic. Even where an individual naturalises in another country, a continuing homeland tie may be facilitated through dual citizenship. Dual citizenship may facilitate remittances and repatriation, for example, in cases where successful business persons return to operate concerns back home. Dual citizenship is also thought to enhance political clout of homeland interests in the country of naturalisation.

It is not clear, however, that dual citizenship actually serves sending-state agendas in these ways. There is nothing necessarily state-enhancing in this deployment of dual citizenship. Retention of home-country citizenship is in most cases essentially cost-free for emigrants, as few states require payment of taxes, military service or other obligations from non-resident citizens. Retention is a passive affair; maintaining original citizenship requires no affirmative act upon naturalisation elsewhere. If action were required, the data might evidence weakness in the state-based tie. One prominent example supports the proposition. When Mexico amended its citizenship law to allow retention of Mexican nationality upon naturalisation elsewhere, it also established a streamlined process for the restoration of nationality for the many hundreds of thousands who had lost it under the prior, dual-citizenship-intolerant regime. However, only 67,000 applied for restoration during an initial 5-year application window.

This experience has been reinforced in the context of non-resident citizen voting patterns. Even as many states move to facilitate exercise of the franchise by non-resident citizens, turnout rates have been low, sometimes remarkably so. Even now that they are eligible to vote from their residence in the United States, only 57,000 Mexicans there out of more than 4 million eligible completed the registration process to vote in July 2006 Mexican presidential elections; as of the spring of 2006, more than half of Mexicans resident in the United States were not even aware that the elections would be taking place. Although external citizen voting participation involves the place of non-resident mono-citizens as well as dual citizens (and participation rates may change as the practice of external voting becomes more entrenched and further facilitated, for instance, through Internet voting), currently low levels of participation may indicate attenuated state connections among external populations (Spiro 2003).

To be sure, dual citizenship has value to external citizen populations. Acceptance of dual citizenship by homeland states allows external populations to secure citizenship in their places of external residence without relinquishing the material and sentimental advantages of retained original citizenship. It allows immigrants to enjoy, in some sense, the best of both worlds. But there is no evidence that dual citizenship necessarily reinforces state ties. Nor is the retention of original citizenship necessarily correlated to the intensity of transnational community ties. As Bosniak notes, not all transnational subjects are dual citizens (Bosniak 2002: 995). Sustained affective connections at the family and subnational level are not contingent on citizenship status, and an emigrant can maintain strong homeland connections consistent with an attenuated state-based identity. The converse is also true; dual citizens need not be transnational. Where dual citizenship is possible at little cost, it may not correlate with affective ties at any level.

The largely instrumental potential uses of dual citizenship—by individuals, rather than states—is more apparent from the perspective of immigrant-receiving states. On the one hand, dual citizenship can be framed as in the interests of receiving states as well as sending states. A system of singular nationality places a high price on naturalisation, where terminating original nationality is perceived as costly by the would-be naturalisation applicant. For some that cost is too steep, and notwithstanding their eligibility to naturalise, they will refuse to opt in. The failure of a large proportion of immigrants to naturalise poses a challenge to receiving states. Such a denizen population will not (almost by definition) be politically assimilable, which may in turn also retard social and cultural integration into the community. At some point, the territorial presence of political non-members will undermine the liberal premises of the modern democratic state, even if the non-membership is a matter of choice. Accepting dual citizenship addresses this challenge. By eliminating the cost of renouncing original citizenship, it facilitates naturalisation and the political incorporation that cannot otherwise be undertaken (Schuck 1998: 231). In this view, plural citizenship emerges as a tool of assimilation.

Instrumental uses of dual citizenship and the dilution of state-based identity

That may make for good naturalisation policy, but plural nationality ultimately evidences and further erodes receiving-state solidarities. Receiving states (especially the United States) were historically in a position to set down naturalisation and sole nationality as a take-it-or-leave-it proposition. Today, that receiving states might have to lower the barriers to naturalisation by way of enticing applications betrays the diminishing bargaining power of receiving states vis-à-vis potential members. Receiving states may no longer dictate the terms of admission, or do so only at the peril of deterring a significant population of permanent residents from becoming full members of the polity and of corroding the representative democratic process as a result. On this score, it is interesting that liberal theorists have moved beyond advocating that naturalisation be at the option of the immigrant (in other words, that naturalisation be reduced to a matter of signing up) to calling for the automatic naturalisation of long-term residents (Rubio-Marin 2000). Such a scheme is improbable as a policy matter and problematic even from a liberal perspective, insofar as it constrains the autonomy of individuals to define their own identities. But the shift shows that immigrants can no longer be assumed to prefer citizenship in their country of resettlement, even if they are eligible for it. In this frame, the increasing difficulty of 'the sale' indicates the diminished quantity that citizenship represents.

But the growing incidence of plural citizenship does more than evidence the decline of citizenship; it will also contribute to that decline and the decoupling of citizenship status from actual parameters of community. There are two conceptual avenues to this conclusion. The first might be deemed the 'second choice' problem. In a world that demanded singular citizenship, individuals could be assumed to opt for a particular citizenship because it was their first choice. On average, that choice would reflect a balancing of the affective and instrumental benefits of one citizenship relative to another. These factors would often point in the same direction, and reflect an actual priority of community membership. Thus, the naturalisation decision would reflect a reprioritisation of identity; the acquisition of receiving-state citizenship— as accompanied by the loss of original citizenship—would (again, on average) reflect a change in the order of community ties. The old ties would not necessarily have been abandoned (in the American immigration tradition, they more often were not), but naturalisation would evidence their subordination to the new affiliation. The result was a community in which citizenship status defined a core, because it coincided with the group for whom receiving-state identity was a first choice among national identities.

This construct is undermined by the acceptance of plural citizenship. There is no longer any implicit ranking in the citizenship choice. One can acquire citizenship in states to which one has subordinate, or even nominal, ties, without sacrificing one's primary attachment. This means that some citizens will sustain a substantial tie to another polity, in terms of their identity and commitments. That possibility may not be identity-dilutive, at least to the extent that identity and commitment are non-zero-sum quantities; an individual can still be meaningfully attached to one state at the same time as he or she holds more significant attachments to others. But plural citizenship also facilitates the citizenship of convenience. There are certain advantages to maintaining or acquiring citizenship, at the same time as obligations specific to citizenship have been reduced virtually to nothing. It is a world in which one can, in effect, collect citizenships at very little cost, and without any meaningful attachment to those states in which citizenship is maintained (Koslowski 2000: 151; Pickus 2005: 181–83). The advantages of citizenship go beyond political rights, the instrumental acquisition of which may benefit states. Naturalisation may, for instance, be under-taken to assure locational security, ensure eligibility for social benefits and immunise the individual from exclusion or deportation. In the near-parody version, citizenship is held for the purpose of securing the privilege of faster passport inspection lines at airports and other ports of entry. In a world of second-, third-, even fourth-choice citizenships, the lesser ones may reflect no actual community ties.

The second-choice phenomenon will be more prevalent with respect to receiving-state citizenship. Receiving-state citizenship is more likely to be subordinated to original citizenship (which, as Peter Schuck suggests, may be akin to first love, never completely eclipsed by later attachments (Schuck 1998: 228)) or secured for the convenience and security it affords residents. The possibility is particularly evident in the US context, in the absence of strong non-citizenship markers of national community. To the extent that plural citizenship does become a commonplace, the United States will become a community of second choicers, with a corresponding loss of filial intensity. Acceptance of dual citizenship in the United States facilitates, in Appadurai's terms, its transformation from 'being a land of immigrants [to] being one node in a postnational network of diasporas' (Appadurai 1996: 171).

But the analysis will be applicable to other citizenships. Emigrant populations that transplant their primary locus of social relations to their new place of residence may retain their original citizenship because retention comes at no cost, the migration of actual identity notwith-standing, especially in subsequent immigrant generations. There may be marginal instrumental benefits to the retention of original citizen-ship, even where identity has shifted from the homeland. Some states continue to restrict certain forms of property ownership to citizens, as well as the franchise and other political rights. Passport lines and visa formalities are a concern for those returning to visit their homelands as well. Insofar as retention becomes the default position from a legal perspective and it is renunciation that requires affirmative action on the part of the individual naturalising elsewhere, one can expect most emigrants not to bother with the formal termination of the original tie.

In either case, the result is the diminished intensity of affiliation indicated by the citizenship tie. Let us assume for the moment that individuals are rational actors. In a regime intolerant of plural citizen-ship, individuals would be forced to choose among citizenships for which they were eligible. In some cases, instrumental factors might have outweighed sentimental ones, but they would have been weighed in a balance, so that in other (and perhaps most) cases affective ties would have determined the citizenship choice. In the wake of prevalent acceptance of plural citizenship, citizenships can be acquired with little or no regard for the affective factor, because the citizenship of greatest sentimental attachment is maintained even as one accumulates additional citizenships. Dual citizenship thus increases the strategic use of citizenship on the part of individuals. The probability that citizenship will be retained or acquired for instrumental purposes has grown with acceptance of multiple citizenship attachments.

Plural citizenship's dilutive effect on state-based identity is also suggested in schematic terms. If one frames the question as one of human geography, the norm against plural citizenship enforces community boundaries. As with territorial delimitation, under the prior regime in which dual citizenship was highly disfavoured, an individual was on one side of the line or the other. There was minimal straddling or overlap between communities. Just as territorial borders created spatial disjunctures—in the days before globalisation, a border was consequential, in terms of social, cultural and (of course) political development, so that a border even on a level field would amount to a barrier as important as a mountain—so too did the boundaries of citizenship. By minimising overlap in state-based communities, the norm against dual nationality made those communities more distinct. That approach eliminated scalar possibilities, instead creating clear binary arrangements which reinforced the sense of other in cross-community perceptions. A world in which the 'us' and the 'them' are rigidly separated is one in which both will loom larger. In this respect, citizenship rules suppressing the incidence of dual nationality contributed to community identification. The rules were themselves consequential in a world that would otherwise lend itself to scalar associations in the wake of immigration and lingering homeland ties.

Acceptance of plural citizenship erodes this distinctiveness among national communities. Bosniak asserts that with the acceptance of dual citizenship, 'state power is not displaced but simply divided' (Bosniak 2002: 998). But the division would seem to dissipate the connection of state and citizen. As Huntington observes, '[f]or a person with two or more citizenships, no one citizenship can be as important as his one citizenship is to a person who only has one' (Huntington 2004: 212). As a matter of human geography, it becomes impossible to say where one community leaves off and another begins. A graphic representation of citizenship status would now be much more complex than a territorial map, characterised by overlapping spaces rather than separated ones. It is as if territory were to come under various joint regimes in which more than one government exercised jurisdiction over the same piece of territory. (Insofar as territorial boundaries once represented, under the doctrine of sovereignty, zones of exclusive jurisdiction, those lines are also being blurred as various forms of trans- and supranational powers emerge. Although our atlases may look basically the same, with the neat carving up of territory, the geographers of globalisation are developing other maps to capture the new geography of power.) The arrangement is no longer binary.

Losing control: Plural citizenship, state interests and international law

If citizenship were a matter of policy within the exclusive control of states, the dilutive tendencies of plural citizenship would be reversible. If acceptance of plural citizenship proved inimical to the interests of a particular state, that state could revert to a position of intolerance for the status. But state decision-making respecting plural citizenship rules may become increasingly constrained by rules of international law, in which reversal would not necessarily be an available option. Short-term state interests-calculation, moreover, may not serve the long-term vitality of state-based association.

It is true that citizenship decisions were long considered within the *domain réservé* of sovereign states, beyond the reach of international law. Insofar as international law concerned itself with citizenship practices, it was with respect to the ascription of citizenship to individuals lacking a genuine connection to the state involved, for purposes of asserting rights of diplomatic protection against other states. This was the holding of the *Nottebohm* case. However, international law did not dictate to states requirements of inclusion. In other words, states were constrained from setting insubstantial citizenship thresholds, at least as against other states, but they were not similarly constrained with respect to exclusionary requirements. States could in effect set the citizenship bar as high as they liked.

It is also true that states have been free to reject dual citizenship (Bosniak 2002: 997). From the mid-nineteenth century until the late twentieth, most states provided for the termination of citizenship upon naturalisation elsewhere. That expatriation practice has never been questioned as inconsistent with international norms. Indeed, dual citizenship was highly disfavoured under international law. Because states were permitted wide discretion in setting citizenship rules, dual citizenship could not be outlawed altogether, but the status was considered highly problematic from the perspective of states. Dual citizens sparked numerous bilateral disputes, especially between the United States and the immigrant-sending European states. If not illegal, the discourse of international relations considered the status with opprobrium (Spiro 1997).

Dual citizenship remains today a status that states may accept or reject at their option consistent with international law. However, there are signs that international norms may come to bear on state practices regarding dual citizenship. The 1997 European Convention on Nationality requires parties to recognise dual citizenship where it results from mixed-national parentage, and its preambular language, for the first time in any international legal instrument, frames dual citizenship as a right. Though a regional agreement not widely acceded to, the Convention could mark a shift in the international conception of dual citizenship. The discourse shift could be reinforced by the nearly unidirectional trend towards wide acceptance of the status. A clear majority of states now allows some form of plural citizenship (Renshon 2005: 6). It is not difficult to articulate a rights basis for the maintenance of dual citizenship, and a matter of personal identity autonomy and freedom of association. To the extent that perceptions of dual citizenship move in that direction and that perception is supported by state practice, dual citizenship may in the long run emerge as a status protected in some contexts under international law.

State postures towards dual citizenship may also be affected by international norm development regarding birthright citizenship and naturalisation, both towards greater liberality. Although there have been some isolated recent restrictions of absolute birthright citizenship (most notably in Ireland, as a result of a national referendum there), the general trend is towards the extension of citizenship on the basis of birth within national territory, and there has also been a global trajectory towards shortened residency requirements for purposes of naturalisation eligibility (Weil 2001). Political theorists have come to situate naturalisation in the landscape of human rights (Benhabib 2004: 134–43). If international norms pull states towards more expansive application of *jus soli* and lower thresholds to naturalisation, entrenched acceptance of dual citizenship may prove an incidental corollary.

In any event, it is possible that states will lose some of their former discretion to limit the incidence of plural citizenship (Spiro 2004). If so, states would be less able to reverse the identity-dilutive implications of larger plural citizen populations, losing the capacity of self-definition. The trend towards acceptance of dual citizenship is unlikely to be reversed for political reasons. Important immigrant domestic political constituencies will work to block such reversals (in the United States, for example, such assimilated immigrant communities as the Italian and Irish with high levels of dual citizenship as well as more recent arrivals among Mexican and Indian immigrants). In any case, states will find their discretion on the issue circumscribed, perhaps prohibitively.

Moreover, the short-term perception of dual citizenship as a tool for reinforcing state identity may mask longer-term costs. As described above, dual citizenship is perceived by sending states to facilitate sustained homeland ties, with corresponding economic returns. For receiving states, dual citizenship facilitates naturalisation which in turn accelerates assimilation. Whether or not such interests are actually advanced, acceptance of dual citizenship comes at little or no short-term material cost from the perspective of the state or existing citizens. Added or retained citizens do not, generally speaking, pose a drain on the public purse or other resources by the fact of their citizenship status. Benefits forthcoming to individuals (as well as obligations owed to states) are generally determined by residence, not citizenship.

The fact that citizenship can be extended on the cheap, as it were, may both explain the willingness to accept plural citizenship as well as evidence the already diminished condition of citizenship as an institution. Citizenship does not get or give much any more. But to the extent that citizenship remains meaningful, that meaning will be further eroded by the rise of dual citizenship. Insofar as citizenship comes to reflect less intensive communal bonds, the state is less likely to serve as a vehicle for robust redistributionist and rights-protective policies, which in turn will result in waning institutional power. This is a key link in establishing the causality of plural citizenship and postnationalism. The dilution of identity is itself not a measurement of state power, but it does have probable implications for state power. The success of the state as a vehicle for vindicating justice has arguably been contingent on its foundations in 'communities of character' (Walzer 1983: 62), which have in the modern era been able to protect their internal solidarities through territorial entry controls. As barriers to physical entry fail, barriers to citizenship might in theory supply a perimeter within which the state could sustain solidarity and continue its good works among members. But citizenship barriers are failing, too, in the face of human rights norms that hold states responsible on the basis of territorial control rather than citizenship affiliation. States are, in other words, being exogenously constrained from a strategy that might otherwise shore up their declining vitality. They are limited in the extent that they can discriminate on the basis of citizenship.

The rise of plural citizenship is a small part of this picture. Dual citizens will, on average, maintain a less affective connection to the state and to fellow members in the community defined on the basis of citizenship. Dual citizenship thus incrementally further weakens the solidarity and trust shared among citizens in the state, which in turn will deplete the power of the state itself. As state-based community wanes, identity will migrate to other forms of association whose membership is defined in other ways and is not always subject to exogenous constraint, and which may be less tolerant of dual affiliations. Religion, race and ethnicity are increasingly salient to identity composites in a global context. These groupings can set the terms of membership (formally or non-formally) and do not typically accept alternate ties. As a result they may be better positioned to maintain the strong communal bonds that are increasingly less evident in the citizenship construct. As individuals seek the strong community that appears inherent to the human condition, their affective attachments to these non-state entities may become more prominent relative to the attachment to state. That may frame the competition for 'post-national solidarity' (Benhabib 2004), in which the prevalence of plural citizenship may help to tip the balance against defining those solidarities in terms of the state.

Conclusion

Although there is paradox in the proposition that dual citizenship undermines the state, it also enjoys intuitive appeal. An institution that has long demanded exclusivity, in the way of religions and marriage, is now surrendering to the possibility of multiple affiliation. This chapter has described the pathways by which dual citizenship will undermine the state. Plural citizenship may emerge as a defining and irreversible feature of a new era in which membership in states is demoted to the level of membership in other forms of association. As citizenship loses the sacral elements of exclusivity, it becomes just another form of belonging.

References

Appadurai, A. (1996) *Modernity at Large: Cultural Dimensions of Globalization.* Minneapolis, MN: University of Minnesota Press.

Benhabib, S. (2004) *The Rights of Others: Aliens, Residents and Citizens.* Cambridge and New York: Cambridge University Press.

Bosniak, L. (2002). 'Multiple Nationality and the Postnational Transformation of Citizenship'. *Virginia Journal of International Law* 42: 979.

Faist, T. (2001) 'Dual Citizenship as Overlapping Membership'. *Willy Brandt Series of Working Papers in International Migration and Ethnic Relations* 3, 1: School of International Migration and Ethnic Relations (IMER). Sweden: Malmö University.

Franck, T. M. (1996). 'Clan and Superclan: Loyalty, Identity and Community in Law and Practice'. *American Journal of International Law* 90: 359.

Huntington, S. P. (2004) *Who are We? The Challenges to America's National Identity*. New York: Simon & Schuster.

Jacobson, D. (1996) *Rights Across Borders: Immigration and the Decline of Citizenship*. Baltimore, MD: Johns Hopkins University Press.

Koslowski, R. (2000) *Migrants and Citizens: Demographic Change in the European State System*. Ithaca, NY: Cornell University Press.

Pickus, N. M. J. (2005) *True Faith and Allegiance: Iimmigration and American Civic Nationalism*. Princeton, NJ: Princeton University Press.

Renshon, S. A. (2005) *The 50% American: Immigration and National Identity in an Age of Terror*. Washington, DC: Georgetown University Press.

Rubio-Marin, R. (2000) *Immigration as a Democratic Challenge: Citizenship and Inclusion in Germany and the United States*. Cambridge and New York: Cambridge University Press.

Schuck, P. H. (1998) *Citizens, Strangers, and In-betweens: Essays on Immigration and Citizenship*. Boulder, CO: Westview Press.

Shain, Y. (1999) *Marketing the American Creed Abroad: Diasporas in the U.S. and their Homelands*. Cambridge and New York: Cambridge University Press.

Soysal, Y. N. (1994). *Limits of Citizenship: Migrants and Postnational Membership in Europe*. Chicago and London: University of Chicago Press.

Spiro, P. J. (1997) 'Dual Nationality and the Meaning of Citizenship'. *Emory Law Journal* 46: 1411.

Spiro, P. J. (2003) 'Political Rights and Dual Nationality'. In D. Martin and K. Heilbroner, eds, *Rights and Duties of Dual Nationals: Evolution and Prospects*. The Hague: Kluwer International.

Spiro, P. J. (2004) 'Mandated Membership, Diluted Identity: Citizenship, Globalization, and International Law'. In A. Brysk and G. Shafir, eds, *People Out of Place: Globalization, Human Rights, and the Citizenship Gap*. New York and London: Routledge, pp. 87–105.

Walzer, M. (1983) *Spheres of Justice: A Defense of Pluralism and Equality*. New York: Basic Books.

Weil, P. (2001). 'Access to Citizenship: A Comparison of Twenty-Five Nationality Laws'. In T. A. Aleinikoff and D. B. Klusmeyer, eds, *Citizenship Today: Global Perspectives and Practices*. Washington, DC: Carnegie Endowment for International Peace, pp. 17–35.

10
Dual Citizenship among Hong Kong Canadians: Convenience or Commitment?

Valerie Preston, Myer Siemiatycki and Audrey Kobayashi[1]

Dual citizenship challenges long-held assumptions regarding the relations of state, society and the individual. It *'disturbs the sense of boundedness'* (original emphasis) that has defined citizenship historically as a spatially rooted concept, within first the city-state and then the nation-state (Miller 2000, Heisler 2001: 229, Isin 2002). Territorially bounded citizenship constituted 'an institutional form of solidarity' (Faist 2000: 202) that bonded the individual citizen to a single state and that strengthened and maintained bonds of belonging and commitment to other citizens in the national society. The concept of dual citizenship challenges traditional views of state attachment and raises this question: to how many different states and societies can one person sustain an attachment?

Sceptics condemn dual citizenship as a measure of convenience rather than commitment that debases and undermines the very currency of belonging (Fritz 1998: 1). Instrumentally acquired to be invoked as circumstances require, they claim it compromises loyalty to the state, national security, social cohesion, international stability and the principle of equality central to citizenship (Hansen and Weil 2002).

Yet, paradoxically, close to 100 countries permit the dual citizenship that allegedly compromises the integrity of the relation between state and citizen. These countries tolerate dual citizenship, not as a simple addition, but as a renegotiation of the concept based on some degree of pluralism that not only recognises the legitimacy of acquired citizenship but also redefines the long-established fixation between national identity and place. Such redefinition has occurred in a context of globalisation and unprecedented human mobility; transnationalism; advances in gender equality giving women rights to pass on nationality to their children; judicial emphasis on individual rights, which curtails the powers of individual states to revoke citizenship; the desire of immigrant-sending states to retain contact with their diaspora; and the desire of immigrant-receiving countries to integrate immigrants and avoid having large numbers of non-citizens in their polity (Pickus 1998, Schuck 1998, Aleinikoff and Klusmeyer 2001, Koslowski 2001, Hansen and Weil 2002, Spiro 2002, Bloemraad 2004, Faist 2004).

Canada's early acceptance of dual citizenship reflects the importance that the Canadian state has always placed on naturalisation of 'suitable' migrants and the influence of a multiculturalism policy[2] that—in principle—expanded the very concept of who is a Canadian. The Immigration Act of 1976 and the Citizenship Act of 1977 removed preferential treatment for immigrants who were British subjects, reduced the time between immigration and obtaining citizenship and removed restrictions on dual citizenship. The combined effect was a diversification of the sources of new immigrants at the same time that the concept of who could be a full citizen was broadened.

The broadened notion of belonging is reflected in citizenship criteria based on attachment to Canada rather than place of birth. Although some migrants are still excluded,[3] the vast majority of immigrants considered permanent residents are naturalised once they meet residency requirements, pass a test demonstrating knowledge of Canada and are not barred because of a criminal record (Citizenship and Immigration Canada 2006). While the Canadian state encourages naturalisation, however, it does not *require* landed immigrants, who are legal permanent residents, to naturalise. Unlike the United States, where many social benefits are currently limited solely to American citizens, the Canadian state places minimal restrictions on the social rights of landed immigrants.

The experience of immigrants from Hong Kong serves as an interesting case study of the complexities and ambiguities of dual citizenship in Canada. It highlights the interplay between the ways in which immigrants shape dual citizenship through their actions and the state policies and regulations—of sending and receiving states—that define the circumstances in which immigrants achieve citizenship and navigate issues surrounding dual citizenship. Such policies include not only those that specifically define the process of immigration and the rights and responsibilities of citizenship, but also those that define the citizen more broadly, such as the Multiculturalism Act and the Charter of Rights and Freedoms, as well as the many policies that affect a citizen's ability to participate fully in society through access to education, health care and other social services. Citizenship participation, or what is often called 'deep citizenship', is also affected by a range of societal factors that include integration into the labour market, experiences of racism and many cultural factors. Dual citizenship in the formal sense, therefore, is fundamentally linked to the informal ways in which people act out their citizenship as well as to the wide range of ways in which their actions are constrained.

We begin this chapter by describing distinctive elements of the Hong Kong migration to Canada. Next, we explore—through surveys and focus group transcripts—the citizenship decisions made by Hong Kong immigrants to Toronto and Vancouver. The findings reveal that immigrants make a wide range of choices about citizenship in the context of a highly commodified regime of citizenship in Canada and a highly complex and uncertain regime of Hong Kong citizenship. Government policies in Canada and Hong Kong have created ideal conditions for the emergence of what some call 'flexible citizenship', and others deride as citizenship of convenience (Ong 1999, Waters 2003). Contrary to prevailing images, there is no monolithic experience of Hong Kong–Canadian citizenship. For many Hong Kong migrants, dual citizenship also entails deep attachment to Canada. Their decisions defy entrenched assumptions about citizenship, identity and belonging. Indeed, our findings lead us to question the validity of framing discussions of dual citizenship around competing, binary norms of 'convenience' or 'commitment'.

Hong Kong exceptionalism – 'debased' citizenship?

Hong Kong's scheduled reunification with China in 1997 prompted widespread unease in the British city-colony. In the decade prior to Hong Kong's reunification with China, the 'expiring' British city-colony of six million experienced an exodus of some 600,000 residents (Meyer 2000: 220–21). More than 300,000 went to Canada. For 11 consecutive years, Hong Kong was the largest source 'country', accounting for one in every seven immigrants who entered Canada between 1987 and 1997 (Citizenship and Immigration Canada 1987–1997).

Its volatile past had made Hong Kong a 'place of transit', with recurring bouts of massive immigration and emigration (Skeldon 1999: 67). While the Japanese takeover of Hong Kong during the Second World War prompted population flight back to China, Mao's postwar triumph there occasioned an even greater migration wave from China to Hong Kong (Buckley 1997). The legacy of history, Ronald Skeldon has observed, was the emergence of a 'refugee mentality' in Hong Kong, whereby its population 'is more fluid, has shallower roots and attachment to place, and is more predisposed to move again' (Skeldon 1999: 68). As Hong Kong's 'appointment with China' approached, anxieties escalated over the impending reunification of Hong Kong's freewheeling market economy with an authoritarian Chinese Communist state (Tsang 1997). China's stated commitment to govern Hong Kong as a Special Administrative Region (SAR) did little to assuage fears. Many Hong Kong residents were anxious to secure a foreign passport 'as an insurance policy against things going wrong after 1997' (Skeldon 1999: 69; see also Tsang 1997, Buckley 1997, Meyer 2000).

Their previous citizenship experiences engendered in these prospective migrants an instrumental relationship to both polity and civil society. The state has long denied its subjects political and civil rights, creating a passive, self-reliant and economistic version of citizenship while promoting a discourse of the 'enterprising individual' contributing to economic prosperity as prototype of the virtuous person (Ku and Pun 2004). According to Thomas Kwan-Choi Tse (2004), the autocratic impulses of both British colonialism and China's current political rulers have fostered a 'deformed citizenry' among Hong Kongnese, whereby materialism, economic contribution, civic deference and conformity all substitute for the politically engaged citizen. As Wai-Man Lam observes,

> The idea of citizenship as promoted by the Hong Kong colonial and SAR governments is depoliticized. It places exclusive importance on the values of economic independence and contribution, and lauds an enterprising characteristic of citizenship. (Lam 2005: 320)

During the 1980s and 1990s, many Hong Kong migrants would be aggressively recruited by Canada precisely for their perceived qualities of 'enterprising citizenship'.

Canadian citizenship and neo-liberal globalisation

'In Canada, as in many other countries', Yasmeen Abu-Laban and Christina Gabriel (2000: 29) have observed, 'issues relating to citizenship, belonging, and justice have taken on renewed salience as a result of globalization'. Many authors have noted that state regimes of citizenship have been particularly influenced by patterns of international migration and transnationalism under neo-liberal globalisation (see Pickus 1998, Abu-Laban and Gabriel 2002, Stasiulis and Bakan 2005, Vertovec 2004, Bloemraad 2004). We contend these dynamics have resulted in a more robust role of the state in forging and promoting an increasingly marketised regime of citizenship. In recent decades, the government significantly expanded its programme for admitting foreign investors into Canada. Domestically, reductions to a host of state social expenditures conveyed the message that citizen well-being should rely on personal or family resources.

In this context, Canadian immigration officials set their sights on Hong Kong. According to two Canadian journalists, 'No other western country has engineered such a blatant grab for Hong Kong's elite and their wealth' (De Mont and Fennell 1989: 81). Canada's business immigration programme facilitated the migration of affluent Hong Kong residents (Ley 2003). In 1986, the Canadian government added an 'investor' category to the 'entrepreneur' category of business immigrants. While entrepreneurs were expected to be hands-on managers of business in Canada, investors were required to have a minimum net worth of $800,000 and to commit to investing at least $400,000 in Canada. Unlike entrepreneurs, investors were not required to establish businesses. Recognising the widespread desire among Hong Kong residents to secure alternate nationality prior to 1997, government recruiters, as well as private immigration agents, actively pitched the programme to the wary wealthy in Hong Kong (Cannon 1989, De Mont and Fennell 1989).

Hong Kong migrants under suspicion

The business-class immigrants who captured public attention in Canada became frequent targets of questions about their loyalty and commitment. Margaret Cannon (1989: 217) sounded the alarm in her book *China Tide: The Revealing Story of the Hong Kong Exodus to Canada*, stating, 'The cold truth is that some Hong Kong Chinese want Canadian citizenship but do not necessarily want Canada.' She describes the newcomers as 'the richest immigrants in Canadian history', arriving 'in Gucci shoes and Giorgio Armani suits' (1989: 10, 11). In a 1996 *Toronto Star* column titled 'Canada Places Too Little Value on Citizenship', University of Toronto economist John Crispo contended that Hong Kong migrants did not sufficiently value their attachment to Canada. The following year, Dal Wagner raised similar concerns in a letter to the *Vancouver Sun*, complaining that for some Hong Kong migrants to Canada '[l]oyalty to country and pride of citizenship apparently are nothing more than a ledger sheet....What a sad day for Canada that we tolerate such attitudes and such people!' (1997: A14). It was not uncommon for media representation and popular discourse to depict Hong Kong migrants as 'standard-bearers for a creed of rootless self-interest' (Siemiatycki and

Preston 2007). Yet ledger sheets and self-interest were hardly absent from Canada's aggressive recruitment of Hong Kong immigrants. Should only states—but not migrants—have a legitimate right to such calculations?

The clearly ambiguous citizenship of Hong Kong migrants

The formal citizenship status of Hong Kong Canadians is at once both clear and ambiguous. Hong Kong immigrants have an extremely high rate of naturalisation. While 84 per cent of all immigrants eligible for naturalisation in 2001 held Canadian citizenship, the rate among Hong Kong–born immigrants stood at 90.7 per cent. Clearly, Hong Kong migrants value Canadian citizenship; but it is less certain whether acquiring Canadian citizenship makes former residents of Hong Kong dual citizens.

Citizenship claims of Hong Kong immigrants are extremely complicated. As residents of a British colony, Hong Kong residents could obtain British National (Overseas) (BNO) passports from the British government. The BNO passports did not confer permanent British residence but they were treated the same as British passports for purposes of visas and other travel requirements. Few Hong Kong residents had British nationality and citizenship at the time Hong Kong was returned to China. Indeed, the United Kingdom limited its offer to repatriate Hong Kong residents to approximately 50,000 carefully chosen Hong Kong residents and their families (Lau 1989, 1990a). After 1997, most Hong Kong residents, including those living abroad, were eligible to become Chinese nationals, provided they were of Chinese ethnic background, had previously resided in Hong Kong for more than 7 years, returned to Hong Kong before 1 January 1999 and did not thereafter remain outside Hong Kong for longer than 36 months. Hong Kong residents of Chinese ethnicity holding a permanent identity card may obtain the Hong Kong Special Administrative Regions (HKSAR) passports, issued by the People's Republic of China (PRC) and conferring the same status as a PRC passport (HKSAR Government 2003). China still does not recognise dual citizenship and extends this prohibition to its citizens in Hong Kong; however, no practical steps have been taken to strip the rights of residency of those who hold Canadian passports, provided they meet the terms of residency in Hong Kong. Chinese nationality is revoked only upon a 'declaration of change of nationality'. Furthermore, Hong Kong residents may also travel using 'relevant documents issued by the foreign governments', although they are not entitled to consular protection when doing so.

In sum, from their homeland, Hong Kong migrants to Canada might hold any combination of four significant documents conveying a range of nationality and citizenship-like status: British Citizenship, a BNO Passport, a Hong Kong Identity Card and a HKSAR Passport. These documents may be combined with documents of a right of permanent abode acquired overseas. While dual citizenship is not technically allowed, a second citizenship must be actively given up. Our research reveals that individual migrants hold diverse views about how this ambiguous status affects their definition of citizenship. For Hong Kong immigrants, self-reported citizenship reflects people's identities more than it describes citizenship rights (Bloemraad 2004).

Research design

This chapter draws on information from questionnaire surveys and transcripts of 23 focus groups participated in by 115 people from Vancouver and 75 from Toronto, including 105 women and 85 men. Participants ranged in age from 18-year-old university students to retirees over the age of 65. Each completed a questionnaire about migration history, settlement experiences in Canada, transnational practices and civic participation in Canada and Hong Kong. Participants then discussed their experiences of immigration and settlement in Canada and participation in civil society.[4] Linking the focus group transcripts with the questionnaire information allows us to connect the social characteristics, immigration histories and transnational behaviours of immigrants with their views of citizenship and participation in Canadian society.

For reasons cited above, establishing participants' citizenship proved problematic. Some Hong Kong immigrants who have naturalised in Canada claim only Canadian citizenship. Many recognise that they are not British citizens because the British government never granted them the right to British residency. A naturalised citizen who has lived in Canada for 11 years, Sam, says:

> I don't think I have dual citizenship. I was born in Hong Kong. I have a Hong Kong ID card and a Canadian passport.... Yes, I can live in Hong Kong, but in reality, I mainly live in Canada. Hence, I don't consider myself to have dual citizenship. (N1, TNM2, 8–87)[5]

Others view the Hong Kong Identity Card and right of abode as equivalent to citizenship since they allow free passage into Hong Kong and

China without jeopardising the right to a Canadian passport. Derek and Sara note,

> Once the mainlanders apply for immigration [to Canada], they have to give up their [PRC] citizenship. We don't need a visa in order to visit Hong Kong. We can use our Hong Kong ID card to go there. (N6, N8, 183–190)
>
> I have Hong Kong and Canadian citizenship. If we use a Canadian passport to go to Hong Kong, we can't stay there for long.... On the other hand, if we use our ID card, it's very convenient when we enter Hong Kong. (N3, TNF2, 67–69)

Sara makes a controversial but common interpretation of formal citizenship enacted by using different documentation on entry to Hong Kong and Canada.

Despite the complicated interpretations of citizenship in Hong Kong, a plurality of participants, 77 of 171,[6] indicated that they were Canadian citizens only. Landed immigrants were the second largest group, accounting for approximately 40 per cent of all participants. Only 26 of the 171 participants, 15.2 per cent, held dual citizenship. The naturalisation rate of approximately 60 per cent is significantly lower than the 90.7 per cent rate for all Hong Kong–born Canadians in 2001. The difference probably occurs because most participants were more recent immigrants. In contrast, however, the rate of dual citizenship for the Hong Kong immigrants in our focus groups is comparable to that recorded for all immigrants, 16.6 per cent in 1996 (Bloemraad 2004: 405).[7] Although the Hong Kong immigrants who participated in the focus groups are taking up dual citizenship at approximately the same rate as all immigrants, we had expected a higher rate. Often portrayed as hypermobile migrants seeking flexible citizenship (Ong 1999) outside China (Lau 1990b), we expected that Hong Kong migrants would be eager to take advantage of Canada's relatively liberal citizenship regulations.

Length of residence plays a crucial role in naturalisation and dual citizenship (Bloemraad 2004). Currently, landed immigrants must have accumulated 3 years of residency within the 4 years prior to application to qualify for citizenship. Prolonged residence is also expected to increase immigrants' attachment to Canada and decrease transnational ties, factors thought to encourage naturalisation. All Hong Kong immigrants who arrived prior to 1986 had Canadian citizenship and two of the seven were dual citizens. In comparison, only 1 of the 45 who arrived after 1996 was naturalised and none of the recent arrivals was a dual citizen. Comparison of the rates of naturalisation and dual citizenship by year of immigration reveals that both increase steadily with longer residence. Naturalisation rates rise from 2.2 per cent of those who arrived after 1996 to 71.4 per cent of those who arrived prior to 1986. Rates of dual citizenship also increase steadily with length of residence. Among those who settled in Canada prior to 1986, more than one quarter, 28.6 per cent, were dual citizens. The largest increases in naturalisation occur within a decade of settling in Canada, another indication that people are claiming citizenship soon after they meet the residency requirements.

Naturalisation and the acquisition of dual citizenship are also linked to changes in immigrants' economic characteristics. In 2001, naturalised citizens had higher employment rates than those who were eligible but had not yet obtained Canadian citizenship (Tran, Kustec and Chiu 2005). Naturalised citizens also had greater economic success than landed immigrants who have not yet naturalised. In this respect, Hong Kong immigrants are similar to Canadian immigrants as a whole. Canadian and dual citizens are much more likely to be employed and to be working full-time than landed immigrants. Only 11 of 65 landed immigrants were employed, however, and an even smaller number, 3 of the 11, were working full-time. In comparison, approximately one third of those who were Canadian citizens and dual citizens were employed, although the majority were working part-time. Among landed immigrants, fully half had household incomes below $20,000, but only about one third, 34.4 per cent, of Canadian citizens and even fewer dual citizens, 13.0 per cent, reported equally low incomes. At the other end of the income spectrum, more than one third of dual citizens, 34.8 per cent, reported household incomes over $50,000 compared with only 9.3 per cent of landed immigrants.

Transnational ties and civic participation

Contrary to the assimilation hypothesis, dual citizenship heightens the passive transnational connections of our participants. Dual citizens were more likely to listen to, read and watch Hong Kong media than those in any other group (Table 10.1). They were equally as likely as landed immigrants, who on average have been in Canada less time, to maintain monthly social contacts by telephone and email. Compared with those who possessed only Canadian citizenship and with landed immigrants, dual citizens were more informed about Hong Kong affairs and culture

Table 10.1   Ties to Hong Kong by citizenship status

	Landed immigrant		Canadian citizen only		Dual citizen	
	N	%	N	%	N	%
Social ties to Hong Kong*	69		80		26	
Immediate family	51	73.9	45	56.3	18	69.2
Extended family	52	75.4	57	71.3	20	76.9
Friends	52	75.4	54	67.5	24	92.3
Hong Kong media*	69		80		26	
TV/radio	44	63.7	53	66.3	21	80.8
Newspapers	51	73.9	60	75.0	21	80.8
Movies	41	59.4	49	61.3	20	76.9
Listservs	12	17.4	7	8.8	8	30.8
Monthly contact*	69		80		26	
Telephone	61	88.4	59	73.8	23	88.4
Email	27	39.1	30	32.5	10	38.5
Letter	8	11.6	9	11.3	0	0
Economic ties to Hong Kong**	69		80		26	
Own property	20	29.0	18	22.5	10	38.5
Run business	12	17.4	9	11.3	6	23.1
Travel to Hong Kong**	67		77		26	
At least once a year	34	50.7	26	33.8	11	42.3
Less than once a year	20	29.9	39	50.6	13	50.0
Never	13	19.4	12	15.6	2	7.7

* Percentages may not sum to 100 because multiple responses were accepted.
** Percentages may not sum to 100 because some respondents reported no economic ties.

and more involved in frequent social contacts. These trends need to be interpreted carefully because of the small number of dual citizens, only 26 participants. Nevertheless, the trends are consistent and marked, suggesting that dual citizens retain more interest in Hong Kong than do those who hold only Canadian citizenship.

The maintenance of transnational ties by dual citizens is doubly surprising because of their length of residence in Canada. Among the three groups of participants, dual citizens had the longest average length of residence. Longer residence is not associated with declining interest in the place of origin. Rather, those who identified themselves as dual citizens had a continuing interest in the popular culture and public affairs of Hong Kong and in maintaining regular social connections.

As expected, the acquisition of Canadian citizenship is associated with more participation in Canadian society, particularly voting, a right

Table 10.2 Civic participation* by citizenship status

	Landed immigrant		Canadian citizen only		Dual citizen	
	N	%	N	%	N	%
	69		80		26	
Donate to Canadian charities	14	20.3	26	32.5	10	38.5
Vote in Canadian elections	0	0	15	18.8	6	23.1
Donate to Hong Kong associations	8	11.6	8	10.0	3	11.5
Volunteer for Hong Kong associations	26	37.7	32	40.0	16	61.5
Member of Hong Kong associations	20	29.0	44	55.0	7	26.9

* These are the activities from a much longer list in which more than 3 or 4 people participated. Percentages may not add to 100 because multiple responses were permitted and some people reported no participation.

available only to citizens. Although naturalised Canadians are less likely to vote than are all eligible Canadians (Stasiulis 1997), their increased probability of voting is associated with increases in other forms of participation, such as donating to charities (Table 10.2). Involvement in Hong Kong society does not diminish much as Hong Kong immigrants become more involved in Canadian society. In addition to participating in Canadian organisations, many Hong Kong immigrants participate in Canadian branches of Hong Kong associations that are valuable sources of social contacts and settlement information. Dual citizens who are more active in Canadian society than naturalised Hong Kong immigrants are also more likely than those who have only Canadian citizenship to donate to and volunteer for Hong Kong associations. Those who are only Canadian citizens do report higher levels of membership in Hong Kong associations than either dual citizens or landed immigrants. But membership is a more passive form of involvement than volunteering, which may indicate greater attachment to Hong Kong among those who are only Canadian citizens than among dual citizens who have lived away from Hong Kong for longer periods.

In sum, dual citizenship among Hong Kong immigrants is associated with enhanced interest in Hong Kong popular culture and public affairs and the maintenance of social and organisational ties to Hong Kong. Such ties do not diminish dual citizens' involvement in Canadian society. Compared with Hong Kong immigrants who hold only Canadian citizenship, dual citizens were more likely to vote. Their involvement is consistent with evidence that dual citizens are well established in Canada with longer residence than those who hold only Canadian citizenship and greater economic success than landed immigrants who arrived more recently.

Meanings of citizenship

By analysing the meanings attached to dual citizenship, we can discern some of the reasons for the complex patterns of dual citizenship. Hong Kong immigrants hold diverse views, confirming that place of origin is only one of the many aspects of social identity that influence citizenship practices and identities. Among our participants, gender and stage in the life course, along with individual differences in settlement experiences, also affect views about dual citizenship. Moreover, to understand the salience and significance of dual citizenship requires examining the rationales for claiming Canadian citizenship and the unwillingness to abandon citizenship status in Hong Kong.

The views about dual citizenship range from rejection of dual citizenship to its pre-eminence as the main reason for migrating. The focus group discussions reflect the dynamic character of people's views about citizenship, framed by the changing context within which Hong Kong migrants migrated and settled in Canada. Acquisition of dual citizenship has occurred in a historical context framed by a history of forced migration after 1948, the experience of colonial government until 1997 and the complicated and fluid citizenship regime that resulted.

Dual citizenship and the family

The participants in our focus groups viewed questions of citizenship through the lens of family needs. Some noted that dual citizenship is not important to them because they plan to stay in Canada, but it is important for their children because it allows them access to job markets in Hong Kong as well as Canada. The discussion confirms Johanna Waters' finding that after graduation students who had studied in British Columbia returned to Hong Kong, where their foreign education and fluency in English enhanced their job opportunities (Waters 2004). Compare the views expressed by Michelle, a landed immigrant living in Vancouver for approximately 3 years, with those of Barbara, a landed immigrant in Vancouver who arrived 3 years earlier. Michelle was married with children, unlike Barbara who was still single. Michelle says,

Actually, for me, in terms of dual citizenship, I don't find it so important. But I want my children to have it because if they can't find a job here, they could go back to Hong Kong. It gives them more options. Actually, there's a lot of pressure here. Even if you grew up and are educated here, you still don't have much opportunity. Why don't we give [them] more opportunities? (N1, N3, 429–439)

Michelle's concerns about her children's economic prospects shape her views about dual citizenship. Barbara appreciates the convenience of dual citizenship and its benefits for children who are not yet born:

I think dual citizenship is good. We do nothing to have it. Dual citizenship gives me convenience. It'll also facilitate my children's careers if they work in Hong Kong in the future. (N2, N6, 98–124)

Men and women shared the view that dual citizenship is important because it offers economic opportunities for their children, although women mentioned it more often as an important reason for naturalising (Preston, Kobayashi and Man 2006). Some youth shared this view, repeating that the main advantages of dual citizenship are economic. According to David, a dual citizen in his early twenties,

If I can't get a job after graduation, I might go back to Hong Kong. ... I have a Hong Kong ID, so I can work in Hong Kong as a Hong Kongnese. (N3, TYM1, 29–33)

Ease of acquisition is another motivation for some to take up dual citizenship.

For Hong Kong immigrants, retaining and updating the Hong Kong Personal Identity Card and their right of abode is a simple administrative process that requires little paperwork since most already possess a personal identity card or evidence of the right of abode. In her comments, Barbara is referring to the ease with which she can retain the right to residency in Hong Kong. Melissa, a Canadian citizen living in Vancouver for six years, notes,

But for us, we have an ID. We have the three stars to indicate that we have lived there seven years. So you're allowed to leave. They don't care. We get the ID because we have lived there a long time. We just need to renew it. (N2, N1, 270–311)

The ease of travel with a Canadian passport was also emphasised. A Canadian passport allows people to travel to more countries without obtaining visas. For Hong Kong immigrants who settled in Canada prior to Hong Kong's handover to China, the Canadian passport is also more widely accepted than their BNO passports that will have to be replaced eventually with HKSAR passports.

Seeking security

Marked by the history of political instability in China during the twentieth century, Hong Kong immigrants also value dual citizenship because of the security it offers. Some have already fled from China once. Migrating again at the prospect of Hong Kong returning to China, they are anxious to have the benefits of protection by a foreign government. Margaret, a student living in Toronto, points out:

> For me, dual citizenship is a form of security. If Hong Kong is politically unstable or a war occurs in the region, we can come back to Canada and vice versa. My family thinks in the same way as I do. (N6, TY2, 55–65)

Others emphasised that they want a Canadian passport so that they can claim the protection of the Canadian embassy in any disputes with the Chinese government. While some participants questioned whether China would recognise their claims to Canadian citizenship, most were anxious to have citizenship from as many countries as possible to provide options in the event of political instability in China and Hong Kong.

The participants emphasised feelings of uncertainty about the future. They reiterated that the future is unknown. Unable to predict the political or economic situations in Hong Kong or Canada, they want to have as many options about places to live and work as possible. Melissa speaks for many of the focus group participants when she says,

> From the individual's point of view, it's better to have as many citizenships as possible, if you're allowed to do so. (N2, N1, 270–311)

Citizenship as belonging

The instrumental value of dual citizenship is readily apparent to our participants, but they also value symbolic aspects of dual citizenship. Like many migrants, they are torn between the identities and loyalties developed in Hong Kong and their commitments to Canada that have been formed through sacrifice and some suffering. Here, we find more differences of opinion among our participants. After living in Canada for almost a decade, Robert expresses a common view:

> It's not important to me at present. . . . I think having a Canadian passport is more convenient. . . . For me, I don't have any special feeling on this issue. It's inconvenient for me to use CI [Personal Identity Certificate] in travelling. Moreover, I've been here a while, and I have no special feelings for Hong Kong. . . . If I have to choose, I prefer the Canadian citizenship. I have already come to Canada. After all, to be a citizen is my major objective of immigration. (N5, TNM1, 85–93)

Robert migrated to Canada in 1994 prior to Hong Kong's return to China with the explicit goal of obtaining Canadian citizenship, and he is ambivalent about the value of dual citizenship. In other passages, however, he notes the advantages of dual citizenship for his children who can look for work in Hong Kong.

Others feel that dual citizenship means they must choose between their familiar identities as Hong Kongnese and Chinese and new Canadian identities. Lisa, who lives in Toronto, expresses the dilemma eloquently:

> I'm a Chinese. I'll never let myself forget it. . . . Although we live here, love our present life, and have citizenship, we should not deny our Chinese ethnicity. . . . I see myself as a Canadian Chinese. Dual citizenship is very important. I hope we won't forget our ethnicity. I have a strong feeling that being a Chinese is extremely important. (N10, TNF3, 85–97)

By retaining Chinese citizenship, Lisa can retain her ethnic identity. But for others, the link between ethnic identity and citizenship is so tight that they will consider abandoning claims to Canadian citizenship to retain their identities as Chinese and Hong Kongnese.

The desire for dual citizenship is also a response to experiences of exclusion in Canada. Aware of the discrimination and violence experienced by Chinese in other countries such as Indonesia, marked by Hong Kong's recent history of forced migration and colonisation, some participants emphasise that dual citizenship enables them to become part of a society that has treated them with hostility. According to Fran, a Canadian citizen who had lived in Canada for 7 years at the time of the focus groups, dual citizenship would give us security. They wanted us to come, but after we came, there are a lot of things that they don't provide for us. In fact, they started finding faults with us for so many different things. That we didn't do this right, we didn't do that right, we're trying to cheat them on this, that we're trying to do something illegal … So even though we really want to become part of Canada, there are no opportunities for us to do so. (N5, N3, 406–427)

Fran's views are typical of many women but particularly those whose husbands are 'astronauts', men who work in Hong Kong while their wives and children settle in Canada (Preston, Kobayashi and Man 2006). Astronauts' rights to permanent residency in Canada and, ultimately, their access to Canadian citizenship are jeopardised by their lengthy periods of absence from Canada. Yet, many women agree with Fran that, faced with economic difficulties in Canada, principally limited employment opportunities, their partners had few options other than to become astronauts. For these women, dual citizenship is an avenue for establishing symbolic attachment to Canada at the same time as it reduces the uncertainty and insecurity that their partners and families face in their efforts to maintain their economic status while settling in Canada. Dichotomies of 'convenience' or 'commitment' simplify and falsely stigmatise the citizenship choices made by migrants.

Conclusion

Hong Kong immigrants have complicated views and behaviours regarding dual citizenship. More immigrants become dual citizens as length of residence increases and as they achieve economic success in Canada; however, rates of dual citizenship are difficult to pin down. The complex and fluid citizenship regime in Hong Kong gives rise to multiple interpretations of citizenship status by Hong Kong immigrants to Canada. Rather than abandoning their ties to Hong Kong, dual citizens maintain passive transnational ties. Compared with those who hold only Canadian citizenship, dual citizens are more likely to be informed about public affairs and popular culture in Hong Kong and equally likely to maintain social ties to Hong Kong. Naturalised Canadians articulate several powerful motives for obtaining Canadian citizenship: desire to vote and participate in Canadian politics; desire to have an unambiguous nationality of which they can be proud; appreciation of Canada's social programmes and international reputation; and desire that full citizenship will eliminate the discrimination they experience in Canada. Many emphasise the instrumental value of dual citizenship, beginning with the ease of retaining the right of residency in Hong Kong. Those looking to Canadian citizenship as protection from political risk have been eager to naturalise at the earliest possible opportunity. Maintaining access to social rights in both Hong Kong and Canada is another reason that some hold dual citizenship. The instrumental value of dual citizenship is framed by concerns about children's economic opportunities and insecurity about the future. With only a few exceptions, participants emphasised that dual citizenship was important for their children, partly to give them more economic options in a globalising world of economic insecurity and partly because of an astute assessment that their children's economic opportunities in Canada are limited by their identities as Chinese Canadians and immigrants. Hong Kong immigrants' sense of unease is heightened by earlier experiences as forced migrants and colonials without secure claims to citizenship anywhere. To the extent that our participants emphasise the instrumental value of dual citizenship, they can be seen as citizens of convenience, but this attitude needs to be understood through the lens of family and the distinct history of Hong Kong. In the current era of globalisation, one needs to ask how much their instrumental views of citizenship differ from those of other Canadians, other institutions and states themselves.

Hong Kong immigrants also value the symbolic aspects of dual citizenship. Many embrace Canadian citizenship eagerly, sometimes even downplaying the value of dual citizenship. Some are torn, feeling their identities as 'Chinese' are threatened by abandoning claims to residency in Hong Kong. Others respond to the exclusion that they experience in Canada by placing more importance on the acquisition of Canadian citizenship. It is the prize that will make difficult settlement experiences more palatable and give them legitimacy in a multicultural setting. The partners of astronauts who often expressed the greatest anguish about their treatment in Canada want the convenience of travelling as a dual citizen and access to economic opportunities in Canada and Hong Kong for themselves, their children and their partners. They also seek a sense of belonging to Canadian society from which many feel excluded.

The alleged instrumentality of Hong Kong dual citizens in Canada may more properly be regarded as manifestations of migrant vulnerability and dedication. Canadians speak from a position of privilege, protection and security in decrying what is perceived as immigrants' citizenship acquisition without adequate love of country. Migrants who seek haven from homeland states they regard—or fear will become—repressive have cause to seek succour in another state. Migrants who face discrimination or unfulfilled promise in their new country have grounds for questioning their belonging. And migrants who base their dual citizenship decisions on what is best for their children may be regarded as entrusting what they love most to a new society.

Instrumental and symbolic meanings of citizenship are thus intertwined. Our analysis suggests that Hong Kong immigrants are settlers both of convenience and of commitment. Responding to the threats and opportunities that result from Hong Kong's distinct history, many value instrumental aspects of dual citizenship. When thinking of Canada and Hong Kong as places in which to live and raise children, their symbolic understanding of citizenship has to do with belonging, even for transnationals who feel a sense of belonging to two places.

The citizenship decisions made by Hong Kong migrants occur within the parameters established by sending and receiving states. Public discourse about dual citizenship often criticises the behaviours of migrants rather than the actions of states. Our analysis shows how individual concerns, centred on the family, through which migrants regulate their movements and organise their households, are connected to numerous public policy issues that range from citizenship regulations to policies that address racism, language training and employment. In the Canadian context, the extensive rights attached to permanent residency reduce the pressure to naturalise at the same time that the Canadian state promotes naturalisation by its minimal citizenship requirements. The contradictory policies raise questions about the role of the state in fostering citizenship take-up and about whether there is a relationship between commitment and convenience. While the complete answers to those questions await further research, we have found that convenience does not reduce commitment and dual citizenship does not compromise it. Rather, transnationalism and dual citizenship raise complex issues of membership and belonging for state, society and migrant.

Notes

1. This research was funded by a Social Science and Humanities Research Council of Canada grant, #829-99-1012, to Audrey Kobayashi and co-investigators David Ley, Guida Man, Valerie Preston and Myer Siemiatycki. We are grateful for the research assistance provided by Ann Marie Murnaghan, Peter Murphy and Julie Young and extremely helpful comments from the editor.
2. The multiculturalism policy was introduced in 1971.

3. For example, temporary agricultural workers who return annually to work in Canada cannot count the months of their sojourns towards the residency required for citizenship.
4. The discussions were conducted mainly in English, but a Cantonese-speaker led many of the focus groups allowing people to speak in the language with which they were comfortable.
5. Pseudonyms are used throughout this chapter. Each quotation is identified by the participant's identification number, the identification code for the focus group and the relevant lines in the transcript of the focus group discussion.
6. Although 190 people participated in the focus groups, only 171 responded to the questions about citizenship. Nineteen participants are not included in the analysis.
7. Under British law, dual citizenship was also permitted in Hong Kong.

References

Abu-Laban, Y. and C. Gabriel. (2002) *Selling Diversity: Immigration, Multiculturalism, Employment Equity, and Globalization.* Peterborough: Broadview Press.
Aleinikoff, T. and D. Klusmeyer, eds. (2001) *Citizenship Today: Global Perspectives and Practices.* Washington, DC: Carnegie Endowment for International Peace.
Bloemraad, I. (2004) 'Who Claims Dual Citizenship? The Limits of Postnationalism, the Possibilities of Transnationalism, and the Persistence of Traditional Citizenship'. *International Migration Review* 38, 2: 389–426.
Buckley, R. (1997) *Hong Kong: The Road to 1997.* Cambridge: Cambridge University Press.
Cannon, M. (1989) *China Tide: The Revealing Story of the Hong Kong Exodus to Canada.* Toronto: Harper Collins.
Citizenship and Immigration Canada (1987–1997) *Immigration Statistics (1987–1996); Facts & Figures: Immigration Overview (1997).* Ottawa: Government of Canada.
Citizenship and Immigration Canada (2006) *Becoming a Canadian Citizen.* (http://www.cici.gc.ca/english/citizen/becoming-howto.html [1 February 2006]).
Crispo, J. (1996) 'Canada Places Too Little Value on Citizenship'. *The Toronto Star*, 14 June: A13.
De Mont, J. and T. Fennell (1989) *Hong Kong Money: How Chinese Families and Fortunes are Changing Canada.* Toronto: Key Porter Books.
Faist, T. (2000) 'Transnationationalization in International Migration: Implications for the Study of Citizenship and Culture'. *Ethnic and Racial Studies* 23: 189–222.
Faist, T. (2004) 'Dual Citizenship as Overlapping Membership'. In D. Joly, ed., *International Migration in the New Millennium: Global Movement and Settlement.* Aldershot, UK: Ashgate, pp. 210–32.
Fritz, M. (1998) 'Pledging Multiple Allegiances'. *Los Angeles Times*, 6 April: A1.
Hansen, R. and P. Weil (2002) 'Dual Citizenship in a Changed World: Immigration, Gender and Social Rights'. In R. Hansen and P. Weil, eds, *Dual Nationality, Social Rights and Federal Citizenship in the U.S. and Europe.* Oxford: Bergahn, pp. 1–15.
Heisler, M. (2001) 'Now and Then, Here and There: Migration and the Transformation of Identities, Borders, and Orders'. In M. Albert, D. Jacobson and

Y. Lapid, eds, *Identities, Borders, Orders*. Minneapolis: University of Minnesota Press, pp. 225–47.

Hong Kong Special Administrative Region (HKSAR) Government. (2003) *A General Guide to HKSAR Passport*. (http://www.immd.gov.hk/ehtml/topical_2.htm [10 March 2005]).

Isin, E. (2002) *Being Political, Genealogies of Citizenship*. Minneapolis and London: University of Minnesota Press.

Koslowski, R. (2001) 'Demographic Boundary Maintenance in World Politics: Of International Norms on Dual Nationality'. In M. Albert, D. Jacobson and Y. Lapid, eds, *Identities, Borders, Orders*. Minneapolis: University of Minnesota Press, pp. 203–23.

Ku, A. and N. Pun. (2004) 'Introduction: Remaking Citizenship in Hong Kong'. In A. Ku and N. Pun, eds, *Remaking Citizenship in Hong Kong: Community, Nation and the Global City*. London and New York: Routledge Curzon, pp. 1–15.

Lam, W.-M. (2005) 'Depoliticization, Citizenship, and the Politics of Community in Hong Kong'. *Citizenship Studies* 9, 3: 309–22.

Lau, E. (1989) 'The Chosen Few'. *Far Eastern Economic Review* 146, 52: 10–11.

Lau, E. (1990a) 'Elites Take All – Britain's Nationality Package Stirs Debate on Fairness'. *Far Eastern Economic Review* 148, 16: 18–19.

Lau, E. (1990b) 'Nationality for Sale: Hong Kong People Scramble for Foreign Passports'. *Far Eastern Economic Review* 147, 11: 17–18.

Ley, D. (2003) 'Seeking *Homo Economicus*: The Canadian state and the Strange Story of the Business Immigration Program'. *Annals of the Association of American Geographers* 93: 426–41.

Meyer, D. (2000) *Hong Kong as a Global Metropolis*. Cambridge: Cambridge University Press.

Miller, D. (2000) *Citizenship and National Identity*. Cambridge: Polity Press.

Ong, A. (1999) *Flexible Citizenship: The Cultural Politics of Transnationality*. Durham: Duke University Press.

Pickus, N. (1998) 'Introduction'. In N. Pickus, ed., *Immigration and Citizenship in the Twenty-First Century*. Lanham, MA: Rowman and Littlefield, pp. xvii–xxxiii.

Preston, V., A. Kobayashi and G. Man (2006) 'Transnationalism, Gender, and Civic Participation: Canadian Case Studies of Hong Kong Immigrants'. *Environment and Planning A* 38, 9: 1633–51.

Schuck, P. (1998) 'Plural Citizenships'. In N. Pickus, ed., *Immigration and Citizenship in the Twenty-First Century*. Lanham, MA: Rowman and Littlefield, pp. 149–91.

Siemiatycki, M. and V. Preston (2007) 'State and Media Construction of Transnational Communities: A Case Study of Recent Migration from Hong Kong to Canada'. In L. Goldring and S. Krishnamurti, eds, *Organizing the Transnational*, Vancouver: University of British Columbia Press.

Skeldon, R. (1999) 'The Case of Hong Kong'. In L. Pan, ed., *The Encyclopedia of the Chinese Overseas*. Cambridge: Harvard University Press, pp. 67–70.

Spiro, P. (2002) 'Embracing Dual Nationality'. In R. Hansen and P. Weil, eds, *Dual Nationality, Social Rights and Federal Citizenship in the U.S. and Europe*. Oxford: Bergahn, pp. 19–33.

Stasiulis, D. (1997) 'Participation by Immigrants/Ethnocultural/Visible Minorities in the Canadian Policity Sytem'. In A. Breton, ed., *Immigration and Civic Participation: Contemporary Policy and Research Issues*. Ottawa: Citizenship and Immigration Canada.

Stasiulis, D. and Bakan, A. (2005) *Negotiating Citizenship: Migrant Women in Canada and the Global System*. Toronto: University of Toronto Press.

Tran, K., S. Kustec, and T. Chiu. (2005) 'Becoming Canadian: Intent, Process and Outcome'. *Canadian Social Trends*, Spring: 8–13.

Tsang, S. (1997) *Hong Kong: An Appointment with China*. London: I. B. Tauris.

Tse, T. (2004) 'Civic Education and the Making of Deformed Citizenry: From British Colony to Chinese SAR'. In A. Ku and N. Pun, eds, *Remaking Citizenship in Hong Kong: Community, Nation and the Global City*. London and New York: Routledge Curzon, pp. 54–73.

Vertovec, S. (2004) *Trends and Impacts of Migrant Transnationalism*. Working Paper 04–03. Oxford: Centre on Migration Policy and Society, Oxford University.

Wagner, D. (1997) 'Uh Oh, Canada! Beware the Return of the Ingrates'. *The Vancouver Sun*, 2 July: A14.

Waters, J. (2003) 'Flexible Citizens? Transnationalism and Citizenship Amongst Economic Immigrants in Vancouver'. *The Canadian Geographer* 47, 3: 219–34.

Waters, J. (2004) *Geographies of Cultural Capital: International Education, Circular Migration and Family Strategies between Canada and Hong Kong*. Doctoral dissertation, Department of Geography, University of British Columbia, Vancouver.

Part IV

Citizenship and Democracy Beyond Borders

11
Dual Citizenship, European Identity and Community-Building in Europe

Waldemar A. Skrobacki

The 'globalisation' of Europe, community-building and dual citizenship

The chapters in this book are testimony to the increasing complexity of dual citizenship, both as a concept and as an institution. The studies not only examine the legal aspect of dual citizenship, but also analyse it in the context of cultural rights, the notion of democracy, the role of the individual in society, civil rights and obligations, not to mention 'pragmatic' considerations, such as security, terrorism or immigration. This complexity is a reflection of the changes in the nature and role of the state. Even if indirectly, these studies are to a degree influenced by 'the roaring nineties' (Stiglitz 2003), when globalisation debates, with their notion of the demise of the 'traditional' state, calls for institutions of 'new governance' and the imagined world-market mobility of the individual, suggested that the planet was changing into a 'global village'.

Although many of these conclusions turned out to be premature, the fact is that the state's role has been changing. And nowhere has it changed more profoundly and more quickly than in post-1945 Europe. Among those changes, the very idea of citizenship, so tightly tied to state authority in the past, is being redefined. As a result, the growing tolerance of dual citizenship, which only a few decades ago was not only strongly disapproved of, but also illegal, is now becoming more the norm, even if not yet fully sanctioned by law. For example, in Sweden, among other places, dual citizenship has already been legally approved (Spång 2007).

The tolerance of dual citizenship would not have happened without growing political acceptance of it by the Europeans. This, in turn, is directly related to the continent's own form of 'globalisation', namely the process of European integration, and its intellectual and political engine, namely Europeanisation. Unlike the version of the 1990s, European 'globalisation' has achieved some measure of success, not least because the European community by design includes a strong ethical dimension (Skrobacki 2005). This is reflected in the fact that the Treaty of Rome included not only economic aspects of integration, for instance Title II (agriculture) and VII (economic and monetary union), but also social ones, such as Title XI (social policy and education) and XIII (public health) (Wyatt 2002).[1] By contrast, the global theory of the 1990s relied almost entirely on 'technical' economic measures, mainly trade and capital mobility, for building the global community. Ethical considerations, for instance those related to the nature of democratic society or the individual's identity, were thought to be of secondary importance.

Dual citizenship studies appropriately capture the ethical dimension of the European 'global' community, and for that reason they can and should be used in general analyses of European integration. However, these studies can shed more light on the nature of European integration only if their scope is extended even further. This is necessary to explain EU, or European, citizenship, which is, as I will argue, *sui generis*.

Created only about a decade ago, and still a work in progress, EU citizenship has the potential to become a critical tool of integration. Moreover, as a tool it is substantially different from most other instruments of integration upon which community-building has relied until now. It may be argued that Europe has come to a point where chiefly political policies have to be employed in order to advance the European project of integration. In other words, most 'traditional' measures of integration, such as various 'common' economic policies, no longer suffice. One more such measure—for instance, the emerging Common Energy Policy—or one less, is unlikely to make an effective difference, as it might have in the past. European integration needs qualitatively different instruments, and dual citizenship is one of them.

In its political aspect, the qualitative change is about tackling sensitive issues that in other times were the primary reasons for continent-wide instability, in particular, national identity. These issues may still appear, especially to decision-makers, 'too hot to handle', but they are no longer so. After all, there have been several decades of continuous democratic politics in Europe; many inter-*national* reconciliations have taken place, for instance between the French and the Germans, or are taking place, such as between the Germans and the Poles; Europeans have become better off and more educated and their penchant for war disappeared a long time ago.

In its cognitive aspect, the qualitative change is about *constructing* a new identity—a European one. This is where dual citizenship, in conjunction with European citizenship, can assist in explaining the scope of change in identity that has taken place thus far and how it might progress further. And it must progress, for community requires a feeling of belonging and a form of identity, in this case European identity. With identity comes loyalty, the kind of bond which makes nationhood into *national* community. But European identity cannot be national, for there is no European nation. Hence, in the foreseeable future, a European community can only be based on political identity. Such identity has to be formed in terms of norms and *values* that are shared by all Europeans, regardless of their national identity.

Dual citizenship and EU citizenship are linked to each other by the state and the nation, which are inherently intertwined in Europe, a continent primarily composed of *nation*-states rather than states. I argue that, chiefly because of the way Europe has developed, dual citizenship is a bridge between national citizenship and EU citizenship, for the growing acceptance of dual citizenship is a catalyst for furthering the construction of European identity. Furthermore, exploring the connection between the two forms of citizenship helps us to comprehend better the changing nature of national citizenship in Europe.

National citizenship and national identity

As Peter Reisenberg observes, 'citizenship presents problems, for "citizenship" may be treated [in] many different ways and has instant associations that must be reckoned with' (Reisenberg 2002: 3). Bernard Crick noted accordingly that citizenship can have four meanings. First, it can refer to rights and duties that are a form of recognition of one's legal status as a permanent resident of a state, regardless of its political system. Second, citizenship can be associated with 'civic republicanism', the belief that inhabitants of a democratic state are to participate actively in political life. Third, it can invoke the ideal of 'global citizenship', a notion 'that we should all act as citizens of one world: that for the sake of peace, justice and human rights, there must be limitations in international law on the sovereignty and power of individual states' powers'. Fourth, citizenship can refer to an educational process of learning and teaching 'how to improve or achieve the aims inherent in the second and third meanings' (Crick 2004: xi). Thus, citizenship has no universally accepted definition, for it involves issues that are of interest to historians, legal scholars, sociologists and political scientists. Its examination requires a combination of many approaches and a consideration of the relevant historical perspective.

Civic republicanism, Crick's second meaning, and citizenship are now often used as if they were synonyms; that they can be used this way is a result of recent developments in Europe. Undoubtedly, the Old Continent has a long and well-established intellectual tradition of civic republicanism; and it has just as long and well-established intellectual tradition of liberal democracy. But Europe has a rather short political history of both. Even though there are some exceptions, notably the United Kingdom and its Magna Carta of 1215, in Continental Europe, by and large, the history of functioning liberal democracies is neither long nor has it been very successful in the past. Consequently, citizenship merged with civic republicanism only within the past few decades. Before 1945, the practice and comprehension of citizenship was antiliberal; and the primary reason for this was the fusion of the state with the nation and citizenship with national identity.

Here is how Diderot explained the nature of citizenship in the *Encyclopédie*:

The Athenians were very loath to grant citizenship to foreigners. They gave the distinction much more value than did the Romans. The title '*citizen*' was never disparaged by them; they never retreated from the high opinion that they had come to about citizenship.... In Athens only those were citizens who were born of Athenian citizens. When a young man reached the age of 20 he was registered, the state now counted him among its members. He then, in a ceremony of entrance (into the community) swore an oath, his eyes toward heaven....

However one could become a citizen of Athens through adoption by an Athenian citizen and by the approval of the people, but this privilege was not frequently granted. If one was not registered as a citizen before he was twenty, he was not viewed as such when age prevented him from fulfilling his (public) obligations....

To be a true Roman *citizen*, three things were necessary: to have a residence in Rome, to be a member of one of the 35 tribes, and to be able to win offices in the Republic. Those who had their citizen rights by grant rather than by birth were only, properly speaking, honorary citizens.... (Diderot, in Reisenberg 2002: 166–67)

Diderot wrote these words in the mid-eighteenth century, the age of the citizen (*citoyen*) and the French Revolution, which was followed by the age of nations in the nineteenth century, when the fusion was completed by the fact that Europe consisted chiefly of nations that formed, or wanted to form, their own states. As a result, the last three centuries in Europe have been about building *nation*-states.[2] Leaving behind the political, economic and social structures of feudalism (although not entirely), the people of Europe were transforming their communities bound by the ties of kinship into communities based on national identity. Moreover, before the formation of nations, societal links were based chiefly on immediate and personal interactions among community members. National ties have become more institutionalised; and citizenship has become one of the institutions. These ties have also become politically potent.

Under the banners of national interest, Europeans waged endless wars, which fused national identity with citizenship even more tightly. This has led to the creation of 'us' vs 'them' divisions; and the notion of citizenship has developed as a reflection of these divisions. It is in this context that the *ethno-national* notion of citizenship was formed (Brubaker 1992). Consequently, the idea of inclusion and exclusion was built into citizenship: the nationals, that is the members of the nation, were included and the non-nationals were not. In turn, citizenship was conceived of, at the most practical level, as a membership card given to nationals that assured them rights and various entitlements along with firmly defined obligations. In short, citizenship became the framework for rights, privileges and duties provided to the members of a nation.

The inclusion–exclusion duality has developed in different ways in Europe's nation-states. For example, in France after the 1789 revolution, the membership card at first included chiefly political rights. Subjects became citizens by claiming the rights that until then had belonged only to a particular segment of society. The principal right was eventually the right to vote and to run for office. France is probably the only country in Europe that from the beginning of its modern statehood has included a notion of civic republicanism in citizenship. Yet, following Diderot's explanation of the nature of citizenship, rights were to be given exclusively to members of the nation. Thus, the French became citizens because they were French nationals, and vice versa. Later, towards the end of the Third Republic and in the Fourth Republic, when the main elements of various schemes of social policy were established, the membership card also covered the benefits of the welfare state. The coupling of citizenship rights and benefits became so firmly entrenched that it is still promoted today, even if by politically extreme forces. As Bell notes, 'The Front [of Le Pen] defends the welfare state but for the French in a familiar form of "welfare chauvinism" ' (Bell 2002: 84).

By contrast, German citizenship at first was centred primarily on welfare state benefits. Since the 1871 unification was the result of a political decision, Bismarck, the first Chancellor of united Germany, had to give citizenship sufficient substance that it would be the binding element for the creation of a nation. Subsequently, legislation introducing various benefits of the welfare state was put forward: workers' health insurance (1883), industrial accident insurance (1884), and, eventually, the 1911 Reich Insurance that covered all segments of the population. The 1919 Constitution of the Weimar Republic guaranteed basic political rights, such as the right to localised self-government. However, given the chaos of the Weimar years and the general lack of acceptance of the Republic by the German public, Hitler had little difficulty in abrogating these rights after coming to power. Only after 1945 were political rights firmly and meaningfully added to citizenship. The 1949 *Grundgesetz* listed them in Articles 1–17, and Article 20 (1) made clear that the Federal Republic of Germany was a democratic and 'social federal state' (Die Bundesrepublik 1949).

The growing tolerance of dual citizenship, again a development of recent decades, is a function of the process of making national citizenship in Europe increasingly synonymous with civic republicanism. The creation of the European Economic Community/European Union (EEC/EU) made this process possible. It is in the framework of European integration that Europeans either have been able to strengthen their previously tenuous democratic experience, as in the French case or, alternatively, have been guided to democracy by the wisdom and foresight of their leaders, as in the German case. As a result, only collectively, across the continent, can Europeans exercise democratic politics in their states and, hence, be citizens. The experience has had a significant impact on national identity and, by extension, national citizenship.

Before the process of European integration began, the Europeans defined their national identity primarily in negative terms—'I am French because I am not German.' Hence the 'us' vs 'them' division was sharp and extremely divisive. Since one nation was in opposition to another nation, one's national loyalty could not be shared with 'outsiders'. Complete loyalty of nationals was required, for the existence of their nation was at stake. As explained by Renan (in Kohn 1981: 139), 'A nation is a soul, a spiritual principle. . . . A nation is a great solidarity, created by the sentiment of the sacrifices which have been made and of those which one is disposed to make in the future. It presupposes a past; but it resumes itself in the present by a tangible fact: the consent, the clearly expressed desire to continue life in common.'

Because the state became the expression of nationhood and, automatically, *the* protector of the nation, dual citizenship was out of the question: one could be loyal only to one nation and belong only to one state, for one has only one soul. The exclusion–inclusion duality was for all practical purposes absolute, for the 'us' vs 'them' dichotomy really meant *us* or *them*. Not surprisingly, Europe in numerous instances became violent, unstable and authoritarian.

To make Europe stable, democratic and prosperous, the designers of European integration—the Community's founders—were faced with a complex task. The complexity was not so much about what was to be changed as how it was to be done. The primary difficulty was the necessity to change the way Europeans thought of themselves. Europeans had to start defining their national identities in positive terms—'I am French because I am French.' As Jean Monnet, one of the founders of the Community, noted in 1962: 'It was necessary to transcend the national framework' (Monnet 2003: 21). Robert Schuman, another founder, continued,

> Europe will not be made all at once, or according to a single plan. It will be built through concrete achievements which first create a *de facto* solidarity. The coming together of the nations of Europe requires the elimination of the age-old opposition of France and Germany. Any action taken must in the first place concern these two countries. (Schuman 2003: 14; emphasis in original)

How could the *de facto* solidarity be achieved?

> In the past, the nations felt no irrevocable commitment [to other nations]. Their responsibility was strictly to themselves, not to any common interest. They had to rely on themselves alone. Relations took the form either of domination if one country was much stronger than the others, or of the trading of advantages if there was a balance of powers between them. This balance was necessarily unstable and the concessions made in an agreement one year could always be retracted the next. (Monnet 2003: 23)

Reaching beyond economic integration, dual citizenship greatly contributes to the creation of solidarity, for it helps to transcend the national framework. Needless to say, it is not the only factor that helps;

and no single factor can be used in isolation from others. But the effectiveness of dual citizenship is undeniable, for it has a direct and immediate impact on the lives of individuals, allowing them to rethink and redefine their loyalties and identities. Once internalised, this redefinition leads to a shift in perception of others, and to a form of civic republicanism. Technically oriented economic institutions cannot do this so directly; nor can this be effectively legislated.

To be sure, national citizenship/civic republicanism still includes the 'us' vs 'them' division. But it has changed in one fundamental respect; now it is us *and* them. Loyalty to one's nation still remains in place, for nations continue to exist in Europe; but the meaning of loyalty has changed and, along with it, its comprehension. The existence of one's nation is no longer at stake. Therefore, loyalty does not have to be absolute; mingling with the others is no longer a form of national betrayal. Moreover, decades of European integration have proved that the coming together of nations has tangible benefits.

Small or big, young or old, all Europe's nations benefit from integration. This is why citizenship, the membership card, now provides benefits that are comparable to those provided by other cards. The building of the welfare state in the EU's member states has made the benefits much less exclusive in national terms. This has also helped to change the inclusion–exclusion duality by making it less exclusionary. Consequently, one of the reasons for the growing acceptance of dual citizenship is the fact that there is not much to be gained by obtaining another citizenship. What can, say, an Irish citizen get by acquiring Italian citizenship? Besides voting rights in the national elections, not much else is at stake.

The dissemination of prosperity across the national borders of the member states is the effect of economic integration. However, precisely because the European Community was never designed to be a mere free trade zone, the benefits of membership could be equalised across the space of the Union. Had it been a trade zone, the national governments would have still jealously guarded any possible gains related to freer and more intense exchange of goods and services among its members. In addition, as a community, the Union has been changing the nation-state in Europe and, inevitably, citizenship.

The Westphalian state, European integration and citizenship

Monnet had no doubt that creation of community was a process that would have to take many forms: 'The need was political as well as economic. The Europeans had to overcome the mistrust born of centuries of feuds and wars. The governments and peoples of Europe still thought in the old terms of victors and vanquished' (Monnet 2003: 21). To transform these sentiments, a revolution of sorts had to take place. While assessing the European Coal and Steel Community (ECSC), which paved the way for the EEC/EU, he said, 'In itself this [ECSC] was a technical step, but its new procedures, under common institutions, created a silent revolution in men's minds' (Monnet 2003: 22).

The silent revolution, when accomplished, is to lead directly to *de facto* solidarity. It would be premature to assert that this revolution has run its course or that complete solidarity has arrived. It can be stated with certainty, however, that in striving to achieve solidarity the Community has had a serious impact on the role and function of the state. For instance, without prior consultation in Brussels the French national parliament would be unable to pass about 80 per cent of its bills (Majone 1996: 57). The very notion of Westpahalian state sovereignty has been altered. Many decisions that only a few decades ago were exclusively in the domain of the state are now either shared in the Council of Ministers by the governments of the member states or have been transferred to EU institutions, in particular the European Commission. Shared decisions, for instance, relate increasingly to security and foreign policy. Those that are transferred involve competition rules or the environment, to name only two examples. Of course, there are powers that still remain the sovereign right of the state; but they, too, have substantially changed in Europe.

One of the powers that continues to be sovereign is the right to accord citizenship, the so-called *domaine réservé* principle. Yet, it is practically impossible for the government of a member state to exercise this right without taking into account EU policies and, equally important, Union law, since the latter takes precedence over national law. The Schengen Agreement, for instance, has significantly changed the *domaine réservé*.[3]

The Agreement has gradually abolished controls at the common frontiers. To do so, it established a new regime regulating the movement of persons within the space of the Union. Thus, even though only the governments of member states can grant citizenship, thus allowing recipients to take advantage of the freedom of movement, they cannot do so in isolation from other governments and from the institutions of the Union.

A case in point is Spanish immigration policy and, by extension, the power of the government in Madrid to grant Spanish citizenship. Various Spanish scholars who have analysed the impact of European integration on the policy usually conclude that Spain is significantly limited in the way it forms and implements the policy by the country's membership in the Union (De Lucas 1996; Piernas 2002). As Belén Agrela puts it rather provocatively, 'A large part of the Spanish political agenda [regarding immigration policy and law] has been conditioned by its relationship to the European Union.... For that reason, Spain has become the southern gate of this fortress [Fortress Europe]' (Agrela 2002: 3). Thus, despite its downward demographic trends, Spain's immigration policy remains restrictive.

Other significant limitations on the *domaine réservé* result from the European Convention on Human Rights[4] and the European Court of Human Rights, both of which are part of the Council of Europe. The same can be said of the European Court of Justice, an institution of the EU. Although neither the Convention nor the courts can directly influence national citizenship law, a member state has to take into account convention obligations and the case-law produced by the two courts. In the United Kingdom, for example, the Convention, since its authority has frequently been referred to by the country's courts, has become a written addition to the British unwritten constitution. For other governments, the Convention has become a political and, equally important, a 'philosophical' check, since rights and freedoms are inherent parts of liberal democracy.

Moreover, using the Convention or the case-law, national citizens can launch complaints against their own government if they believe their rights are being violated. This has significantly changed the relationship between the citizen and the national government and the state; in this case, national citizenship—not so much its legal aspect as its 'spirit'—has been altered. The liberal dimension of national citizenship, that is the legal framework for the rights and duties of citizens vis-à-vis their own governments, has been extended beyond the nation-state.

This extension greatly contributes to the acceptance of dual citizenship. For one thing, citizens have yet another reason for rethinking their previously undivided loyalty to the state. For another, they strengthen their attachment to the principles of liberal democracy, however protected. As a result, the extension reinforces their civic republicanism on the national level and facilitates its extension to the EU level, thus helping the development of EU citizenship, as I will explain shortly. It also creates conditions for enriching the ideal of the global citizen (Crick's third meaning) and undoubtedly makes more effective the teaching and learning of citizenship (Crick's fourth meaning). Finally, it gives this meaning a different substance.

When the Union was in its early stages, the chief and, for all practical purposes, the only agents of implementing the principles of liberal democracy in European politics were the governments of the member states. The publics were neither ready nor necessarily eager to become civic republicans. In order for them to become eager, ethno-nationalism had to give way. Since this could only be accomplished by real, as opposed to declaratory, cooperation among nations, the Europeans first had to live it. Needless to say, the living had to be given a direction and a framework. The direction became inter-governmental cooperation, to be followed by the supranationalism of European integration; the framework became the European polity, which has been built on the extension of identity beyond the nation-state. In practical terms, this means that having learned the value of liberal democracy at the national level, the Europeans have to take learning a step further by carrying liberal democracy beyond the nation-state, for which it was originally designed, and placing it on the level of the EU. This requires the creation of a non-national political identity. Thus, in addition to being national civic republicans, they also have to become Community civic republicans, namely EU citizens.

EU citizenship and European identity

Examining European citizenship must be an exercise in patience, for it seems to exemplify just about any problem one has to cope with while dealing with European integration and the Union. The EU is often referred to as a project, that is something that is being worked upon and may or may not succeed. Although the Community is constantly changing, its foundation is well established and the Union has become an important part of the lives of the Europeans. At the same time, many of its elements have yet to be defined fully. European citizenship is one such element, which is why it continues to be a project. Also, the EU is frequently described as *sui generis*, a model unto itself. Although the Union appears to be becoming more and more institutionalised, it still contains many components that validate this description. EU citizenship is one such components, for it is truly *sui generis*.

The Rome Treaty at first harmonised the national citizenships of the member states of the EEC by insisting that they referred to both political rights and the benefits of the welfare state. This has entailed the sharing of values and norms, which requires both time and, certainly, a greater degree of integration. Equally important, the sharing could not be determined exclusively from above. The nascent citizenries of the member states had to be drawn into the integration process and become organically involved. To change the 'us' or 'them' divisions, international amity and goodwill had to take root, for only then could the hatred between nations fade away. Not surprisingly, the very notion of, and the legal framework for, Union citizenship appeared only after several decades of integration.

The 1993 Treaty of Maastricht established EU citizenship.[5] Article 8 extended a number of rights, which until then were the exclusive domain of national citizenship, to the whole space of the Union. Since then, EU citizens have the right to vote or stand as a candidate in municipal or European Parliament elections conducted outside their home countries; the right to be protected outside the Union's borders by the diplomatic or consular authorities of any member state; the right to petition the European Ombudsman and the European Parliament; and the right to move freely within the space of the EU (Maastricht Treaty 1992).

In the 1995 *Report on the Operation of the Treaty on European Union*, the Commission noted that the extension of citizenship beyond the framework of the nation-state was to enhance democracy by giving it a supranational dimension:

> One of the Treaty's basic innovations in terms of democracy is the concept of European citizenship. The object of this is not to replace national citizenship, but to give Europe's citizens an added benefit and strengthen their sense of belonging to the Union. The Treaty makes citizenship an evolving concept, and the Commission recommends developing it to the full. Moreover, although the task of building Europe is centred on democracy and human rights, citizens of the Union have at this stage no fundamental text which they can invoke as a summary of their rights and duties. The Commission thinks this gap should be filled, more especially since such an instrument would constitute a powerful means of promoting equal opportunities and combatting [sic!] racism and xenophobia. (Report on the Operation)

Yet the extension of rights associated with the membership card beyond the borders of nation-states was such a radical change that it might have been introduced prematurely. The 1997 Amsterdam Treaty had to 'correct' this by restating the relationship between national citizenships and European citizenship. Article 17.1 (ex article 8[1]) of the Union Treaty was edited to show clearly the relationship: 'Every person holding the nationality of a Member State shall be a citizen of the Union. Citizenship of the Union shall complement and not replace national citizenship' (Treaty of Amsterdam 1997). The 2003 draft of the Constitution for Europe changed the wording of Amsterdam slightly: 'Every national of a Member State shall be a citizen of the Union. Citizenship of the Union shall be additional to national citizenship; it shall not replace it. All citizens of the Union, women and men, shall be equal before the law'; and stressed that the rights of the citizenship 'shall be exercised in accordance with the conditions and limits defined by this Constitution and by the measures adopted to give it effect' (Draft Treaty: 13–14).

The introduction of European citizenship triggered a small avalanche of studies on its nature and role (see Holmes and Murray 1999; Bellamy and Warleigh 2001; Delgado-Moreira 2000; O'Leary 1996). The main focus of these studies has been a comparison of European citizenship and national citizenships. Hence, European citizenship is either *thin*, or, to use Meehan's terminology, *minimalist*, for it has a whole lot less to offer than national citizenship, or it is *thick*, or *dynamic*, for it has plenty to offer, but just not yet. And when it finally does, its offerings will be more or less similar to those offered by national citizenships (Meehan 1993; see also Wiener 2003: 400).

That national citizenship is the main reference point for students of European citizenship is not surprising. After all, the very concept of citizenship is tightly connected to the nation-state. Besides, EU citizenship has not eliminated the duality of inclusion and exclusion—it has only extended the inclusion to the whole space of the Union, while remaining exclusionary towards third-country nationals.[6] While drawing comparisons and elucidating differences between national and European citizenship is conceptually useful, it is insufficient to examine fully the *sui generis* nature of European citizenship, for such comparisons mainly show what European citizenship is *not* about.

First, European citizenship cannot be a simple extension of national citizenships. Since by now the latter firmly guarantee rights and entitlements, there is no real need for the former to be another form of assurance. From this perspective, European citizenship will remain minimalist. Furthermore, it is not even its primary role to extend the privileges of the membership card to the Union's space, for this is done by other mechanisms and institutions of the EU. The single market, or rules of competition, is more effective in extending the privileges than European citizenship. Also, the rulings of the European Court of Justice on various aspects of integration and, in this context, of rights and entitlements are equally, if not more, effective.[7]

Second, national citizenships come with well defined duties. One of them is the duty to defend the homeland and, if need be, to serve in the national army. If such an obligation ever becomes a part of European citizenship, it will be a long time from now. To begin with, a European nation—a form of an extension of Europe's nations and, consequently, a creation that would absorb them—would have to come into being first. This is probably not possible; nor is it necessary for the Union to exist and develop and for EU citizenship to be fully formed.

Third, national citizenships have already been developed. They are a reflection of Europe's history and, hence, of the Westphalian system. However, after 1945, and certainly after the creation of the EEC, Europe has been steadily moving away from this system, which is why the supranational part of the Union has been constantly growing and strengthening. Therefore, European citizenship is certainly thick, but its dynamism is not leading, nor is it supposed to lead, to a recreation of national citizenship at the Union level.

Finally, since the Union was designed from the very beginning to be a community, EU legislation, such as directives of the Commission and rulings of the European Court of Justice, has prevented the occurrence of social dumping in the Union. Hence, none of the member states has been allowed to lower taxes, curtail welfare-state benefits or limit rights, such as the right to strike, in order to attract investment, either from within or from outside of the EU. This, in itself, has been more effective in extending the rights and benefits of national citizenships outside member states than the introduction of European citizenship by Maastricht.

All in all, EU citizenship, when merely compared to national citizenship, shows its distinctiveness. To find out what it is, EU citizenship also has to be examined in its own right. What makes EU citizenship *sui generis* is the way it has been designed, the context in which it is placed and the role it is to play.

European citizenship is not tied to, nor is it designed to be tied to, the state or nationhood. Instead, EU citizenship extracts the philosophical 'core' principles of liberal democracy, which, to repeat, are intended for the state, and places them in the context of the European polity. Yet, since citizenship is a political institution, rather than a product of philosophy, the placement has clearly defined political 'practicalities'. From this perspective, it is also a form of a membership card, for it has a citizenry that lives in a space with firm boundaries, albeit ones that may change from time to time. However, because EU citizenship relies almost entirely on philosophical 'core' principles, it is also an ideal. At the same time, because it exits in reality, the ideal is carried into the political life of the Community through civic republicanism. Last but not least, since citizenship encompasses the whole Union space, its internal national partitions are to be overcome by practising civic republicanism on the EU-level.

In short, European citizenship entails and affirms the values and norms of civic republicanism. The political role of citizenship is to instil these norms and values, in part through enlargement of the Union, and to strengthen them across the EU until they are fully and unquestionably entrenched in political practice. European citizenship is based on the continent's intellectual history of civic republicanism and on the process of European integration. In this respect it is non-Westphalian or, to be more precise, post-Westphalian. This is the very essence of the *sui generis* nature of European citizenship.

The values and norms of civic republicanism will become fully entrenched when European identity is formed. Jürgen Habermas distinguishes between *ethnos* and *demos* (Habermas 2001a). European citizenship involves the creation and upholding of a European demos, in essence, a society of people who have internalised the norms of civic republicanism. And as the demos emerges, it will presumably change the ethnos, the national identities of Europeans. In this way they will progress from a backward, non-democratic Europe of nations towards a modern and democratic *postnational constellation* (Habermas 2001a) based on European identity. But what, exactly, is European identity, and can it be formed?

As Habermas points out, the identity of a person and, in this context, of a citizen, is partly a result of institutions (Habermas 1998: xxiii). Thus, European identity requires democratic institutions functioning across the EU. Such institutions cannot function without the involvement of EU citizens. Otherwise, the institutions will be hollow and insignificant. Why would EU citizens be willing to become involved in EU institutions? The answer is that their European identity is, or will be, based upon and affirmed through civic republicanism, or *practical* commitment to the 'core' philosophical *principles*.

Habermas distinguishes between a *civic* and an *ethnic* identity. Following this distinction, European citizens do not have to shed their national identity and, by extension, their citizenship. In fact, there is no reason why a person should have only one identity. European identity, reflected through European citizenship, is the other identity. The same is true of European citizenship; it is the other citizenship.

Since loyalty usually comes with identity, does (or will) European identity (and citizenship) entail loyalty to EU institutions and values? If so, what has to happen with the loyalty to nation? 'As within the nation-state', says Habermas, 'inherited regional loyalties could be subordinated to... constitutional patriotism, so a similar process might take shape at the supranational level' (Habermas 1998: xxiii). Indeed, it can; and European citizenship can greatly assist with the development of constitutional patriotism. In fact, this is the only kind possible so long as there is no European nation. Patriotism, therefore, is about the internalisation of the values of civic republicanism exercised at the Community level.

Habermas, without a doubt, wants republicanism at a supranational level. This should not be too difficult to achieve, since the corresponding values are not alien to the Europeans. All they have to do is look at their intellectual past to realise this. However, until 1945 the Europeans mainly preached such values; now they have to live by them. European citizenship and European institutions are the framework that makes such a life possible (Habermas 2001b). But can a European identity, or any other, for that matter, really be 'made'? Habermas certainly believes this is the case. He writes,

A process of democratic will-formation that can cross national borders needs a unified context, and this in turn requires the development of a European public sphere and a common European political culture.... an awareness of collective membership needs to emerge from the background of an already existing fabric of interests.... collective identities are made, not found. But they can only unify the heterogeneous. Citizens who share a common political life are others to one another, and each is entitled to *remain* an Other. (Habermas 2001a: 18–19)

Can such a collective identity in otherness of Europeans endure? Just as identity expanded in the past from the village and the manor to the nation, so Habermas believes a European identity can emerge and endure. This newly emerging identity does not negate national identity, but it does require agreement on constitutional principles to institutionalise a European public space for the democratic formation of political will. The duties and rights of European citizenship may prove more difficult to exercise than in the case of national politics, and a European citizen has to be more civic-minded and more republican than at the national level, for high principles will be at issue, not just particular policies. At the same time, however, European citizenship promotes and consolidates precisely the values needed to affirm civic republicanism at the national level. If each process will reinforce the other, the result should be to consolidate a European political community that upholds and at the same time transcends traditional national identities.

Habermas assumes that the Europeans have already become, or are about to become, civic republicans at the supranational level, for they have internalised the values and the norms. He may or may not be correct. Whichever the case, there is no doubt that dual citizenship is a vital component in the growth of continent-wide civic republicanism.

Conclusions: Dual citizenship and the process of community-building

Dual citizenship is an interaction between states and, in Europe, between nations. This means it can be used for various reasons and may contribute to the success of numerous policies, including those of a purely technical and economic nature. But it is also an interaction between citizens, whose horizons are in the process of extending beyond the historical limitations of their particular states and nations. Since the Europeans gain no additional tangible benefits by acquiring another citizenship, the tolerance of dual citizenship is but a sign of the growing awareness and conviction that national loyalty need not be absolute. Europeans are becoming civic republicans on the level of the EU.

At the same time, the potential of dual citizenship to advance community-building is also limited to some degree, for it still operates within the state and respects national identity and loyalty. When Irish nationals acquire, say, Italian citizenship, they will still be Irish. They may speak fluent Italian; they may cook pasta that will satisfy even the most discerning Italian palate; they may know Italian history better than many Italians; and they may make many Italian friends. Yet, for as long as Europe consists of nations, they will still be Irish living in Italy.

In societies that do not have national identity, but have nevertheless developed a political identity, people can have a hyphenated identity, as many Italian-Canadians do, for instance. In Europe, however, this is probably not possible, at least not yet, for it goes directly against Europe's historical development. Habermas wants to move in the direction of postnationalism. But as things stand today, this may be easier said than done. Even for Habermas, this is always a question of *moving in a post-national direction*, for, as I have previously noted, 'Citizens who share a common political life are others to one another, and each is entitled to *remain* an Other' (Habermas 2001a: 18–19). EU citizenship, in this sense, can be thought of as a process that incorporates national identity and loyalty while adding to it a European identity that is non-national. EU identity must be a political achievement, and its fundamental presupposition is practical commitment to 'core' philosophical principles that inherently make a claim, as Habermas would say, to universal validity.

Dual citizenship is a bridge between national citizenship and EU citizenship. It connects the history of European states with the continent's future. To borrow from Benedict Anderson, if national community is 'imagined' (and in some sense it may be), then dual citizenship involves *reimagining* community in a post-Westphalian, political (and ethical) community of European citizens (Anderson 1991: 5–6).

Notes

1. The texts of the European Treaties can be found at http://www.eurotreaties. com/index.html (accessed 11 March 2006).
2. For a good survey of nation-building in Europe, see Kriesi et al. 2004.
3. A good study on the Agreement and its impact on European integration is Pauly 1994.
4. The text of the Convention for the Protection of Human Rights and Fundamental Freedoms is available at http://www.echr.coe.int/ECHR/EN/ Header/Basic+Texts/Basic+Texts/The+European+Convention+on+Human+ Rights+and+its+Protocols/ (accessed on 11 March 2006).
5. The EEC was renamed into the EU by the Maastricht Treaty.
6. The exclusionary nature may be changing, although it is too early to say that this trend will continue successfully and smoothly. See Perchinig (n.d.).
7. An example of the Court's ruling that helped to extend the rights and benefits associated with national citizenship to the whole territory of the EU is the 1998 *Martinez Sala v. Freistaat Bayern*. In essence, the court ruled that an unemployed Spanish person, Ms. Martinez Sala, had the right to apply for a child-raising allowance in Germany, despite not having German citizenship or even residence permit: http://europa.eu.int/abc/doc/off/rg/en/1998/x1051.htm (accessed on 11 March 2006).

References

Agrela, B. (2002) 'Spain as a Recent Country of Immigration: How Immigration Became a Symbolic, Political and Cultural Problem in the "New Spain" '. Working Paper 57. San Diego: The Center for Comparative Immigration Studies, University of California. http://www.ccis-ucsd.org/PUBLICATIONS/ wrkg57.PDF (accessed 11 March 2006).

Anderson, B. R. O. G. (1991) *Imagined Communities: Reflections on the Origin and Spread of Nationalism*. London, New York: Verso.

Bell, D. S. (2002). *French Politics Today*. Manchester: Manchester University Press.

Bellamy, R. and A. Warleigh eds. (2001) *Citizenship and Governance in the European Union*. London and New York: Continuum.

Brubaker, R. (1992) *Citizenship and Nationhood in France and Germany*. Cambridge, MA: Harvard University Press.

Crick, B. (2004) 'Foreword'. In D. Heater, ed., *Citizenship. The Civic Ideal in World History, Politics and Education*. Manchester and New York: Manchester University Press pp. xi–xii.

De Lucas, J. (1996) *Puertas que se cierran. Europa como fortaleza*. Barcelona: Icaria.

Delgado-Moreira, J. M. (2000) *Multicultural Citizenship of the European Union*. Aldershot: Ashgate.

Die Bundesrepublik Deutschland. (1949) Grundgesetz (GG) für die Bundesrepublik Deutschland 'Die Bundesrepublik Deutschland ist ein demokratischer und sozialer Bundesstaat'. Artikel 20 (1). http://www.datenschutzberlin.de/recht/de/gg/gg1_de.htm#art15 (accessed 11 March 2006).

Draft Treaty Establishing a Constitution for Europe. *Adopted by Consensus by the European Convention on 13 June and 10 July 2003. Submitted to the President of European Council in Rome 18 July 2003* (2003) Luxembourg: Office for Official Publications of the European Communities, pp. 13–14.

Habermas, J. (1998) *The Inclusion of the Other: Studies in Political Theory*. Cambridge, MA: MIT Press.

Habermas, J. (2001a) *The Postnational Constellation: Political Essays*. Cambridge, MA: MIT Press.

Habermas, J. (2001b) 'Why Europe Needs a Constitution'. *New Left Review* 11, Sept–Oct: 5–26.

Holmes, L. and P. Murray, eds. (1999) *Citizenship and Identity in Europe*. Aldershot: Ashgate.

Kohn, H. (1981) *Nationalism: Its Meaning and History*. Malabar, FL: Robert E. Krieger Publishing Company.

Kriesi, H., K. Arimingeon, H. Siegrist and A. Wimmer, eds. (2004) *Nation and National Identity. The European Experience in Perspective*. West Lafayette, IN: Purdue University Press.

Maastricht Treaty. (1992) http://www.eurotreaties.com/maastrichtec.pdf (accessed 11 March 2006).

Majone, G. (1996) 'The Rise of Statutory Regulation in Europe'. In Giandomenico Majone, ed., *Regulating Europe*. New York: Routledge, pp. 47–60.

Meehan, E. M. (1993) *Citizenship and the European Community*. London: Sage.

Monnet, J. (2003) 'A Ferment of Change'. In Brent F. Nelsen and Alexander Stubb, eds, *The European Union. Readings on the Theory and Practice of European Integration*, 3d ed. Boulder, CO and London: Lynne Rienner Publishers, pp. 19–26. Originally published in the *Journal of Common Market Studies* in 1962.

O'Leary, S. (1996) *The Evolving Concept of Community Citizenship. From the Free Movement of Persons to Union Citizenship*. The Hague: Kluwer Law International.

Pauly, A., ed. (1994) *Schengen en panne*. Maastricht: European Institute of Public Administration.

Perchinig, B. (n.d.) 'Union Citizenship and the Status of Third Country Nationals'. EIF Working Paper Series: Working Paper Nr: 12. Wien: Österreichische Akademie der Wissenschaften, Institut für Europäische Integrationsforschung, n.d.

Piernas, C. J. (2002) 'La comunitarización de las políticas de inmigración y extranjería: especial referencia a España'. *Revista de Derecho Comunitario Europeo* 13, septiembre/diciembre: 857–94.

Reisenberg, P. (2002) *A History of Citizenship Sparta to Washington*. Malabar, FL: Krieger Publishing Company.

Report on the Operation of the Treaty on European Union SEC(95) 731 Final. http://www.unizar.es/euroconstitucion/Treaties/Treaty_Amst_Prep.htm (accessed 11 March 2006).

Schuman, R. (2003) 'The Schuman Declaration'. In Brent F. Nelsen and Alexander Stubb, eds, *The European Union. Readings on the Theory and Practice of European Integration*, 3d ed. Boulder, CO and London: Lynne Rienner Publishers.

Skrobacki, W. A. (2005) 'The Community of Europe and Globalization'. *Perspectives on Global Politics and Technology*, 4, 3–4: 447–64.

Spång, M. (2007) 'Pragmatism all the Way Down? The Politics of Citizenship in Sweden'. In Thomas Faist, ed., *Dual Citizenship in Europe: From Nationhood to Societal Integration*. Aldershot: Ashgate, pp. 103–25.

Stiglitz, J. E. (2003) *The Roaring Nineties: A New History of the World's Most Prosperous Decade*. New York: W. W. Norton & Company.

Treaty of Amsterdam (1997) http://www.eurotreaties.com/amsterdamtreaty.pdf (retrieved on March 11, 2006).

Wiener, A. (2003) 'Citizenship'. In Michelle Cini, ed., *European Union Politics*. Oxford: Oxford University Press, pp. 397–414.

Wyatt, D., ed. (2002) *Rudden & Wyatt's EU Treaties and Legislation*. Oxford: Oxford University Press.

12
Twilight of Sovereignty or the Emergence of Cosmopolitan Norms? Rethinking Citizenship in Volatile Times[1]

Seyla Benhabib

In several works in the last decade I have documented the disaggregation of citizenship rights, the emergence of an international human rights regime and the spread of cosmopolitan norms (Benhabib 2001, 2002, 2004a, b). Briefly, national citizenship is a legal and social status which combines some form of collectively shared identity with the entitlement to social and economic benefits and the privileges of political membership through the exercise of democratic rights. I have argued that in today's world the civil and social rights of migrants, aliens and denizens are increasingly protected by international human rights documents.[2] The establishment of the European Union (EU) has been accompanied by a Charter of Fundamental Rights and by the formation of a European Court of Justice. The European Convention for the Protection of Human Rights and Fundamental Freedoms, which encompasses non–member states as well, permits the claims of citizens of adhering states to be heard by a European Court of Human Rights. Parallel developments can be seen on the American continent through the establishment of the Inter-American System for the Protection of Human Rights and the Inter-American Court of Human Rights. African states have accepted the African Charter on Human and Peoples' Rights in 1981 through the Organization of African Unity and to date it has been ratified by 49 states (Henkin et al. 1999).

Despite these developments, the link between national citizenship and the privileges of democratic participation such as voting rights that restricts these privileges to nationals alone is retained, but in this domain as well changes are visible throughout the EU in particular: in

Denmark, Sweden, Finland and the Netherlands, third-country nationals can participate in local and regional elections; in Ireland these rights are granted at the local level. In the United Kingdom, Commonwealth citizens can vote in national elections.

These developments are not limited to Europe. Increasingly, Mexico and some Central American governments such as El Salvador and Guatemala are permitting those who are born to immigrant citizen parents in foreign countries to retain voting rights at home and even to run for office; the practice of recognising dual citizenship is becoming widespread. In South Asia, particularly among economic elites who carry three or more passports and navigate three or more national economies, the institution of 'flexible citizenship' is taking hold (Ong 1999).

Yet these changes in modalities of political belonging have been accompanied by other, more ominous, forms of exclusion: first, the condition of refugees and asylum seekers has not benefited equally from the spread of cosmopolitan norms. While their numbers the world over have increased as a result of the global state of violence (see Zolberg and Benda 2001), most liberal democracies since 11 September 2001, and even before then, had already shifted towards criminalising the refugee and asylum seeker either as a dissembler attempting to gain access to economic advantages or as a potential security threat. The politics of refuge and asylum have become sites of some of the world's most intense global distributive, as well as racialised, confrontations. Even within the EU, the establishment of refugee processing transit camps (RPTCs) outside the borders of the EU, for the purpose of catching refugees and illegal migrants before they land on European soil, have been advocated by the United Kingdom and Denmark and are in operation in Spanish-held territories in North Africa and in transit camps in Libya.

Furthermore, as Hannah Arendt observed more than half a century ago, 'the right to have rights' remains an aporetic longing.[3] For who is to grant 'the right to be a member', the right to belong to a community in which one's right to have rights is to be protected by all? Within a permanently divided mankind it is only through membership in a polity in which one's right to have rights is defended through the solidarity of all that the aporias of statelessness can be resolved. The right to have rights must combine the liberal vision of citizenship as entitlement to rights with the republican-democratic vision of membership through full democratic participation. Disaggregated citizenship, in my view, does not replace membership in bounded communities; rather, it ought to be seen as a modality of it.

The disaggregation of citizenship rights through the extension of cosmopolitan norms, the continuing liminality of the condition of refugees and asylum seekers, and the increasing criminalisation of migrants as a consequence of the global state of confrontation between the forces of political Islam and the United States have led a number of scholars to interpret these developments in quite a different light than I have in recent writings. For some, the spread of an international human rights regime and of cosmopolitan norms presents a Pollyannaish narrative which does not account for the growing condition of a global civil war (Agamben 2005; Hardt and Negri 2001). For others, while these trends are real, the defence of republican federalism seems inadequate in that it does not acknowledge the more radical political potentials of the present moment (Balibar 2004; Held 2004).

The very great disparity among these diagnoses of our contemporary condition, which extend from predictions of global civil war and a permanent state of exception to the utopia of citizenship beyond the state and transnational democracy, may itself be an indication of the volatile and obscure moment we are traversing. What has become crystal clear is that the changing security situation after 11 September 2001 has destabilised the principle of formal sovereign equality of states. The spread of cosmopolitan norms and transformations of sovereignty inevitably accompany one another. The rise of an international human rights regime, which is one of the hallmarks of post-Westphalian changes in sovereignty, also heralds alterations in the jurisdictional prerogative of nation-states. As Jean L. Cohen (2004: 2) rightly observes,

> Talk of legal and constitutional pluralism, societal constitutionalism, transnational governmental networks, cosmopolitan human rights law enforced by 'humanitarian intervention', and so on are all attempts to conceptualize the new global legal order that is allegedly emerging before our eyes. The general claim is that the world is witnessing a move to cosmopolitan law. . . . But . . . if one shifts the political perspective, the sovereignty-based model of international law appears to be ceding not to cosmopolitan justice but to a different bid to restructure the world order: the project of empire.

The rise of cosmopolitan norms or the spread of empire? Indeed, it is crucial to unravel this ambivalent potential: while the emergence of cosmopolitan norms is intended to protect the individual in a global civil society, there are dangers as well as opportunities created by the weakening of state sovereignty. The fact that the internationalisation of human rights norms and the weakening of state sovereignty are developing in tandem with each other decidedly does not mean that the one can be reduced to the other; the genesis of these developments as well as their normative logics are distinct.[4] Nor should concerns about the weakening of state sovereignty, some of which I share, lead one to reject the spread of human rights norms for fear that they can be used to justify humanitarian interventions.

Since these transformations are altering norms of state sovereignty as well as impacting the actual capacity of states to exercise sovereignty, it is important at the outset to distinguish between *state sovereignty* and *popular sovereignty*. The concept of 'sovereignty' ambiguously refers to two moments in the foundation of the modern state, and the history of modern political thought in the West since Thomas Hobbes can plausibly be told as a negotiation of these poles: first, sovereignty means the capacity of a public body, in this case the modern nation-state, to act as the *final* and *indivisible* seat of authority with the jurisdiction to not only wield 'monopoly over the means of violence', to recall Max Weber's famous phrase, but also distribute justice and manage the economy.

Sovereignty also means, particularly since the French Revolution, *popular sovereignty*, that is the idea of the people as subjects and objects of the law, or as makers as well as obeyers of the law. Popular sovereignty involves representative institutions, the separation of powers and the guarantee not only of liberty and equality, but of the 'equal value of the liberty of each'. Etienne Balibar (2004: 152) has expressed the interdependence between state sovereignty and popular sovereignty thus: '...state sovereignty has simultaneously "protected" itself from and "founded" itself upon popular sovereignty to the extent that the political state has been transformed into a "social-state"... passing through the progressive institution of a "representation of social forces" by the mechanism of universal suffrage and the institutions of social citizenship...'.

My question is, how does the new configuration of state sovereignty influence popular sovereignty? Which political options are becoming possible? Which are blocked? Today we are caught not only in the reconfiguration of sovereignty but also in the *reconstitutions of citizenship*. We are moving away from citizenship as national membership increasingly towards a *citizenship of residency* which strengthens the multiple ties to locality, to the region and to transnational institutions.

Cosmopolitan norms enhance the project of popular sovereignty while prying open the black box of state sovereignty. They challenge the prerogative of the state to be the highest authority dispensing justice over all that is living and dead within certain territorial boundaries. In becoming party to many human rights treaties, states themselves 'bind' their own decisions. Very often this can lead to collusions between the will of majorities and international norms—as we can observe with regard to issues of women's rights and the rights of cultural, ethnic and linguistic minorities, for example. But such collusions have become all too frequent only because the world is moving towards a new form of post-Westphalian politics of global interdependence.

Distinct from the influence of cosmopolitan human rights norms is the undermining of state sovereignty through the demands of global capitalism. Global capitalism is indeed creating its own form of 'global law without a state' (Teubner 1997), as well as sabotaging the efforts of legislators to conduct open and public deliberations on legislation impacting the movements of capital and other resources. Furthermore, many states are privatising their own activities by disbursing authority over prisons and schools to private enterprises (see Apter 2001). Whereas cosmopolitan norms lead to the emergence of *generalisable human interests and the articulation of public standards of norm justification*, global capitalism leads to the *privatisation and segmentation of interest communities* and the *weakening of standards of public justification through the rise of private logics of norm generation*. This results in the deterioration of the capacity of states to protect and provide for their citizens.

The following sections of this chapter document in broad strokes changes in the relationship of territoriality and jurisdiction in the evolution of the modern state: transnational migrations, the emergence of global law and the rise of fast-track legislation. The latter two socioeconomic and legal transformations are leading to the undermining of popular sovereignty and the privatisation of state sovereignty. I conclude with normative considerations on democratic iterations, which I define as processes whereby cosmopolitan norms and the will of democratic majorities can be reconciled, though never perfectly, through public argumentation and deliberation in acts of normative iterations.

Territorialisation and law: Colonialism vs. transnational migrations

Modern state formation in the West begins with the 'territorialisation' of space. The enclosure of a particular portion of the earth and its demarcation from others through the creation of protected boundaries, and the presumption that all that lies within these boundaries, whether animate or inanimate, belongs under the dominion of the sovereign, is central to the territorially bounded system of states in Western modernity. In this 'Westphalian' model, territorial integrity and a unified jurisdictional authority are two sides of the same coin; protecting territorial integrity is the obverse side of the power of the state to assert its jurisdictional authority (*dominium*).

The modern absolutist states of western Europe were governed, in Carl Schmitt's terms (1997: 99), by the 'jus publicum Europaeum' as their international law. However, this model was unstable from its inception—in Stephen Krasner's (1999) famous phrase, 'sovereignty is hypocrisy'. The discovery of the Americas, the imperialist ventures into India and China, the struggle for domination over the Indian Ocean and the nineteenth-century colonisation of Africa destroyed this form of state sovereignty and international law by chipping away at the peripheries.[5] The limitations of this order were revealed not only by the West's confrontation with other continents but also by the question as to whether the non-Christian Ottoman Empire belonged to the *jus publicum Europaeum*. Though Schmitt himself is not far from idealising this moment in the evolution of 'the law of the earth', his own account documents its inherent limits and eventual dissolution.[6] The 'deterritorialisation' of the modern state goes hand in hand with its transformation from early bourgeois republics into European empires, whether they be those of England, France, Spain, Portugal, Belgium, the Netherlands or Italy.

The evolution of bourgeois republics into empires destroys the overlap of territorial control with jurisdictional authority, which governs, at least in principle, the motherland. Europe's colonies become the sites of usurpation and conquest in which *extra-juridical spaces*, removed from the purview of liberal principles of consent, are created. As Edmund Burke was to express it pithily with respect to 'administrative massacres' in India, and the impeachment of their architect, Warren Hastings, by the British House, this needed to be done so that 'breakers of the law in India might [not] become "the makers of law for England"'.[7]

With the rise of bourgeois and democratic republics the 'subject' of the absolutist state is transformed into the 'citizen'. As the Westphalian paradigm of sovereignty meets its limits outside Europe, it is constitutionalised at home by social struggles for increased accountability, universal suffrage, expanded representation, democratic freedoms and social rights. These struggles are the site of popular sovereignty, of demands to make the state apparatus responsive and transparent to its citizens. In ways that much scholarship has not even begun to fathom, modern citizenship and popular sovereignty struggles at home and imperialist ventures abroad go hand in hand (see Brodie 2004; Ikeda 2004).

This legacy of empire has come back today to haunt the resource-rich countries of the northern hemisphere through the rise of transnational migrations. Transnational migrations also cause a disaggregation of territoriality, sovereignty and citizenship but in different ways than colonialism. Whereas in the nineteenth and twentieth centuries, European imperialism spread jurisdiction to colonial territories but was shielded from democratic consent and control, contemporary migratory movements give rise to overlapping jurisdictions which are often protected by international norms.

In 1910 roughly 33 million migrants lived in countries other than their own; by the year 2000 their number had reached 175 million (Zlotnik 2001: 227). During this same period (1910–2000), the population of the world grew from 1.6 to 5.3 billion, roughly threefold. Migrations, by contrast, increased almost sixfold over the same time span. Strikingly, more than half of this growth occurred in the last three decades of the twentieth century, between 1965 and 2000. In this period 75 million people undertook cross-border movements to settle in countries other than those of their origin (UN, Department of Economic and Social Affairs 2002).

Transformations in patterns of migration are leading more and more individuals to retain ties with their home countries and to resist total immersion in their countries of immigration. Globalised networks of transportation, communication, electronic media, banking and financial services make it easier to produce guest workers, seasonal workers, dual nationals and diasporic commuters. Migrations no longer bring with them total absorption and socialisation in the culture of the host country—a process poignantly symbolised by the assignment to immigrants to the United States of new family names in Ellis Island, for example.

Today nation-states encourage diasporic politics among their migrants and ex-citizens, seeing in the diaspora not only a source of political support for projects at home, but also a resource of networks, skills and competencies that can be used to enhance a state's own standing in an increasingly global world. Notable examples of such diasporas are the large Indian, Chinese and Jewish communities across the globe. Their continuing allegiance to the so-called 'home country' is carefully cultivated.

Migrations thus lead to a pluralisation of allegiances and commitments and to the growing complexity of nationals who, more often than not, in today's world are also ex-, post- and neocolonials. We are witnessing increasing migration from periphery to centre, encouraged by wide differentials in standards of living between regions of the world, and facilitated by the large presence of family and kin already at the centre of what was once the Empire. Indians, Pakistanis, Kashmiris and Sri Lankans in the United Kingdom; Algerians and Moroccans in France; Surinamese and Moluccans in the Netherlands; Latin Americans in Spain; Libyans in Italy—all are population groups whose history is deeply bound up with European empires. The Westphalian state which extended towards the rest of the world now finds that its borders are porous in both directions and that it is not only the centre which flows to the periphery but the periphery which flows towards the centre.

State sovereignty, which is imminently tied to the ability to protect borders, now more than ever is revealed to depend upon skilful negotiations, transactions, agreements and flows with other states. Of course, states and regions differ widely in their ability to assert their sovereignty and to throw their weight around. The poorer economies of Central America, South Asia and Africa are less able to police their borders; the world's largest refugee populations are also settled in some of the world's poorest regions such as Chad, Pakistan and Ingushetia (Benhabib 2004b: 5ff.).

Migrations are the site of intense conflicts over resources as well as identities. In the contemporary world, strong states militarise and increasingly criminalise migratory movements. The poor migrant becomes the symbol of the continuing assertion of sovereignty. Migrants' bodies, both dead and alive, strew the path of state's power.

Transnational migrations reveal the pluralisation of sites of sovereignty in that, with the changing patterns of acculturation and socialisation, migrants begin to live in multiple jurisdictions. Although they are increasingly protected by cosmopolitan norms in the form of the various human rights treaties, they are still vulnerable to a system of state sovereignty which privileges national citizenship while restricting dual and multiple citizenship regimes.

Militarisation and criminalisation are defensive responses which states use to reassert their sovereignty in the face of transnational migrations. But is it possible to think about sovereignty in terms other than those suggested by the model of autochtonous impermeability? Is it conceivable to think of sovereignty in relational terms? Is it possible to disaggregate sovereignty's functions and yet create modalities of cooperation? Can we still maintain the ideal of popular sovereignty and democratic rule if the state-centred model of sovereignty is itself becoming dysfunctional?

Deterritorialisation of law: Global capitalism

Transnational migrations reveal the dependence of states upon the worldwide movement of peoples as well as each other's policies. Since every inch of the earth's surface, with the exception of the North and South Poles, is now etatised and governed by a state which has territorial jurisdiction, cross-border movements initiated by migrants as well as refuge and asylum seekers bring to light the fragility as well as the frequent irrationality of the state system. Vis-à-vis peoples' cross-border movements, the state remains sovereign, albeit in much reduced fashion. Indeed, given the movement of capital and commodities, information and technology across borders, the state today is more hostage than sovereign.

A great deal has been written in recent years about globalisation as a worldwide phenomenon and the diminished capacity of states. I am persuaded by the argument that to understand this phenomenon it is analytically more useful to use the term 'stateness', meaning the dynamic capacity of states to react to and control their environments in multiple ways (Evans 1997; see also Nettl 1968: 559). There is tremendous variation across the globe in the capacity of 'stateness'. The affluent democracies of North America, Europe, Australia and New Zealand can manipulate, tame and channel the forces of global capitalism as well as the worldwide flow of information, communication and transportation technologies. This is obviously much less true for many states in North Africa, the Middle East, Latin America and Asia. The rise to global prominence of China, India, Brazil, as well as the Asian 'tiger' economies, is in large measure due to the capacity of these states to channel economic globalisation to their own advantage.

In her analysis of Southeast Asian economies, Aihwa Ong gives a compelling example, namely the creation of 'multinational zones of sovereignty' in the form of Growth Triangles (GTs). These 'straddle borders between neighboring states such as to maximize the locational advantage and attract global capital' (Ong 1999: 221). The three GTs formed by linking neighbouring countries are Indonesia–Malaysia–Singapore (Sijori), Indonesia–Malaysia–Thailand, and Brunei–Indonesia–Malaysia–Philippines. Transnational corporations such as

Nike, Reebok and the Gap now employ millions of women who work 12 hours a day and make less than $2 a day. Ong observes that these

> growth triangles are zones of special sovereignty that are arranged through a multinational network of smart partnerships and that exploits the cheap labor that exists within the orbit of a global hub such as Singapore. It appears that GT workers are less subject to the rules of their home country and more to the rules of companies and to the competitive conditions set by other growth triangles in the region. (Ong 1999: 222)

A parallel account is provided by Carolin Emcke of the workings of the *maquiladoras* in Central America. These are established by foreign capital in El Salvador, Guatemala and Costa Rica under the protection of their respective governments often as tax-free zones to attract foreign investment. They protect the zones they occupy through the use of private security guards and forces; crush any attempt to organise the labour force; and fiercely defend themselves against international and even national control and supervision. They resemble medieval warlords who have taken the native populations hostage.

Whether it is the Growth Triangles of Southeast Asia or the *maquiladoras* of Central America, this form of economic globalisation results in the disaggregation of states' sovereignty with their own complicity. As in the case of colonisation and imperialism, there is an uncoupling once more of *jursdiction* and *territory* in that the state transfers its own powers of jurisdiction, whether in full knowledge or by unintended consequence, to non-state private and corporate bodies. The losers in this process are the citizens from whom state protection is withdrawn or, more likely, who never had strong state protection in the first place and who become dependent upon the power and mercy of transnational corporations and other forms of venture capitalists.

Despite the great variation across countries with respect to the interactions of the global economy and states, one generalisation can be safely made: economic globalisation is leading to a fundamental transformation of legal institutions and of the paradigm of the rule of law. Increasingly globalisation is engendering a body of law which is self-generating and self-regulating and which does not originate through the legislative or deliberative activity of national legislators.

Law without a state?

In his influential article '"Global Bukowina": Legal Pluralism in the World Society', Gunther Teubner (1997: 5) makes this case: 'Today's globalization is not a gradual emergence of a world society under the leadership of interstate politics, but is a highly contradictory and highly fragmented process in which politics has lost its leading role.' As examples of global law without a state Teubner cites *lex mercatoria*, the transnational law of economic transactions; labour law, where enterprises and labour unions, acting as private actors, become lawmakers; and the technical standardisation and professional self-regulation engaged worldwide by the relevant parties without the intervention of official politics.

This emergent body of law is 'a legal order', even if it has no specific point of origination in the form of law-producing institutions, and even less, a single and visible law-enforcing agency. The boundaries of global law are not set by national borders but by ' "invisible colleges," "invisible markets and branches," "invisible professional communities," "invisible social networks" . . . ' (Teubner 1997: 8). Territorial boundaries and jurisdictional powers are once more uncoupled.

As Teubner acknowledges (1997: 21), this form of law has serious democratic deficits: 'It is a law that grows and changes according to the exigencies of global economic transactions and organizations. This makes its extremely vulnerable to interest and power pressures from economic processes, because it is "indeterminate" and can change in its application from case to case.' Soft law is law without the characteristics traditionally associated with the rule of law: transparency, predictability and uniformity of application. These features of the rule of law, however, are not mere procedural characteristics, but they act as guarantees of the equality of persons and citizens before the law. Global law, by contrast, is not equality-guaranteeing and equality-protecting; rather it is law that enables global corporations and other bodies to carry out their transactions in an increasingly complex environment by generating self-binding and self-regulating norms.

There are important clashes and tensions between these features of *lex mercatoria* and human rights law and cosmopolitan norms: both the GTs and the *maquiladoras* are characterised by a *suspension* of human rights norms in zones of special economic and business privilege. Furthermore, individuals working in these zones are not only citizens of the countries in which these zones of privileged economic sovereignty operate; very often they are themselves transnational migrants from neighbouring countries, whose human rights are regularly trampled upon. Thus Malaysians, Thai, Burmese and others work in Indonesia; illegal Chinese labourers abound in the *maquilodoras* of central America. While without a doubt the flow of global capital is itself responsible for the flow of transnational migrations, we see that the norms which ought to protect migrants and the laws which enable global capitalism are not compatible. *Lex mercatoria*, the law of international commercial transactions, and human rights law collide and conflict.[8]

That economic globalisation threatens core features of the rule of law and thereby challenges the prospects for liberal democracy as well is emphatically argued by Scheuerman:

> Contemporary capitalism is different in many ways from its historical predecessors: economies driven by huge transnational corporations that make effective use of high-speed communication, information, and transportation technologies represent a relatively novel development. The relationship of capitalism to the rule of law is thereby transformed as well... As high-speed social action 'compresses' distance, the separation between domestic and foreign affairs erodes, and the traditional vision of the executive as best suited to the dictates of rapid-fire foreign policy making undermines basic standards of legality in the domestic sphere as well. (Scheuerman 2004: 145)

The transformation of the rule of law gives rise to 'fast-track legislation', pushed by national legislators without adequate debate and deliberation; the power of deliberative bodies is eclipsed and that of the executive increases. 'The main problem posed by globalization is less that transnational business can only preserve its autonomy by limiting state power by means of the rule of law than that the democratic nation-state can only hope to maintain its independence in relation to global business by counteracting the virtually universal competitive rush to provide transnational firms with special rights and privileges' (Scheuerman 2004: 169). States have to avoid the 'race to the bottom', that is to embrace neoliberal reforms, cutting back on the welfare state and relaxing labour and environmental legislations.

Law without a state? Or race to the bottom? In the first part of this chapter I had asked, the rise of cosmopolitan norms or imperialism? Again we seem confronted by alternatives and disjunction. Surely, these are not the only alternatives offered up by globalisation processes, but in either case the model of liberal sovereignty—based upon the unity of jurisdiction administered over a defined territory, assuring citizen's equality through the administration of the rule of law and guaranteeing social welfare through economic redistribution—appears more and more to be a memory of a quaint past. It is important to emphasise that sovereign states are players with considerable power in this process: they themselves often nurture and guide the very transformations that curtail their own powers.

Whether it be through the changing patterns of transnational migrations; through the emergence of GTs and new global forms of law without a state in the accelerated and fluid global market place; or through the pressure to adapt state bureaucracies to the new capitalism, an epochal change is under way in which aspects of state sovereignty are being dismantled chip by chip. State jurisdiction and territoriality are uncoupled, as new agents of jurisdiction in the form of multinational corporations emerge. In some cases, the state offloads its own jurisdiction to private agencies in order to escape the territorial control of popular legislators. The social contract is increasingly frayed.

If the analysis presented above is partially accurate, does the 'twilight of state sovereignty' mean the end of citizenship and of democratic politics, the displacement of the political or may be even its eventual disappearance in the evolution of world societies? What are the normative consequences of these transformations? What light does this social-theoretic analysis shed on the political philosophies of the present period?

Twilight of sovereignty and global civil society

Just as the capacity of nation-states to exercise their stateness varies considerably, so do their reactions to the shrinking sphere of state autonomy and activity. To meet the economic, ecological and legal challenges posed by the growing fluidity of worldwide migrations, the states of Europe have chosen *the cooperative restructuring of sovereignty;* juxtaposed to this cooperative restructuring of sovereignty is the *unilateral reassertion of sovereignty.* At the present time not only the United States, but also China, Iran and India are taking this route, not to mention Russia, North Korea and Israel. The strategy here is to strengthen the state via attempts to gather all the markers of sovereignty in the public authority with the consequence of increased militarisation, disregard for international law and human rights, regressive and hostile relations with neighbours, and criminalisation of migration. The third alternative is the *weakening* of the already fragile institutions of *state sovereignty* in vast regions of Africa, Central and Latin America, and South Asia. In these cases global market forces further destabilise fragile economies; they break up the bonds between the vast army of the poor and the downtrodden and their local elites, who now network with their global counterparts, thus leaving the masses to the mercy of *maquiladoras*, paramilitaries, drug lords and criminal gangs. The state withdraws into a shell, as has happened in the Ivory Coast, the Congo, the Sudan, El Salvador, Burma, some parts of Brazil, and elsewhere. Under such conditions popular sovereignty takes the form, at best, of guerrilla warfare and, at worst, of equally criminal groups fighting to gain a piece of the pie. Neither the contraction of stateness nor its militarised reassertion enhances popular sovereignty.

The volatile and often ambivalent configurations of institutions such as citizenship and sovereignty which have defined our understanding of modern politics for the last three hundred and fifty years since the Treaty of Westphalia (1648) have understandably given rise to conflicting commentaries and interpretations in contemporary political thought. These can be characterised as theories of empire, theories of transnational governance and theories of postnational citizenship.

Empire, according to Michael Hardt and Antonio Negri (2004), is the ever-expanding power of global capital to bring more and more of the world into its reach. Unlike the extractive and exploitative empires of the past, however, the new empire encourages the spread of human rights norms; it pushes the new technologies of networking, thus destroying the walls of separation and generating a new global connectivity consonant with this new age.[9]

Since the webs of empire are so ubiquitous, sites of resistance to it are diffuse, decentred and multiple. The 'multitude' resists the total penetration of life structures by the empire in organising demonstrations against the G7, the World Bank, the Gulf War, the Iraq War and the violation of international law. The multitude focuses on power as a global phenomenon and attempts to generate a counter-force to empire.[10]

The metaphors of networking, entanglement, binding, spread of communicative forms and the like which underlie this social-theoretical analysis are one-sided precisely because they present a world without institutional actors and without structured centres of resistance.[11] The multitude, Hardt's and Negri's revolutionary subject, is not the citizen. The multitude is not even the carrier of popular sovereignty since it lacks the drive towards the constitutionalisation of power, which has been the desiderata of all popular movements since the American and French revolutions. The multitude gives expression to the rage of those who have lost their republics: the multitude smashes institutions and resists power. It does not engage in what Hannah Arendt has called the 'constitutio libertatis' (Arendt 1963; see also Benhabib 2003; 130–172). By contrast, popular sovereignty aims at widening the circle of representation among all members of the demos in an enduring form; popular sovereignty aims at the control of state power via the separation of powers between the judiciary, the legislative and the executive; popular sovereignty means creating structures of accountability and transparency in the public exercise of power. This is a far cry from the politics of the multitude.

This aspect of the legitimate exercise of power is well noted in contemporary debates by theorists of transnational governance such as Anne-Marie Slaughter and David Held. At the roots of empire's extension, argue advocates of transnational democracy, lies a problem of legitimation. We are in the grip of forces and processes which resemble the galloping horseman without a head. Decisions are made in exclusive board meetings of the IMF, WTO and the World Bank, affecting the lives of millions, while nation-states refuse to sign multilateral treaties such as the Kyoto Convention or the Rome Treaty leading to the establishment of the International Criminal Court. Theorists of the multitude seem to confuse politics with carnival. Only transnational institutions can build permanent structures to counteract the forces of empire.

We need transparent and accountable structures of world governance and coordination. Some of these structures are already in sight through the networking of economic, judicial, military, immigration, health and communication experts. They form horizontally networked sites of information, coordination and regulation. The future of global citizenship lies in becoming actively involved in such transnational organisations and working towards global governance. Whether this implies world government or not is at this stage beside the point: what matters is to increase structures of global accountability and governance.[12]

In the version of the global governance thesis advocated by Anne-Marie Slaughter, who focuses less on the normative possibilities for democratic governance beyond borders and more on the horizontal networks linking government officials in judicial, regulatory and administrative organisations across state boundaries, a realm of law 'beyond the state' has already been created and the reach of global law is extended without the agency of the state and its institutions.

Whereas followers of the late Niklas Luhmann, such as Gunther Teubner, see structures of global governance resulting *per impossibile* through the self-regulating interlocking of anonymous systems of norm-generation which act as each other's environment, Anne-Marie

Slaughter places her faith in the networking of actual elites in the judiciaries across the world, administrative bureaucracies and so on. The hope is that new norms and standards for public behaviour will result through such interlockings.

Defenders of transnational governance have a point: the current state of global interdependence requires new modalities of cooperation and regulation. Certain markers of sovereignty in the domain of arms control, ecology, combating disease and epidemics and fighting the spread of poverty must be global joint ventures which will require the work of all people of good will and good faith in all nations of the world. As David Held in particular has argued powerfully, the goal is not only to form new institutions of transnational governance but to render existing ones such as the WTO, IMF and AID more transparent, accountable and responsive to their constituencies' needs. This in turn can only happen if popular movements within donor and member countries force the elites who govern these institutions towards democratic accountability. It is naïve to assume, as Guther Teubner and Anne-Marie Slaughter seem to do, that the good faith of elites or the miraculous sociological signals of anonymous systems alone will move such structures towards democratisation and accountability. They will not. Transnational structures need to be propelled towards a dynamic where they can be controlled by public law.

Here, however, we reach a dilemma: precisely because state-centred politics has become so reduced in effectiveness today, new theoretisations of the political have emerged. Yet my critique of the models of empire and transnational governance seems to presuppose a form of popular sovereignty, a *global demos*, which is nowhere in existence. Where is the popular sovereign who can counter empire or who can be the bearer of new institutions of transnational governance?

Today we are caught not only in the reconfiguration of sovereignty but also in the *reconstitutions of citizenship*. We are moving away from citizenship understood as national membership increasingly towards a *citizenship of residency* which strengthens the multiple ties to locality, to the region and to transnational institutions. In this respect defenders of postnational citizenship are correct. The universalistic extension of civil and social rights and, in some cases, of political participation rights as well to immigrants and denizens within the context of the European Union in particular is heralding a new institution of citizenship. This new modality decouples citizenship from national belonging and being rooted in a particular cultural community. Not only in Europe, but all around the globe we see the rise of political activism on the part of non-nationals, postnationals and ex-colonials. They live in multicultural neighbourhoods, they come together around women's rights, secondary language education for their children, environmental concerns, jobs for migrants, representation in school boards and city councils. This new urban activism, which includes citizens as well as non-citizens, shows that political agency is possible beyond the member/non-member divide. The paradoxes of the 'right to have rights' (Hannah Arendt) is ameliorated by those who exercise their democratic-republican participation rights with or without the correct papers.

The local level is not the only site of postnational citizenship. New modalities of citizenship and a nascent public sphere are also emerging at the global level through the meetings of the World Social Forum in which activists from all nations—representing women, ecology, ethnic rights, cultural self-determination, and economic democracy groups, NGOs and INGOs gather together, and plan strategy and policy. They are, in many cases, the ones who articulate and bring to global awareness problems to which transnational structures of governance have to respond. These citizens' groups and social activists are the transmitters of local and global knowledge and know-how; they generate new needs and demands that democracies have to respond to. They are members of the new global civil society. This new global civil society is inhabited not only by multinationals and transnationals, whether public and private, but also by citizens, movement activists and constituents of various kinds. This emergent global civil society is quite complementary to republican federalism, which in my opinion constitutes the only viable response to the contemporary crisis of sovereignty.[13]

Republican federalism and democratic sovereignty

I will define 'republican federalism' as the constitutionally structured reaggregation of the markers of sovereignty, in a set of interlocking institutions each responsible and accountable to the other. There is, as there must be in any structuring of sovereignty, a moment of finality, in the sense of decisional closure, but not a moment of ultimacy, in the sense of being beyond questioning, challenge and accountability. As the legal scholar Judith Resnik notes, the development of international law and of cosmopolitan human rights treaties are creating new modalities for the exercise of federalism.

> ... federalism is also a path for the movement of international rights across borders, as it can be seen from the adoption by mayors, local

city councils, state legislatures, and state judges of transnational rights including the United Nations Charter and the Convention to Eliminate All Forms of Discrimination Against Women (CEDAW) and the Kyoto Protocol on global warming. Such actions are often trans-local – with municipalities and states joining together to shape rules that cross borders. (Resnik 2006)

I call such processes of 'law's migration' (Resnik) across state boundaries and institutional jurisdictions, whether institutionalised or popular, 'democratic iterations'. By 'democratic iterations' I mean complex processes of public argument, deliberation, and exchange through which universalist rights claims and principles are contested and contextualised, invoked and revoked, posited and positioned throughout legal and political institutions, as well as in the associations of civil society. Democratic iterations can take place in the 'strong' public bodies of legislatives, the judiciary and the executive, as well as in the informal and 'weak' publics of civil society associations and the media.

In the process of repeating a term or a concept, we never simply produce a replica of the first original usage and its intended meaning; rather, every repetition is a form of variation. Every iteration transforms meaning and enriches it in ever-so-subtle ways. In fact, there really is no 'originary' source of meaning, or an 'original' to which all subsequent forms must conform. Even if the concept of 'original meaning' makes no sense when applied to language as such—for to identify the original we would already need to use language itself—it may be, though, that it would not be so ill placed in conjunction with documents such as the law and institutional norms. Thus, every act of iteration might refer to an antecedent which is taken to be authoritative. The iteration and interpretation of norms, and of every aspect of the universe of value, however, is never merely an act of repetition. The antecedent thereby is reposited and resignified via subsequent usages and references. Meaning is enhanced and transformed; conversely, when the creative appropriation of that authoritative original ceases or stops making sense, then the original loses its authority upon us as well.

Democratic iterations are processes of linguistic, legal, cultural and political repetitions-in-transformation, invocations which are also revocations.[14] Through such iterative acts a democratic people who considers itself bound by certain guiding norms and principles reappropriates and reinterprets these, thus showing itself to be not only the *subject* but also the *author of the laws*. Whereas natural right doctrines assume that the principles which are the basis of democratic politics are impervious to transformative acts of will, and whereas legal positivism identifies democratic legitimacy with the correctly posited norms of a sovereign legislature, jurisgenerative politics signals a space of interpretation and intervention between transcendent norms and the will of democratic majorities.[15] On the one hand, the rights claims which frame democratic politics must be viewed as transcending the specific enactments of democratic majorities in specific circumstances; on the other hand, such democratic majorities *reiterate* these principles and incorporate them into the democratic will-formation of the people through argument, contestation, revision and rejection. *Popular sovereignty no longer refers to the physical presence of a people gathered in a delimited territory, but rather to the interlocking in a global public sphere of the many processes of democratic iteration in which peoples learn from one another.*

There will be an inevitable tension between the border- and boundary-transcending discourses of democratic iterations and state sovereignty. In fact, democracy is the process through which the popular sovereign tries to tame state sovereignty by making it responsive, transparent and accountable to the people. The spread of cosmopolitan norms which aim to protect the human being as such, not as a member of a national group but rather as a citizen of a global civil society, reinforces and is reinforced by popular sovereignty. Whereas in the case of the decline of state sovereignty it is the receding of the public exercise of state power which is at stake, in the case of the augmentation of popular sovereignty, international and cosmopolitan norms subject agencies of the public exercise of power. First and foremost the state itself is submitted to heightened public and juridical scrutiny, thus aiding the assertion of popular sovereignty. The supposed conflict between the spread of cosmopolitan norms and popular sovereignty is based upon a mistaken equation of state with popular sovereignty.

Whereas cosmopolitan norms lead to border-crossing interlockings and coordinations of democratic iterations among those who are organised in human rights, women's rights, ecology and indigenous rights movements, *lex mercatoria* and other forms of law without the state generated by global capitalism, by contrast, strengthen private corporations vis-à-vis public bodies. Thus, in the case of the North American Free Trade Agreement (NAFTA) firms are granted rights hitherto generally limited to nation-states. Chapter II (B) of the Treaty allows private businesses to submit complaints against member-states to a three-member tribunal. One of the members is chosen by the affected state, another by the firm, and the third jointly by the parties. As Scheuerman observes, 'NAFTA thereby effectively grants states and corporations equal authority in some crucial decision-making matters.' And he adds, 'In a revealing contrast the procedures making up NAFTA's labor "side agreement" deny similar rights to organized labor' (Scheuerman 2004: 268–69, fn. 52).

There is an interesting parallel here to the growing power of individuals to bring before the European Court of Human Rights charges for human rights violations against states that are signatories to the European Convention for the Protection of Human Rights and Fundamental Freedoms. In this case as well, states are defendants and no longer immune to legal prosecution. In both cases, the 'black box' of state sovereignty has been pried open but with very different normative presuppositions: in the case of NAFTA and other forms of *lex mercatoria*, states becomes liable to prosecution by corporate bodies which do not represent *generalisable interests* but only their particular interests and those of their constituents. Interestingly, they also disempower organised labour and environmental groups from enjoying similar jurisdictional privileges in bringing charges against the state.

In the case of charges brought against states for human rights violations, by contrast, there is a potential *generalisable interest* shared by all citizens and residents of a state alike, namely to prevent the use of torture and other forms of the widespread violation of human rights. Human rights trials against sovereign states even go beyond the generalisable interest of the national citizens involved, to establish universalisable norms of human rights which would protect individuals everywhere and in any part of the world. There is a context-transcending power to these human rights iterations which feed into the normative power of cosmopolitan norms.

The boundaries of the political have shifted today beyond the republic housed in the nation-state. The deterritorialisation of law brings in its wake a displacement of the political. It is clear that only multiple strategies and forms of struggle can reassert the ruptured link between consent and the public exercise of power which is the essence of democratic sovereignty. Transnational structures of governance are fundamental in order to tame the forces of global capitalism; but the accountability of transnational elites can be only demanded by their own constituencies who mobilise for post- and transnational citizenship projects. The interlocking networks of local and global activists in turn form an emergent global civil society in which new needs are articulated for a worldwide public, new forms of knowledge are communicated to a world-public opinion and new forms of solidarity across borders are crafted.

Popular sovereignty cannot be regained today by returning to the era of the 'black box' of state sovereignty: the formal equality of sovereign states must mean the universalisation of human rights across state boundaries; respect for the rule of law and democratic forms of government all over the globe. It is an insult to the dignity and freedom of individuals everywhere to assume, as so many today are tempted to do, that human rights and cosmopolitan norms, such as the prohibition of 'crimes against humanity', are products of Western cultures alone whose validity cannot be extended to other peoples and other cultures throughout the world. Not only is this a very inadequate view of the spread of modernity as a global project, but it is also a philosophical conflation of genesis and validity, that is to say, of the conditions of the origin of a norm with the conditions of its validity. Global human rights and cosmopolitan norms establish new thresholds of public justification for a humanity that is increasingly united and interdependent.[16] New modalities of citizenship, not only in the sense of the privileges of membership but also in the sense of the power of democratic agency, can only flourish in the transnational, local as well as global spaces created by this new institutional framework. The multiplying sites of the political herald transformations of citizenship and new configurations of popular sovereignty.

Notes

1. The research leading to this chapter was first undertaken during my sabbatical stay at the Remarque Institute in New York University during the Winter of 2005. Special thanks to Thomas Faist, who has helped me clarify the complex interconnections between transnational migrations and other developments considered in this chapter. A version of this chapter has appeared as S. Benhabib (February 2007) 'Twilight of Sovereignty or the Emergence of Cosmopolitan Norms? Rethinking Citizenship in Volatile Times'. *Citizenship Studies* 11, 1: 19–36.
2. The most prominent of these are the Universal Declaration of Human Rights of 1948, the International Covenant on Civil and Political Rights, the International Covenant on Economic, Social and Cultural Rights, the Convention on the Elimination of All Forms of Racial Discrimination, the Convention of the Elimination of All Forms of Discrimination Against Women, the Convention Against Torture and other Cruel, Inhuman or Degrading Treatment or Punishment, and the Convention on the Rights of the Child.
3. For a more extensive treatment of Arendt's concept, see Benhabib (2004a, b: ch. 2).
4. The genesis of cosmopolitan norms goes back to the experiences of the two World Wars, European colonialism and anti-colonial struggles, the

Armenian genocide in the late stages of the Ottoman Empire and the Holocaust. It is wrong to confuse *lex mercatoria*, which is also global law, with the development of cosmopolitan human rights norms. For a masterful account of the development of international law, see Koskenniemi (2002). See also Taner Akcam's (1996) accounts of the trials against members of the 'Union and Progress Party' in the Ottoman Empire, which was responsible for the Armenian genocide; for the Nueremberg trials, see Marrus (1997); and for Ralph Lemkin and his efforts to pass the Genocide Convention, see Power (2003).

5. For a masterful account, which is also a sustained critique of Schmitt, see Koskenniemi (2002: 98–179). See also the statement of the Belgian legal historian Ernest Nys: 'A state uses the territories that constitute its private domain as it wishes; it sells them, it rents them out, it attaches such conditions to the concessions it grants as it sees warranted...in none of this does it owe an explanation to other States.' From 'L'Etat Independent du Congo et les dispositions de l'acte generale'. Quoted in Koskenniemi (2002: 161).

6. Schmitt's elogue to the *Jus Publicum Europaeum* (the public law of Europe) emphasises that this system 'neutralises' war by moving away from the medieval notion of 'just war'. In this transformation the enemy is no longer viewed as *inimicus* but a *justi hostes* (categories which also return in Schmitt's concept of the 'political'). This 'neutralised' concept of war is also called 'the non-discriminatory concept of war' (*der nicht-diskriminierende Kriegsbegriff*). '*All inter-state wars upon European soil, which are carried out through the militarily organized armies of states recognized by European law of nations (Voelkerrecht), are just in the sense of the European law of nations of this inter-statal period*' (Schmitt 1997: 115 [emphasis in the original]). Schmitt here conflates 'justice' and 'legality', not out of some logical error, but because he rejects all normative standards in judging wars.

7. Cited in Arendt (1951: 183). See also Hannah Arendt's powerful treatment, 'The only grandeur of imperialism lies in the nation's losing battle against it', ibid., 32.

8. Andreas Fischer-Lescano and Gunther Teubner discuss this extensively in their article: 'Regime-Collisions: The Vain Search for Legal Unity in the Fragmentation of Global Law,' trans. By Michelle Everson, in: *Michigan Journal of International Law* 25 (Summer 2004), pp. 999–1046. Particularly interesting is the collusion between the economic interests of patent holders, such as big pharmaceuticals Merck, Pfeizer, Rocheand so on, which in 2001 asked the WTO to investigate Brazil, which had permitted the domestic production of generic drugs via copying patented medicines. Brazil defended itself by pointing out that the AIDS epidemic had taken 150,000 lives since 1981 and that with preventive measures annual infections could be reduced to less than 5,000. This case, entailing a clear human rights claim to health and public protection from epidemic disease, in turn led to a major renegotiation of the terms of TRIPS (Trade Related Intellectual Property Rights) and to further negotiations between WHO and WTO about the preventive and non-commercial use of patented drugs and led all the way to a resolution of the UN Commission on Human Rights in 2000 protecting the preventive use of generic drugs whenever possible to help combat the spread of disease

and epidemics. At the Doha meetings in 2002, a Declaration on the TRIPS agreement and Public Health was issued, which affirmed the safeguards provided in TRIPS with regard to rights of states to issue such measures as compulsory licensing to cope with health crises in their respective countries. Company representatives in general preferred methods of differential pricing but accepted that they must accept the decision of states to deal with their own health problems. Since the DOHA round in 2002, however, trends have apparently gone in the direction of bilateral rather than multilateral agreements. See the publication 'Intellectual Property Rights', Results of a Stakeholder Dialogue between the World Business Council for Sustainable Development and the Wissenschaftszentrum Berlin fuer Sozialfoschung. (Reprint April 2004). Contact: wbcsd@earthprint.com.

9. Although first translated into English in 2001, the Italian version of *Empire* was written in the period between the Persian Gulf War of 1991 and the Yugoslav Civil War of 1994. Its view of American power is more benevolent than the subsequent work by Hardt and Negri (2004).

10. The last chapter of Hardt and Negri (2004) is entitled 'May the Force be With You.' On carnival (341–48) the authors state 'The various forms of carnival and mimicry that are so common today at globalization protests might be considered another form of weaponry. Simply having millions of people in the streets for a demonstration is a kind of weapon, as is also, in a rather different way, the pressure of illegal migrations... A one-week global biopolitical strike would block any war' (Hardt and Negri 2004: 347).

11. Just as in Michel Foucault's theory of power the subjects of power are interpellated by it, that is constituted in part through the network of power rather than preceding it, similarly in Hardt and Negri's analysis states and other world institutions disappear as agents and sites of resistance that have prior constitution. I disagree with this theory of power. One can stipulate the existence of very distinct and structured institutions and patterns of resistance to power without presupposing a metaphysical primordiality of either the state or the subject. The reach of empire is neither as ubiquitous nor as omniscient as Hardt and Negri would like us to think.

12. See Held (2004), Kuper (2004) and Slaughter (2004). There is something all too cheery and optimistic in these proposals which downplay the danger of dissociating constitutionalism from democracy and from citizens' will and reason by transferring it to an expertocracy, even if as good and willing an expertocracy as the judges and practitioners of international law.

13. Global civil society, as defended here, should not be confused with the appeal to voluntarism and private associations, so characteristic of the neoliberals, who aim at curtailing state power. I endorse the public provision of public goods in a system of nested interdependencies of public authorities. Global civil society is a space of global civic activism and the counterpart to the model of 'republican federalism' which I develop below.

14. Since I have introduced the concept of 'democratic iterations', in *The Rights of Others* (Benhabib 2004b: ch. 5), I have been asked to clarify, first, the relationship between practical discourses of justification and democratic iterations and, second, whether democratic iterations can also be regressive and non-meaning enhancing.Democratic iterations are processes of *legitimation* and not *justification*. They stand in the same relationship to normative

discourses of justification as John Rawls's *Theory of Justice* stands to a theory of democracy; second, yes, 'jurispathic' democratic iterations, which block the enhancement of meaning and the augmentation of rights claims, are possible.(Benhabib, ed. by Robert Post, 2006).
15. For the concept of the 'jurisgenerative', see Cover 1983.
16. On the idea of a threshold of justification, see Benhabib (2004b: 15–21).

References

A revised version of this article has appeared as S. Benhabib (February 2007) 'Twilight of Sovereignty or the Emergence of Cosmopolitan Norms? Rethinking Citizenship in Volatile Times'. *Citizenship Studies* 11, 1: 19–36.

Agamben, G. (2005) *State of Exception*. Trans. Kevin Attell. Chicago and London: The University of Chicago Press.

Akcam, T. (1996) *Armenien und der Voelkermord. Die Istanbuler Prozesse und die tuerkische Nationalbewegung*. Hamburg: Hamburger Edition.

Apter, D. (2001) 'Globalization, Marginality and the Specter of the Superfluous Man'. *Journal of Social Affairs* 18, 71: 73–94.

Arendt, H. (1951) *The Origins of Totalitarianism*. New York: Harcourt Brace.

Arendt, H. (1963) *On Revolution*. New York: Viking Press.

Balibar, E. (2004) *We, the People of Europe? Reflections on Transnational Citizenship*. Trans. James Swenson. Princeton and Oxford: Princeton University Press.

Benhabib, S. (2001) *Transformation of Citizenship. Dilemmas of the Nation-State in an Era of Globalization. The Spinoza Lectures*. Amsterdam: Van Gorcum.

Benhabib, S. (2002) *The Claims of Culture. Equality and Diversity in the Global Era*. Princeton, NJ: Princeton University Press.

Benhabib, S. (2003) *The Reluctant Modernism of Hannah Arendt*, 2nd edn. New York: Rowman and Littlefield.

Benhabib, S. (2004a) 'Kantian Questions, Arendtian Answers'. In Seyla Benhabib and Nancy Fraser, eds, *Pragmatism, Critique and Judgment. Festschrift for Richard J. Bernstein*. Cambridge, MA: MIT Press, pp. 171–97.

Benhabib, S. (2004b) *The Rights of Others. Aliens, Citizens and Residents. The John Seeley Memorial Lectures*. Cambridge, UK: Cambridge University Press.

Benhabib, S. (2006) 'Reply to my Critics'. In Robert Post, ed., *Another Cosmopolitanism: Hospitality, Sovereignty and Democratic Iterations*, with Commentaries by Jeremy Waldron, Bonnie Honig and Will Kymlicka. New York and Oxford: Oxford University Press.

Brodie, J. (2004) 'Introduction: Globalization and Citizenship Beyond the National State'. *Citizenship Studies* 8, 4 (December): 323–33.

Cohen, J. L. (2004) 'Whose Sovereignty? Empire vs. International Law'. *Ethics and International Affairs* 18, 3: 1–24.

Cover, R. (1983) '*Nomos* and Narrative'. *Harvard Law Review*, 97, 1: 4–68.

Evans, P. (1997) 'The Eclipse of the State? Reflections on Stateness in an Era of Globalization'. *World Politics* 50, 1: 62–87.

Fischer-Lescano, A. and G. Teubner. (2004). 'Regime-Collisions: The Vain Search for Legal Unity in the Fragmentation of Global Law'. Trans. Michelle Everson. *Michigan Journal of International Law* 25 (Summer 2004): 999–1046.

Hardt, M. and A. Negri (2001) *Empire*. Cambridge, MA: Harvard University Press.

Hardt, M. and A. Negri (2004). *Multitude. War and Democracy in the Age of Empire.* New York: Penguin Press.

Held, D. (2004) *Global Covenant. The Social Democratic Alternative to the Washington Consensus.* London: Polity Press.

Henkin, L., G. L. Neuman, D. F. Orentlicher, and D. W. Leebron (eds). (1999) *Human Rights.* New York: Foundation Press, Ch. 1, pp. 147ff.

Ikeda, S. (2004) 'Imperial Subjects, National Citizenship, and Corporate Subjects: Cycles of Political Participation/Exclusion in the Modern World System'. *Citizenship Studies* 8, 4 (December): 333–49.

Koskenniemi, M. (2002) *The Gentle Civilizer of Nations. The Rise and Fall of International Law 1870–1960.* Cambridge, MA: Cambridge University Press.

Krasner, S. D. (1999) *Sovereignty: Organized Hypocrisy.* Princeton, NJ: Princeton University Press.

Kuper, A. (2004) *Democracy Beyond Borders. Justice and Representation in Global Institutions.* Oxford: Oxford University Press.

Marrus, M. (1997) *The Nuremberg War Crimes Trial 1945–46: A Documentary History.* New York: Bedford/St. Martin's.

Nettl, J. P. (1968) 'The State as a Conceptual Variable'. *World Politics*, 20, 4 (July): 559–92.

Ong, A. (1999) *Flexible Citizenship. The Cultural Logic of Transnationality.* Durham and London: Duke University Press.

Power, S. (2003) *A Problem from Hell: America in the Age of Genocide.* New York: Basic Books.

Resnik, J. (2006) 'Law's Migration: American Exceptionalism, Silent Dialogues, and Federalism's Multiple Ports of Entry'. *The Yale Law Journal* 115, 7: 1564–1670.

Scheuerman. W. E. (2004) *Liberal Democracy and the Social Acceleration of Time.* Balimore and London: Johns Hopkins University Press.

Schmitt, C. (1997) *Der Nomos der Erde im Voelkerrecht des Jus Publicum Europaeum*, 4th ed. Berlin: Duncker and Humblot.

Slaughter, A. -M. (2004) *A New World Order.* Princeton, NJ: Princeton University Press.

Teubner, G., ed. (1997) *Global Law Without a State. Studies in Modern Law and Policy.* Aldershot and Brookfield, Vermont: Dartmouth Publishing Company.

UN (2002) *International Migration Report.* Department of Economic and Social Affairs, ST/ESA/SER.A/220, 2002.

Zlotnik, H. (2001) 'Past Trends in International Migration and Their Implications for Future Prospects'. In M. A. B. Siddique, ed., International Migration into the Twenty-First Century: Essays in Honor of Reginald Appleyard. Boston: Edward Elgar.

Zolberg, A. and P. Benda (2001) *Global Migrants. Global Refugees: Problems and Solutions.* New York: Berghahn Books.

13
Conclusion: The Boundaries of Citizenship in a Transitional Age

Peter Kivisto

In the past, including the recent past, dual citizenship was considered to be a problem. Today it is increasingly viewed instead as a possibility that needs to be negotiated from standpoints ranging from a simple pragmatic tolerance to active encouragement. Such a bald statement needs immediately to be qualified lest the contemporary significance of dual citizenship be misconstrued as yet another of those claims about a radical rupture between past and present—reflected for instance in many accounts of postmodernism, postnationalism, and various other 'posts'. It needs to be stressed, moreover, that those actors treating the phenomenon as either a problem or a possibility include in various ways agents of states—including of course political elites, government bureaucrats and cultural elites concerned with offering ideological defences of particular national identities.

Since the birth of modern nation-states and the emergence of the idea of citizenship within the boundaries of such political entities, the issue of dual citizenship has been addressed by those elites (Kivisto and Faist 2007). Modern nation-states claim a monopoly not only on violence, but on determinations of membership. Indeed, it is the state that arbitrates the distinctions between citizen and alien, between insider and outsider, between member and non-member. States have been averse to ceding the power to decide who is and who is not qualified to become a citizen and this has led to certain inherent dilemmas for both individuals and states. If each state establishes its own citizenship laws, individuals may well find themselves in situations where they can legally become citizens of two or more states. On the other hand, other individuals may find that they can potentially become stateless.

Historical excursus

Dual citizenship became a matter of concern in the nineteenth century, due chiefly to the impact of emigration from Europe to the United States. It came to a head when immigrants seeking to become naturalised citizens of their new homeland were confronted with the challenge posed by the refusal of their states of origin to allow them to renounce their original citizenship. The refusal was at some level perplexing given the fact that both political and cultural elites at the time also tended to denounce the emigrants as traitors to the homeland. Traitors they may be, but the very same states were not prepared to release them from the obligations of citizenship. Although this may seem ironic, in fact it was a product of rational calculation, particularly because of a desire to maintain their émigré population as a potential source for military conscription.

These sending states, quite simply, sought to reinforce their claim to determine all matters involving citizenship, ranging from the matter of inclusion to the matter of exit. For its part, concerned about what was seen as the problem of dual loyalties, American immigration law called for naturalising citizens to renounce their previous allegiances. But, as Peter Spiro (2002: 22) has pointed out, the issue did not only concern the relationship between the state and the citizen. Rather, it involved interstate relations. Specifically, the monopoly of control over its citizenry was not questioned by other states provided that the citizen did not hold dual citizenship. If an individual did, questions were raised about the ability of the nation to do whatever it wished to its citizens because there were limits as to what could be done to citizens of other countries.

The tide of immigration was not going to be stemmed by this intrastate conflict over competing citizenship regimes. Thus, in the end a negotiated settlement had to be worked out, commencing with the treaties between the United States and various West European nations that collectively became known as the Bancroft Treaties. The guiding principle behind these treaties was that dual citizenship should be avoided as much as possible. The states did not seek to eradicate dual citizenship entirely, but rather attempted to contain it. In particular, from the perspective of a settler society such as the United States, it was understood that nation building could not proceed unless the huge infusion of newcomers arriving at the nation's shores could repudiate their earlier national identities and, in effect, start over.

The significance of treating national identity in civic rather than ethnic terms was that by making the choice to become an American volitional, the message was that earlier claims to primordial allegiances were to be viewed as suspect. Meanwhile, the sending states learned that it was best to cut their losses. Several factors led them to this conclusion, including the growing power of the United States, both politically and economically. Second, some states discovered that when their émigré populations maintained an interest in homeland politics the results could be a mixed bag. While they might work to support existing regimes, they might work equally to overthrow them. Although the factors at play differed depending on the particular state in question, it was clear by the early decades of the twentieth century that a growing consensus between sending and receiving nations was emerging. This consensus was codified in 1930 in the Hague Convention Concerning Certain Questions Relating to the Conflict of Nationality, in which the signatories established the principle that all people should be citizens of one and only one state. Two things were to be avoided: promoting dual citizenship and constructing policies that resulted in statelessness.

This has been the guiding thread of state policies in the world's liberal democracies until very recently, when fissures in this consensus have developed. That being said, it was never the case that states attempted to eliminate dual citizenship altogether. In the case of a settler state like the United States, the goal was to ensure that naturalised citizens did not maintain citizenship in their nation of origin. However, in other instances dual citizenship was permitted, due to the competing claims of four criteria that can factor into the citizenship laws of particular states: the *jus soli* principle, the *jus sanguinis* principle, marital status and residential location (Hansen and Weil 2002: 2). For example, children born in the United States of non-citizen parents will be both citizens of the United States and citizens of their parents' homeland(s), which in some cases might mean that at birth the child actually has three legitimate citizenships (if the parents were from two different countries). Meanwhile, those nations of Western Europe that were once primarily sending nations have since the second half of the twentieth century become immigrant-receiving nations—and as a consequence have had to wrestle with the issue of naturalisation that since the nineteenth century has primarily preoccupied the historic settler states.

It is in this historical context that current developments in the expansion of dual citizenship need to be understood, including those related to state efforts to reconsider the principle of the Hague Convention and changes that are a consequence of the growing role of transstate entities in shaping citizenship regimes. Stephen Legomsky (2003: 81) has pointed to the inherent instability of this approach to citizenship by noting that there are three factors shaping citizenship regimes that have the capacity to interact to yield dual or plural citizenship in spite of opposition to it in principle: (1) 'each state decides who its own nationals are'; (2) 'a state typically provides alternative multiple routes to nationality'; and (3) 'the rules vary from state to state'.

Contemporary developments

Until the last decades of the twentieth century, this instability did not lead to a dramatic escalation of dual citizenship. When it did, it would occur as a consequence of mass immigration and, to a lesser extent, of the reconfiguration of national boundaries or the willingness to embrace expatriates in nearby countries in certain parts of Central and Eastern Europe. Elsewhere, Seyla Benhabib (2004: 1) has provided the following backdrop to recent developments:

> The modern nation-state has regulated membership in terms of one principal category: national citizenship. We have entered an era when state sovereignty has been frayed and the institution of national citizenship has been disaggregated or unbundled into diverse elements. New modalities of membership have emerged, with the result that the boundaries of the political community, as defined by the nation-state system, are no longer adequate to membership.

In discussing the disaggregation of citizenship, Benhabib (2004: 145) distinguishes the following three parts: 'collective identity, privileges of political membership, and social rights and claims'. In the introduction to her contribution to this book, she observes that linked to the disaggregation of citizenship are two other developments that serve to frame the factors shaping traditional perspectives on citizenship: the rise of an international human rights regime and the expansion of cosmopolitan norms. Later in the chapter, she points to the role of global capitalism in effecting the growing 'deterritorialisation of law'. Though the implications and impacts of each vary by case, in combination they have undermined state sovereignty. This being said, undermining means that state sovereignty has been eroded or weakened, not that it has been replaced.

It is in this context that one can discuss the recasting of citizenship from being rooted in the nation-state to becoming not unfettered from the state, but located in an expanding circle of ties that move from the locality through the region to the transnational level. Benhabib refers to this as a 'citizenship of residency', contending that this shift constitutes support in part for the postnational thesis. Such a reconfigured citizenship is predicated on multicultural engagements in all three spatial sectors. This is, thus, nested citizenship—and as such it is more evident in the nations of the European Union than in the United States. Although she provides some concrete examples of the ways that activist citizens are exemplifying the cosmopolitan sensibility underpinning a citizenship of residency, Benhabib makes it clear that this is an incipient form of citizenship, far more aspiration than actualisation. Indeed, her chapter ends by stressing that it is only possible if provided with the institutional structure to nurture and sustain it.

Dual citizenship is not the focus of the chapter. Implicitly, however, it offers a partial answer to the question of why so many states have been willing in recent years to entertain the prospect of legitimising, or barring that, tolerating dual citizenship. The erosion of the sovereignty of nation-states makes them vulnerable to pressures exerted by transstate institutional actors and a transnational citizenry.

Dual citizenship and solidarity

Peter Spiro does focus on the impact of postnationalism on dual citizenship. Like Benhabib, he is not particularly sanguine about what the erosion of state sovereignty will yield—at least in the short term, at a point characterised by 'immature postnational structures'. Spiro expresses concern about the lack of the institutional structures needed to ensure the robustness of an international human rights regime. Not knowing precisely what will happen in the longer term, he makes the following claims about the present and the near-term. First, dual citizenship will continue to grow and will become part of the political landscape. Second, the prospect of dual citizenship will be perceived and pursued in largely instrumental terms. Transnational migrants can find it advantageous to possess multiple passports. While receiving states sometimes operate with the assumption that easing naturalisation requirements will facilitate incorporation into the new society of residence, Spiro does not think this is a given.

He does think that one of the consequences of the cheapening of citizenship is that it 'does not get or give much any more'. Thus, while citizenship continues to speak to in-group membership, such membership is devalued as both the rights that accrue to citizenship status and the obligations flowing from it become increasingly thin. An instrumental attitude towards citizenship derives from this fact. What this suggests is that the bases for solidarity predicated on emotional ties to the political community and to fellow citizens are lacking, or at least are insufficiently powerful to be efficacious.

There is a large claim being advanced here: dual citizenship serves to undermine the state-based societal community. If this is true, the prevalence of dual citizenship represents a challenge to theorists building on the tradition of T. H. Marshall who have invested citizenship with the capacity to unite individuals in a transcendent community. Parsons' (1971, forthcoming 2007) work constitutes the primary example of such a position, arguing that modern citizenship contains the capacity for overcoming the divisiveness of religious, racial and ethnic identities without necessitating the elimination of difference. Parsons thought that these particularistic identities could persist over time as long as their salience was tempered. Key to this happening was the emergence of cross-cutting allegiances and social ties, the likes of which would serve to tamp down the potentially incendiary character of these particularistic identities. Citizenship, in this scheme, would become the overarching identity of individual members, containing and constraining all other identities.

Parsons operated within a theoretical perspective that treated society and the nation-state as isomorphic. His theoretical framework was not conceived in terms of a recognition of transnational or globalising forces that located nations within a larger, transstate and global context. Moreover, although he thought difference might persist, he did so without a consideration of the potential for a multicultural perspective to emerge and to promote the idea of group rights complementing individual rights. Equipped in his later years with an evolutionary schema, Parsons' work strikes us today as naively optimistic.

Such cannot be said of the work of Jeffrey Alexander, who though deeply influenced by Parsons has also moved beyond the Parsonian imprint. In his recent book, *The Civil Sphere* (2006), Alexander claims that multiculturalism properly understood can have a positive impact on the incorporation of marginalised groups—immigrants and others. The civil sphere becomes for him the site where both difference and solidarity are possible. Rather than being conceived as mutually exclusive (as critics of multiculturalism often claim), they are seen as having the potential to coexist. Stripped of any notion of evolutionary movement, the project of civil society is conceived in terms of possibilities, not inevitabilities. Civil society must be achieved not once and for all, but over and over again.

Spiro does not address such theoretical projects in his chapter, but his bottom-line conclusion does reflect a significant challenge. If dual citizenship undermines solidarity at the national level, those particularistic identities will fill the void, offering themselves as alternatives. This is a disturbing prospect insofar as it can be taken to suggest the balkanisation of a nation. Douglas Hartmann and Joseph Gerteis (2005) refer to this situation as 'fragmented pluralism', which occurs when the centre does not hold. Given the abundant evidence we have, not from the world's existing liberal democracies, but from such failed states as Yugoslavia, Rwanda, Congo and Iraq, fragmented pluralism can produce hell on earth. This is not to suggest that such a scenario is likely in the liberal democracies. Even those who see an erosion of such states know that they remain powerful. What Spiro seems to think the future might portend for such nations is a situation in which the capacity of the state to forge allegiances does not disappear, but national identity should be seen as increasingly competing with other identities and solidarities. No longer the overarching mode of identity containing others, it is becoming merely one among others.

Given the fact that we are early into what will be a long process, it is impossible to provide sufficient evidence to either support or refute the assertion that dual citizenship serves to undermine the state. There are some clues, however, that can be distilled from other chapters in this book that offer a variety of concrete empirical examples to assess this thesis at least provisionally. Herein we find support for Benhabib and Spiro as well as evidence that calls their claims into question, leading to an appreciation of the fundamental ambiguity of the present. These clues might be taken as key elements to consider in future research agendas aimed at ascertaining the precise impact of dual citizenship.

Beyond 9/11

Since the events of 11 September 2001, the US government has aggressively pursued policies aimed at reasserting the singular role of the state in promoting national security. In response to the tragic events of that fateful day, the Bush administration orchestrated a public relations campaign aimed at convincing the citizenry that their safety rested in the hands of government that of necessity would have to operate in new ways to meet the terrorist threat. The colour-coded national alerts were intended to be a device to calibrate levels of fear among the public at large. The administration acted without transparency and argued that secrecy was essential if they were to succeed in protecting the nation. At the same time, administration officials argued that their conduct had to be unilateral, that, in other words, they would not be tied to a variety of international agreements (thus, the Attorney General described certain features of the Geneva Convention as quaint). Not surprisingly, the United Kingdom, America's closest ally in the 'war on terror', pushed the securitisation envelope close to that of the United States. However, even states opposed to the Americans' approach and critical of the war in Iraq have also, in more limited ways, reasserted the power of the state in security matters.

Audrey Macklin's discussion of the impact of securitisation on dual citizenship is a lesson in point. Her argument can be summarised in two words: membership counts. In examining the relationship between membership and the rights and obligations substance of citizenship, she indicates just how much it counts in her case studies of the Khadr family in Canada and Yaser Hamdi in the United States. The awesome power of the state is being asserted here and elsewhere as ideas such as revoking citizenship—as she points out, most acutely in the United Kingdom and Germany—have gained currency in some policy circles and among the public at large. While these have not always been acted on, far more consequential at the moment is the widespread resistance to the continued entry of asylum seekers and refugees.

Macklin sees these and related developments as challenging the idea of dual citizenship due to the suspicion of the divided loyalties of newcomers. In this she is no doubt quite right. This suggests that we have not yet moved decisively past the old concerns that informed the Hague Convention. Given the right circumstances, state authorities can find themselves in a position to ratchet up public suspicions of foreigners, and cast into doubt the wisdom of granting citizenship rights to people who might also maintain their legal attachments to their nation of origin.

This position is echoed in Triadafilos Triadafilopoulos's chapter, which locates what he refers to as the current post-9/11 'security norms' in broader historical context. Three interrelated topics are discussed, beginning with the role of war in the formation of modern nation-states, moving to changes that have occurred since the middle of the twentieth century, and finally engaging the debate on postnationalism. The needs of states in making available loyal subject bodies for both the protective and the expansionist activities of militaries and the ability to extract

needed funds via taxation required the forging of bonds of national-
istic solidarity. As Triadafilopoulos puts it, this amounted early on to a
'revolution in loyalties'. In his view, the primacy of warfare meant that
the loyalty of subjects had to be sufficient to yield a willingness to make
blood sacrifices on behalf of the state.

In such a situation, dual nationalities were inherently problematic
and thus from the vantage of states were to be prevented whenever
possible. This particular perspective was codified in the aforementioned
1930 Hague Convention. Writing at around the same time as the Hague
Convention, German political theorist Carl Schmidt (1996) argued that
states could not exist without enemies. Triadafilopoulos views the post–
Second World War era as a watershed in the history of the modern
state insofar as war was no longer normative in the same sense and
intrastate rivalries took on a new character. While this is no doubt an
apt characterisation of most of the world's major liberal democracies, it
looks somewhat different from the vantage of the United States, where
the Cold War, which stretched over four decades, quickly gave way to
the new war on combating non-state terrorists, a war that the Bush
regime and its British allies have frequently described as never-ending
and as shaping the political agenda of the twenty-first century. Wars
in various guises continue, but they tend no longer to require the mass
mobilisation of the citizenry.

Triadafilopoulos stresses what he refers to as the reprivatisation of war,
by which he means the increasing reliance on a professional military
rather than conscription. The significance of such a shift is that the issue
of dual loyalties ceases to have the same urgency as it did prior to the
Second World War. This, he contends, goes some distance in explaining
why so many states are today willing to entertain the prospect of dual
citizenship. It is not that the states support dual nationality, but rather
that the reasons for avoiding it become less compelling. Although he
does not rule out a reversal of this trend due to fears of terrorism
and thus in the interest of state security, in contrast to Macklin he
sees little evidence that the trend will be reversed anytime in the near
future.

Thomas Faist's and Jürgen Gerdes' chapter observes and attempts to
explain why it is that Germany managed to pass a new citizenship
law that was among the most liberal in Europe in terms of its *jus soli*
component, while at the same time was averse to passing legislation
that would have legitimised dual citizenship. In their view, one might
have expected that liberalisation in one aspect of citizenship law would
be linked to liberalisation in the other. If it is true that the shift from an

ethnic to a civic definition of citizenship would appear to be predicated on a republican model, the claim can be made (despite voices of protest being registered on the extreme right) that 'we are all republican now'. To the extent that this claim was embraced on the left and elicited sufficient support on the right, the introduction of a more tolerant civic version of citizenship was possible.

At the same time, however, dual citizenship proved to be problematic insofar as it highlighted differences between the left and the right over the respective weights to be accorded to rights versus obligations. The left, endorsing a liberal individualist perspective, placed an emphasis on individual rights, including the right to maintain dual citizenship. On the other hand, the right operated from what Faist and Gerdes call a 'state-communitarian standpoint' or what would commonly be seen as a republican rather than liberal perspective. The concern with dual citizenship from this perspective emanates from the conviction that citizenship must be predicated on a type of solidarity rooted in an emotional attachment to the nation and a willingness to entertain the prospect that one might actually have to sacrifice on its behalf. From this vantage, dual citizenship is inherently suspect because it smacks of promoting an instrumental attitude towards membership.

The current German stance on dual citizenship parallels that of the United States. Of course, the United States was from its founding—at least in principle—based on a civic rather than ethnic base. National solidarity was thus conceived in voluntaristic terms rather than rooted in bloodlines. This generated a conception of national identity that allowed for considerable ethnic diversity. If there was a suspicion that ethnic allegiances would trump national solidarity—and there often was in the nation's history—in terms of any particular group, this tended with the passage of time and generational succession to give way to a view that ethnicity could be safely subsumed within the overarching solidarity of national identity. National elites often sent mixed messages about ethnic involvements in homeland politics. At times, such involvements worked in the interests of elites, such as anti-Castro Cubans during the Cold War. At other times, the prospects of homeland engagements, real or perceived, were seen as threatening, with the Japanese case in the Second World War being the most obvious and troubling example.

In this context, dual citizenship could be problematic, but was not necessarily so. This may account for the fact that American policy for the past half century can be characterised as ambivalent. On the one hand, there has been no effort to permit naturalising citizens to maintain their earlier citizenships. On the other hand, there has been no attempt to impose criminal sanctions on individuals who do maintain dual citizenship. This amounts to a 'don't ask, don't tell' policy.

Impacts of dual citizenship

What do we know about the actual impacts of dual citizenship and about whether or not the substantive content of citizenship has been changed due to cross-cutting national loyalties? Three chapters in this collection offer empirical evidence that together provide partial and somewhat contradictory answers. Irene Bloemraad is interested in whether or not a state's openness to dual citizenship has an impact on the willingness of immigrants to naturalise, which she sees as a central indicator of incorporation. In her chapter and in considerably more detail in her book *Becoming a Citizen* (2006), she enters into a comparative analysis of a select number of immigrant groups in the United States and Canada. What she discovered is that immigrants are more inclined to naturalise in Canada compared to those locating in the United States. The question is why? If the primary reason for naturalising was instrumental, one might expect the rates to be essentially the same. Given that this is not the case, Bloemraad offers a counter explanation. The United States still demands a renunciation of prior citizenship at naturalisation proceedings. Though immigrants tend to know that this will not be acted on, it does set a tone that implies dual nationality may be tolerated, but is not embraced by the state. This approach stands in contrast to Canada, where dual nationality is valorised in official government statements.

Bloemraad interprets this valorisation as significant at the symbolic rather than the instrumental level. In short, it defines Canada as an accepting and inclusive multicultural nation—a place that is sufficiently attractive for immigrants to want to forge a permanent legal attachment. In a sense, this might strike one as counter-intuitive given that one's willingness to reject a previous allegiance might be taken to signal a desire to attach at an emotional level with a nation. However, I would suggest that what Bloemraad has identified is a manifestation of what Barbara Ballis Lal (1990: 3) has referred to as the 'ethnicity paradox', which contends that in the process of seeking to remain attached to their ethnic origins, group members paradoxically prepare themselves for incorporation into the host society. Although Bloemraad does not say so in so many words, what this might suggest is that dual citizenship is in some sense a temporary phenomenon insofar as with the passage of time, the salience of the citizenship of the nation of origin progressively declines.

This could be a conclusion that one can draw from José Itzigsohn's study of dual citizenship among Mexicans and Dominicans in the United States. In both instances, homeland political officials confronted the reality of well-established migratory networks and a new political climate brought about by the end of rule of entrenched political elites. Realising the economic significance of remittances, these officials promoted dual citizenship as a mechanism designed to maintain loyalty to the homeland while simultaneously encouraging incorporation into the United States. The anticipated consequences of dual citizenship included the perpetuation of the remittance system and the willingness of the émigré population to serve a lobbying function on behalf of the homeland.

Itzigsohn has discovered that in both cases these expectations have not been realised, concluding that what he refers to as transnational citizenship has produced 'paradoxical and contradictory' results. One of the findings most relevant to the assessment of the significance of dual citizenship is that in case of both Mexicans and Dominicans, a very small percentage of the eligible populations living in the United States have opted to participate in their respective homeland's electoral process. Although Itzigsohn is hesitant to draw broad conclusions about what this means for dual citizenship, his evidence would appear to suggest that in becoming naturalised citizens, immigrants have opted to hang their political loyalties on the receiving country's peg rather than on the homeland's peg. This is not to suggest that transnational practices will cease, for this shift of political allegiances does not necessarily mean the end to transnational economic, cultural and personal ties.

The complex character of dual citizenship is also evident in Valerie Preston, Myer Siemiatycki and Audrey Kobayashi's study of Hong Kong Canadians. If there are any recent immigrants more inclined to operate with a purely instrumental view of citizenship, it is the members of Hong Kong's business community attempting to sort out the implications of the transition from British to Chinese rule. As it turns out, however, the picture is considerably more complex. Although the small sample size cautions against broad generalisations, it does appear that for most immigrants instrumental and symbolic factors are interwoven. That being said, it is not clear what that might mean for the future. Dual citizenship could conceivably be important in both ways for those economic 'argonauts' that are exemplars of economic transnationalism. However, for those Hong Kong Chinese who over time find their economic future is chiefly located in North America, dual citizenship may increasingly become symbolic in the sense of Gans' (1979) concept of symbolic ethnicity—an ethnicity based primarily on nostalgia, with few behavioural consequences.

Dual citizenship in Central and Eastern Europe

As Rainer Bauböck and Mária M. Kovács's chapters on dual citizenship in Central and Eastern Europe suggest, there is yet another way that the phenomenon has become a significant issue—a way quite different from what is occurring elsewhere. In these cases, a history of disputed territories and political boundaries, the product of the demise of the Austro-Hungarian Empire and more recently the collapse of the Soviet Union, has resulted in states reaching out by providing dual citizenship to residents of neighbouring nations who are perceived to be former citizens of the state in question. The objective is to expand the size of the nation by including people who do not live within current state borders. Baucöck cautions against reading what has occurred in Hungary, Romania and Moldova as reflective of the promotion of an ethnic conception of citizenship versus the civic conception in Western Europe and North America. He is correct that if posed as a stark dichotomy it fails to capture the complex character of these different geographic regions, where these ideal types are just that, ideal types. Nevertheless, at some level it strikes me that this distinction is in no small part accurate, particularly in the case of Hungary.

Kovács chronicles the political conflict surrounding the dual citizenship debate in Hungary, pointing out that the political left opposed the policy while nationalists on the right supported it. This would lend credence to the argument that what is at stake here is indeed a dispute over whether contemporary citizenship in the nation ought to be defined in primarily civic terms, as one would expect the left would advocate, or in ethnic terms, which would be congruent with conservative nationalist ideology.

Bauböck offers a typology of political and identity options for transborder minorities. In his scheme there are seven types, four that he describes as main alternatives and three as mixed. The former include emigration, assimilation, autonomy and secession. The latter include diasporic identity, ethnic identity and condominium. The political likelihood of these different options varies considerably. Some of them are not conducive to stable forms of dual citizenship. Such is the case for emigration to the country of ancestral origin, assimilation into the nation of residence, claims of political autonomy and an irredentist campaign. Other options lend themselves to less unstable forms of dual citizenship. Part of Bauböck's agenda is to call into question those who would simultaneously make claims in favour of dual citizenship in the context of immigration to the world's liberal democracies, while expressing opposition to dual citizenship in the Central and Eastern European case. Without getting into the normative issues, suffice it to say that I fully agree with him when he notes that the latter situation contains an inherent problem that is absent in the former: the fact that built into the issue of dual citizenship are questions about the legitimacy of existing political boundaries. Later in the chapter, Bauböck moves from his geographical focus to discuss briefly some 'complex cases' from around the world, including Cyprus, Kashmir, Northern Ireland and Israel/Palestine. These are, of course, particularly troubling examples of the potential for violence that territorial disputes engender.

The Future of dual citizenship

It is useful to be reminded that in many respects the study of dual citizenship is in its infancy, reflective of the fact that contemporary developments have only recently begun to receive the scholarly attention they deserve. It is also useful to note that social scientists have a rather checkered record of predicting how the future is likely to unfold. It behoves us to be keenly appreciative of the fact that there is much we do not know about dual citizenship and we should therefore be rather circumspect in making predictions about future trends. Instead, we ought to be engaged in the business of developing comprehensive comparative research agendas. In an era of mass immigration, it can safely be assumed that levels of dual citizenship will remain high. What we know relatively little about at the moment—but about which the chapters in this book provide tantalising clues—is the larger significance and the meaning attached to dual citizenship.

One track of research ought to focus on state actors as they either embrace or resist dual citizenship. We know less than we should at the moment about the actual constellation of political forces at play in getting dual citizenship onto the legislative agenda. Why, for example, has this matter been the focus of parliamentary debate in Germany while it has not received comparable attention in the United States? What is the role of political elites and how do the divisions among elites structure discourse? Similarly, we need to know more about the role of non-elites, ranging from the impacts of organised anti-immigration social movements to the lobbying efforts of pro-immigrant forces and the immigrants themselves. Contrary to postnationalist theorists who would argue that the focus of policy-related research on dual citizenship ought to be focused on the role of transstate entities, I would argue—backed in part by the essays on the post-9/11 security state—that states continue to be the central locus of decision-making regarding all aspects of dual citizenship. At the same time, it is true that transstate institutions have come increasingly to play a role in this process, particularly in Europe, where the significance of the EU in such matters has expanded in recent decades.

The second research locus ought to be on dual citizens themselves. How did they become dual citizens and why? Was it a conscious choice or not? Did they opt to become a dual citizen for instrumental reasons or for deeply held attachments—with similar emotional valences—to two places? Do they perceive dual citizenship as a temporary or permanent aspect of their lives? What is their understanding of the issue of divided loyalties? How do they define citizenship: in thin, but rights-bearing terms, or in thicker, more republican terms involving emotional and behavioural solidarity with particular polities? At the moment, we actually know precious little about these and related questions, though some of the contributors to this book have begun to redress this situation.

> Posed in this way, what I am suggesting is that we need to know much more about the phenomenology of dual citizenship. While true, this is not sufficient. It is important to conduct research into the social psychology of dual citizens, but this needs to be complemented with research into the impacts of dual citizenship on the political systems of both the nation of origin and the receiving nation. (Deaux 2006)

This is, indeed, a transitional age where the previous international consensus about the undesirability of dual citizenship has broken down. It has not been replaced by a comparable international consensus that definitively rejects that earlier consensus. Rather, we live at present in an interstitial moment, where much remains indeterminate. In such a time, research ought to be framed in a way that appreciates dual citizenship's fluid and ambiguous character, and which carefully distinguishes its long-term implications from those of the short term.

References

Alexander, J. C. (2006) *The Civil Sphere*. New York: Oxford University Press.
Benhabib, S. (2004) *The Rights of Others: Aliens, Residents, and Citizens*. Cambridge: Cambridge University Press.

Bloemraad, I. (2006) *Becoming a Citizen: Incorporating Immigrants and Refugees in the United States and Canada*. Berkeley: University of California Press.

Deaux, K. (2006) *To Be an Immigrant*. New York: Russell Sage Foundation.

Gans, H. (1979) 'Symbolic Ethnicity: The Future of Ethnic Groups and Cultures in America'. *Ethnic and Racial Studies* 2, 1: 1–20.

Hansen, R. and P. Weil (2002) 'Dual Citizenship in a Changed World: Immigration, Gender, and Social Rights'. In Randall Hansen and PatrickWeil, eds., *Dual Nationality, Social Rights, and Federal Citizenship in the U.S. and Europe: The Reinvention of Citizenship*. New York: Berghahn, pp. 1–15.

Hartmann, D. and J. Gerteis (2005) 'Dealing with Diversity: Mapping Multiculturalism in Sociological Terms'. *Sociological Theory* 23, 2: 218–40.

Kivisto, P. and T. Faist (2007) *Citizenship: Discourse, Theory, and Transnational Prospects*. Malden, MA: Blackwell.

Lal, B. B. (1990) *The Romance of Culture in an Urban Civilization: Robert E. Park on Race and Ethnic Relations in Cities*. London: Routledge.

Legomsky, S. (2003) 'Dual Nationality and Military Service: Strategy Number Two'. In David A. Martin and Kay Hailbronner, eds., *Rights and Duties of Dual Nationals: Evolution and Prospects*. The Hague: Kluwer Law International, pp. 79–126.

Parsons, T. (1971) *The System of Modern Societies*. Englewood Cliffs, NJ: Prentice Hall.

Parsons, T. (2007) *American Society: A Theory of the Societal Community*. Ed. Giuseppe Sciortino. Boulder, CO: Paradigm.

Schmidt, C. (1996) *The Concept of the Political*. Chicago: University of Chicago Press.

Spiro, P. (2002) 'Embracing Dual Nationality'. In Randall Hansen and Patrick Weil, eds., *Dual Nationality, Social Rights, and Federal Citizenship in the U.S. and Europe: The Reinvention of Citizenship*. New York: Berghahn, pp. 19–33.

Index

Growth Triangles (GTs), 255–6, 259
sovereignty, 6–9, 20, 43–4, 85, 100,
153, 235
crisis of, 259–63
democratic, 263–7
meaning of, 250
response to, 261–3
see also popular sovereignty; state
sovereignty
Soysal, Yasemin, 2
Spain, 235
special economic zones, 257
Spiro, Peter, J., 16, 189, 273, 278
state boundaries, relevance of, 133
state security, 9–11, 19, 42, 145,
278–84, 280
state sovereignty, 2, 6–9, 94, 252–4
and popular sovereignty, 250, 265–7
weakening of, 2, 237, 251–2, 258,
261–7, 277–8; by demands of
global capitalism, 253, 261–2;
by internationalisation of
human rights, 19, 249–50,
256–60, 266–7, 275
stateless persons, *see* asylum seekers
Sweden, 7, 14, 227
advocation of dual citizenship,
144–5
civic-republican nationhood, 137
opposition to dual citizenship,
144–5
Switzerland, 172–3

territorialisation of space, 251–2
and jurisdictional authority, 252–2,
257
terrorism, 9, 19–20, 37, 43–4, 52–3,
60, 131, 278, 280
link to asylum seekers, 43–4
military intervention to combat, 9
Teubner, Gunther, 257, 261–2
Tilly, Charles, 28–9
transborder minorities, 75–7
dispersed, 86–7; Roma, 84–5
without kin states, 84–6; Basques,
85; Catalans, 85; Kurds, 85
transnational citizenship, *see* dual
citizenship

transnational corporations, as new
agents of jurisdiction, 255–9
transnational law of economic
transactions, 257–8
see also lex mercatoria
transnational migration, 45, 74–6,
113–18, 125, 132, 205–9, 251–5,
259–9
transnational nationalism, *see* dual
nationalism
Treaty of Amsterdam, 238–9
Treaty of Maastricht, 238–9
Treaty of Rome, 228, 237, 261
Treaty of Westphalia, 260
Triadafilopoulos, Triadafilos, 10, 27,
279, 280
Trudeau, Pierre, 165
Trujillo, Rafael Leonidas, 124–5

undocumented migrants, 28, 116,
123, 131
see also asylum seekers
unitary citizenship, 32, 36
United Kingdom, 2, 6, 31, 38, 60
citizenship law amendment, 60–1
nationality law, 53
subway attacks, 60
United Nations High Commissioner
for Refugees (UNHCR), 45–8
United States Bureau of Citizenship
and Immigration Services
(USCIS), 159
United States of America, 6, 15, 16,
32, 159–66, 281
dual citizenship, 159–66, 282
migration from Mexico, 114–15
migration from the Dominican
Republic, 114–18, 125
urban activism, 263
Uruguay, 172–3
US Declaration of Independence, 162

Van Gogh, Theo, 45
Verdonk, Rita, 45–6
vertical multiple citizenship, 79, 85
see also dual citizenship
voting rights, 7, 81, 86, 102, 114
argument against, 73
in Canada, 164, 213–14